Endorsements

'The editorial team and contributors' knowledge and understanding of the broad intersections of cyberpsychology research is second-to-none, given their years of experience teaching and writing about the impact of technology on human behaviour. This is a must have book for those starting to learn about, or wanting to keep pace with, the multi-disciplinary field of cyberpsychology'.

Dr Andrew J. Campbell, *Associate Professor of Cyberpsychology, The University of Sydney, Australia*

'The second edition of *An Introduction to Cyberpsychology* offers a comprehensive and thought-provoking critical analysis of a range of contemporary topics in this ever-evolving field. With supporting online resources, this is an essential read for interested scholars and students across a range of disciplinary areas, not least in psychology. Highly recommend'.

Neil Coulson, *Professor of Health Psychology, University of Nottingham, UK*

'The second edition of *An Introduction to Cyberpsychology* shares the most-up-to-date research on contemporary issues in cyberpsychology in accessible, easy-to-understand language. It is thorough and considers the multiple ways in which human behaviour shapes and is shaped by digital technology across all facets of life from developmental ages (youth and older age), work, education, sport, and interpersonal and romantic relationships. Chapters are written by leaders in the field and the online learning activities would enhance any cyberpsychology curriculum. I'm looking forward to using this in my own classrooms!'

Dr Melanie Keep, *Director of Academic Education, Sydney School of Health Sciences, Faculty of Medicine and Health, The University of Sydney*

'This book provides a comprehensive overview of cyberpsychology. It applies evidence-based literature from psychology and related disciplines to explore the impact of online technologies on a diverse range of topics including but not limited to health, education, social identity, consumer behaviour, and the workplace. In doing so it provides an invaluable resource for students, instructors, policymakers, and any other stakeholders with an interest in the increasingly important discipline of cyberpsychology. The supplementary online resources provided that can be accessed by students are engaging and will provide a deeper understanding of the issues that the book discusses'.

Prof. John McAlaney, *University of Bournemouth, UK*

'As technology progresses, the importance of cyberpsychology as an essential part of the wider psychology curriculum becomes more apparent. This book acts as an excellent introduction to the field, providing an in-depth overview of all the subject has to offer. Through interactive discussion questions and additional reading lists, the book provides a valuable and accessible resource for students and anyone intrigued to find out more about our digital behaviours. An essential addition to the existing literature, with contributions from leading experts in the field. A great read!'

Dr Lisa Orchard, *Senior Lecturer in Psychology, University of Wolverhampton, UK*

'The new edition of *An Introduction to Cyberpsychology* by Irene Connolly, Marion Palmer, Hannah Barton, and Gráinne Kirwan demystifies the relatively new field of cyberpsychology. Moreover, it communicates the nuts and bolts of strategies from several up-to-date approaches for studying digital technologies. The companion website provides informative supplementary materials that are easy to follow. This is an important addition to the cyberpsychology literature'.

Thomas D. Parsons, PhD, *Grace Center Professor for Innovation in Clinical Education, Simulation Science, and Immersive Technology, Director: Computational Neuropsychology and Simulation (CNS) Lab, Arizona State University, USA*

'The second edition of *An Introduction to Cyberpsychology* is a valuable and much needed addition to the field. A must-read for those who are new to cyberpsychology as well as those who are looking to update their understandings. *An Introduction to Cyberpsychology* covers diverse topics at the forefront of cyberpsychology, which are highly applicable to life in the digital age. Importantly, *An Introduction to Cyberpsychology* provides readers with the building blocks to develop a nuanced and critical understanding of key issues in cyberpsychology'.

Dr Catherine Talbot, *Senior Lecturer in Psychology, Bournemouth University, UK*

'*An Introduction to Cyberpsychology* does an amazing job of covering the current state of cyberpsychology and how its basic premises extend interdisciplinarily in both positive and potentially destructive ways. In addition to including many opportunities for the reader to think critically about this growing applied discipline within psychology, the editors and chapter authors have included many resources and relevant references that allow for extending the utility of the textbook outside of the very pages they appear on. As a cyberpsychological researcher and an academic teaching cyberpsychology at the graduate level, I found the focus on conducting online research particularly well-suited to my students' needs, with several of the other chapters uniquely capturing the essence of what I want all of my first-year students to be aware of'.

Dr Scott Debb, *Associate Professor,*
CyberPsychology Research and Program Coordinator,
Norfolk State University, USA

AN INTRODUCTION TO CYBERPSYCHOLOGY

An Introduction to Cyberpsychology provides a comprehensive introduction to this rapidly growing discipline. Fully updated in its second edition, the book encourages students to critically evaluate the psychology of online interactions and to develop appropriate research methodologies to complete their own work in this field.

The book examines cyberpsychology and online research methodologies, social psychology in an online context, practical applications of cyberpsychology, and the psychological aspects of other technologies. This new edition has been carefully updated to include additional coverage of:

- Expanded content relating to major developments in the field and new content on gaming and screentime
- A new chapter examining the relationship between older adults and technology
- Cyberpsychology in focus feature boxes in each chapter that examine topics in depth
- Interviews with professionals working in fields relating to cyberpsychology

Each chapter includes key terms and a glossary, content summaries, discussion questions, and recommended reading to guide further study.

Supported by extensive online resources for students and instructors, this authoritative book is an essential core text for undergraduate modules in cyberpsychology, and an ideal primer for students of postgraduate programs in cyberpsychology.

To view the additional student and instructor resources for this book, please visit bpscoretextbooks.routledge.com

Gráinne Kirwan is a Lecturer in Psychology at Dún Laoghaire Institute of Art, Design and Technology, Ireland.

Irene Connolly is Lecturer in Developmental and Educational Psychology at Dún Laoghaire Institute of Art, Design and Technology, Ireland.

Hannah Barton is a Lecturer in Psychology at Dún Laoghaire Institute of Art, Design and Technology, Ireland.

Marion Palmer is the former Head of the Department of Technology and Psychology at Dún Laoghaire Institute of Art, Design and Technology, Ireland.

BPS Core Textbooks Series
Series editor: Simon Goodson

Routledge in partnership with British Psychological Society are pleased to present their flagship textbook program, the *BPS Core Textbooks Series*. Aimed at a global undergraduate readership, these volumes are designed to be core texts for course adoption, covering all key subject areas in Psychology.

Diversity, equity and inclusion is at the heart of the series. Each book includes a strong focus on all aspects of diversity, including decolonising the curriculum and an understanding of the value of multiple perspectives. There is also a spotlight on employability, to explain why a grounding in basic theoretical areas is necessary for careers in Psychology. There is also a focus on real-world applications and life skills, to help students explore the use of psychological theory to answer real-world questions. These full colour books include a range of pedagogical features, illustrations and figures, with content to emphasise critical thinking and study skills and the unpicking of pseudoscience.

Books are available in traditional print format, as well as our innovative enhanced eBook format. This includes integrative features such as pop-up keyword definitions, hypertext links to web-based resources, short-answer/open-ended questions, multiple-choice and true/false quizzes and video clips. There is a series website hosting additional digital resources for both students and instructors to tie in with learning objectives.

The books in the *BPS Core Textbooks Series* are essential reading in the core areas in any Psychology honours degree or conversion-level course. They are also relevant as secondary reading in related disciplines.

Titles in the series:

Cognitive Psychology in a Changing World
Linden Ball, Laurie Butler, Sue Sherman & Helen St Clair-Thompson

For more information about this series, please visit: www.routledge.com/our-products/book-series/BPSCT

AN INTRODUCTION TO CYBERPSYCHOLOGY

2nd Edition

EDITED BY GRÁINNE KIRWAN, IRENE CONNOLLY, HANNAH BARTON AND MARION PALMER

Routledge
Taylor & Francis Group

LONDON AND NEW YORK

Designed cover image: © Getty

Second edition published 2024
by Routledge
4 Park Square, Milton Park, Abingdon, Oxon, OX14 4RN

and by Routledge
605 Third Avenue, New York, NY 10158

Routledge is an imprint of the Taylor & Francis Group, an informa business

© 2024 selection and editorial matter, Gráinne Kirwan, Irene Connolly, Hannah Barton, and Marion Palmer; individual chapters, the contributors

First edition published by Routledge 2016

British Library Cataloguing-in-Publication Data
A catalogue record for this book is available from the British Library

Library of Congress Cataloging-in-Publication Data
Names: Kirwan, Grainne, 1978- editor. | Connolly, Irene, editor. |
Barton, Hannah (College teacher), editor.
Title: An introduction to cyberpsychology / [edited by] Gráinne Kirwan,
Irene Connolly, Hannah Barton and Marion Palmer.
Description: Second edition. | Abingdon, Oxon ; New York, NY : Routledge,
2023. | First edition published by Routledge 2016. |
Includes bibliographical references and index. |
Identifiers: LCCN 2023026232 (print) | LCCN 2023026233 (ebook) |
ISBN 9780367636418 (hardback) | ISBN 9780367552299 (paperback) |
ISBN 9781003092513 (ebook) | ISBN 9781032603520
Subjects: LCSH: Cyberspace–Psychological aspects. |
Virtual reality–Psychological aspects. | Telematics–Social aspects.
Classification: LCC HM1017 .I58 2023 (print) | LCC HM1017 (ebook) |
DDC 303.48/34–dc23/eng/20230902
LC record available at https://lccn.loc.gov/2023026232
LC ebook record available at https://lccn.loc.gov/2023026233

ISBN: 978-0-367-63641-8 (hbk)
ISBN: 978-0-367-55229-9 (pbk)
ISBN: 978-1-003-09251-3 (ebk)
ISBN: 9781032603520 (eBook+)

DOI: 10.4324/9781003092513

Typeset in Stone Serif
by Deanta Global Publishing Services, Chennai, India

Access the instructor and student resources: bpscoretextbooks.routledge.com

Printed and bound in Great Britain by
TJBooks Limited, Padstow, Cornwall

MIX
Paper from
responsible sources
FSC® C013056

Dedicated to our families

Contents

List of Figures and Table

Figures

Table

Notes on Contributors

Hannah Barton holds an MA in Psychology from University College Cork and is a previous coordinator of the MSc in Cyberpsychology. She has been lecturing in personality and social psychology in IADT for over 20 years, teaching on both the BSc (Hons) in Applied Psychology and the MSc in Cyberpsychology degrees. Her research has included altruism and positive psychology, mobile learning (podcasting), and group dynamics in both online and offline settings.

Liam Challenor, PhD, is a chartered psychologist accredited by the Psychological Society of Ireland and Psychology Lecturer in IADT. He lectures undergraduate and postgraduate students on research methods and statistics, cyberpsychology, persuasion, and cybersecurity and computer-mediated communication. Dr Challenor's research interests focus on technology and its impact on human behaviour and wellbeing. This includes misinformation, cybersecurity, social media use, cyberbullying, and their impact in workplace and educational settings. ORCID iD: 0000-0002-1974-9535.

Irene Connolly, PhD, is a Lecturer of Developmental and Educational Psychology at Dún Laoghaire Institute of Art, Design and Technology (IADT) and a member of the Psychological Society of Ireland. Irene holds a PhD in Educational Psychology from Trinity College Dublin, specialising in the area of bullying. Her research has focused on areas such as bullying, cyberbullying, and online learning. She is also a research fellow with the National Anti-Bullying Research and Resource Centre, Dublin City University (DCU). ORCID iD: 0000-0001-7843-7657.

Andrew Errity, PhD, is a Senior Lecturer and Head of Department of Technology and Psychology at IADT. This department includes the complementary disciplines of computing, design, and psychology. He is a graduate of Dublin City University, having been awarded both a BSc (Hons) in Computer Applications [Computer Science] and a PhD in Speech Signal Processing. His areas of expertise and research interests include software development, UX design, human–computer interaction, and spoken dialogue systems. He has actively taught, supervised, reviewed, published, and consulted in these areas. ORCID iD: 0000-0002-4041-1408.

Cliona Flood holds an MSc in Work and Organisational Psychology from Dublin City University and a BSc in Psychology from the Open University and has studied counselling and psychotherapy with Dublin Business School. Cliona also holds a postgraduate diploma in teaching and learning awarded by Athlone Institute of Technology. Cliona lectures on the Psychology programme at IADT and is currently a PhD candidate with Lancaster University. Her research is related to how images in presentation technologies enhance teaching and learning. ORCID iD: 0000-0003-3925-9629.

Nicola Fox Hamilton, PhD, holds an MSc in Cyberpsychology from IADT and a PhD from the University of Wolverhampton. Her research examines the connection between language, personality, culture and attraction, and the consistency of expression of personality in online platforms. Nicola was founding secretary of the Psychological Society of Ireland's Special Interest Group for Media, Art and Cyberpsychology. ORCID iD: 0000-0002-6334-704X.

John Greaney, PhD, is a Lecturer in Applied Psychology at IADT. He holds a BSc (Hons) in Mathematics and Psychology and a PhD in Psychology, and has worked for the Royal National Institute for the Blind, Hewlett Packard Labs, and Frontend. He has held lectureships at the Universities of Birmingham and Manchester, and is an associate fellow of the British Psychological Society.

David Hayes is a PhD candidate in the School of Psychology, University College Dublin. His research focuses on conceptualising the psychological experience of video game entertainment and, through this, he has developed the Integrated Gameplay Entertainment Model – a comprehensive and validated account of the player experience. David has also lectured on video game effects at both undergraduate and postgraduate level and has most recently published a systematic scoping review on the use of gamification and serious games for addressing pollution. ORCID iD: 0000-0003-0484-4182.

Olivia A. Hurley, PhD, holds a BSc (Hons), an MSc, and a PhD in Psychology from University College Dublin (UCD). She is a lecturer on the BSc (Hons) Applied Psychology programme at the Institute of Art, Design and Technology (IADT, Dún Laoghaire). She is also a guest lecturer in RCSI and UCD. Olivia is a chartered psychologist with the Psychological Society of Ireland (PSI). She is also one of Sport Ireland's Approved Sport Psychology Consultants. Olivia has published numerous academic papers and book chapters, as well as speaking at national and international conferences. She is a frequent guest on various media outlets. Her first solo book, *Sport Cyberpsychology*, was published by Routledge in 2018. ORCID iD: 0000-0003-1357-3951.

Gráinne Kirwan, PhD, is a chartered psychologist with the British Psychological Society and a Lecturer in Psychology in IADT. She teaches on both the BSc (Hons) in Applied Psychology and the MSc in Cyberpsychology. Gráinne holds a PhD in Criminology as well as an MSc in Applied Forensic Psychology, a Postgraduate Certificate in Third Level Learning and Teaching, and an MLitt in Psychology. She has co-authored two books on forensic cyberpsychology with Dr Andrew Power: *Cybercrime* (Cambridge University Press, 2013) and *The Psychology of Cybercrime* (IGI Global, 2012) as well as co-editing *Cyberpsychology and New Media* (Psychology Press, 2014). ORCID iD: 0000-0001-6011-5510.

Derek A. Laffan currently works as a researcher in the Dublin City University Anti-Bullying Centre and teaches on the MSc Cyberpsychology programme in Dún Laoghaire Institute of Art, Design, and Technology. He has published peer-reviewed research related to cyberpsychology across areas such as digital gaming, adolescent wellbeing, online schooling during the COVID-19 lockdown, anti-cyberbullying, and K-Pop fandom. Derek sits on the committee of the Special Interest Group for Media, the Arts, and Cyberpsychology (SIGMAC) at the Psychological Society of Ireland. ORCID iD: 0000-0002-5780-1840.

Emma Mathias, PhD, is a Lecturer in Applied Psychology in the Institute of Art, Design, and Technology (IADT) and an Occasional Lecturer in the School of Politics and International Relations, University College Dublin (UCD). Emma teaches a cognitive psychology module to second-year undergraduate students in IADT and a module on the application of psychology to IT. Emma's PhD research focused on the interactions between culture and mental health using qualitative research methods. She is currently working on a project to develop an ethical toolkit for use by researchers across disciplines such as business, psychology, and design.

Marion Palmer, PhD, is a higher education consultant. She retired as Head of the Department of Technology and Psychology at Dún Laoghaire Institute of Art, Design and Technology, Ireland, in 2016. Marion worked on the MSc in Cyberpsychology with a particular focus on learning in cyberspace. She researched teaching in Irish Institutes of Technology for a doctorate in education from Queen's University Belfast and was a national Award of Teaching Excellence winner in 2011. Marion is a member of the Board of the National Forum for the Enhancement of Teaching and Learning, (www.teachingandlearning.ie). ORCID iD: 0000-0003-0678-9025.

Brendan Rooney, PhD, is an Assistant Professor in the UCD School of Psychology and Director of the Media and Entertainment Psychology Lab. He previously held appointments at Columbia University, the Dún

Laoghaire Institute of Art, Design and Technology, and the National College of Art and Design. Brendan's research interests include social cognition, (visual) perception, and how cognitive and emotional processes interact in the context of media, arts, and entertainment. Through his research and teaching, he has worked in a number of interdisciplinary and international research teams, with creative and entertainment industry experts (such as animators, filmmakers, and designers), philosophers, computer scientists and engineers, film and humanities scholars, and cognitive neuroscientists. Brendan founded the Psychological Society of Ireland's Special Interest Group for Media, the Arts and Cyberpsychology, and he is a member and fellow of the Society for the Cognitive Studies of the Moving Image (www.scsmi-online.org). ORCID iD: 0000-0001-9842-1492.

Audrey Stenson, PhD, holds a PhD from the University of Wolverhampton in Psychology. She holds an MSc in Cyberpsychology from IADT, an MA in Psychoanalysis by Clinical Specialisation from Dublin Business School, and a BSc in Information Systems from Trinity College Dublin. She is currently a graduate member of the British Psychological Society. In addition to this, Audrey has over ten years of industry experience in software development and project management roles. She is a lecturer in the field of business, technology, information systems, project management, psychoanalysis, and psychology. ORCID iD: 0000-0002-3388-9868.

Conall Tunney, PhD, completed a PhD by research at University College Dublin in the area of technology for well-being. He works on the *Pesky Gnats* project, which designs and develops technology-based cognitive behavioural therapy interventions for children who are experiencing anxiety or low mood. His research uses mixed methods, including systematic reviews and meta-analyses, qualitative focus groups, and randomised controlled trials. He has also lectured at IADT on the psychology of new media and entertainment and on gaming and media psychology. Conall maintains a clinical focus in psychology with a part-time post as an assistant psychologist at the Children's University Hospital, Temple Street, Dublin. ORCID iD: 0000-0002-9667-5832.

Foreword

It is a great honour to be able to provide a foreword for the second edition of *An Introduction to Cyberpsychology*. This is especially humbling for me as I was also the invited guest to launch the first edition of the book back in 2016. It is great to see the positive reception that this book has brought about, and what a useful resource it continues to be for students, researchers, and enthusiasts of cyberpsychology. This is a resource I include on my own reading list for students on my specialist cyberpsychology course, as it serves as a helpful introduction for those new to this field to navigate the common topic areas and issues in this field.

Even since the book's first release in 2016, the landscape and opportunities for cyberpsychology have somewhat advanced. The COVID-19 pandemic has undoubtedly cast cyberpsychology further into public discourse, and helped us recognise the far-reaching value of internet-enabled technology and online environments for supporting our work, play, socialising, leisure, business, education, and health, to name a few. The technology innovation landscape also continues to evolve, with proposals for a more inter-connected Metaverse infrastructure where the boundaries between online and offline become increasingly even more blurred.

All these advancements present opportunities for cyberpsychology to take a front seat in exploring the digitally connected human experience and how this operates on an individual and societal level. This may relate to our identity experiences – how we express our identity through our online behaviours and digital traces; our social experiences – the nature of our social connections on social media; or our thinking experiences – how human decision-making may be enriched or compromised by algorithms. These are all fascinating areas of the human experience which cyberpsychology is well-positioned to help us further explore.

This book has consolidated a wide range of topics from prominent scholars in the field, to provide a comprehensive introduction to cyberpsychology. This includes topics which cover key theoretical areas as well as many applied avenues of the field. I welcome the inclusion of a new chapter on "older adults in the digital age" which goes some way to represent key issues for understanding older users' psychological experiences of using technology and the internet. The chapter authors present the ideas in an accessible and engaging way, whilst also integrating the academic bases which underpin their assertions. Each chapter includes some useful thinking activities and features boxes to help readers apply their learning.

The last 15 years or so of my career have been dedicated to advancing the field of cyberpsychology. I have been heavily involved in advancing the reputation of the field both nationally and internationally, largely through leading on the development of a specialised section for cyberpsychology in the British Psychology Society. I have engaged widely in thought-leadership, and developed an array of methods to encourage a more external-facing role of cyberpsychology for informing public debate, increasing public awareness of evidence, supporting practitioners and researchers, and working with policy-makers. Alongside this, I readily apply cyberpsychology in the services delivered by my company The CyberDoctor® to support businesses in maximising their online communications and marketing. I am a huge advocate for the value of cyberpsychology in society and am always encouraged to learn of key texts such as *An Introduction to Cyberpsychology* which are written in a way which is accessible to wide audiences.

I am sure that the success of *An Introduction to Cyberpsychology* will continue to be realised through the publication of its second edition. The authors and editors have done a tremendous job (again) of helping the reader navigate this wide-ranging and fascinating field.

Dr Linda K. Kaye
Past Chair of BPS Cyberpsychology Section
Associate Head of Psychology, Edge Hill University

Acknowledgements

As an editorial team, we are very grateful to all of those who helped us at each stage of the book's development. In particular, we would like to extend our gratitude to Eleanor Taylor, Tori Sharpe, Emilie Coin, Andrew Corrigan, and the production team at Taylor & Francis/Routledge for their enthusiasm for this project, their guidance, and the many cheerful answers that they provided to our queries.

We would like to thank Dr Linda Kaye of Edge Hill University for kindly writing the Foreword for this edition, and for launching the first edition of this textbook. Our appreciation also goes to our esteemed colleagues who wrote endorsements for the book at very short notice, and to those who shared their real-life experience of the practical aspects of psychology in the interviews at even shorter notice. A special word of thanks to Dr Nicola Fox Hamilton who provided advice and professional insight on the cover design, and to Dr Andrew Errity, our Head of Department, who supported our work on this edition.

We would also like to thank each of the chapter authors. Their expertise in their respective fields and their dedication to teaching combine to form chapters that are rich in content and full of engaging pedagogic material. We know that the preparation of these chapters required a great deal of time, effort, and patience, and we appreciate the authors' adherence to our schedule and quick responses to our requests, despite so many conflicting demands on their time.

While textbooks such as this can be read by people from many backgrounds, they are primarily developed with students in mind. Over the years, our own students on both the MSc in Cyberpsychology and our undergraduate programmes have helped us to develop our ideas, push beyond our perceived capabilities, and view online behaviour in new ways. We hope that this textbook will help future generations of students to become as excited about online interaction as they have made us.

We would also like to make some individual acknowledgements.

From Irene: To my husband Tom, to my children Lauren, Jamie, and Tom, and to my parents, Ita and Michael, a huge thank you for everything you do. To my fantastic colleagues, each of you is simply brilliant.

From Marion: To my co-editors, thank you for all the work over the years. It's been a privilege to work with you. To my fellow authors, thank you for a valuable book. Last but not least thanks to Peter for the unending support.

From Hannah: To Ashling for being you, and to my friends and colleagues for unlimited patience, good humour, and endless cat jokes.

From Gráinne: To my mother, Marie Kirwan, for decades of encouragement in all things academic. To Glen, for infinite patience – again. Most of all, to Ben, for being the wonderful person that you are and for making me smile and laugh every single day.

PART 1

Introduction

Cyberpsychology in Professional Practice

Interview 1

Itayi Viriri has been the Senior Regional Media and Communications Officer and Spokesperson for the International Organization for Migration (IOM-UN Migration) Asia-Pacific for the past three years. Prior to that he worked for an additional three years as Head of IOM Global Online Communications.

What are your main responsibilities and/or daily activities in this post?

As head of media and communications covering IOM's vast Asia Pacific region which covers countries from Afghanistan to Vanuatu, I oversee and manage the regional office's digital/online platforms and advise our chiefs of mission on media aspects. I am also the senior spokesperson meaning that I deal with all media requests pertaining to migration and related topics.

When did you first become interested in cyberpsychology, and how did you develop this interest into part of your career path?

I first became interested in cyberpsychology in the early 2000s just as social media channels started gaining prominence. Of course, back then I didn't know this was "cyberpsychology" but as someone keenly interested in social media, especially how it is utilised in journalism (my initial tertiary qualification and

3

DOI: 10.4324/9781003092513-2

first profession), I grabbed the opportunity when it came up to combine my personal and career interests and affirm them with some sound academic basis and foundation. The MSc in Cyberpsychology at IADT provided exactly that.

What cyberpsychological knowledge is of most relevance to your current role?

I would definitely say aspects that focus on understanding which message fits best with which medium and audience. This understanding helps ensure that our external communications are fit for purpose.

Are there any theories in cyberpsychology which you find applicable to your work? If so, which one(s), and how are they relevant to your responsibilities in your role?

Any theory that brings me to closer understanding the nuances of human–computer interaction, especially in these sometimes fraught times in the digital space, is applicable to my current work, particularly when it applies to tackling disinformation (I co-wrote a chapter on this, for IOM's flagship World Migration Report 2022).

What do you think are the most important real-world applications of cyberpsychology?

As a trained journalist and now a media practitioner, the best real-world application of cyberpsychology is understanding the what, when, where, why, and how human beings utilise social and traditional media.

Is there anything else that you'd like to add about cyberpsychology in your professional life?

First of all, it was an honour and privilege to be part of the very first cohort of the MSc in Cyberpsychology and for years I have enjoyed and sometimes even revelled in explaining to curious family, friends, and even strangers who were curious as to what cyberpsychology entailed. Cyberpsychology has featured significantly in my professional life particularly when I was previously IOM's head of global online communications, managing teams running and operating IOM's extensive digital platforms around the world.

Itayi Viriri
Bangkok, Thailand

Introduction to Cyberpsychology

Gráinne Kirwan

Chapter Overview

Cyberpsychology is a relatively new field within applied psychology, although there is now a growing library of research and scholarship examining the topic. As an area of study, it assesses how we interact with others using technology, how we can develop technology to best fit our requirements, and how our behaviour and psychological states are influenced by technology. The most commonly studied technology in cyberpsychology research is the Internet, although the area considers human interactions with many devices which may not necessarily be online, including mobile computing, games consoles, virtual reality, and artificial intelligence. This chapter provides a brief overview of some areas of research in cyberpsychology, including a short introduction to each of the chapters that follow.

Key Terms

Cyberpsychology "is a scientific inter-disciplinary domain that focuses on the psychological phenomena which emerge as a result of the human interaction with digital technology, particularly the Internet" (British Psychological Society, n.d., Title section). It examines how we interact with others using technology, how our behaviour is influenced by technology, how technology can be developed to best suit our needs, and how our psychological states can be affected by technologies. Much research in cyberpsychology has been driven by the Internet, and in particular the advent of **social media**. However, other technologies have also been closely examined, including **gaming** (both online and offline), **mobile computing**, **artificial intelligence**, **virtual reality**, and **augmented reality**.

Cyberpsychology: A Brief Synopsis

Psychology as a discipline does not stand still for long. It changes and adjusts as new research, theories, and developments arise, and it aims to face new advances while challenging concepts that were previously widely accepted.

DOI: 10.4324/9781003092513-3

It is not surprising that the advances in technologies, especially those over the past quarter of a century, have drawn the interest of so many academics and practitioners in the area. Probably the most significant change in human behaviour and interaction in the past two decades has been the rise in popularity of the Internet (in a general sense) and **social media** and online interactions (in a more specific sense). It is unsurprising that psychologists have not only embraced these technologies as methods of improving general well-being but have also been drawn to examine how these technologies can impact our behaviour and our relationships with others. The research of psychologists in this field complements the research of other social scientists across the globe who also examine online interactions.

Cyberpsychology is a broad topic, and it encompasses many aspects of research, some of which have been in existence for some time, and some of which are more recent. Generally, cyberpsychology encompasses three main aspects. First, it assesses how we interact with others using technology. This has been of particular interest since the advent of social media technologies, but our interactions with others have been affected by technologies for a considerably longer period of time through the use of communication mechanisms such as email and websites. To consider this for a moment, think about one of the people that you communicate with the most often. Now imagine under what circumstances you might talk to them in person, or when you might call them, or send them a direct message on social media, or tag them in a post on social media. What would be different about your communications with them in each of these contexts? Also, take a moment and think about if you know someone who you communicate with online fairly regularly, but have never met offline (for example, through online gaming). What is your impression of that person? Do you think that this might change if you met them offline now? Do you think that you might have a different impression of them if you had met them offline in the first instance, and only later started communicating with them online?

A second aspect of cyberpsychology considers how we can develop technology to best fit our requirements and desires. Some attributes of this type of cyberpsychology often come under the heading of **human–computer interaction**, although this is also considered as an entire specialism in itself. One example of advances in this area involves programming the recording of programmes from television channels. Up until fairly recently this was a complex affair – blank video cassettes needed to be purchased and placed in the video cassette recorder (VCR), the store-bought television guide magazine needed to be consulted to determine the start time, end time, day, and channel that a programme was on, the VCR clock needed to be checked to ensure that it was accurate, the appropriate option within the VCR's menu needed to be identified, and all the date, time, and channel details needed to be inputted correctly. An error at any stage, a power outage, or a change in the scheduled time of the programme meant that the recording would fail. Now, most digital television providers include all the necessary hardware, including storage space, and allow users to select a programme from the on-screen listings and record an entire season of the programme with a single button press. Changes in running schedule are no longer a problem as the system can compensate for it. The almost ubiquitous nature of "on demand" and "catch-up" services now adds an extra layer of ease, as the viewer no longer needs to even be aware of the programme in advance of it airing to watch it in its entirety. And watching entire series on streaming services is even easier. The interaction between the human and the computer has become considerably easier and less prone to error.

Of course, there are many other ways in which research in human–computer interaction makes our daily lives easier – we only need to briefly look at a computer's operating system, or the difference in mobile phones over the past 15 years, to identify such improvements. Another key example is the touchscreen – this technology was very rare before the advent of smartphones, but has become a common feature of daily life. Interacting with a computer in this way requires a different set of skills from using other interface methods, such as keyboards. One of the goals of human–computer interaction includes determining which interface methods are the most appropriate for a given situation, realising that one approach does not answer all problems.

The third key aspect of cyberpsychology examines how our behaviour and psychological states can be affected by technologies. Again, there are many examples of this, but one that many will have experienced is a distorted sense of time when using technologies, particularly when gaming. This phenomenon is one of several characteristics of a "flow" state, as identified by Csikszentmihalyi (1990), and applied to interactions with technology by many researchers (see, for example, Kaye et al., 2018). Of course, technology can affect us in many other ways as well. For example, theorists and researchers have identified the aspects of online communication that can result in our feeling closer to others whom we are interacting with online (see, for example, Walther's hyperpersonal model, 1996, 2007, which is discussed in more detail in Chapter 3). This may result in our disclosing our innermost thoughts in what might be unsuitably public settings. Others have identified some core psychological reasons why it is easier for some people to be hostile or harassing online (see, for example, Lee & Jin, 2019; Suler, 2004, 2015). These disruptive behaviours are evident through a variety of online actions, such as cyberbullying, trolling, and flaming. A deeper understanding of these psychological principles can help us to advise Internet users of safer and more appropriate behaviour online – simply being aware of why we might engage in certain activities can often give us the tools we need to make wiser decisions regarding our online interactions. It can also provide us with the skills to manage such behaviours should we find ourselves on the receiving end of a hostile communication.

Much research in cyberpsychology also examines how we manage the impressions that others form of us based on our online personae, and the roles of anonymity and self-disclosure in this area (see, for example, Fullwood, 2019; Joinson et al., 2007; Joinson et al., 2010). In some online fora (such as online gaming) we have the opportunity to create entirely new personas, even choosing to act as a different gender from our own if we wish. In others, such as many social media platforms, we will normally adopt our own persona – we use our own name and photograph, and we will generally include our offline friends as our primary contacts (although many factors can influence what we present on these platforms; see, for example, the discussion by Keep et al., 2019, on image sharing on social networking sites; that by Talbot et al., 2022, which examines identity management by LGBTQ+ individuals on social media; and the research by Chadwick and Fullwood, 2018, which explores the use of social networking by those with intellectual disabilities). In these settings we do not tend to use pretence or change much about ourselves, although there are many individual differences which can affect how and why we use such platforms (Orchard et al., 2014). However, we will tend to present ourselves in a more positive light than we normally would – we emphasise the good things that happen to us, and the exciting activities that we engage in, without focusing on the more mundane or negative aspects of our lives. As such, on social media, our impression management is usually relatively minimal, but we still put a positive spin on our communications.

Another time when we might engage in very careful impression management is if we are considering seeking a romantic partner using an online dating application. While once these applications involved the completion of a relatively simple profile, as technology has advanced, these applications have become more complex in some cases (including the possibilities of multiple photographs, video messages, and many more). But in other cases the technology has simplified – smartphone dating applications often show a minimal profile along with a single image, and the user can decide whether or not they are interested in the individual with a simple swipe to the left or the right. While online dating has resulted in countless romantic relationships and marriages, there are many risks involved, and care must be taken (see Buchanan & Whitty, 2014, for a description of some of these risks).

The Internet has also become a rich territory for research in linguistics. While abbreviations and acronyms are not new, the frequency of use in modern times and the rate at which new instances are noted have resulted in these becoming a much more prevalent aspect of modern parlance. Similarly, the use of emoji (and previously, emoticons/smileys) is of particular interest – the development of new methods of communicating emotion and mood when the primary methods by which these are normally communicated (facial expression and tone of voice) are absent (see, for example, Fullwood et al., 2013; Jones et al., 2020). The presence of an emoji can completely change the meaning of a sentence, so their importance in modern linguistics must not be ignored.

Much research has also examined "applied" cyberpsychology. This refers to any application of our online behaviours to other aspects of our daily lives. For example, technologies allow us to stay in touch with our workplace, even when we cannot be there. Being geographically distant from our workplace no longer means that we cannot immediately respond to any matters that require our attention. While many workplaces offered some individuals the opportunity to work remotely for many years, the extent of the possibilities of remote working became evident in March 2020, as significant proportions of the planet's population switched to working from home at very short notice due to the COVID-19 pandemic. The ability to work from home using such technologies meant that many (but far from all) services and organisations continued to function, to some extent or another, while keeping their employees in a safer environment. Of course, there are negative aspects to this as well – we may feel pressure to respond to emails throughout the night, or at weekends, resulting in negative effects on our home and family lives, and in the long term, potentially negative effects on our health. That said, cyberpsychology can also have positive effects on our health – we now have access to more information on well-being, medicine, and healthy living than ever before. This, coupled with support from others online who might be facing the same health problems as ourselves (see, for example, Coulson, 2019), can greatly enhance resilience and resources for an individual facing a worrying situation. Of course, seeking such support and information can also hold risks – such as distinguishing between useful and irrelevant (or even harmful) information, knowing who to trust with our personal details, and even the unnecessary escalation of worry. Using insights from both psychology generally and cyberpsychology specifically can help users to make good decisions regarding their online behaviours so that their online actions can be beneficial to them while avoiding harmful consequences.

Another important aspect of online life is our increased tendency to use the Internet to purchase goods and services, or to manage our financial arrangements. Trust is particularly important in understanding consumer behaviour online. A thorough understanding of how and why we trust, and what features might cause us to lose trust, is essential in building a consumer base and ensuring the continuance of online commerce. The affordances of technology also allow online retailers to provide each consumer with the technological equivalent of a personal shopper – artificially intelligent interfaces that compare your prior purchases and viewing behaviour to all those who have gone before you, and, using this information, suggest the next product that you are likely to desire, even though you never knew of its existence. These personalised recommendations can result in increased revenue for the retailer, a more interesting experience for the consumer, and a healthier long-term prospect for economies. Similarly, the impact of influencers online can determine what purchases we make, but also how we respond to and behave in a variety of situations (see Chapter 9).

The very nature of technology has also been harnessed by psychologists to improve well-being. We can see this in particular with regard to gaming – terms like serious games, gameful design, and gamification all refer to methods by which game elements and gaming principles can be applied to help people and organisations to reach goals, while also adding some entertainment value. Many of these draw from other areas of psychology, such as positive psychology and learning theories. One of the key tasks in cyberpsychology is determining when our online behaviour is fundamentally similar to our offline behaviour (in which case, we can draw from the vast literature in psychology as a whole), but also determining when online behaviour differs significantly from our offline responses (in which case, new theories may need to be developed and new research conducted to fully understand the ways in which the technology has changed us).

Unfortunately, along with the good that technology brings, there are also negative aspects. When the American Psychiatric Association (2013) updated their *Diagnostic and Statistical Manual* (DSM) to the fifth edition, they included "Internet gaming disorder" as a phenomenon which requires further research. This was retained by the association in the text-revision to the fifth edition (DSM-5-TR), where it is listed as a "condition for further study" (American Psychiatric Association, 2022, pp. 913–15). The World Health Organisation (WHO, 2018) also includes "gaming disorder" in the 11th revision of the International Classification of Diseases (ICD-11) as a "disorder due to addictive behaviours". Similar to other behavioural control problems, the diagnoses for these conditions are primarily based on the impact that the behaviour has on the individual's life (rather than the actual number of hours spent playing games). So, if an individual plays video games to the extent that they experience tolerance and withdrawal, they relapse if they try to stop playing, they have pervasive thoughts about playing, or their playing impacts on their family, work, or education, then it may be something that needs professional attention. Similar concerns have been raised about the potential problematic use of smartphones and the Internet generally, and some studies have explored perceptions of smartphone over-reliance (see, for example, Conroy et al., 2022). It is not without a certain degree of irony that someone with such problems can seek help online – Internet-mediated therapy is offered by an increasing number of practitioners, especially since the COVID-19 pandemic commenced, although the benefits of online platforms for therapeutic interventions had been explored prior to the pandemic (see, for example, Campbell et al., 2019). Such therapy offers advantages for both clients and therapists, including ease of access and increased confidentiality.

Another fear that has arisen with the proliferation of our daily interactions with technology is cybercrime victimisation. There are many dangers online for all users, although understandably we pay particular attention to the Internet activity of children and adolescents who can be at particular risk of sexual exploitation (Merdian et al., 2021; Quayle & Koukopoulos, 2019). Cyberpsychology can provide insights into why some individuals who would never engage in criminal activity offline might be attracted to such behaviours online (Kirwan, 2019; Kirwan & Power, 2013). Researching this field can provide insights into the tactics used by offenders to ensnare their victims and the aspects of human behaviour which can make us more vulnerable to such attacks (see, for example, McAlaney & Hills, 2020). Finally, we can also design educational programmes to help users to protect themselves and their loved ones against victimisation.

Part of such protection involves the consideration of the careful maintenance of our privacy. Much recent research in cyberpsychology examines how and why we share information with others (Joinson et al., 2011; Kirwan, 2015; Paine et al., 2007; Vasalou et al., 2015), or the management of our online security (see, for example, Debb et al., 2020; Hadlington, 2017). This becomes even more important as we carry an increasing amount of personal data with us in the form of mobile devices. These mobile devices may also result in our sharing information about ourselves unwittingly – such as our previous or current locations. The more that we use technology and share information about ourselves, the more we risk. However, the benefits of such sharing often outweigh the potential risks for many, and some authors (for example, Finkelhor et al., 2021) have suggested that teaching privacy as a strategy for children's online safety may be problematic.

As mentioned, cyberpsychology examines technologies other than the Internet. This includes common activities, such as gaming, and less common activities, such as the use of virtual reality, augmented reality, and robotics. But the use of these technologies is increasing as they become more affordable, and as larger companies take more of an interest in creating consumer-level versions. Also of interest in cyberpsychology is human behaviour when interacting with artificial intelligence, whether or not it is coupled with a robotic device. There is an increase in the use of artificially intelligent chatbots as a frontline in customer service, as well as understanding the potential use of artificially intelligent robots as caregivers and companions. Of course, we interact with some forms of artificial intelligence much more regularly, such as the artificial intelligence within certain websites, and that which controls non-player characters in games. While human interaction with robots is still at an early stage, it is the role of cyberpsychology research to determine how we can aid a transition into greater levels of interaction when necessary.

FEATURE BOX: THINKING CRITICALLY ABOUT CYBERPSYCHOLOGY IN THE NEWS

Many aspects of cyberpsychological research are fascinating to a wide range of people, including those with no previous psychological knowledge or training. Because of this, news reports frequently include items relating to cyberpsychology, and often enlist a researcher or practitioner in the field to provide insights into our behaviours with technology. The quality of these insights, and the expertise of the researcher or practitioner, can vary greatly. Additionally, some media sources are keen to present their item in a way which gathers as many viewers/listeners/readers as possible, and this may include the use of sensationalist headlines and/or pieces which are focused towards fear-mongering, regardless of whether or not that induced fear is a valid one. When reviewing content in cyberpsychology, especially that prepared for a general audience, always consider carefully the empirical evidence relating to the subject, and attempt to determine if a balanced perspective of the relevant research is being presented.

Cyberpsychology Journals, Conferences, and Research Groups

While cyberpsychology is a relatively new field, there are many resources available for students and scholars to further their knowledge of this important area.

Several journals focus primarily on cyberpsychology, or welcome papers with such a focus. These include *Technology, Mind, and Behavior*; *Media Psychology*; *Social Media and Society*; *Cyberpsychology, Behavior, and Social Networking* (previously *Cyberpsychology and Behavior*); *Computers in Human Behavior*; *Journal of Computer-Mediated Communication*; *Behaviour & Information Technology*; *New Media & Society*; *Human-Computer Interaction*; *Interacting with Computers*; *International Journal of Human-Computer Studies*; *Virtual Reality*; and *Games for Health*, among many more.

Similarly, there are many academic conferences which focus on or include cyberpsychological research, including the BPS Cyberpsychology Section conference, the APA Technology, Mind & Society conference, the Cyberpsychology, Cybertherapy & Social Networking Conference (organised by the International Association of CyberPsychology, Training & Rehabilitation – iACToR), the Social Networking in Cyberspace Conference (organised by the Cyberpsychology Research at the University of Wolverhampton research group), and the Internet Research Conference (organised by the Association of Internet Researchers).

There are also other excellent research and professional groups internationally, such as the British Psychological Society "Cyberpsychology Section", the Oxford Internet Institute at the University of Oxford, the Cyberpsychology Research at the University of Wolverhampton (CRUW) group, the Cyberpsychology Research Group at the University of Sydney, and the Research Centre for Virtual Environments and Behavior at the University of California Santa Barbara, among many others. Finally, if you would like to consider a structured academic programme within this area, there are various options, including the MSc in Social Science of the Internet (at the Oxford Internet Institute) and numerous undergraduate and postgraduate programmes in cyberpsychology at a variety of higher education institutions (for example, the Dun Laoghaire Institute of Art, Design and Technology in Ireland; the University of Wolverhampton; Bournemouth University; Norfolk State University; and many others).

Aims and Structure of the Book

This book aims to provide readers with an introduction to the field of cyberpsychology, with a particular focus on applied aspects of the field. It is designed to encourage readers to critically evaluate the psychology of online interactions and to develop appropriate research methodologies to complete their own research in this field. The book may be used as a core text for undergraduate modules in cyberpsychology or psychology of the Internet, and a fundamental reading for students of postgraduate programmes in cyberpsychology.

Each chapter of the book includes additional resources which may be useful for the reader, especially those who are using the book as part of a structured course. For example, activities are suggested that can help to illustrate the everyday applications of the content being covered. Additional readings are recommended for those who would like to know more about the content in each chapter, and definitions of keywords are provided within glossaries. Topics for discussion are also provided, and these can be used both online and offline. A variety of other resources are also available to instructors and students online.

The book comprises four main Parts. The first section introduces the field, while the second examines human interactions online. The third section considers applications of cyberpsychology, while the final section considers psychology and technology. More information on each chapter is provided below.

Part 1: Introduction

The first section of the book comprises this introductory chapter and a chapter by Dr Brendan Rooney describing the fundamentals of online behavioural research. It provides an introduction to behavioural research and reviews the main types of online research methodologies, such as experiments, self-report measures, interviews, focus groups, and observational studies. The chapter also reflects on the main ethical considerations of online research.

Part 2: Human Interactions Online

The second section of the book concerns itself with the interactions between people online. Much cyberpsychological research draws from social psychological and cognitive psychological constructs, and so this section of the book often utilises similar topics to introduce the reader to many aspects of online life.

The second section commences with a chapter examining computer-mediated communication and online media. This chapter describes the history of online communication and the types of communication prevalent online, while also identifying the ways in which online communication is different from offline methods. It also demonstrates the applicability of communication theories to online interactions. Chapter 4, by Dr Irene Connolly, considers the self and identity in cyberspace. It introduces the main theories of the self-concept and personality and relates them to how we present ourselves online. It is designed to show how specific personality types use the Internet and how the Internet, especially social media, allows us to manage who we want to be online. It also focuses on impression management – our portrayal of ourselves to others online.

In Chapter 5, Derek A. Laffan and Hannah Barton examine the dark side of cyberspace, such as flaming, trolling, prejudice, stereotyping, and harassment. Chapter 6 identifies how we are attracted to others online, and here Dr Nicola Fox Hamilton differentiates between how relationships are formed online and offline. In Chapter 7, Dr John Greaney and Dr Emma Mathias examine attention and distraction online, noting how recent technological developments have resulted in many individuals being in a relatively constant state of divided attention.

In Chapter 8, Dr Olivia A. Hurley considers the dynamics of groups online, comparing them to offline groups in terms of norms, group identity, group formation, and group regulation, whereas Chapter 9 includes insights by Hannah Barton on social influence, persuasion, and compliance online. The final chapter in this section considers privacy and trust online, why we sacrifice privacy in order to make other perceived gains, and how we can improve our online security.

Part 3: Applied Cyberpsychology

Applied psychology takes many forms, and this section identifies how each branch of applied psychology has importance in cyberpsychology. It starts by considering cybercrime, identifying different types of cybercrime, describing how forensic psychology differs from media portrayals of the area, and identifying how forensic psychology can aid our understanding of cybercriminals and their victims. In Chapter 12, Cliona Flood and Dr Audrey Stenson examine some of the psychological problems which may emerge with technology use, such as pathological Internet use. They also identify how the Internet can be used as a therapeutic tool. In Chapter 13, Dr Olivia A. Hurley then examines the applications of sport psychology and health psychology in technological developments, including the influence of social media and health-promoting applications. In Chapter 14, Cliona Flood and Dr Audrey Stenson consider the modern workplace and the challenges that emerging technologies pose to organisations, including constant connectedness, work–life balance, telecommuting, and organisational design.

The Internet has also changed the way that we study, teach, and learn, and Dr Marion Palmer investigates this in Chapter 15, considering both formal and informal learning. Chapter 16 considers consumer cyberpsychology, with Dr Nicola Fox Hamilton evaluating the roles of trust and credibility in online transactions, and providing guidelines for advertising and marketing online. In Chapter 17, Dr Irene Connolly writes about young people online, particularly examining aspects of development and the risk of cyberbullying. The final chapter of Part 3 is new to this edition, and here Dr Liam Challenor considers older adults' use of technologies.

Part 4: Psychology and Technology

This final section of the book examines the application of psychology to technologies other than the World Wide Web. It commences with a chapter by Dr Andrew Errity describing the history and current state of the field of human–computer interaction. In Chapter 20, David Hayes, Dr Andrew Errity, Dr Brendan Rooney, and Dr Conall Tunney write about the psychology of online gaming, which has diversified in terms of platforms and goals. They consider the impact of the increased realism of graphics, the phenomenon of gamification, and the identification of gaming disorders.

Chapter 21 describes the psychological applications of virtual reality. There are a wide variety of virtual reality technologies currently available, and these are increasingly being aimed at the consumer market. The potential for such technologies in psychological treatments has been explored for many years, particularly as a component in the treatment of anxiety disorders, but also as interventions in distraction from pain (see, for example, Ahmadpour et al., 2020, for a discussion of this in relation to managing pain in children and adolescents). Virtual reality can also be used in other settings, such as stress management in workplaces (Naylor et al., 2020). The final chapter examines the psychology of artificial intelligence, with particular focus on the potential for artificially intelligent robotic devices to be used as companions.

Conclusion

Cyberpsychology as a topic of research is expanding at an extraordinary rate, and it is not difficult to see why – more and more of our daily activities are being conducted in online environments and we cannot help but be influenced by the medium. Cyberpsychology researchers have a crucial role to play in understanding our behaviours and determining how best to design technologies and information strategies to ensure that users can make the best possible use of such developments. The remainder of the book considers each of the points in this chapter in more detail, particularly with regard to the Internet, but also other technologies such as online gaming, virtual reality, and artificial intelligence.

Activity

Keep a diary of your use of Internet technologies for one week. What apps do you use, which websites do you visit, what social media do you use, what other communication technologies do you employ? If possible, try to keep a log of how long you spend on each activity, and what the goal of each activity was (many smartphones will have a log of how much time you spend within each app). Try to determine how you would achieve these goals if Internet technologies didn't exist. How were similar goals achieved before the Internet was invented?

Discussion Questions

1 What technological developments do you think were significant in making cyberpsychology important as a field of study?
2 Are human behaviours online different from those offline? If there are differences, what are they, and what reasons might be behind their occurrence?
3 Should Internet gaming disorder/gaming disorder have been included in the DSM/ICD? Why or why not?
4 Are there any emergent technologies not listed in the chapter that should be considered by cyberpsychology? What are they?

Recommended Reading List

The Psychology of Online Behavior is an audiobook written and narrated by Dr Nicola Fox Hamilton. This audiobook provides an excellent introduction to many of the topics which are covered within this book.

> Fox Hamilton, N. (2022). *The psychology of online behavior* [Audiobook]. Audible. https://www.audible.co.uk/pd/The-Psychology-of-Online -Behavior-Audiobook/B0B194S215

There are many ongoing debates within cyberpsychology, and these are explored in fascinating detail by Dr Linda Kaye in *Issues and Debates in Cyberpsychology*.

> Kaye, L. K. (2022). *Issues and debates in cyberpsychology*. Open University Press.

The *Oxford Handbook of Cyberpsychology* provides an excellent overview of the breadth of this interesting field.

> Attrill-Smith, A., Fullwood, C., Keep, M., & Kuss, D. J. (Eds.). (2019). *The Oxford handbook of cyberpsychology*. Oxford University Press.

There are many ethical issues which are especially concerning to those who study cyberpsychology. This excellent text by Thomas Parsons considers many of these in detail.

> Parsons, T. D. (2019). *Ethical challenges in digital psychology and cyberpsychology*. Cambridge University Press.

An interesting collection of research in the field of cyberpsychology is included in *Cyberpsychology and Society.*

> Power, A. (Ed.). (2018). *Cyberpsychology and society.* Routledge.

A considerable volume of research considers how technology affects various aspects of cognition. Lee Hadlington's *Cybercognition* reviews much of this content in a single volume.

> Hadlington, L. (2017). *Cybercognition: Brain, behaviour, and the digital world.* Sage.

Glossary

Artificial intelligence: The creation of intelligent machines and computer systems.

Augmented reality (AR): The visual portrayal of virtual objects over real world displays using technologies such as cameras and screens.

Cyberpsychology: "Is a scientific inter-disciplinary domain that focuses on the psychological phenomena which emerge as a result of the human interaction with digital technology, particularly the Internet" (British Psychological Society, n.d., Title section).

Gaming: The use of video games online or offline.

Human–computer interaction: Refers to the field that studies the design and testing of interactive computer systems that exist at the point where humans and computers meet.

Mobile computing: The use of smartphones, tablets, laptops, and other mobile devices as computers.

Social media: Websites, applications, and online social networks which individuals use to make contact with others and to communicate and share information online.

Virtual reality: The use of computer technologies to create three-dimensional virtual worlds or objects which users can interact with.

References

Ahmadpour, N., Keep, M., Janssen, A., Rouf, A., & Marthick, M. (2020). Design strategies for virtual reality interventions for managing pain and anxiety in children and adolescents: Scoping review. *JMIR Serious Games, 8*(1), 1–11.

American Psychiatric Association. (2013). *Diagnostic and statistical manual of mental disorders* (5th ed.). https://doi.org/10.1176/appi.books.9780890425596

American Psychiatric Association. (2022). *Diagnostic and statistical manual of mental disorders* (5th ed., text rev.). Author. https://doi.org/10.1176/appi.books.9780890425787

British Psychological Society. (n.d.). *Cyberpsychology section.* Retrieved April 23, 2023, from https://www.bps.org.uk/member-networks/cyberpsychology-section

Buchanan, T., & Whitty, M. T. (2014). The online dating romance scam: Causes and consequences of victimhood. *Psychology, Crime and Law, 20*(3), 261–283. https://doi.org/10.1080/1068316X.2013.772180

Campbell, A., Ridout, B., Amon, K., Navarro, P., Collyer, B., & Dalgleish, J. (2019). A customized social network platform (kids helpline circles) for delivering group counseling to young people experiencing family discord that impacts their well-being: Exploratory study. *Journal of Medical Internet Research, 21*(12), 1–10.

Chadwick, D. D., & Fullwood, C. (2018). An online life like any other: Identity, self-determination, and social networking among adults with intellectual disabilities. *Cyberpsychology, Behavior, and Social Networking, 21*(1), 56–64.

Conroy, D., Chadwick, D., Fullwood, C., & Lloyd, J. (2022). "You have to know how to live with it without getting to the addiction part": British young adult experiences of smartphone overreliance and disconnectivity. *Psychology of Popular Media.* Advance online publication. https://doi.org/10.1037/ppm0000425

Coulson, N. S. (2019). Online support communities. In A. Attrill-Smith, C. Fullwood, M. Keep, & D. J. Kuss (Eds.), *The Oxford handbook of cyberpsychology* (pp. 241–260). Oxford University Press.

Csikszentmihalyi, M. (1990). *Flow: The psychology of optimal performance.* Cambridge University Press.

Debb, S. M., Schaffer, D. R., & Colson, D. G. (2020). A reverse digital divide: Comparing information security behaviors of generation Y and generation Z adults. *International Journal of Cybersecurity Intelligence & Cybercrime, 3*(1), 42–55.

Finkelhor, D., Jones, L., & Mitchell, K. (2021). Teaching privacy: A flawed strategy for children's online safety. *Child Abuse and Neglect, 117,* Article 105064. https://doi.org/10.1016/j.chiabu.2021.105064

Fullwood, C. (2019). Impression management and self-presentation online. In A. Attrill-Smith, C. Fullwood, M. Keep, & D. J. Kuss (Eds.), *The Oxford handbook of cyberpsychology* (pp. 35–56). Oxford University Press.

Fullwood, C., Orchard, L., & Floyd, S. (2013). Emoticon convergence in Internet chat rooms. *Social Semiotics, 23*(5), 648–662. https://doi.org/10.1080/10350330.2012.739000

Hadlington, L. (2017). Human factors in cybersecurity; examining the link between Internet addiction, impulsivity, attitudes towards cybersecurity, and risky cybersecurity behaviours. *Heliyon, 3*(7), e00346.

Joinson, A. N., Houghton, D. J., Vasalou, A., & Marder, B. L. (2011). Digital crowding: Privacy, self-disclosure, and technology. In S. Trepte & L. Reinecke (Eds.), *Privacy online: Perspectives on privacy and self-disclosure in the social web* (pp. 33–45). Springer.

Joinson, A. N., Reips, U.-D., Buchanan, T., & Paine Schofield, C. B. (2010). Privacy, trust, and self-disclosure online. *Human-Computer Interaction, 25*(1), 1–24. https://doi.org/10.1080/07370020903586662

Joinson, A. N., Woodley, A., & Reips, U.-D. (2007). Personalisation, authentication, and self-disclosure in self-administered Internet surveys. *Computers in Human Behavior, 23*(1), 275–285. https://doi.org/10.1016/j.chb.2004.10.012

Jones, L. L., Wurm, L. H., Norville, G. A., & Mullins, K. L. (2020). Sex differences in emoji use, familiarity, and valence. *Computers in Human Behavior, 108,* 106305. https://doi.org/10.1016/j.chb.2020.106305

Kaye, L. K., Monk, R. L., Wall, H. J., Hamlin, I., & Qureshi, A. W. (2018). The effect of flow and context on in-vivo positive mood in digital gaming. *International Journal of Human-Computer Studies, 110*, 45–52. https://doi.org /10.1016/j.ijhcs.2017.10.005

Keep, M., Janssen, A., & Amon, K. (2019). Image sharing on social networking sites: Who, what, why, and so what? In A. Attrill-Smith, C. Fullwood, M. Keep, & D. J. Kuss (Eds.), *The Oxford handbook of cyberpsychology* (pp. 349–369). Oxford University Press.

Kirwan, G. (2015). Psychology and security: Utilising psychological and communication theories to promote safer cloud security behaviours. In R. Ko & K.-K. R. Choo (Eds.), *The cloud security ecosystem: Technical, legal, business and management issues* (pp. 269–281). Syngress.

Kirwan, G. H. (2019). The rise of cybercrime. In A. Attrill-Smith, C. Fullwood, M. Keep, & D. J. Kuss (Eds.), *The Oxford handbook of cyberpsychology* (pp. 627–644). Oxford University Press.

Kirwan, G., & Power, A. (2013). *Cybercrime: The psychology of online offenders.* Cambridge University Press.

Lee, J., & Jin, C. (2019). The relationship between self-concepts and flaming behavior: Polarity of the online comments. *Journal of Theoretical and Applied Information Technology, 97*, 2518–2529.

McAlaney, J., & Hills, P. J. (2020). Understanding Phishing email processing and perceived trustworthiness through eye-tracking. *Frontiers in Psychology, 11*, 1756. https://doi.org/10.3389/fpsyg.2020.01756

Merdian, H. L., Perkins, D., McCashin, D., & Stevanovic, J. (2021). Integrating structured individual offending pathway analysis into group treatment for individuals who have accessed, shared, and/or distributed child sexual exploitation material: A feasibility study and preliminary outcome evaluation. *Psychology, Crime and Law, 27*(6), 579–605. https://doi.org/10 .1080/1068316X.2020.1849690

Naylor, M., Ridout, B., & Campbell, A. (2020). A scoping review identifying the need for quality research on the use of virtual reality in workplace settings for stress management. *Cyberpsychology, Behavior, and Social Networking, 23*(8), 506–518.

Orchard, L. J., Fullwood, C., Galbraith, N., & Morris, N. (2014). Individual differences as predictors of social networking. *Journal of Computer-Mediated Communication, 19*(3), 388–402.

Paine, C., Reips, U.-D., Stieger, S., Joinson, A., & Buchanan, T. (2007). Internet users' perceptions of 'privacy concerns' and 'privacy actions'. *International Journal of Human – Computer Studies, 65*(6), 526–536. https://doi.org/10.1016 /j.ijhcs.2006.12.001

Quayle, E., & Koukopoulos, N. (2019). Deterrence of online child sexual abuse and exploitation. *Policing: A Journal of Policy and Practice, 13*(3), 345–362. https://doi.org/10.1093/police/pay028

Suler, J. (2004). The online disinhibition effect. *Cyberpsychology and Behavior, 7*(3), 321–326. https://doi.org/10.1089/1094931041291295.

Suler, J. (2015). *Psychology of the digital age: Humans become electric.* Cambridge University Press.

Talbot, C. V., Talbot, A., Roe, D. J., & Briggs, P. (2022). The management of LGBTQ+ identities on social media: A student perspective. *New Media and Society, 24*(8), 1729–1750.

Vasalou, A., Joinson, A. N., & Houghton, D. (2015). Privacy as a fuzzy concept: A new conceptualization of privacy for practitioners. *Journal of the American Society for Information Science and Technology, 66*(5), 918–929. https://doi.org/10.1002/asi.23220

Walther, J. B. (1996). Computer mediated communication: Impersonal, interpersonal and hyperpersonal interaction. *Communication Research, 23*(1), 3–43. https://doi.org/10.1177/009365096023001001

Walther, J. B. (2007). Selective self-presentation in computer mediated communication: Hyperpersonal dimensions of technology, language and cognition. *Computers in Human Behaviour, 23*(5), 2538–2557. https://doi.org/10.1016/j.chb.2006.05.002

World Health Organization. (2018). *International classification of diseases for mortality and morbidity statistics* (11th rev.). https://icd.who.int/browse11/l-m/en

Conducting Online Research

Brendan Rooney

Chapter Overview

The chapter will begin by briefly considering the key characteristics of good research. Next, this chapter will review the main types of online research methods (online observational studies, online interviews and focus groups, web experiments, and online questionnaires and surveys), and provide key considerations for researchers seeking to choose an online method. Finally, the chapter will consider how the main ethical issues that apply when collecting data online can (and must) be considered.

Key Terms

The **research population** is the entire group of people (or animals or other things), with the characteristic(s) a researcher wishes to explore; the whole group of interest. The **research sample** is a subset of the population, from which the researcher can collect data so as to make claims about the population.

Introduction: Good Research

Research is the systematic process of collecting and analysing information in an effort to make a contribution to knowledge on a particular phenomenon; it is looking for an answer to a research question. It typically involves (a) considering what is currently known about a topic and articulating a specific question about it, (b) designing a way to collect information, (c) executing the information-finding strategy, (d) analysing the findings, and (e) communicating the results so as to make a contribution to knowledge.

The important thing to remember about research is that any or all outcomes (from good research) constitute a contribution to knowledge and can be equally valuable to discovery. Research students can often feel like their research project needs to produce a specific outcome, such as a statistically significant difference between groups, in order for it to be worthwhile. This is not the case. Sometimes very bad research can produce seemingly novel and exciting findings, but it is still bad research. So how do we know what makes research good

DOI: 10.4324/9781003092513-4

or bad? If we don't evaluate research by its findings, then how might we evaluate research?

All good research builds upon what has come before and aims to pave the way for more research. Any single research project is conducted in the context of many other questions and studies. It is part of a bigger process, part of a community of knowledge-making. To evaluate research, reviewers should scrutinise the *claims* that are being made about the phenomenon in question and whether or not there is sufficient basis for these claims. In short, producing good research requires careful consideration and design.

The Internet and Research

Throughout history various developments in society and technology have afforded researchers the opportunity to conduct better quality research in line with the characteristics described above. One of the most influential developments was the rise of the internet. Since the start of the millennium, internet use has seen a 1,392% increase to over 5 billion internet users (over 65% of the world's population) by 30 June 2022 (InternetWorldStats.com, 2022). This exponential penetration of the internet into daily life has revolutionised the way in which research is conducted. This chapter explores this revolution and considers some of the associated issues for researchers wishing to collect data online.

Secondary Research Online

Using the internet, researchers can more easily communicate with each other, collaborate in teams, and coordinate their research activities. This efficient communication can facilitate multi-disciplinary and international collaborations on bigger research projects using larger skill-sets and greater expertise. Researchers can also more successfully and efficiently disseminate their work using online journals, interactive websites, and social and e-learning media. In turn, researchers can search and access this existing body of published work much more efficiently than before using the internet. When a researcher collects, reviews, or synthesises existing research, when they assimilate and evaluate previous theory and findings, it is referred to as **"secondary research"**. High-quality research is built upon a systematic and thorough review of what has been done before and the internet allows researchers to conduct this secondary research at an enormous rate using search engines and specialist databases. (See the activity section of this chapter for some advice on conducting your own online literature search.)

When researchers conduct and report a formal structured and transparent review of the literature in a particular area, it is referred to as a systematic review. A systematic review attempts to collate and analyse the findings from an entire set of research studies that fit particular criteria (e.g. all studies exploring workplace cyberbullying, conducted in the past ten years). By including multiple studies from different research groups, while minimising bias, systematic reviews can present a more reliable picture of the current findings and knowledge of a particular topic (Chandler et al., 2021). By using predefined search and inclusion criteria, the systematic reviews can be replicated by other researchers and thus are available for scrutiny and peer review (one of the most important quality control checks for research). In many cases, systematic reviews can also use statistical techniques, referred to as meta-analysis, so as to combine data from multiple studies and provide more precise estimates of the size of statistical effects, than individual studies (Glass, 1976). For these reasons, systematic reviews make powerful and important contributions to our understanding of phenomena. Thus, using the internet, researchers can access and synthesise previous research but importantly, they can do so using a quantifiable and transparent system that can then be disseminated widely.

Primary Research Online

In addition to allowing researchers to access previous research more efficiently, the internet also allows them to collect their own data for new research (referred to as **primary research**) more efficiently. As mentioned earlier, so much of modern human life is lived online. People use smartphone apps to take pictures, navigate cities, and monitor daily food intake or physical activity. They use the internet to socialise and date, to study, bank, and shop. High-quality rich quantifiable data about all these activities can be accessed by researchers and explored. Thus researchers can efficiently access immeasurable amounts of information about human communication, behaviour, and social interactions, by observing them directly as they happen. Indeed, in recent times so much of these data from so many people are being rapidly channelled through and collected by servers, that the field of "Big Data" has emerged to tackle ways to link and analyse data to extract useful information. In response, lobbying groups have called on governments to regulate the use of such information in the interest of privacy and data protection (Mostert et al., 2018).

Observation

While some form of observation is present in all research, here "**observation**" refers to a method by which researchers can collect data about participants' behaviour as they naturally go about or live through particular experiences. These methods have also been referred to as "**non-reactive data collection**" (NRDC; Janetzko, 2008) because, typically, it is the participants' normal behaviour that is observed in an unobtrusive or non-invasive fashion, rather than their response to questions or their performance in a specifically designed task.

    The use of observation and NRDC studies is characterised by its directness, that is, they allow for direct observation of how people are behaving online.

This means that peoples' reactions to events can be observed as they occur and in some cases rare behaviours can be documented. For example, Koustuv Saha and colleagues (2020) collected more than 50 million tweets from US users of Twitter/X during a 2-month period in 2020 during the COVID-19 global pandemic and compared them with more than 30 million posts from a comparable period in the previous year, before the pandemic. From these tweets they could "observe" a 14% increase in people's mental health symptomatic expressions. This directness of NRDCs is most characteristic when the researchers are hidden, when participants never know they are being observed. However, it is important to note that this sort of research comes with ethical dilemmas and, as discussed later, researchers need to give careful consideration to the implications of the way in which they collect data.

Interviews, Questionnaires, and Experiments

Interviews are one of the most flexible tools available to researchers, but when used for research, it is important that they are conducted using a predefined or systematic approach. Research interviews can vary along a spectrum from extremely structured interviews that follow a strict inflexible schedule, perhaps with closed-response questions (where responses have been predefined), to extremely unstructured discussions that allow for any topic to be discussed in any way. Typically, in order to allow the researcher to efficiently probe a specific topic, while allowing for unanticipated responses, researchers will carefully design and use an interview schedule that guides the agenda of the discussion. Interviews are flexible enough to be used with prompts or activities. For example, Robards and Lincoln (2017) have developed and documented the use of the "social media scroll back" interview, where researchers and participants revisit the activity of the participant's social media to prompt reflection or discussion. This is a particularly innovative way to give participants a voice in the work and include them as co-analysts. A variant of the interview method conducted with small groups of people has become a useful research tool. These **focus groups** allow the researcher to conveniently collect data from more than one person at a time and they allow for the examination of group interaction (see Brown et al., 2021, for a useful discussion of conducting web-based focus groups with young people).

Another way to ask questions in research is by using a survey or questionnaire. **Questionnaires** are one of the most commonly used methods for data collection (Berends, 2006), and this is also true online where increasingly researchers are using online surveys and questionnaires (Buchanan, 2007; Gosling et al., 2004). Questionnaires allow researchers to collect rich data similar to the interview technique, but can also be used to identify quantified patterns and relationships that emerge in the data. If researchers want to make claims that go beyond patterns and relationships, if they want to test causal hypotheses and explore the *influences* or *causes* of events, thoughts, or behaviour, then they often collect data using an experiment. Experiments allow researchers to hold many variables constant while manipulating only one or two factors, thus allowing the researcher to identify the role of various possible causes. By conducting experiments and questionnaires online, all sorts of things, from questions or stimuli to execution of the design and testing, can be precisely constructed, manipulated, automated, and delivered to large numbers of participants all over the world.

Considerations for Online Data Collection

The characteristic features of the internet that have redefined the way people communicate are the very same features that have supported online researchers in their ability to collect data online. Online methods provide several advantages over traditional delivery. Executing research online can be faster and cheaper than traditional offline methods (e.g. Gosling et al., 2004; Kwak & Radler, 2002). Furthermore, using online research methods like these can give a researcher greater control of the design and greater flexibility and functionality (Bandilla et al., 2003; Boyer et al., 2002). Researchers can conduct interviews with participants using video call technology such as Zoom (Archibald et al., 2019) or they might decide to conduct an interview through text by exchanging email messages. Thus participating in an online study can be a more comfortable experience (e.g. Naus et al., 2009; Archibald et al., 2019). The increased comfort and convenience can help participants feel trusting of the research, which in turn encourages them to answer questions around sensitive topics (Tourangeau, 2004), to disclose more information about themselves (Weisband & Kiesler, 1996), and to respond with reduced social desirability (Frick et al., 2001; Joinson, 1999). (See Reips, 2021, for further discussion of the benefits of using online methods.)

Online research methods provide researchers with the opportunity to access large samples of participants which can in turn increase the statistical power of the research (Buchanan & Smith, 1999; Cantrell & Lupinacci, 2007; Gosling et al., 2004). In addition to large samples, the internet provides an opportunity for researchers to access diverse or difficult-to-reach populations, giving a voice to some previously underrepresented populations. For example, Russomanno et al. (2019) used targeted Facebook advertisements to recruit transgender participants for their research. Some research even suggests that conducting interviews and discussions online (referred to as computer-mediated communication or CMC) is superior to face-to-face communication (Jonassen et al., 1999; Smith et al., 2011). However, other researchers criticise the lack of context and nonverbal cues in CMC (Liu, 2002; Rovai, 2000). Importantly, these strengths and weaknesses vary depending on whether the CMC is synchronous (e.g. video chat, instant messaging) or asynchronous (e.g. email, SMS) (Abrams et al., 2014) and whether it is an audio-visual display (e.g. talking face display) or text-based (Walker et al., 1994). This point highlights that despite apparent benefits, online research methods also have some characteristic challenges that require consideration and attention, if they are to be used successfully.

One major criticism of online research concerns the quality of the data collected and whether or not it is equivalent to data collected offline. Some researchers have reported that online questionnaires produced different responses to their offline counterparts and even different psychometric properties (T. Buchanan, 2002; Chmielewski & Kucker, 2020; Gosling et al., 2004). While others have argued that online methods are generally valid and sometimes generate higher quality data than offline studies (Birnbaum, 2001; Kees et al., 2017; Paolacci & Chandler, 2014). A potential threat to the quality of the data in online research is "drop-out", that is, when a participant decides to abandon the research before it has been completed. Zhou and Fishbach (2016) observed rates of between 31.9% and 51% drop-out in online social psychology paradigms. Researchers have suggested various techniques for reducing drop-out that may suit various research projects such as using rewards or incentives for completion (Frick et al., 2001; Musch & Reips, 2000). For further suggestions on how to improve the design of web experiments and questionnaires see Zhou and Fishbach (2016) and Reips (2021).

Related to the issue of drop-out, self-selection to participate has also been discussed as a potential threat to the quality of online data. This is because the group of people who decide to participate (called the research sample) might not be very representative of the group of people we want to study (the research population). This problem is not unique to online research, but what is unique is the magnitude to which this issue can be escalated online, due to typically large samples recruited. Whereas in offline research, increasing the sample size typically improves the quality of the data, issues such as self-selection challenge this assumption with online research (Bethlehem, 2010).

The issue of self-selection draws attention to the need for researchers to consider their recruitment procedures. In the past many have argued that online recruitment is problematic, as it excludes those who do not have internet access (e.g. Bethlehem, 2010). However, more recently various user analyses have shown that, in developed economies such as Western Europe and the USA, the population of internet users is very similar to the general population in all surveyed characteristics (e.g. Internet Society, 2014; Pew Research, 2014). The pace at which the online population profile is converging with the offline population may serve as an important advantage of internet research over offline methods. However, it is important to note that just because a normal population is using the internet, this does not mean that the sample derived from an online study is representative and free from bias.

Finally, there has been much discussion and concern raised about the varied setting in which people participate in online research (e.g. Buchanan & Smith, 1999; Fouladi et al., 2002; Heath et al., 2007; Hewson & Charlton, 2005; Lewis et al., 2009; Nosek et al., 2002; Whittier et al., 2004). Some people might participate in research while watching TV or talking on the phone, while others might be more seriously attentive and considerate of their responses. As with drop-out and many other potential problems in research design, the varied research setting is particularly problematic if it systematically differs between conditions or groups of people. Otherwise, the potential problems with this issue might be regulated using carefully worded instructions, by asking participants to provide a note about the context in which they participated so it can be reported, or by recruiting a large sample (to balance or average out the issue).

Overall, it appears as though conducting research online brings advantages that balance out the scientific and practical disadvantages. Converging evidence shows that online research methods result in qualitatively comparable findings to traditional research methods and where differences in online and offline are found, there is often an explanation in the way in which the study was designed or the sample was recruited. For this reason, it is important to remember that while the internet can become an increasingly more efficient choice of research context, careful design is still important. Indeed, careful research design becomes even more important when online research methods are the only option. With the public health restrictions associated with the COVID-19 pandemic, researchers found themselves with no choice but to use online methods of data collection. The large increase in studies that used online methods brought increased emphasis on the importance of evaluation of research methods and the impact of design (see, for example, Ali et al., 2020, or other articles in the recommended reading list).

CYBERPSYCHOLOGY IN FOCUS: THINKING CRITICALLY ABOUT MEASUREMENT TOOLS

Researchers collect information using measurement tools (like surveys or questionnaires) that they or others have designed and they design scientific studies to try to describe "the nature of things", to get at the "truth". But it is vital to remember that such research doesn't simply collect information, it constructs information. That is, the data are collected using tools that have been designed by the researchers and so they are quite likely to already presuppose the researchers' views and values. For example, consider an online survey that uses closed multiple choice questions to explore participants' reasons for deactivating their social media account. The available response options could not possibly include everything and so the researcher will likely create categories of response options. In doing so, the researcher is *constructing* the possible results. If they are not from a minority group, they may not see it as important to separate out hate-speech experiences from things like cyberstalking, doxxing, or impersonation, using something broad like "Negative online experiences" as the response option. The results of their research will not emphasise these specific reasons for deactivating a social media account. When designing research we need to remain critical and ask whose values are being built into this view of the world? Whose perspectives/experiences are being overlooked? Why is this so? And what can be done?

Internet Research Ethics

As the internet became more popular for data collection, ethicists and research-ers attempted to apply traditional offline research ethics protocols to online research. However, the internet has some particular features that have presented researchers with unique ethical dilemmas. For example, back at the start of the century, Bakardjieva and Feenberg (2001) pointed out that the way in which online electronic records of discussions are freely accessible constituted an unprecedented ethical problem for researchers. When data were openly accessi-ble to all online, their use in any and all research seemed acceptable. Over time, with the exponentially increasing amount of data available online, users and governments became concerned about the way in which people's information was being used. Governments introduced legislation such as the EU's General Data Protection Regulation (GDPR) to try to manage the way in which data are used. While this legislation went a long way in regulating how data can be accessed and used, the ethical principles (and dilemmas) remain. Just because a researcher complies with legislation in how they access data does not mean they are free of ethical concerns. Something might have been posted on a web-site but this doesn't mean it is available to be used in research or that the author "owns" the data. For example, in their *Ethics Guidelines for Internet-Mediated Research*, the British Psychological Society (2021) identified the social respon-sibilities of conducting research online and how researchers need to consider how their work might disrupt or harm social groups. King (1996) presents an illustrative case of a researcher who publishes research based on the discussions of an online support group, and when the members of the group learn of the way their discussions were used, they discontinue participation in the group and the support group dissolves. Bakardjieva and Feenberg (2001) also discuss research that uses peoples' online stories and communications. They argue that what is even worse than invasions of privacy is that such research *alienates* people and objectifies their lives in a way that is unethical. They go on to argue that this is particularly unjust as "cyberspace provides unique opportunities for empowering subjects [participants] by involving them as *contributors* in the research project" (p. 233). Conducting research online has also raised important discussions about ethical dissemination and children's rights to online protec-tion (for a more in-depth discussion of online ethical issues and guidelines for researchers see Oates, 2020; Gupta, 2017; Buchanan & Zimmer, 2013; Social Sciences and Humanities Research Ethics Special Working Committee, 2008; and the additional resources section for this chapter). As the internet, tech-nology, and society evolve, so too do the issues surrounding internet research ethics and so researchers need to stay continuously sensitive, considerate, and informed about current debates and best practice.

Conclusion

Technological developments continue to shape the internet and society, and the ways in which they are shaping research needs to be seen as a dynamic process that requires continuous re-consideration. While much of the research exploring features of online data collection methods suggests that the advantages outweigh the challenges, researchers need to give careful consideration to the way in which they use the internet and design online research if they are to obtain high-quality data from appropriate samples of individuals. In addition, the use of online research methods requires additional ethical considerations if the principles of ethical research are to be maintained. While conducting research online brings issues that are unique, two trends are worth noting. Firstly, because the internet provides researchers with increasing efficiency of data collection and researchers are improving their online data collection skills, internet research is becoming more and more commonplace. Secondly, as the internet develops, many features of the offline and online worlds are converging. For example, research has demonstrated that users of online virtual worlds operate under the same nonverbal social norms (such as eye-gaze and personal space) that exist offline (Yee et al., 2007). For both of these reasons, the particular features of internet research may soon be indistinguishable from "traditional" offline research.

Activity

The capacity to access previous research online is one of the main ways in which the internet has revolutionised research. Indeed, the amount of research literature online can be overwhelming and for this reason it is important to filter and select the relevant and credible information from the rest. When conducting a review of the current literature it is important to plan your approach.

Try to conduct an online search of the literature on a particular topic of interest. Start by articulating the main keywords for your topic (e.g. "mobile phone" and "addiction"). As part of your plan, consider alternative terms or cultural variants of keywords (e.g. "cell phone", "dependency", "obsession", "nomophobia"). Your plan might start with a broad search by superficially scanning a large number of potentially relevant findings. After this, you can narrow the search to a more manageable number of highly relevant articles. To get a broad sense of an area, course syllabi (can be searched online) or websites such as Wikipedia can offer helpful situational context. For more detailed information, the use of up-to-date review articles on a topic or special issues of relevant journals can be particularly helpful. Many databases also feature particular tools to support your search such as Boolean operators (i.e. combining keywords together with words such as "AND" or "OR").

Discussion Questions

- Can you think of any other advantages or disadvantages to conducting research online?
- Do you think the internet provides greater advantage to observation studies over other types such as questionnaires and experiments? Say why you think so.
- Are there certain types of topics that are better suited to online research than offline research? If so, which ones? And why?
- Discuss the idea that, if someone posts something online, and it is publicly accessible to everyone, then researchers should be allowed use it for their research.

Recommended Reading List

Ulf-Dietrich Reips is a leader in the area of online research. He has been publishing on how online research has changed science since the 1990s. This article reviews trends over the past 25 years and introduces important new methods such as attention checks. Pitfalls and best practices are also described. Indeed the entire special issue of this journal includes other insightful papers.

Reips, U. D. (2021). Web-based research in psychology. *Zeitschrift für Psychologie, 229*(4), 198–213. http://doi.org/10.1027/2151-2604/a000475

The public health measures that came about in response to the COVID-19 pandemic rapidly increased the pace at which research methods and practices moved online. In the context of the COVID-19 pandemic this short article weighs up the strengths of online research against the weaknesses, particularly with regard to the diversity of recruited samples.

Lourenco, S. F., & Tasimi, A. (2020). No participant left behind: Conducting science during COVID-19. *Trends in Cognitive Sciences, 24*(8), 583–584. https://doi.org/10.1016/j.tics.2020.05.003

These two research synthesis reports by Barroga and Matanguihan (2020) and Nind et al. (2021) also reflect on COVID-19 as they chart how social research methods have been successfully adapted to operate under the public health measures such as social distancing during the pandemic conditions of COVID-19.

Barroga, E., & Matanguihan, G. J. (2020). Fundamental shifts in research, ethics and peer review in the era of the COVID-19 pandemic. *Journal of Korean Medical Science, 35*(45). https://doi.org/10.3346/jkms.2020.35.e395

Nind, M., Coverdale, A., & Meckin, R. (2021). Changing social research practices in the context of Covid-19: Rapid evidence review. UK National Centre for Research Methods. http://eprints.ncrm.ac.uk/4398/. https://doi.org/10.5258/NCRM/NCRM.00004458

These guidelines published by the British Psychological Society provide an excellent overview of some of the main ethical issues surrounding online research.

> British Psychological Society. (2021). Ethics guidelines for Internet-mediated research. https://www.bps.org.uk/news-and-policy/ethics -guidelines-internet-mediated-research

Glossary

Experiment: A research situation or activity that has been specifically designed and controlled so as to allow researchers to establish causal inference (i.e. the role of some condition or characteristic in causing some outcome).

Focus groups: A variant of the interview method conducted with small groups of people, that allows for discussion to answer the interviewer's questions.

Interview (research): A method of data collection where questions are asked by the interviewer so as to collect information from the interviewee.

Non-reactive data collection: When the researcher collects data using an unobtrusive observation method.

Observation (research): A non-experimental research method whereby the researcher observes behaviour.

Primary research: When the researcher collects original data, specifically for their research project.

Questionnaire: A series of predefined questions or other statements distributed so as to collect information from respondents.

Research: The systematic process of collecting and analysing information in an effort to make a contribution to knowledge of a particular phenomenon.

Research population: The entire group of people (or animals or other things), with the characteristic(s) a researcher wishes to explore; the whole group of interest.

Research sample: A subset of the population, from which the researcher can collect data so as to make claims about the population.

Secondary research: When the researcher collects, reviews, or synthesises existing research.

References

Abrams, K., Wang, Z., Song, Y. J., & Gonzalez-Galindo, S. (2014). Data richness tradeoffs between face-to-face, online audio-visual, and online text-only focus groups. *Social Science Computer Review, 33*(1). https://doi.org/10.1177 /0894439313519733

Ali, S. H., Foreman, J., Capasso, A., Jones, A. M., Tozan, Y., & DiClemente, R. J. (2020). Social media as a recruitment platform for a nationwide online survey of COVID-19 knowledge, beliefs, and practices in the United States: Methodology and feasibility analysis. *BMC Medical Research Methodology, 20*(1), 1–11. https://doi.org/10.1186/s12874-020-01011-0

Archibald, M. M., Ambagtsheer, R. C., Casey, M. G., & Lawless, M. (2019). Using Zoom videoconferencing for qualitative data collection: Perceptions and experiences of researchers and participants. *International Journal of Qualitative Methods.* https://doi.org/10.1177/1609406919874596

Bakardjieva, M., & Feenberg, A. (2001). Involving the virtual subject. *Ethics and Information Technology, 2*(4), 233–240. https://doi.org/10.1023/A:1011454606534

Bandilla, W., Bosnjak, M., & Altdorfer, P. (2003). Survey administration effects? A comparison of Web-based and traditional written self administered surveys using the ISSP environment module. *Social Science Computer Review, 21*(2), 235–243. https://doi.org/10.1177/0894439303021002009

Barroga, E., & Matanguihan, G. J. (2020). Fundamental shifts in research, ethics and peer review in the era of the COVID-19 pandemic. *Journal of Korean Medical Science, 35*(45). https://doi.org/10.3346/jkms.2020.35.e395

Berends, M. (2006). Survey methods in educational research. In J. L. Green, G. Camilli, & P. B. Elmore (Eds.), *Handbook of complementary methods in education research* (pp. 623–640). Erlbaum. https://doi.org/10.4324/9780203874769

Bethlehem, J. (2010). Selection bias in web surveys. *International Statistical Review, 78*(2), 161–188. https://doi.org/10.1111/j.1751-5823.2010.00112.x

Birnbaum, M. H. (2001). A web-based program of research on decision making. In U.-D. Reips & M. Bosnjak (Eds.), *Dimensions of internet science* (pp. 23–55). Pabst.

Boyer, K. K., Olson, J. R., Calantone, R. J., & Jackson, E. C. (2002). Print versus electronic surveys: A comparison of two data collection methodologies. *Journal of Operations Management, 20*(4), 357–373. https://doi.org/10.1016/S0272-6963(02)00004-9

British Psychological Society. (2021). Ethics guidelines for Internet-mediated research. https://www.bps.org.uk/news-and-policy/ethics-guidelines-internet-mediated-research

Brown, C. A., Revette, A. C., de Ferranti, S. D., Fontenot, H. B., & Gooding, H. C. (2021). Conducting web-based focus groups with adolescents and young adults. *International Journal of Qualitative Methods, 20.* https://doi.org/10.1177/1609406921996872

Buchanan, E. A., & Zimmer, M. (2013). Internet research ethics. In E. N. Zalta (Ed.), *The Stanford encyclopedia of philosophy* (Fall 2013 ed.). https://plato.stanford.edu/entries/ethics-internet-research/

Buchanan, T. (2002). Online assessment: Desirable or dangerous? *Professional Psychology: Research and Practice, 33*(2), 148–154. https://doi.org/10.1037/0735-7028.33.2.148

Buchanan, T. (2007). Personality testing on the Internet: What we know, and what we do not. In A. Joinson, K. McKenna, T. Postmes, & U.-D. Reips (Eds.), *Oxford handbook of Internet psychology* (pp. 447–459). Oxford University Press. https://doi.org/10.1093/oxfordhb/9780199561803.001.0001

Buchanan, T., & Smith, J. L. (1999). Using the Internet for psychological research: Personality testing on the World Wide Web. *British Journal of Psychology, 90*(1), 125–144. https://doi.org/10.1348/000712699161189

Cantrell, M. A., & Lupinacci, P. (2007). Methodological issues in online data collection. *Journal of Advanced Nursing, 60*(5), 544–549. https://doi.org/10.1111/j.1365-2648.2007.04448.x

Chandler, J., Cumpston, M., Thomas, J., Higgins, J. P. T., Deeks, J. J., & Clarke, M. J. (2021). Chapter I: Introduction. In J. P. T. Higgins, J. Thomas, J. Chandler, M. Cumpston, T. Li, M. J. Page, V. A. Welch (Eds.), *Cochrane handbook for systematic reviews of interventions version 6.2* (updated February 2021). Cochrane. www.training.cochrane.org/handbook.

Chmielewski, M., & Kucker, S. C. (2020). An MTurk crisis? Shifts in data quality and the impact on study results. *Social Psychological and Personality Science, 11*(4), 464–473. https://doi.org/10.1177/1948550619875149

Fouladi, R. T., McCarthy, C. J., & Moller, N. P. (2002). Paper-and-pencil or online? Evaluating mode effects on measures of emotional functioning and attachment. *Assessment, 9*(2), 204–215. https://doi.org/10.1177/10791102009002011

Frick, A., Bächtiger, M. T., & Reips, U.-D. (2001). Financial incentives, personal information and drop-out in online studies. In U.-D. Reips & M. Bosnjak (Eds.), *Dimensions of internet science* (pp. 209–219). Pabst. http://citeseerx.ist.psu.edu/viewdoc/download?doi=10.1.1.567.8057&rep=rep1&type=pdf

Glass, G. V. (1976). Primary, secondary and meta-analysis of research. *Educational Researcher, 5*(10), 3–8.

Gosling, S. D., Vazire, S., Srivastava, S., & John, O. P. (2004). Should we trust web-based studies? A comparative analysis of six preconceptions about Internet questionnaires. *American Psychologist, 59*(2), 93–104. https://doi.org/10.1037/0003-066X.59.2.93

Gupta, S. (2017). Ethical issues in designing internet-based research: Recommendations for good practice. *Journal of Research Practice, 13*(2), D1. http://jrp.icaap.org/index.php/jrp/article/view/576/476

Heath, N. M., Lawyer, S. R., & Rasmussen, E. B. (2007). Web-based versus paper-and-pencil course evaluations. *Teaching of Psychology, 34*(4), 259–261. https://doi.org/10.1080/00986280701700433

Hewson, C., & Charlton, J. P. (2005). Measuring health beliefs on the Internet: A comparison of paper and Internet administrations of the Multidimensional Health Locus of Control Scale. *Behavior Research Methods, 37*(4), 691–702. https://doi.org/10.3758/BF03192742

Internet Society. (2014). Global Internet user survey 2014. http://www.internetsociety.org/sites/default/files/Global_Internet_Report_2014_0.pdf

InternetWorldStats.com. (2022). Internet usage and world population statistics for. Retrieved 11 September 2023, from http://www.internetworldstats.com/stats.htm

Janetzko, D. (2008). Nonreactive data collection on the Internet. In N. Fielding, R. M. Lee, & G. Blank (Eds.), *The SAGE handbook of online research methods* (pp. 161–174). Sager, K.

Joinson, A. (1999). Social desirability, anonymity, and Internet-based questionnaires. *Behavior Research Methods, Instruments and Computers, 31*(3), 433–438. https://doi.org/10.3758/BF03200723

Jonassen, D., Prevish, T., Christy, D., & Stavulaki, E. (1999). Learning to solve problems on the Web: Aggregate planning in a business management course. *Distance Education, 20*(1), 49–63. https://doi.org/10.1080/0158791990200105

Kees, J., Berry, C., Burton, S., & Sheehan, K. (2017). An analysis of data quality: Professional panels, student subject pools, and Amazon's Mechanical Turk. *Journal of Advertising, 46*(1), 141–155. https://doi.org/10.1080/00913367.2016.1269304

King, S. (1996). Researching Internet communities: Proposed ethical guidelines for the reporting of results. *Information Society, 12*(2), 119. https://doi.org/10.1080/713856145

Kwak, N., & Radler, B. (2002). A comparison between mail and web surveys: Response pattern, respondent profile, and data quality. *Journal of Official Statistics*, *18*(2), 257–274.

Lewis, I. M., Watson, B. C., & White, K. M. (2009). Internet versus paper-and-pencil survey methods in psychological experiments: Equivalence testing of participant responses to health-related messages. *Australian Journal of Psychology*, *61*(2), 107–116. https://doi.org/10.1080/00049530802105865

Liu, Y. (2002). What does research say about the nature of computer-mediated communication: Task-orientated, social-emotion-orientated, or both? *Electronic Journal of Sociology*, *6*(1), A1.

Lourenco, S. F., & Tasimi, A. (2020). No participant left behind: Conducting science during COVID-19. *Trends in Cognitive Sciences*, *24*(8), 583–584. https://doi.org/10.1016/j.tics.2020.05.003

Mostert, M., Bredenoord, A. L., Van Der Slootb, B., & Van Delden, J. J. (2018). From privacy to data protection in the EU: Implications for big data health research. *European Journal of Health Law*, *25*(1), 43–55. https://doi.org/10.1163/15718093-12460346

Musch, J., & Reips, U.-D. (2000). A brief history of web experimenting. In M. H. Birnbaum (Ed.), *Psychological experiments on the Internet* (pp. 61–88). Academic Press. https://doi.org/10.1016/B978-012099980-4/50004-6

Naus, M. J., Philipp, L. M., & Samsi, M. (2009). From paper to pixels: A comparison of paper and computer formats in psychological assessment. *Computers in Human Behavior*, *25*(1), 1–7. https://doi.org/10.1016/j.chb.2008.05.012

Nind, M., Coverdale, A., & Meckin, R. (2021). Changing social research practices in the context of Covid-19: Rapid evidence review. UK National Centre for Research Methods. http://eprints.ncrm.ac.uk/4398/. https://doi.org/10.5258/NCRM/NCRM.00004458

Nosek, B. A., Banaji, M. R., & Greenwald, A. G. (2002). E-research: Ethics, security, design, and control in psychological research on the Internet. *Journal of Social Issues*, *58*(1), 161–176. https://doi-org.ucd.idm.oclc.org/10.1111/1540-4560.00254

Oates, J. (2020). Research ethics, children, and young people. In *Handbook of research ethics and scientific integrity* (pp. 623–635). https://doi.org/10.1007/978-3-319-76040-7_28-1

Paolacci, G., & Chandler, J. (2014). Inside the Turk: Understanding Mechanical Turk as a participant pool. *Current Directions in Psychological Science*, *23*(3), 184–188. https://doi.org/10.1177/0963721414531598

Pew Research. (2014). Internet project: Internet user demographics. http://www.pewinternet.org/data-trend/social-media/social-media-user-demographics/

Reips, U. D. (2021). Web-based research in psychology. *Zeitschrift für Psychologie*, *229*(4), 198–213. http://doi.org/10.1027/2151-2604/a000475

Robards, B., & Lincoln, S. (2017). Uncovering longitudinal life narratives: Scrolling back on Facebook. *Qualitative Research*, *17*(6), 715–730. http://journals.sagepub.com/doi/abs/10.1177/1468794117700707

Rovai, A. P. (2000). Building and sustaining community in asynchronous learning networks. *The Internet and Higher Education*, *3*(4), 285–297. https://doi.org/10.1016/S1096-7516(01)00037-9

Russomanno, J., Patterson, J. G., & Tree, J. M. J. (2019). Social media recruitment of marginalized, hard-to-reach populations: Development of recruitment and monitoring guidelines. *JMIR Public Health and Surveillance*, *5*(4), e14886. https://doi.org/10.2196/14886

Saha, K., Torous, J., Caine, E. D., & De Choudhury, M. (2020). Psychosocial effects of the COVID-19 pandemic: Large-scale quasi-experimental study on social media. *Journal of Medical Internet Research, 22*(11), e22600. https://doi.org/10.2196/22600

Smith, G. G., Sorensen, C., Gump, A., Heindel, A. J., Caris, M., & Martinez, C. D. (2011). Overcoming student resistance to group work: Online versus face-to-face. *The Internet and Higher Education, 14*(2), 121–128. http://doi.org/10.1016/j.iheduc.2010.09.005

Social sciences and humanities research ethics special working committee. (2008). *Extending the spectrum: The TCPS and ethical issues in Internet-based research.* Interagency Advisory Panel on Research Ethics.

Tourangeau, R. (2004). Survey research and societal change. *Annual Review of Psychology, 55*(1), 775–802. https://doi.org/10.1146/annurev.psych.55.090902.142040

Walker, J., Sproull, L., & Subramani, R. (1994). *Using a human face in an interface.* Paper presented at the In Proceedings of the Conference on Human Factors in Computers. https://doi.org/10.1145/191666.191708

Weisband, S., & Kiesler, S. (1996). *Self-disclosure on computer forms: Meta-analysis and implications.* Paper presented at the CHI96, Vancouver, British Columbia, Canada.

Whittier, D. K., Seeley, S., & St. Lawrence, J. S. (2004). A comparison of Web- with paper-based surveys of gay and bisexual men who vacationed in a gay resort community. *AIDS Education and Prevention, 16*(5), 476–485. https://doi.org/10.1521/aeap.16.5.476.48735

Yee, N., Bailenson, J. N., Urbanek, M., Chang, F., & Merget, D. (2007). The unbearable likeness of being digital: The persistence of nonverbal social norms in online virtual environments. *The Journal of Cyberpsychology and Behavior, 10*(1), 115–121. https://doi.org/10.1089/cpb.2006.9984

Zhou, H., & Fishbach, A. (2016). The pitfall of experimenting on the web: How unattended selective attrition leads to surprising (yet false) research conclusions. *Journal of Personality and Social Psychology, 111*(4), 493. https://doi.org/10.1037/pspa0000056

PART 2

Human Interaction Online

Cyberpsychology in Professional Practice

Interview 2

Lee Kelly is the digital marketing, content, and community manager for a global cybersecurity platform and has been working in this role for six months. He has worked in digital content management and communication for over a decade.

What are your main responsibilities and/or daily activities in this post?

Website build and maintenance. Content creation and management. Content and social media strategy. Working with other departments to make sure their content is kept up to date and that the information for their area of the business is being represented correctly in any outward-facing content and communications. Working closely with internal stakeholders to translate their requirements into usable digital assets and on-site user journeys. Working with the team to build an active community within the online platform.

When did you first become interested in cyberpsychology, and how did you develop this interest into part of your career path?

DOI: 10.4324/9781003092513-6

I've been a giant tech geek since I was a child. I was obsessed with *Star Trek: The Next Generation* and the way it depicts how computers and technology will play a major role in humanity's future. Deanna Troi, the ship's counsellor and psychologist, was my favourite character and role model. Combining this with natural people-watching skills and an endless fascination for observable human behaviour brought me into the world of psychology.

In the final year of my undergrad degree, we did a module on cyberpsychology (which was literally in its infancy at that time) and I thought to myself, "wow – this is the good stuff". I went from not really knowing what my next move would be to having a focused interest area. When the chance to enter into an MSc in cyberpsychology came along, a light switch went on in my mind and my transition to the path of being a super geek was complete.

What cyberpsychological knowledge is of most relevance to your current role?

The scientific method and data-driven decision-making are areas of knowledge that have stuck with me to this day. I'm a really big advocate of the phrase "don't bring your opinion to a data fight". To explain this more, in my professional life as a digital content manager, everyone in the company has a brilliant idea about what they subjectively think is the most important-thing-ever that we should be working on or adding to our website or app or whatever it is that we are pushing at the time. Sometimes it's a good idea, sometimes not. I'm not a big fan of time wasting so I would generally go out and do some research using readily available data such as our website analytics or keyword search tools to see if search data or online behaviour patterns support the claim that something is important. Success leaves clues and the answer will always be there somewhere in the data. If the suggested idea (a pseudo hypothesis) is supported by the data as something would be of interest to our target audience, then that will get the green light to proceed. If not then it can go into a backlog for future consideration. It is a good way of managing and prioritising workloads and using resources effectively. It is also an excellent way of appeasing idea-suggesting egos in various different states of inflation who feel that their input has been explored. They'll have moved on to the next shiny thing by then. That's more of an area for an organisational psychologist to explore.

Are there any theories in cyberpsychology which you find applicable to your work? If so, which one(s), and how are they relevant to your responsibilities in your role?

Mental models:

I always start with the tenet that users will already have a mental model of how something works. There is no need to reinvent the wheel or create a new type of website or app that would cause a barrier to adoption. Often in business, there is a perception that every challenge faced is a totally unique problem that needs a newly invented solution. In reality, the problem is mostly new to that particular business only and they don't want to look outside for help. I've previously worked across many industries and in digital agencies and know that we just need to replicate something based on a model already being used somewhere else. Once again success leaves clues.

Addiction:

I am very ethically driven which is a fundamental of psychology. Addiction in the form of online gambling is a major problem with relatively weak regulation. In a previous role, I worked in an organisation with elements of online gameplay. That organisation (unlike most of the industry) was also heavily regulated and I took up a secondary role in problem-play prevention to help detect and prevent addictive behaviours from manifesting early in the user lifecycle.

Research in the area was thin on the ground and for the most part, it seems to be a hidden problem. I would be a firm advocate of introducing robust far-reaching regulation of the gambling industry as well as ethical standards around online ad targeting. From experience at the time, most regulatory bodies had a very low-level understanding of how digital advertising and targeting worked so were for the most part ignored or worked on the basis that the entity running the ads would self-regulate themselves. This can sometimes be at odds with a business's internal ethos to generate as much revenue as possible.

Measures to prevent the use of misleading descriptors such as "gaming" rather than "gambling" as a way to soften the image of the industry should also be introduced.

What do you think are the most important real-world applications of cyberpsychology?

I think the most widely identifiable area would be in user experience and UX design. Many of my contemporaries went on to work in these areas. I suppose I am biased but I think anyone I know who has a psychology background is light years ahead of others on how they approach the human-centred element of design.

I have a particular interest in social and consumer cyberpsychology which brought me down my career path in digital content management and social media communication. In the last couple of years, the realisation of the power that large social platforms have to change and sometimes manipulate human behaviours has come to light. This can lead to undesirable consequences such as an unfavourable election or referendum results. These outcomes would have been unthinkable previously and the manipulation may leave long-lasting polarising societal effects.

Is there anything else that you'd like to add about cyberpsychology in your professional life?

Cyberpsychology has been a real door opener for me. Not only has it provided me with a network of other people with qualifications and interests in cyberpsychology, but it is also always an instant conversation starter. People may not have heard of the term cyberpsychology but know quite well that their phone, computer, wearable, or other devices are changing their own and society's behaviours and are very inquisitive about what the effects of these are.

I supposed we are lucky to get to see the effects of technology on human behaviour unfolding before our eyes over very short time frames: the rise and fall of social media platforms, the dangers of algorithms that may be skewing people's perceptions, and the triggering of younger generations who recognise the power and effect of technology who are becoming politically active at much earlier stages in life. These are all things that have occurred in the last decade. Gen Z is undoubtedly much savvier than the Millennials and other generations before them. Gen Alpha is just entering into the equation and will undoubtedly push further ahead again. Hopefully, they will bring a new and innate wave of critical thinking and move us beyond the post-truth world in which we currently live.

Lee Kelly
Dublin, Ireland

3 Computer-Mediated Communication and Online Media

Gráinne Kirwan

Chapter Overview

This chapter will consider the variety of communication tools used online, as well as the history of computer-mediated communication (CMC), with particular focus on how the Internet has become an increasingly interactive medium in recent years. The language used online will be examined, especially in relation to abbreviations, acronyms, paralanguage, and emoji. The chapter will consider how various communication theories can be used to understand online communications, especially considering Walther's (1996) hyperpersonal communication model. Finally, the chapter will provide a brief introduction to the concepts of impression management, anonymity, disinhibition, and privacy that will be considered in more detail in the following chapters.

Key Terms

While **computer-mediated communication** (CMC) is a term that most individuals may not have heard of, it describes a great deal of what they do on a daily basis. Put simply, it encompasses all communications that use computers as a medium. Every time that you send an email, or send a message on social media, or comment on an online video, you are engaging in CMC. Indeed, it is even broader than that – for example, it can include text messages (or Short Message Services – SMS) from mobile phones and Voice over Internet Protocol (VoIP) or videoconferencing. Crystal (2011) suggests that CMC incorporates all forms of communication online, including music, photos, drawings, video, and language.

Within these types of online communication, we often engage in **paralanguage**. In general parlance, this refers to methods of modifying meaning through the use of volume, intonation, or other adjustments. For example, even the simple expression "fascinating" could be interpreted as its literal meaning if it is said in an enthusiastic, high-volume manner with the accompaniment of a gasp. Alternatively, it could be interpreted as the complete opposite if said in a

DOI: 10.4324/9781003092513-7

dull, subdued intonation and accompanied by a sigh. In CMC such distinctions might be expressed via punctuation or other devices to enrich the communication – turning the CMC from a **lean medium** into a more nuanced and sometimes playful experience. Other methods of increasing nuance can include the use of abbreviations, acronyms, excessive punctuation, or even the inclusion of indicators of various expressions and icons, such as **emoji** (which developed from earlier **emoticons** and **smileys**).

Many communication theories have been proposed to help us to develop a deeper understanding of what occurs within a communication, and in some cases to give us an ability to predict the future path which that communication will take. Several of these communication theories are considered in this chapter. Some theories are specific to mediated communication, such as **hyperpersonal communication** (Walther, 1996, 2007), which examines how the formation and development of relationships can be affected by the characteristics of CMC. Other communication theories also have relevance for our online interactions and are also discussed here.

Communication Tools Online

Think for a moment about your online communications. Do you use email to contact lecturers? Perhaps you contact your classmates via a virtual learning environment, but use instant messaging or other CMC devices on social media to stay in touch with closer friends and family. Maybe you enjoy online gaming and use the variety of voice and text messaging systems that are used to communicate with fellow gamers. It could be that you stay in touch with family members using videoconferencing, while you use direct messages to arrange meet-ups with your closest friends. Perhaps you're a member of a social media discussion group that allows you to communicate with others with similar interests, or perhaps you use online forums or boards to fill that purpose. Perhaps you write a blog, or keep a Twitter/X account, or maybe you're an influencer on one of the video-based media platforms. Maybe you contribute to a wiki or other collaborative online environment. You might even share files with friends, classmates, or colleagues using a system that permits **computer-supported co-operative work** (CSCW).

There are some important concepts to consider when using CMC. For example, is our usage **synchronous** or **asynchronous**? Synchronous refers to a communication medium where all communicators are simultaneously exchanging messages. This might include voice communications in gaming or chat facilities within virtual learning environments. Asynchronous communications refer to situations where it is expected that the users are not simultaneously communicating – for example, email or forums. There can sometimes be confusion regarding these, especially due to the popularity of smartphones which allow constant access to communications. An individual may become upset if they feel that they are within a communication medium which they consider to be synchronous, but the person that they are communicating with does not respond immediately.

The **fluidity** of online communication tools is also an important factor for consideration. Printed media remains static – it is not possible to change or edit the content once printed (although the information may be revised in newer editions). In contrast, online resources can change in very short periods of time. Consider, for example, an entry on particle physics in an online encyclopaedia – as new developments are made, this article can be updated so the content is fluid when compared to a printed encyclopaedia article on the same topic. This can make online encyclopaedias extremely useful for staying abreast of modern developments, although it is worth noting that unless the entries are maintained by reliable experts in the area it is possible for intentional or unintentional inaccuracies to creep in.

A related concept is the distinction between whether we consider our communications to be more like written language or oral speech. Historically, it required a great deal of effort for most people to publish a piece of written content in a medium where it could be read by many others – for example, they needed to publish a book or have an article included in a newspaper. Even one-to-one written communication such as business and personal letters had a tone that was very different from speech. But modern online communication tends to be much more similar to spoken expression, using a relaxed tone and informal language even with individuals who we do not know, or celebrities with whom we otherwise would not get the opportunity to interact.

A Very Short History of Computer-Mediated Communication

Computers and online communication are such a prevalent part of modern society that it is difficult for many to imagine life without them. Yet as recently as 25 years ago many offices had a very small number of Internet-enabled computers, which were frequently shared among many staff and used for specific purposes (such as bank transfers or payroll).

One of the first books considering CMC was written by Hiltz and Turoff (1978). In particular, it examined the business use of email, and described how early users of this technology noted that many non-verbal cues were lost – an early acknowledgement of the **lean medium** (as noted above), or alternatively a **cues-filtered out** situation. Hiltz and Turoff noted that many early users would attempt to re-establish this information by using a visit or a telephone call to supplement their email.

Soon users started to identify ways of including socioemotional content into their online communications (see, for example, Rice & Love, 1987). However, it was noted that this was not always appropriate in online communications (in a similar way that it is not always appropriate in offline communications).

Indeed, Derks et al. (2008) noted that online communication has similar emotional content to offline communication.

Of course, there have been many changes in the way that online communication occurs since the work of earlier writers such as Hiltz and Turoff (1978) and Rice and Love (1987). Most notably, the much wider variety of methods used in more recent times demonstrates how we use CMC for a mixture of mass communication (to a wide group of people) and personal communication (to a smaller group or individual). While the Internet has allowed communication via computers for around five decades, the **World Wide Web**, as a method of linking documents online, is a much more recent phenomenon (it was conceptualised by Tim Berners-Lee in 1989). Most of the early webpages were relatively static – users could visit them and follow links on their pages, but could rarely interact with them. While some remain this way, many now encourage some degree of interactivity from their users.

While images and video existed online prior to such increased interactivity levels, this development has also resulted in an increase in **multimodality**. Instead of simply reading text on a page, we often now have such text supplemented or replaced by other modes of communication, such as audio files, images, or video files, among many others. The impact of this is evident in terms of the changes in social media – early versions simply allowed text updates, but more recently images and videos have become the norm, with several newer social media platforms being specifically created for the sharing of such content. It is now possible to document our own lives, and the lives of others, in ways previously impossible.

Language and Online Communication

The complexity of communication is seldom clearer than when you travel to a country where you do not speak the native language. Disorientation and frustration can be common, although eventually a few words are learned, and gradually communication becomes easier. One of the main reasons why this occurs is because language is symbolic. A word does not have a meaning until it is given one and that association between the word and its meaning is accepted by the communicators involved.

Similarly, communication is not restricted to verbal language. Meaning can be altered through intonation, facial expression, gestures, and context. Despite the increase in multimodal communication indicated above, the majority of CMC still occurs in the form of written language. The role of this medium can affect how the messages are interpreted (this is considered in more detail in the section on hyperpersonal communication below), but various mechanisms have been adopted to add non-verbal cues to written communication online, thus reducing the lean medium effect. One method of doing this, as already mentioned, involves the use of punctuation or other cues to illustrate paralanguage. Other communication strategies online include the use of abbreviations, acronyms, and emoji.

Paralanguage

We may not be conscious of our own use of paralanguage in our verbal communications. We may often gasp, sigh, or make noises indicative of hesitancy or uncertainty without realising that we're doing it. Writers of fiction have developed many ways of including cues for such paralanguage in the conversations of their characters, often through the use of punctuation or grammar. Many of these cues have been adopted or adapted by users of CMC to illustrate nuances in their own expressions. For example, ellipses (a series of dots such as "…") might be used to indicate a pause or that something is being left unsaid. Extra letters or exaggerated punctuation might be used to indicate strong emotional reactions, and capital letters can also be used for this purpose, or to indicate shouting. In some cases an approximation of the actual sound used might be typed, such as "Ummm", "Hmmm", or "Eh". Finally, the paralanguage may be so subtle that it is easily missed by a user who is unfamiliar with online communication. For example, the inclusion of a full stop after "OK" can indicate frustration or anger in the writer in response to a request from their communication partner (the absence of the full stop indicates a more amicable acceptance of the request).

Acronyms and Abbreviations

Acronyms and abbreviations are popular communication tools for many reasons. They can speed up response times and use fewer characters in communications where space might be limited (for example, Twitter/X) or where longer messages incur additional costs (such as in text messaging). They also avoid the need for repetitive writing or reading of frequently occurring longer terms or phrases. Acronyms and abbreviations may be spontaneously invented by groups or individuals as required.

The usefulness of such acronyms and abbreviations is dependent on the familiarity of the receiving communicator with the term. While some are pervasive across many types of online communication (for example, LOL – an extremely common acronym which stands for "laugh out loud"), others might be rarely seen outside of a specific type of online communication (for example, ELI5 – seen on particular online forums and meaning "explain like I'm 5 [years old]"). Other examples might only be seen in communications that consider particular topics – the acronym "FMIL" (future mother-in-law) makes frequent appearances on forums dedicated to wedding planning, while "PEBKAC" (problem exists between keyboard and chair) is used by the software engineering community to indicate user error.

Several authors, such as De Jonge and Kemp (2012) have developed typologies and taxonomies of such abbreviations, acronyms, and other "textisms". Some of the most common types include "initialism" (which primarily describes acronyms), "contraction" (where letters within words are omitted), "shortening" (where letters are omitted from the start or end of words), and "combined letter/number homophones", such as "GR8" in place of "great".

CYBERPSYCHOLOGY IN FOCUS: ACRONYMS AND ABBREVIATIONS AROUND THE WORLD

There are cultural differences in the use of acronyms and abbreviations. A popular Malaysian one, "TCSS" (talk cock, sing song – derived from "cock and bull story"), refers to hanging out and chatting (C. Teoh, personal communication, 2 December 2014), while "FFK" (Fong Fei Kei) is a Cantonese acronym whose literal translation approximates "leaving on an aeroplane" but is used to indicate being stood up for a planned meeting or date (R.H.C. Goh, personal communication, 21 April 2015). A Thai alternative to "LOL" is "5555", as "5" is pronounced "ha", but in Cantonese "555" means "fast fast fast" (A.J. Jegathesan, personal communication, 3 December 2014).

Emojis/Graphic Accents/Smileys/Emoticons

While many modern online communications allow text to be easily supplemented with video or images, the early Internet was not capable of managing such files easily, and they were used much less frequently. When users wished to indicate an emotional expression with the message that they were sending they were restricted to a basic set of characters, including letters, numbers, punctuation, and commonly used mathematical symbols. Using these characters, Internet users began creating miniature facial expressions, termed "emoticons", with the most common one being the 'smiley' – :-). Variations of emoticons have been given different designations, such as "graphic accents". More recently, "emojis" or "emoji" (both terms have been accepted by various sources as the plural for "an emoji") have overtaken those earlier emotional expressions, and at the time of writing the full emoji list includes over 3,660 options to select from (https://home.unicode.org/). As with paralanguage, different emoji can adjust the meaning of a message. Emoji of various types can be used to denote irony, flirtatiousness, sarcasm, anger, sadness, humour, and many other emotional states, although they are not always used with the purpose intended for them, or understood with accuracy by all recipients. Certain emoji also have dual meanings – what may seem like a simple image of a fruit or vegetable may mean something very different, depending on the context (see, for example, Thomson et al., 2018).

Many researchers have examined the use of emoticons and emoji. Early research by Derks et al. (2007) noted that socioemotional discussions evoke more use of emoticons than task-oriented discussions. Kato et al. (2009) found that fewer emoticons were used when there were strong negative emotions (such as anger and guilt) present. More recently, Kaye et al. (2021) noted that emoji may be subject to being processed emotionally, and perhaps in a similar way that face stimuli are.

Some research has focused on the use of emoticons and emoji across genders. For example, Tossell et al. (2012) found that in text messages, females sent more emoticons but males had more diversity in the range of emoticons sent. This was similar to the findings of Fullwood et al. (2013), who also identified women as more likely to use emoticons, but identified no difference in range. More recent work by Jones et al. (2020) regarding emoji noted that women reported using emojis more, and interestingly also found that women rated negative emojis as more negative than men did.

Communication Theories

So far, this chapter has concerned itself with describing online communication and aspects of it which are different from offline communication. However, it is useful to examine theories of communication relating to both online and offline interactions to gain an understanding of why online interactions take the form that they do. We shall examine a selection of these theories now.

Hyperpersonal Communication

Several theories have attempted to examine CMC specifically, and the most famous of these is probably Walther's (1996) **hyperpersonal** model. This suggests that emotion and levels of affection developed through CMC can sometimes surpass those developed through offline interactions. Specifically, Walther felt that various elements influence this: the receiver, the sender, feedback, and the asynchronous channels of communication.

The receiver may assume positive and idealised characteristics about their communication partner when there is uncertainty. Walther also suggests that the sender of CMC messages has increased control in that they can selectively choose what aspects of themselves they present, carefully editing and curating the information disseminated to enhance others' opinions. This is especially true as they are usually geographically distant from each other and have fewer distractions preventing them from concentrating on their self-presentation. As many online communications are asynchronous, there is a reduction in the time constraints normally evident in offline tasks, permitting social interactions to occur without having a detrimental effect on task completion and allowing more time to construct responses. Finally, the importance of any feedback received during the interaction is magnified, which might lead to idealisation.

Many researchers have examined the hyperpersonal model in experimental studies. For example, Jiang et al. (2011) had participants communicate with a confederate who made either high- or low-intimacy self-disclosures either face to face or in a CMC condition. CMC was found to lead to intensified disclosures and perceived intimacy compared to offline interactions. Scott and Fullwood (2020) note that there has been significant empirical support for the hyperpersonal model, but that there have been some conflicting findings, and that the model requires modification to reflect changes in our online communications due to the increased use of photographs and videos in our online presentation.

The SIDE Model

Another important model of communication which is targeted towards CMC is the social identity model of deindividuation effects (SIDE), which suggests that a social identity might replace individual identity in CMC (the potential positive and negative effects of which are investigated by Postmes et al., 1998). Specifically, Postmes et al. suggest that "when communicators share a common social identity, they appear to be more susceptible to group influence, social attraction, stereotyping, gender typing, and discrimination in anonymous CMC" (1998, p. 689).

Again, there has been considerable support for the SIDE model, although not always in the manner expected (see, for example, Rains et al.'s (2017) research on incivility and political identity online). The model has significant potential in explaining many kinds of online behaviour, such as cyberactivism (Stiff, 2019), although again the changes in online interactions in recent years, resulting in less anonymity in some settings, may affect its applicability to all CMC.

The Shannon–Weaver Mathematical Model

Not all communication theories include a strong psychological focus, but they may still have considerable psychological implications. The mathematical model proposed by Shannon and Weaver (1949) is one such model. Fundamentally, it focuses on the mechanical exchange of information from a source to a destination via a transmitter, channel, and receiver. However, it also considers how other factors, such as noise, entropy, redundancy, and channel capacity, can affect the quality of the message received (or whether it is received at all). If we think about the various things that can go wrong during a communication exchange using computers, it is clear that the Shannon–Weaver model is important. This is probably particularly the case in videoconferencing technologies, where some computers and Internet connections struggle to keep up with the volume of information that is being communicated. The video image may become distorted, the sound may be muffled, or there may be considerable lag. It is easy for information to be lost and, in some cases, for frustration to occur as a result.

While the Shannon–Weaver model has an important part to play in understanding communication, it does not consider many different aspects that are important in interpreting and responding to a message. For example, it does not consider the relationship between the communicators, the context of the communication, or how the receiver of a message extracts the meaning from the communication. Thankfully, these gaps have been identified by other researchers and theorists.

Rules Theory/Co-Ordinated Management of Meaning (CMM)

Pearce and Cronen (1980) suggested rules theory and the co-ordinated management of meaning to help understanding of human communication in a broad sense (i.e. not restricted to CMC). Their theory suggests that human communication is guided by rules and the social patterns of our culture.

Pearce and Cronen proposed that there is a hierarchy of meanings that needs to be borne in mind when interpreting a communication. At the lowest level, there is the literal content of the expression. Using the "fascinating" example from earlier, the literal meaning is just that. But at the next level, "speech act", the word indicates further meaning – for example, indicating interest in the information. Other levels of meaning include episodes, relationships, autobiography, and cultural patterns. For example, the use of the word "fascinating" in a particular tone and manner could be employed by fans of the original *Star Trek* series to denote humour, relationships, and cultural group.

Different levels in the hierarchy are co-ordinated by rules, and these rules form two main types – constitutive rules and regulative rules. Constitutive rules refer to what certain communications mean – for example, if someone provides instructions or mentoring, they are demonstrating leadership, while if they offer sympathies during a crisis this often demonstrates affection and care. Regulative rules tell us when it's appropriate to do certain things and what we should do next in an interaction. For example, if a person stops speaking, we should pick up the conversation unless it has been drawn to a close.

It is easy to see how communications in various online settings are regulated by the hierarchy of meaning, constitutive rules, and regulative rules. But it must also be noted that different settings have different rules, and what is acceptable in some online groups is highly offensive in others.

Herb Clark's Grounding Theory

In a series of papers, Herb Clark (see, for example, Clark & Brennan, 1991) outlines how conversation is collaborative and requires shared understanding by building common ground based on mutual knowledge. This process is referred to as grounding, and participants collaborate to add information to their common ground. We can easily see this as we teach young children new words –repeating the word and indicating what it means by pointing to a picture or engaging in an action provides the child with the common ground to use the word in future conversations.

It should be noted that making an utterance in itself does not automatically add to the common ground. If the adult repeatedly says the word "computer" to a child but does not show them what a computer is or explain what it does, then the child cannot absorb the information effectively. However, when a child understands what a computer is, and can identify or describe one, then they have provided evidence of sufficient understanding.

The applications of grounding theory to CMC are particularly clear in terms of the use of abbreviations, acronyms, and emoji. It is easy for a novice user to be confused or misunderstand a communication that includes these components. For example, there have been several anecdotal instances of individuals telling a friend or family member about a recent bereavement via text message, signing off with "LOL". As noted above, this is generally accepted as meaning "laugh out loud", but the senders in these cases confused the meaning for "lots of love".

Other Theories of Communication

In addition to the above, there are many other theories of communication that can help us to understand both online and offline communications. For example, Paul Watzlawick proposed the interactional view of communications (Watzlawick et al., 1967) which proposes several axioms, including how it is impossible not to communicate (even silence is a communication in itself), how the nature of relationships depends on how the communicators punctuate the sequence, and how power is asserted within communications. Berger (1979) suggested that when strangers commence communicating there is a high level of uncertainty between them, and in order to progress the relationship, this uncertainty needs to be reduced. A similar concept is Altman and Taylor's (1973) social penetration theory, which suggests that intimacy is reached as communicators progress through the disclosure of information at various layers, progressing from superficial layers (such as liked aspects of popular culture), through middle and inner layers (such as social attitudes, deep fears, hopes, spiritual values, etc.), and finally to the core personality. Even established relationships may run into problems, however, and Baxter and Montgomery's dialectical theory (e.g., Baxter, 1988; Baxter & Montgomery, 1996) examines how internal conflicts can affect communication patterns within relationships. Of course, it is also possible that we adjust our communication patterns to accommodate others, a position taken by Howard Giles in communication accommodation theory (see, for example, Giles, 2008).

It should be noted, of course, that all these theories, as well as all those listed above, are partial – none completely describes all human communication. Most specialise in one particular area of communication (e.g., information transfer, relationship development) and few integrate different aspects together. Few of the theories directly compete with each other and most provide new insights not present in others. It is only when we consider several theories together that we can hope to gain an overview of the complexity of human communication in both online and offline arenas.

Related Concepts

It is important to note that communication does not occur in a vacuum. Many other factors impact on what is said, who it is said by, and how it is said. It is not possible to cover all these within this chapter, so it is recommended that the reader also consults other related chapters in this text, depending on their area of interest. For example, authors of online communications often attempt to manage the impressions that others form of them, and carefully control their online self and identity, and this is considered in the next chapter. This is particularly the case for those seeking to find potential romantic partners online, and Chapter 6 examines this phenomenon. Chapter 5 considers the disruptive sides of online behaviour, including communication behaviours such as flaming and trolling, while the methods by which persuasion occurs online are described in Chapter 9. Factors relating to privacy, trust, and anonymity are described in Chapter 10, including communication privacy management theory – another communication theory that describes how and why we share information that we deem private. Finally, communication in online gaming is considered in Chapter 20.

Conclusion

This chapter has provided an introduction to CMC, considering how our communications have changed as computers have become more popular, and examining the range of communications that we now engage in. It has identified how language can be different online from offline, particularly focusing on paralanguage, abbreviations, acronyms, and emoji. Finally, online communication was considered in the light of communication theories, both those specifically developed for online communication and ones developed with offline communication in mind, but which have applications for online interaction.

Despite all this, communication in itself is a complex topic – by its very nature, the vast majority of our communications are discussing something else, or are made to reach a goal. Any consideration of online communication must also consider the context, topic, and aim of that communication, and many of the following chapters consider these aspects of online life.

Activity

Look for a few examples of interesting conversations on publicly accessible forums online (for ethical reasons, please ensure that you do not need to log in to the relevant websites to see the conversations, and protect the individuals' anonymity and confidentiality if discussing this activity with others). It is best if the conversations include several communications by one or more of the writers. Consider how each of the communication theories outlined above help us to form insights into the process of the communication, the relationship between the communicators, and the eventual outcome.

Discussion Questions

1 What do you use online communication for? Do you use different communication methods to communicate with different people or to discuss different topics?
2 Which of the communication theories mentioned do you think provides the greatest understanding of CMC? Is it necessary to combine different theories to get a better overview of the phenomenon?
3 During what computer-based activities do you experience flow? What do you think it is about these activities that results in flow?
4 Does CMC have an adverse effect on interpersonal relationships?

Recommended Reading List

Hyperpersonal communication theory provides interesting insights into our online communications. Walther's original (1996) article is well worth a read.

> Walther, J. B. (1996). Computer-mediated communication: Impersonal, interpersonal and hyperpersonal interaction. *Communication Research*, *23*(1), 3–43. https://doi.org/10.1177/009365096023001001

As well as reviewing Walther's original article, it is worthwhile reading the evaluation of the current applicability of the theory as presented by Scott and Fullwood (2020).

Scott, G. G., & Fullwood, C. (2020). Does recent research evidence support the hyperpersonal model of online impression management? *Current Opinion in Psychology, 36,* 106–111. https://doi.org/10.1016/j.copsyc.2020 .05.005

The SIDE model is also important when considering online behaviour, and again it is interesting to read one of the early articles on this important theory.

Postmes, T., Spears, R., & Lea, M. (1998). Breaching or building social boundaries? Side-effects of computer-mediated communication. *Communication Research, 25*(6), 689–715. https://doi.org/10.1177 /009365098025006006

Emoji are a core research area in CMC, and their impact on us is a topic which has fascinated researchers. This paper by Kaye et al. provides particular insights on this topic.

Kaye, L. K., Rodriguez-Cuadrado, S., Malone, S. A., Wall, H. J., Gaunt, E., Mulvey, A. L., & Graham, C. (2021). How emotional are emoji?: Exploring the effect of emotional valence on the processing of emoji stimuli. *Computers in Human Behavior, 116,* 106648. https://doi.org/10.1016/j.chb .2020.106648

Glossary

Asynchronous communication: Communications where it is expected that the users are not simultaneously communicating.
Computer-mediated communication (CMC): Human communication that relies on the medium of computer technology.
Computer-supported co-operative work (CSCW): The use of computing technology to support work by groups.
Cues-filtered out: A description of CMC as a medium where there are limited nonverbal cues available (see also lean medium).
Emojis: The use of symbols to indicate mood or to illustrate concepts in communication.
Emoticons: Variation of emojis, usually indicating facial expression.
Fluidity: In CMC, refers to content that can be changed easily and frequently.
Hyperpersonal communication: A model by Walther (1996) describing how computer-mediated communication can lead to enhanced feelings of intimacy.
Lean medium: A description of CMC as a medium where limited non-verbal cues are available.
Multimodality: The use of multiple modes of communication, such as text with video, images, or sound.
Paralanguage: Modifying meaning through the use of volume, intonation, or other adjustments.
Smileys: Variation of emoticons, usually indicating a smiling face.

Synchronous communication: Communications where it is expected that users are simultaneously communicating, such as instant messaging.

World Wide Web: An application of the Internet which allows the linking of documents online.

References

Altman, I., & Taylor, D. (1973). *Social penetration: The development of interpersonal relationships*. Holt, Rinehart & Winston.

Baxter, L. A. (1988). A dialectical perspective on communication strategies in relationship development. In S. Duck (Ed.), *Handbook of personal relationships* (pp. 257–273). Wiley.

Baxter, L. A., & Montgomery, B. M. (1996). *Relating: Dialogues and dialectics*. Guilford.

Berger, C. R. (1979). Beyond initial interaction: Uncertainty, understanding and the development of interpersonal relationships. In H. Giles & R. St. Clair (Eds.), *Language and social psychology* (pp. 122–144). Blackwell.

Berners-Lee, T. J. (1989). *Information management: A proposal* (No. CERN-DD-89-001-OC). https://cds.cern.ch/record/369245/files/dd-89-001.pdf

Clark, H. H., & Brennan, S. A. (1991). Grounding in communication. In L. B. Resnick, J. M. Levine, & S. D. Teasley (Eds.), *Perspectives on socially shared cognition* (pp. 127–149). APA Books.

Crystal, D. (2011). *Internet linguistics: A student guide*. Routledge.

De Jonge, S., & Kemp, N. (2012). Text-message abbreviations and language skills in high school and university students. *Journal of Research in Reading, 35*(1), 49–68. https://doi.org/10.1111/j.1467-9817.2010.01466.x

Derks, D., Bos, A. E. R., & von Grumbkow, J. (2007). Emoticons and social interaction on the Internet: The importance of social context. *Computers in Human Behavior, 23*(1), 842–849. https://doi.org/10.1016/j.chb.2004.11.013

Derks, D., Fischer, A. H., & Bos, A. E. R. (2008). The role of emotion in computer-mediated communication: A review. *Computers in Human Behavior, 24*(3), 766–785. https://doi.org/10.1016/j.chb.2007.04.004

Fullwood, C., Orchard, L., & Floyd, S. (2013). Emoticon convergence in Internet chat rooms. *Social Semiotics, 23*(5), 648–662. https://doi.org/10.1080/10350330.2012.739000

Giles, H. (2008). Communication accommodation theory. In L. A. Baxter & D. O. Braithewaite (Eds.), *Engaging theories in interpersonal communication: Multiple perspectives* (pp. 161–173). Sage Publications.

Hiltz, S. R., & Turoff, M. (1978). *The network nation: Human communication via computer*. Addison-Wesley.

Jiang, L. C., Bazarova, N. N., & Hancock, J. T. (2011). The disclosure-intimacy link in computer-mediated communication: An attributional extension of the hyperpersonal model. *Human Communication Research, 37*(1), 58–77. https://doi.org/10.1111/j.1468-2958.2010.01393.x

Jones, L. L., Wurm, L. H., Norville, G. A., & Mullins, K. L. (2020). Sex differences in emoji use, familiarity, and valence. *Computers in Human Behavior, 108*, 106305. https://doi.org/10.1016/j.chb.2020.106305

Kato, S., Kato, Y., & Scott, D. (2009). Relationships between emotional states and emoticons in mobile phone email communication in Japan. *International Journal on E-Learning, 8*(3), 385–401.

Kaye, L. K., Rodriguez-Cuadrado, S., Malone, S. A., Wall, H. J., Gaunt, E., Mulvey, A. L., & Graham, C. (2021). How emotional are emoji?: Exploring the effect of emotional valence on the processing of emoji stimuli. *Computers in Human Behavior, 116*, 106648. https://doi.org/10.1016/j.chb.2020.106648

Pearce, W. B., & Cronen, V. E. (1980). *Communication, action and meaning: The creation of social realities.* Praeger.

Postmes, T., Spears, R., & Lea, M. (1998). Breaching or building social boundaries? Side-effects of computer-mediated communication. *Communication Research, 25*(6), 689–715. https://doi.org/10.1177/009365098025006006

Rains, S. A., Kenski, K., Coe, K., & Harwood, J. (2017). Incivility and political identity on the Internet: Intergroup factors as predictors of incivility in discussions of news online. *Journal of Computer-Mediated Communication, 22*(4), 163–178. https://doi.org/10.1111/jcc4.12191

Rice, R. E., & Love, G. (1987). Electronic emotion: Socioemotional content in a computer-mediated communication network. *Communication Research, 14*(1), 85–108. https://doi.org/10.1177/009365087014001005

Scott, G. G., & Fullwood, C. (2020). Does recent research evidence support the hyperpersonal model of online impression management? *Current Opinion in Psychology, 36*, 106–111. https://doi.org/10.1016/j.copsyc.2020.05.005

Shannon, C. E., & Weaver, W. (1949). *The mathematical theory of communication.* University of Illinois Press.

Stiff, C. (2019). Social media and cyberactivism. In A. Attrill-Smith, C. Fullwood, M. Keep, & D. J. Kuss (Eds.), *The Oxford handbook of cyberpsychology* (pp. 370–393). Oxford University Press.

Thomson, S., Kluftinger, E., & Wentland, J. (2018). Are you fluent in sexual emoji?: Exploring the use of emoji in romantic and sexual contexts. *The Canadian Journal of Human Sexuality, 27*(3), 226–234. https://doi.org/10.3138/cjhs.2018-0020

Tossell, C. C., Kortum, P., Shepard, C., Barg-Walkow, L. H., Rahmati, A., & Zhong, L. (2012). A longitudinal study of emoticon use in text messaging from smartphones. *Computers in Human Behavior, 28*(2), 659–663. https://doi.org/10.1016/j.chb.2011.11.012

Walther, J. B. (1996). Computer-mediated communication: Impersonal, interpersonal and hyperpersonal interaction. *Communication Research, 23*(1), 3–43. https://doi.org/10.1177/009365096023001001

Walther, J. B. (2007). Selective self-presentation in computer-mediated communication: Hyperpersonal dimensions of technology, language and cognition. *Computers in Human Behaviour, 23*(5), 2538–2557. https://doi.org/10.1016/j.chb.2006.05.002

Watzlawick, P., Beavin, J., & Jackson, D. (1967). *Pragmatics of human communication.* W. W. Norton.

Self and Identity in Cyberspace

Irene Connolly

Chapter Overview

This chapter will introduce the main theories of the self and identity in cyberspace. In recent years our relationship with the online world has changed substantially, firstly with much larger numbers accessing social media but now, in the aftermath of COVID-19, its use for education, counselling, working, and of course socialising has transformed our experience.

The role of identity in identifiable settings, where one's identity is known, is compared to anonymous environments, where identity is not known. It is designed to show how specific personality types use the Internet and how the Internet, especially social media, allows us to manage who we want to be online. It will highlight how we can use self-enhancing tools to show ourselves in a positive light, using impression management.

Key Terms

Identity is the development of one's self-concept, including one's thoughts and feelings about oneself (Rosenberg, 1986). Suler (2016) talks about the identity dimension as the first of eight dimensions in cyberpsychology architecture. This emphasises that constant interaction online, without reflection, can affect the development of a sense of self. In the online world, the role of identity is complex, as multiple versions of the **self** can be expressed (Ellison et al., 2006). Further exploration of the self by Higgins (1987) proposes three domains: the "actual self" or "now self" (Markus & Nurius, 1986), the characteristics an individual possesses; the "ideal self", the characteristics a person would like to possess; and the "ought self", the characteristics a person feels that they should possess. The actual self is who you are in different situations, with the ideal self being how you would like those who communicate with you online to perceive you, and the ought self is how you feel you should project yourself for others, the person you believe others would like you to be. Online, our identities exist within a vacuity; we choose the social media handle, the profile photo, email address, or character design, reflecting how we wish people to perceive us. The reason may be a desire to connect with other individuals or anonymity, but

DOI: 10.4324/9781003092513-8

many times these choices provide insight into our identities, especially as people can use different platforms to explore different presentations of themselves (Wiederhold, 2018).

Online anonymity gives people the chance to present any of these three selves and hence permits individuals to better present aspects of their true selves than they would feel capable of doing in a face-to-face (FtF) interaction (Ellison et al., 2006). The concept of "true selves" has been used to refer to the "hidden aspects of what we need or wish to be" (Suler, 2002, p. 458), and "hidden" has meant "anti-normative" or "deviant" in this context. Potentially, identity empowerment may occur in the online environment.

In a fully **identifiable** (Zhao, 2006) real-life world (where a person's identity is known), any deviance from established social norms may be punished or ridiculed, the masks people wear in everyday life become their "real" or known identities (Goffman, 1959), and a person's "true" self is often inhibited (Bargh et al., 2002). Zhao et al. (2008) challenge the distinction between "real selves" and "virtual selves" or "true selves" and "false selves". Where "virtual selves" commonly refer to online selves and "real selves" to offline selves, the authors reported that Facebook identities are clearly real in the sense that they have real consequences for the lives of the individuals who construct them.

Research has challenged the distinction between "real selves" and "virtual selves" or "true selves" and "false selves". While "virtual selves" commonly refer to online selves and "real selves" to offline selves, Zhao et al. (2008) reported that Facebook identities are real in the sense that they have real consequences for the lives of the individuals who construct them. As larger numbers of people have joined the world of social media, we have seen some who promote positivity, while missing profile pictures and fake accounts can be used to roam public and private conversations to ignite an argument.

In contrast, in a fully **anonymous** online world where responsibility is absent, the masks people wear offline are often discarded and their "true" selves allowed to emerge. The identifiable online world, however, emerges as a third type of environment where people may tend to express what have been called the "hoped-for possible selves" (Yurchisin et al., 2005). Hoped-for possible selves are a subcomponent of possible selves (Markus & Nurius, 1986) that differs from the suppressed or hidden "true self" on the one hand and the unrealistic or fantasised "ideal self" (Higgins, 1987) on the other. Hoped-for possible selves are socially pleasing identities a person wishes to assert under receptive conditions such as an anonymous online environment. Looking at the continuing development of the self, the online world may provide an area for growth, where people can find a voice when they don't have one in the real world. The question is whether these are distinctive or whether they all become a part of the same thing eventually.

CYBERPSYCHOLOGY IN FOCUS: EMERGING ADULTHOOD SOCIAL ANXIETY AND ONLINE SELF-PRESENTATION

Further investigation into this area was carried out by Michikyan (2020) who examined the role of social media in psychosocial development and adjustment in emerging adulthood. This revealed that emerging adults high in general identity coherence conveyed the real self and the ideal self on Facebook, proposing that they were more honest and positively accurate in their online self-presentation. Emerging adults high in general identity confusion reported presenting the ideal self and the false self on Facebook, signifying that they were less ingenuous and more socially desirable in their virtual self-presentation. Additionally, emerging adults who experienced both identity coherence and identity confusion reported presenting a false self on Facebook motivated by self-exploration. Michikyan (2020) suggested that emerging adults who experienced high social anxiety reported presenting a false self on Facebook; they engaged in an extensive self-exploratory and socially desirable online self-presentation. Further, emerging adults experiencing both high identity confusion and high social anxiety reported presenting themselves on Facebook in a less truthful manner. More research by Fullwood et al. (2020) found that individuals with higher self-concept clarity and self-monitoring are more likely to present a single consistent online and offline self. Younger adults and those with greater social anxiety are more likely to present idealised self-images online, while participants with higher social anxiety and lower self-esteem are more likely to prefer online, rather than offline communication. Psychosocial development and adjustment in adulthood appear to play a role in the type of identity and self-presentation that people project on social media, emphasising the importance of understanding that psychological adjustment in the real world can play a factor in online behaviour.

Online Behaviour Theories

Several theories have been put forward to analyse the variation of online behaviour in anonymous and identifiable environments. Two prominent theories include the **equalisation hypothesis** and the **social identity model of deindividuation effects (SIDE)**. In FtF interaction a person's gender, age, or ethnicity are apparent and social power hierarchies all play a role in these social interactions (Allport, 1954; Hatfield & Sprecher, 1986).

Equalisation Hypothesis

The **equalisation hypothesis** suggests that with the removal of these social cues, a reduction of associated stereotypes may occur, therefore possibly leading to increased social power in the online world (Kieser et al., 1984). Without this inhibitory information, it is hypothesised that individuals who hold less power in society should have increased power in the online environment; however complete anonymity is not fundamental to the **equalisation hypothesis** (Dubrovsky et al., 1991). The following research has supported the idea of the equalisation hypothesis. Research conducted by Siegel et al. (1986) investigated whether or not there were more equal amounts of participation in a group decision-making process in computer-mediated communication (CMC) discussions than in FtF discussions. Anonymity was manipulated with participants indicating their first names or remaining completely anonymous in their communications. Results indicated that there was significantly more equalisation in the CMC condition than in the FtF condition. Dubrovsky et al. (1991) further explored these findings by studying the effect of status as well as the effect of anonymity. This research supported the hypothesis that CMC would diminish inequality; each group member submitted an equal number of responses as the other members, regardless of status, even when the status differences of the group members were revealed to the participants in the CMC condition.

Social Identity Model of Deindividuation Effects (SIDE) Theory (Leary and Kowalski, 1990)

The SIDE theory is a reinterpretation of the classic deindividuation theory (Zimbardo, 1969) which highlights the importance of the identifiable variables in a social situation. SIDE theory incorporates two components of the effect and use of anonymity in CMC. Firstly, a cognitive element of anonymity exists which focuses on how group dynamics and individual behaviour within groups are facilitated by anonymity and the depth of an individual's identification with the group (Postmes et al., 2001). SIDE theory anticipates that when complete anonymity exists within a group, then group salience will be enhanced, with those members' identification with the group growing stronger. However, where an individual can identify group members while remaining anonymous to the group, SIDE theory predicts that the one anonymous individual will identify more strongly with themselves rather than with the group. This individual's behaviour will not be advantageous to the group. Researchers such as Joinson (2000), Lea et al. (2001), and Postmes et al. (2001) working on the cognitive component of SIDE theory support these assertions by Spears and Lea (1992).

Secondly, the SIDE theory comprises a strategic component, which includes the deliberate use of anonymity in CMC, as a method to benefit from this anonymity (Spears & Lea, 1994). It strengthens the influence of social norms and their effect when social identity is strong. Also, anonymity will lessen the effect of social norms where a person's own identity is more conspicuous (Spears & Lea, 1992). Therefore, social norms are more likely to be adhered to when the individual has a high awareness of social identity and personal identity is less important. In conclusion, SIDE theory proposes that to achieve goal-directed groups, where each member strives to achieve the group's goal and not their personal goals, circumstances call for the complete anonymity of each member of the group or complete identity transparency across the group (Spears & Lea, 1992).

Impression Management

Social networking communication is more closely related to FtF communication than other forms of text-based computer-mediated communication (CMC) (Walther, 2007). One aspect of these online environments which allows people to alter their self-representation is known as impression management (IM). Impression management is selectively self-presenting or editing messages to reveal socially desirable attitudes and dimensions of the self (Walther, 1996). The more critical the impression is thought to be concerning one's goal fulfilment, the more motivated a person may be to realise an anticipated impression. There are three reasons why an individual manages impressions; these include attempting to persuade others to respond in the desired manner, creating and preserving one's private self-identity and self-esteem, and standardising one's emotional practices (Leary, 1996). Furthermore, Goffman (1959) suggested that people want to convince others to see them as fair, decent, and ethical individuals, and also sustain established positive impressions (Lemert & Branaman, 1997).

The Role of Anonymity in Impression Management

Impression management may be affected by several factors, including the effect of anonymous versus identifiable environment, identity, and self-development. Pedersen (1979) suggested that there are six different types of privacy, *reserve*, *isolation*, *intimacy with family*, *intimacy with friends*, *solitude*, and *anonymity*. *Reserve* refers to the reluctance to reveal personal information about one's self. *Isolation* is the wish to be alone and away from others. *Intimacy with family* and *intimacy with friends* involve the desire to be alone with either group. *Solitude* comprises being free of scrutiny from other people, and *anonymity* involves interacting with others, without being scrutinised by them. Anonymity occurs when a person cannot be identified by others in a social networking situation. Within this concept, there appear to be two aspects, that is, *technical anonymity* (Hayne & Rice, 1997) or *discursive anonymity* (Qian & Scott, 2007) and *social anonymity* (Hayne & Rice, 1997) or *visual anonymity* (Qian & Scott, 2007). The former terms refer to identifying material from online communication, such as names and email addresses. The latter refer to the perception of others or one's self as unidentifiable as a result of a lack of signs to provide an identity for that person. The role of anonymity in the online world can have both positive and negative effects, where traditional research such as Zimbardo (1969) has highlighted the negative aspects of anonymity with increases in aggressive behaviour. Anonymity can have a positive effect on the role of privacy or the amount of contact that someone has with others. While privacy can enhance psychological wellbeing (Werner et al., 1992), the absence of it can lead to aggression and anti-social behaviour (Heffron, 1972). Anonymity can also provide autonomy, where people can try out new behaviours without fear of social consequences, or the fear of reprisal. However, the online world may not be completely anonymous, as real-world communities can interact with online communities, disallowing complete anonymity. While the identifiable nature of the environment does seem to make people more "realistic and honest" (Ellison et al., 2006) in their self-presentation, the reduction of "gating obstacles" in the online setting enables the users to be more liberal with the truth (Yurchisin et al., 2005). This occurs in particular when attempting to project a self that is more socially desirable, and better than their "real" offline identity. The rules of engagement, even in an anonymous online environment, seem to be affected by cues provided by the participants of the group. The consequences of anonymity and engagement in a virtual breast cancer patient support group were examined by Kang (2017). Visually identifiable group members were more likely to get supportive responses than visually anonymous members. Also, when support group members are visually and discursively identifiable, they are more likely to get supportive messages than those who are visually and discursively anonymous. In essence, the more identifiable support group members are, the more they receive positive messages (Kang, 2017).

Lying or Impression Management?

Within the area of impression management, a person's willingness to deceive is paramount. Research has suggested that social networking site (SNS) users possess more risk-taking attitudes than non-users (Fogel & Nehmad, 2009), where this is demonstrated largely with males in the online world (Zuckerman & Kuhlman, 2000) and also by DePaulo et al. (1996) in the offline world, where male students told significantly more self-centred lies than did female students. Over half of their total lies were self-oriented, involving impression management and self-promotion. There is a great variation between a person telling "white lies" and participating in the full deception of another individual (DePaulo, et al., 1996; Hancock et al., 2004). DePaulo et al.'s (1996) taxonomy of lies proposes four main features: (1) The content of the lie, (2) the reason for the lie, (3) the type of lie, or its seriousness, and (4) the referent of the lie, which is who the lie concerns. Zhao et al. (2008) assert that different behaviours in anonymous and identifiable online environments exist. The research found that, while anonymous environments often do support an identity closer to that of the individual's real-world identity, the degree to which this is so differs across individuals.

Broadcasters and Communicators

The Underwood et al. (2011) study identified differences in online net-working behaviours. An opportunity sample of 113 undergraduate students within a UK university, aged between 18 and 36 years, participated in this study. The key criterion for inclusion in the study was an active Facebook account. The study has provided evidence for two identifiable modes of interaction when using an SNS, termed *broadcasting* and *communicating*, and provided compelling information on the underlying behavioural characteristics in helping to explain such online activity. At one end of the continuum are group-focused *communicators* while at the other are the self-focused *broadcasters*. *Broadcasting* is one-to-many with the primary flow outwards from the one, and *communicating* involves one-to-few with reciprocal exchanges (Underwood et al., 2011). Broadcasting can be identified as a public communication style as part of an individual's self-projection (Pempek, et al., 2009) and can involve impression management (Walther, 1996). It can result in a low quality of interaction, particularly concerning blogs (Instone, 2005; Zhou & Hovy, 2006). Broadcasters who engage in such self-promotion and self-oriented lies attempt to provide a more desirable self (Hancock, 2007; Walther, 2007). In this sense, the broadcasters' behaviours are closer to those within anonymous online environments (Bargh et al., 2002). They are also characterised by higher levels of out-going personality, risk-taking behaviour, mild social deviance (MSD), and a willingness to engage in lying behaviours. Risk-taking leads to a greater willingness to disclose personal information online and engage in deviant or risky behaviours (Fogel & Nehmad, 2009). However, the act of communicating between individuals who know one another and have shared interests tends to produce high-quality interactions (Skinstad, 2008). *Communicators* are more likely to have anchored relationships. That is, the communicators talk to individuals who are liked and well known, focus on the maintenance of a strong close-knit social friendship group, have regular high-quality interactions, and support smaller online network communities. Moreover, communicators are uncomfortable about lying even though their lies tend to be those everyday lies that oil social interaction (Skinstad, 2008). The conclusion here is that communicators work to support group coherence and to maintain their membership in the group. This is corroborated by Zhao et al.'s (2008) finding that users stress group identities over personal identities in their postings on Facebook. In recent years identifiable online environments have grown exponentially; examples include video conferencing, online counselling, online gaming, and online dating. With the occurrence of the pandemic, online communities were joined by people, including older members of our communities, who may never have used technology to communicate previously. Game nights on Zoom or drinks with friends became a way of socialising that, pre-COVID-19, would simply never have been entertained by most. Therefore, future research will need to look at this developing aspect of communication and interaction online. One area that has been studied extensively already is online dating (see Chapter 6, "Love and Relationships Online").

Identifiable Online Environments

Studies have examined identity construction in Internet dating which is a uniquely identifiable online environment (Ellison et al., 2006; Gibbs et al., 2006; Yurchisin et al., 2005). Internet dating sites are different from the role-playing games (RPGs), which are anonymous. Internet dating sites are designed to facilitate the exchange of personal information. Individuals have to find a balance between presenting "the best self" on their profile and providing precise information (Ellison et al., 2006; Whitty, 2007). There is a narrowed discrepancy between "actual selves" and "ideal selves" in people's online self-presentation when dealing with being identified in the online world. The identifiable nature of the environment, particularly the expectation of ensuing face-to-face encounters, had been theorised to narrow the incongruity between "actual selves" and "ideal selves" in people's online self-presentation (Ellison et al., 2006). Identities produced on Internet dating sites differ from the identities produced in face-to-face situations because people on the Internet dating sites tend to "stretch the truth a bit" (Yurchisin et al., 2005, p. 742) in their online self-presentation. Regardless of those "truth-stretching" behaviours, identities formed on Internet dating sites were found to be both honest and realistic. Perhaps in an attempt to avoid objectionable encounters in offline meetings that occur, the possibility of FtF interaction in the future may in itself act as a buffer to reduce the variation between actual and ideal selves. In the realm of online dating, participants reported using the profile to ideate a version of self they desired to experience in the future. This suggests that for some individuals online profile construction may encompass self-growth, the aim of which is to diminish the difference between the actual and ideal selves (Ellison et al., 2006). Online dating is examined in greater detail in Chapter 6.

Identity and Self in Anonymous versus Identifiable Online Environments

The Zhao et al. (2008) research examined identity construction on Facebook, which is another identifiable online environment. The research methodology combined same-ethnic focus groups, interviews with administrators involved in student services and student organisations, and structured in-depth interviews as well as online Facebook analyses. Using content analyses of 63 users, the research found that the identities devised by those in an identifiable environment do vary from those created in an anonymous environment. The authors reported that the hoped-for possible selves that users projected on Facebook were neither the "true selves" often seen in anonymous online environments nor the "real selves" people presented in FtF communications. The

Facebook selves appear to be highly socially desirable identities that people wish to have in the real world but cannot achieve. This is a similar result to Ellison et al.'s (2006) study of Internet dating. Being identifiable in the online world seems to produce a more honest presentation of the self (Ellison et al., 2006), but the lack of social cues seems to allow them to present themselves more favourably than in the real world (Yurchisin et al., 2005). Zhao et al. (2008) have suggested some implications arising from their study. One is that identity is not an individual character but is a social product. Individuals will produce identities based on the context of the environment. Hence, they suggest that "true selves", "real selves", and "hoped-for possible selves" are produced within the environment rather than the characteristics of the person. Secondly, in an identifiable environment, where a person's identity can be recognised, individuals are more likely to present themselves within the normal expectations of the real world. Whereas in an anonymous environment, either online or offline, where individuals are unidentifiable and thus cannot be held responsible, people are more likely to behave as they wish, ignoring normative restrictions (Cinnirella & Green, 2007). Thirdly, Zhao et al. (2008) suggest that there are few distinctions between online behaviour and offline behaviour and consequences. Individuals need to coordinate their behaviours in both environments. "Digital selves" are real, and they can serve to enhance users' overall self-image and identity claims and quite possibly increase their chances to connect in the offline world. Finally, the researchers challenge the distinction between "real selves" and "virtual selves" or "true selves" and "false selves". "Virtual selves" commonly refers to online selves and "real selves" to offline selves, as they found the Facebook identities are real in the sense that they have real consequences for the lives of the individuals who constructed them.

Two studies on the impact of identity cues within anonymous online environments were carried out by Tanis and Postmes (2007). In the first study, identity cues were manipulated by showing the participants a photo and first name of the alleged partner and themselves or not. The researchers found that more positive impressions did result minimally with the presence of cues to one's identity; this supported earlier findings by Tanis and Postmes (2003) where even the smallest identity cues affected a person's impression management. Additionally, in this study, Tanis and Postmes reported that identity cues had negative effects on variables related to assessments of the contact. People had slightly more positive impressions of their partners but they felt less certain about and were less satisfied with the interaction. The subsequent study by Tanis and Postmes (2007) demonstrated that when performing an online communication task (discussing a paper for college), participants felt more confident, were more pleased with the interaction, and thought they had performed better in the absence of identity cues. Therefore, this study supports the supposition that interactions that allow the communication of identity cues such as face-to-face interactions are better, as they make the interaction more personal, but that these effects are not reflected by the appraisal of the contact. Perhaps the existence of identity cues positively affects social perceptions, while decreasing perceptions of cohesion. The results of these studies conflict with expectations resulting from social presence theory (see Short, 1974; Short et al., 1976), the reduced social cues approach (see Culnan & Markus, 1987), and the cuelessness model (see Rutter & Stephenson, 1979), all of which predict that identity cues benefit the interaction.

Conclusion

The role of self and identity in cyberspace is complex. One's identity impacts one's thoughts and feelings and hence can influence the type of person one wishes to associate with. Many factors in cyberspace can affect interactions, such as the anonymity or identifiable nature of sites visited. The equalisation hypothesis and SIDE attempt to explain the impact of anonymity in SNS on behaviour. Impression management occurs in both anonymous and identifiable environments but to varying extents, with the issue of telling lies being linked to the personality type. Online environments appear to encourage impression management for personal gain or status; for some this may be used negatively and for others it may be used positively.

Activity

"Who am I?" Provide five sentences that answer this question about yourself. Then go to your social media (whichever one you use the most!). This time look at your profile and your comments and write down five sentences that answer the "who am I?" question based on your online persona. Compare the real-life answers with those of the online persona. Do the "offline" you and the "online" you match or are they completely different?

Discussion Questions

1. Do you think that people are different in the online world compared to the real world? Explain.
2. Should anonymity exist in the online world? Support your answers.
3. Is impression management simply a nicer way of saying that people lie online? Elaborate.
4. Can online dating be successful if people are managing their identities rather than showing their true selves? Discuss.

Recommended Reading List

Rosenberg and Egbert found that personality traits and secondary goals are theoretically and empirically sound components for the conceptualisation of online impression management.

Rosenberg, J., & Egbert, N. (2011). Online impression management: Personality traits and concerns for secondary goals as predictors of self-presentation tactics on Facebook. *Journal of Computer-Mediated Communication*, *17*(1), 1–18. https://doi.org/10.1111/j.1083-6101.2011 .01560.x

Carolyn Cunningham offers a critical inquiry into how identity is constructed, deconstructed, performed, and perceived on SNSs, such as Facebook and LinkedIn.

Cunningham, C. (Ed.). (2013). *Social networking and impression management: Self-presentation in the digital age.* Rowman & Littlefield.

John Suler's work spans over two decades of participant-observation field research in diverse online environments. His book offers insights for improving lifestyles and enhancing wellbeing in the digital age.

Suler, J. R. (2016). *Psychology of the digital age: Humans become electric.* Cambridge University Press. https://doi.org/10.1017/CBO9781316424070

Allison Attrill-Smith's work on the online self is intriguing and informative. The work examines the self in the online world, in relation to the offline self, but equally how an individual may generate diverse forms of the self online.

Attrill-Smith, A. (2019). The online self. In A. Attrill-Smith, C. Fullwood, M. Keep, & M. J. Kuss (Eds.), *The Oxford handbook of cyberpsychology* (pp. 17–35). Oxford University Press. https://doi.org/10.1093/oxfordhb /9780198812746.013.37

Glossary

Anonymous: Your identity is hidden from others.
Broadcasting: One-to-many with the primary flow outwards from the one.
Communicating: One-to-few with reciprocal exchanges.
Identifiable: Your identity can be seen by others.
Identity: Recognition of one's potential and qualities as an individual, especially with social context.
Impression management: Selectively self-presenting or editing messages to reveal socially desirable attitudes and dimensions of the self.
Online dating: Searching for a romantic or sexual partner on the Internet, typically via a dedicated website.
Self: A person's essential being that distinguishes them from others, especially considered as the object of introspection or reflexive action.

References

Allport, G. W. (1954/1979). *The nature of prejudice.* Addison-Wesley.

Attrill-Smith, A. (2019). The online self. In A. Attrill-Smith, C. Fullwood, M. Keep, & M. J. Kuss (Eds.), *The Oxford handbook of cyberpsychology* (pp. 17–35). Oxford University Press. https://doi.org/10.1093/oxfordhb/9780198812746 .013.37

Bargh, J. A., McKenna, K. Y., & Fitzsimons, G. M. (2002). Can you see the real me? Activation and expression of the "true self" on the Internet. *Journal of Social Issues*, *58*(1), 33–48. https://doi.org/10.1111/1540-4560.00247

Cinnirella, M., & Green, B. (2007). Does "cyber-conformity" vary cross-culturally? Exploring the effect of culture and communication medium on social conformity. *Computers in Human Behaviour*, *23*(4), 2011–2025. https://doi.org/10.1016/j.chb.2006.02.009

Culnan, M., & Markus, M. L. (1987). Information technologies. In F. M. Jablin, L. L. Putnam, K. H. Roberts, & L. W. Porter (Eds.), *Handbook of organizational communication: An interdisciplinary perspective* (pp. 420–444). Sage.

DePaulo, B. M., Ansfield, M. E., & Bell, K. L. (1996). Theories about deception and paradigms for studying it: A critical appraisal of Buller and Burgoon's interpersonal deception theory and research. *Communication Theory*, *3*, 297–310. https://doi.org/10.1111/j.1468-2885.1996.tb00131.x

DePaulo, B. M., Kashy, D. A., Kirkendol, S. E., Wyer, M. M., & Epstein, J. A. (1996). Lying in everyday life. *Journal of Personality and Social Psychology*, *70*(5), 979–995. https://doi.org/10.1037/0022-3514.70.5.979

Dubrovsky, V. J., Kiesler, S., & Sethna, B. N. (1991). The equalization phenomenon: Status effects in computer-mediated and face-to-face decision-making groups. *Human-Computer Interaction*, *6*(2), 119–146. https://doi.org/10.1207/s15327051hci0602_2

Ellison, N., Heino, R., & Gibbs, J. (2006). Managing impressions online: Self-presentation processes in the online dating environment. *Journal of Computer-Mediated Communication*, *11*(2), Article 2. https://doi.org/10.1111/j .1083-6101.2006.00020.x

Fogel, J., & Nehmad, E. (2009). Internet social network communities: Risk-taking trust, and privacy concerns. *Computers in Human Behaviour*, *25*(1), 153–160. https://doi.org/10.1016/j.chb.2008.08.006

Fullwood, C., Wesson, C., Chen-Wilson, J., Keep, M., Asbury, T., & Wilsdon, L. (2020). If the mask fits: Psychological correlates with online self-presentation experimentation in adults. *Cyberpsychology, Behaviour and Social Networking*, *23*(11), 737–742. https://doi.org/10.1089/cyber.2020.0154

Gibbs, J. L., Ellison, N. B., & Heino, R. D. (2006). Self-presentation in online personals the role of anticipated future interaction, self-disclosure, and perceived success in Internet dating. *Communication Research*, *33*(2), 152–177. https://doi.org/10.1177/0093650205285368

Goffman, E. (1959). *The presentation of self in everyday life*. Doubleday.

Hancock, J. T. (2007). Digital deception: When, where and how people lie online. In A. N. Joinson, K. McKenna, T. Postmes, & U. Reips (Eds.), *Oxford handbook of internet psychology* (pp. 287–301). Oxford University Press. https://doi.org/10.1093/oxfordhb/9780199561803.013.0019

Hancock, J. T., Thom-Santelli, J., & Ritchie, T. (2004). Deception and design: The impact of communication technologies on lying behaviour. In *Proceedings of the conference on computer human interaction* (Vol. 6, pp. 130–136). ACM.

Hatfield, E., & Sprecher, S. (1986). *Mirror, mirror. . . The importance of looks in everyday life*. State University of New York Press.

Hayne, S. C., & Rice, R. E. (1997). Attribution accuracy when using anonymity in group support systems. *International Journal of Human–Computer Studies*, *47*(3), 429–452. https://doi.org/10.1006/ijhc.1997.0134

Heffron, M. H. (1972). The naval ship as an urban design problem. *Naval Engineers Journal, 12*, 49–64. https://doi.org/10.1111/j.1559-3584.1973.tb04807.x

Higgins, E. T. (1987). Self-discrepancy: A theory relating self and affect. *Psychological Review, 94*(3), 319–340. https://doi.org/10.1037/0033-295X.94.3.319

Instone, L. (2005). Conversations beyond the classroom: Blogging in a professional development course. In *Proceedings of the balance, fidelity, mobility: Maintaining the momentum* (Vol. 1, pp. 305–308). Ascilite.

Joinson, A. N. (2000). Self-disclosure in computer-mediated communication: The role of self-awareness and visual anonymity. *European Journal of Social Psychology, 31*(2), 177–192. https://doi.org/10.1002/ejsp.36

Kang, K. K. (2017). Anonymity and interaction in an online breast cancer social support group. *Communication Studies, 68*(4), 403–421. https://doi.org/10.1080/10510974.2017.1340902

Kiesler, S., Siegel, J., & McGuire, T. (1984). Social psychological aspects of computer-mediated communication. *American Psychologist, 39*(10), 1123–1134. https://doi.org/10.1037/0003-066X.39.10.1123

Lea, M., Spears, R., & de Groot, D. (2001). *Knowing me, knowing you*: Anonymity effects on social identity processes within groups. *Personality and Social Psychology Bulletin, 27*(5), 526–537. https://doi.org/10.1177/0146167201275002

Leary, M. R. (1996). *Self-presentation: Impression management and interpersonal behaviour*. Westview Press.

Leary, M. R., & Kowalski, R. M. (1990). Impression management: A literature review and two-component model. *Psychological Bulletin, 107*(1), 34. https://doi.org/10.1037/0033-2909.107.1.34

Lemert, C., & Branaman, A. (1997). *The Goffman reader*. Blackwell.

Markus, H., & Nurius, P. (1986). Possible selves. *American Psychologist, 41*(9), 954–969. https://doi.org/10.1037/0003-066X.41.9.954

Michikyan, M. (2020). Linking online self-presentation to identity coherence, identity confusion, and social anxiety in emerging adulthood. *British Journal of Developmental Psychology, 38*(4), 543–565. https://doi.org/10.1111/bjdp.12337

Pedersen, D. M. (1979). Dimensions of privacy. *Perceptual and Motor Skills, 48*(3), 1291–1297. https://doi.org/10.2466/pms.1979.48.3c.1291

Pempek, T. A., Yermolayeva, Y. A., & Calvert, S. L. (2009). College students' social networking experiences on Facebook. *Journal of Applied Developmental Psychology, 30*(3), 227–238. https://doi.org/10.1016/j.appdev.2008.12.010

Postmes, T., Spears, R., Sakhel, K., & de Groot, D. (2001). Social influence in computer-mediated communication: The effects of anonymity on group behaviour. *Personality and Social Psychology Bulletin, 27*, 1242–1254. https://doi.org/10.1080/15391523.2010.10782562

Qian, H., & Scott, C. R. (2007). Anonymity and self-disclosure on weblogs. *Journal of Computer-Mediated Communication, 12*(4), 1428–1451. https://doi.org/10.1111/j.1083-6101.2007.00380.x

Rosenberg, J., & Egbert, N. (2011). Online impression management: Personality traits and concerns for secondary goals as predictors of self-presentation tactics on Facebook. *Journal of Computer-Mediated Communication, 17*(1), 1–18. https://doi.org/10.1111/j.1083-6101.2011.01560.x

Rosenberg, M. (1986). Self-concept from middle childhood through adolescence. In J. Suls & A. G. Greenwald (Eds.), *Psychological perspectives on the self* (Vol. 3, pp. 107–135). Lawrence Erlbaum.

Rutter, D. R., & Stephenson, G. M. (1979). The role of visual communication in social interaction. *Current Anthropology, 20*(1), 124–125. https://doi.org/10.1086/202217

Short, J. A. (1974). Effects of medium of communication on experimental negotiation. *Human Relations, 27*(3), 225–234. https://doi.org/10.1177/001872677402700303

Short, J., Williams, E., & Christie, B. (1976). *The social psychology of telecommunications*. Wiley.

Siegel, J., Dubrovsky, V., Kiesler, S., & McGuire, T. W. (1986). Group processes in computer-mediated communication. *Organizational Behaviour and Human Decision Processes, 37*(2), 157–187. https://doi.org/10.1016/0749-5978(86)90050-6

Skinstad, M. (2008). Facebook: A digital network of friends. In Paper presented at the 24th conference of the Nordic sociological association (pp. 1–14). University of Aarhus.

Spears, R., & Lea, M. (1992). Social influence and the influence of the "social" in computer-mediated communication. In M. Lea (Ed.), *Contexts of computer-mediated communication* (pp. 30–65). Harvester-Wheatsheaf.

Spears, R., & Lea, M. (1994). Panacea or panopticon? The hidden power in computer-mediated communication. *Communication Research, 21*(4), 427–459. https://doi.org/10.1177/009365094021004001

Suler, J. R. (2016). *Psychology of the digital age: Humans become electric*. Cambridge University Press. https://doi.org/10.1017/CBO9781316424070

Suler, J. R. (2002). Identity management in cyberspace. *Journal of Applied Psychoanalytic Studies, 4*(4), 455–459. https://doi.org/10.1023/A:1020392231924

Tanis, M., & Postmes, T. (2003). Social cues and impression formation in CMC. *Journal of Communication, 53*(4), 676–693. https://doi.org/10.1111/j.1460-2466.2003.tb02917.x

Tanis, M., & Postmes, T. (2007). Two faces of anonymity: Paradoxical effects of cues to identity in CMC. *Computers in Human Behaviour, 23*(2), 955–970. https://doi.org/10.1016/j.chb.2005.08.004

Underwood, J. D. M., Kerlin, L., & Farrington-Flint, L. (2011). The lies we tell and what they say about us: Using behavioural characteristics to explain Facebook activity. *Computers in Human Behaviour, 27*(5), 1621–1626. https://doi.org/10.1016/j.chb.2011.01.012

Walther, J. B. (1996). Computer-mediated communication: Impersonal, interpersonal, and hyperpersonal interaction. *Communication Research, 23*(1), 3–43. https://doi.org/10.1177/009365096023001001

Walther, J. B. (2007). Selective self-presentation in computer-mediated communication: Hyperpersonal dimensions of technology, language, and cognition. *Computers in Human Behaviour, 23*(5), 2538–2557. https://doi.org/10.1016/j.chb.2006.05.002

Werner, C. C., Altman, I., & Brown, B. B. (1992). A transactional approach to interpersonal relations: Physical environment, social context, and temporal. *Journal of Social and Personal Relations, 9*(2), 297–323.

Whitty, M. T. (2007). Revealing the 'real' me, searching for the 'actual' you: Presentations of self on an Internet dating site. *Computers in Human Behaviour, 24*(4), 1707–1723. http://doi.org/10.1016/j.chb.2007.07.002

Wiederhold, B. K. (2018). When second life becomes real life: The evolution of self-presentation. *Cyberpsychology, Behavior, and Social Networking, 21*(1), 1–2. https://doi.org/10.1089/cyber.2017.29095.bkw

Yurchisin, J., Watchravesringkan, K., & McCabe, D. B. (2005). An exploration of identity re-creation in the context of Internet dating. *Social Behavior and Personality, 33*(8), 735–750. https://doi.org/10.2224/sbp.2005.33.8.735

Zhao, S. (2006). *Cyber-gathering places and online-embedded relationships.* Paper presented at The Annual Meetings of the Eastern Sociological Society. Boston.

Zhao, S., Grasmuck, S., & Martin, J. (2008). Identity construction on Facebook: Digital empowerment in anchored relationships. *Computers in Human Behaviour, 24*(5), 1816–1836. https://doi.org/10.1016/j.chb.2008.02.012

Zhou, L., & Hovy, E. (2006). On the summarization of dynamically introduced information: Online discussions and blogs. In *Proceedings of the AAAI spring symposium on computational approaches to analysing weblogs.*

Zimbardo, P. G. (1969). The human choice. Individuation, reason, and order vs. deindividuation, impulse and chaos. *Nebraska Symposium on Motivation, 17,* 237–307.

Zuckerman, M., & Kuhlman, D. M. (2000). Personality and risk-taking: Common biosocial factors. *Journal of Personality, 68*(6), 999–1029. https://doi.org/10.1111/1467-6494.00124

5 The Dark Side of the Internet

Hannah Barton and Derek A. Laffan

Chapter Overview

The landscape of negative behaviour online is a rapidly changing one. A recent example of this is when many young people across Europe reported significant increases in exposure to online hate content in recent years (Wachs et al., 2021). There are well-known benefits and opportunities of digital technology such as social support and keeping people connected and entertained. However, the Internet can also facilitate much negative behaviour, causing all sorts of consequences and pain to those who experience them. Negative behaviour online can be so broad a topic that it is important to all areas related to cyberpsychology. This is because certain negative behaviours (e.g. trolling) can occur in almost any digital space where people interact with others. Yet despite some commonalities, negative behaviour online might look different depending on the context it is in. For example, in online dating, negative behaviour could be considered as cyber dating abuse involving harm and coercive control by means of digital technology towards an intimate partner (Branson & March, 2021). This could look very different to the dynamics of interpersonal behaviour that occurs in substantially more risky online environments such as the Dark Web (Kloess & van der Bruggen, 2021). This chapter provides an overview of some of the processes (i.e. the how and why) involved in the more common anti-social behaviours, e.g. trolling, flaming, online sexual harassment, cyberstalking, and digital game-based dark participation, which can occur across various online contexts. It will also examine how the online environment can facilitate prejudice, stereotypes, and ostracism.

Key Terms

Trolling occurs when there are "deliberate attempts to provoke other participants into any reaction, thus disrupting communication on the forum and potentially steering the discussion from its original topic" (Hopkinson, 2013, p. 5). Trolls operate by participating in a discussion just like any other member, but then post a comment which is the bait and is designed to be upsetting.

DOI: 10.4324/9781003092513-9

Flaming occurs when personal insults including verbal aggression are directed at the other participants in the discussion. **Prejudice** can be an umbrella term for discrimination, negative attitudes, and stereotyping towards a social group and its members (Allport, 1954). Prejudice can extend online into digital gaming spaces, machine learning agents such as robots, and in computer-mediated communication between humans and avatars. **Sexual harassment online** can manifest as unwanted gender-based violence and can extend into different online environments. **Cyberstalking** is a pathological set of behaviours similar to that of stalking but using the Internet or other forms of technology such as smartphones to pursue and harass another. Negative behaviour online is also evident in digital games in forms such as griefing, toxic gamer cultures, and **dark participation** more broadly.

The Internet and Trolling

When we think of a troll from the fairy tales, we think of an ugly brute that hides under a bridge or in a dark cave, just waiting for an unsuspecting victim who they can then terrorise. Well, online trolls behave in a similar fashion. They frequent discussion pages and online communities' support pages and wait for an opportune moment to pounce with a provocative comment before sitting back and watching the sparks fly. To the trolls, this can be just fun. The Internet by its nature can facilitate trolling. In many online discussions, the participants do not actually see each other or, more importantly, comprehend the impact their words and behaviours can have on the people they interact with. It has been suggested that this lack of visibility can lead to a dehumanising effect, making us feel detached and remote from the effects of our words and behaviours. This, coupled with the anonymity that most individuals feel when online, can trigger online disinhibition (Suler, 2004), leading us to do and say things that we would not do in a face-to-face situation. As Widyanto and Griffiths (2011, p. 15) describe it, "the internet provides anonymity which removes the threat of confrontation, rejection and other consequences of behaviour". We do not feel responsible or accountable for our behaviour. This loss of self-consciousness is akin to **deindividuation** which occurs when we become submerged in a group and which results in anti-social behaviour.

Sometimes, individuals do not have to rely on anonymity in order to intentionally antagonise or provoke others online (Ortiz, 2020). Instead, some identifiable individuals – particularly those in positions of power – can carry out forms of collective trolling behaviour (Fichman, 2022). This trolling does not always involve explicit abusive words or targeted harassment. For example, *evocative trolling* is when an individual posts information online in order to encourage mass agreement, disagreement, and resonance among Internet users

(Hong & Cheng, 2018). Another example is when an individual with greater **online social capital** encourages an Internet *pile-on* (Thompson & Cover, 2021) so that a target is ridiculed, trolled, and shamed by a mass number of users across social media. Such individuals can be famous figures protected by organisations and supported by other Internet users and groups. In recent years, some well-known media figures, politicians, and celebrities have been accused of promoting trolling behaviour. In some cases, these figures have been suspended or even banned from social media platforms. Whereas in other cases, the consequences of mass online trolling have been considered to be a factor in celebrity cancel culture, and more worryingly, incidents of suicide.

Why Do the Trolls Do It?

Empirical research evidence on trolling is growing. Some of the earlier empirical studies found that the motivations of typical trolls included boredom, attention seeking, revenge, to provoke a reaction, and trolling simply for the fun of it (Herring, 2004; Shachaf & Hara, 2010). But sometimes these motivations can be much more sinister. Herring's (2004) study examined trolling in online feminist discussion forums and found that certain environments and support sites are prime targets for trolling. These are ones that are regarded as non-mainstream and according to Herring (2004, p. 371) provide a "new arena for the enactment of power inequalities such as those motivated by sexism, racism and heterosexism". Mantilla (2013) described gendertrolling to be trolling predominantly motivated by misogyny.

Researchers have also found that dark personality can also explain trolling (Buckels et al., 2014). Craker and March (2016) found that trait psychopathy and sadism were predictors of trolling behaviour among Facebook users. Gylfason et al. (2021) found that the entertainment of trolling was a mediator of Machiavellianism, sadism, and trolling behaviour. This could mean that the manipulative, callous, and sadistic personality of trolls is greatly helped by the entertainment they get from trolling others. Trolls also participate in flaming.

Flaming can be interpreted as a game or contest of verbal wit. It can be seen in many online communities and group behaviour as a marker of how status and prestige are awarded. O'Sullivan and Flanagin (2003) defined flaming as hostile and aggressive interactions via computer-mediated communication. The verbal contest between the core members who retaliate against the troll turns into an online show, and the defending members are often rewarded by praise, support, and respect from the other members of the community. Thus, often a troll and their attack on an online community can enhance cohesion in the group when the members unite to defend their community against a common enemy.

CYBERPSYCHOLOGY IN FOCUS: THINKING CRITICALLY ABOUT NEGATIVE BEHAVIOUR ONLINE WITH A GENDER LENS

One of the reasons for the gender focus in this chapter is that much negative behaviour online can be understood within a wider intersectional context. This means that we can better understand the dynamics, reasons, and consequences of this behaviour when we also consider the individual, group social, and contextual factors involved such as gender, ethnicity, disability, identity, sexuality, and religious beliefs. Many global human rights organisations such as Amnesty International, the United Nations, and Plan International have long argued that women tend to experience a disproportionately high amount of violence online and offline. Being aware of this when we are discussing negative behaviour online could help us determine if such negative behaviour is a manifestation of a wider societal problem.

How Do Trolls Operate?

Trolls get pleasure out of watching the other participants react to their bait and continue to draw them in through ever-increasing provocative comments. Herring (2004) described three different ways trolls try to cause this disruption: (1) their messages appear outwardly sincere, (2) messages are deliberately designed to provoke a reaction, and (3) messages are designed to waste time through fruitless argument. Hardaker (2010) went a little further and identified four main characteristics of trolling: (1) aggression – *baiting* the other users through the use of annoying or offensive comments, (2) success – assessing whether or not the bait has been taken and has provoked an angry response from the other users. This is also known as *biting*, (3) disruption, where the troll changes the course of the discussion into a series of personal insults, and (4) deception, where the troll often uses a virtual or false identity created with the sole intention of disrupting the group discussion and creating conflict. This fake identity can change when users realise it is a troll. The troll can then discard that identity and create a new one to continue to stay in the group.

Though a substantial amount of research has focused on the identification, motivations, and behaviours of trolls, much less research exists about how trolling can be prevented. Sun and Shen (2021) conducted a social network analysis of reactions to trolls and found that users who are most active within their online communities were more likely to respond to negative trolling messages. The researchers followed up with recommendations for online communities to consider for keeping the trolls away. They suggested that establishing and implementing group norms to react before trolling occurs can prevent further trolling. Individuals who breach these norms by responding to trolls in their communities can arguably encourage further trolling towards themselves and other users. Perhaps "don't feed the trolls" is a useful and somewhat evidence-based mantra?

Prejudice and Stereotyping Online

Prejudice has traditionally been an umbrella term that covers discrimination, negative attitudes, and stereotyping. They are interrelated but separate topics. Prejudice is a negative attitude towards a social group and its members (Allport, 1954). It works by viewing the targets as being less than human. This dehumanisation of a group can then make discrimination and other unacceptable behaviours seem acceptable as the targets are falsely considered "less than human". Traditionally, Allport (1954) viewed prejudice as being composed of three components. These are the cognitive – the beliefs about the person; the affective – the strong feelings, usually negative, about the person; and the conative – the intention to behave in a certain way towards the person. The historic LaPiere experiment in 1934 showed that people often do not behave in accordance with their attitudes. An example of this is how prejudice is often expressed implicitly – as microaggressions, subtle cues, body language etc. – but not so much explicitly. Though researchers have traditionally tested implicit associations using the **implicit association test (IAT)** by Greenwald et al. (1998), some empirical advances have sharply questioned the IAT as a valid measure of implicit associations in recent years (Kurdi et al., 2021; Schimmack, 2021).

Real world prejudice also happens in the digital world. Some researchers such as Tynes et al. (2008) have found that participants had a 59% chance of experiencing or witnessing racial prejudice in unmonitored chat rooms and a 19% chance in a monitored chat room. Other researchers have commented on the over-prevalence of White avatars and White supremacy evident in some virtual environments such as greater distances being kept from Black avatars and more compliance to requests online reported by White avatars (Dotsch & Wigboldus, 2008; Kafai et al., 2007). It demonstrates that we can judge and treat avatars using the same criteria and rules that people are judged with in the real world. This can make the virtual world rather threatening to minority groups and it compromises their sense of belonging and feeling when they participate in spaces online.

Stereotyping

Stereotyping is an over-generalised belief about an individual based on their group membership. Stereotypes are culturally defined, and knowledge of a stereotype does not indicate agreement. This is due to our tendency to put people, just like we do with objects, into groups, based on a perceived or actual similarity. This is a psychological process called social categorisation and it works like a mental shortcut or heuristic. Indicators of social group identification, such as physical features indicating gender or race, can activate concepts or stereotypes relating to those social groups. Stereotypes are culturally created from our tendency to categorise.

This idea of forming categories of people into groups such as in-group (like me/us) and out-group (not like me/us) as a natural and universal one is one of the core tenets of **social identity theory** devised by Tajfel and Turner (1979). This theory also suggests that our group membership is an important source of our self-identity and self-esteem. An attack on our group (in-group) is an attack on us and on our self-esteem. However, this bond allows other in-group members to become a viable source of information about social reality, thus making possible processes of mutual social influence and persuasion. This means that we can often pay more attention to our in-group than to our own values and ideas. These differences between the groups that stimulate the bias may be trivial, such as eye colour, which was experimented with by Jane Eliot in 1968 to show how quickly behaviour could be modified on the basis of a stereotype based on a trivial difference.

Sometimes these stereotypes are far from trivial. In recent years, there has been plentiful discussion about the prejudices involved in machine learning (ML) agents such as robots. In an experimental study, Hundt et al. (2022) found that human-designed robots acted out malignant gender-based and race-based stereotype behaviour. The researchers asserted that the robots acted in racial and gendered hierarchies putting men first and women second, and with an additional racial hierarchy putting Whites first followed by Asian, Hispanic, and Black people. The explanation for this is that such injustices are implicitly encoded into the algorithms and programming of such ML agents, and that problematic existing code is used in the development of new technologies.

Effects of Online Ostracism and Prejudice

The effects of online **ostracism** and prejudice are just as strong and real to the people who experience them and to their self-esteem. Williams et al. (2000) demonstrated that people can feel ostracised when playing an online game with competitors they visualise, even when what they see on the screen are simple coloured representations. Even when people are told that the game is controlled by a computer, the effects of ostracism are about as negative as when they are ostracised by actual others (Zadro et al., 2004).

How Can We Reduce Prejudice Online?

One method of reducing prejudice (Allport, 1954) is the **contact hypothesis** which asserts that positive contact between an in-group and an out-group reduces the intergroup bias. This effect is enhanced if there is a common goal for both groups. Where there is a need to work cooperatively to achieve a common goal and there is a shift in thinking from "us" and "them" to "we", then intergroup bias will also be reduced. Contact must also be between people of equal status and occur frequently and in a range of situations. Tynes et al. (2008) showed that the more time spent online interacting with out-groups by European and American participants, the more open they were to diverse groups. Walther et al. (2015) investigated the contact hypothesis involving Arab and Jewish students in Israel who participated in an online course. They collaborated by doing assignments for a year and the researchers could show that the students who participated in the virtual groups experience had significantly less prejudice towards these respective out-groups at the end of the course.

Another way of reducing prejudice is to enhance similarity between people. This is often done when we feel empathy – the experience of emotion congruent with another person's situation (Batson et al., 2002). Empathy is linked with decreased prejudice. Someone who is high in trait empathy is likely to identify with someone who is victimised or ostracised and to experience concern for the victim. In terms of harassment, lower levels of empathy are associated with greater acceptance of sexual harassment and prejudice. Interventions using immersive virtual environments (IVEs) have shown successful reductions in ageism (Yee & Bailenson, 2006).

Sexual Harassment Online

There are different forms of **sexual harassment online**. It can be an environment where women are perceived as "cyberbabes" with whom one can have cyber-sex (Doring, 2000). It can be more direct involving increased negative comments when female voices are heard (Kuznekoff & Rose, 2013), receiving emails with lewd content/pictures, and other forms of general harassment (Ballard & Welch, 2017). Some online environments can be highly sexualised, and sometimes anyone with a female name may receive unwanted comments or approaches from strangers. The anonymity that the Internet provides can heighten the problem leading to sexual harassment. More worryingly, online sexual harassment can include forms of gender-based violence such as threats of rape, death, and reputational damage (Ging & Siapera, 2018).

Gender stereotyping is one explanation for why sexual harassment occurs online. Fox and Tang (2014) asked online game players to relate the last incident of harassment they had witnessed or experienced; 10% of these incidents reported sexist remarks ranging from traditional sexism to sexual harassment. One of the reasons for this may be the stereotypical roles that female game characters play. A study by Yao et al. (2010) revealed that playing games with sexualised characters leads players to normalise sexual harassment, and some men can indicate a greater likelihood to harass women after play. Fox et al. (2013) found that women who were embodied in sexualised avatars that resembled the self demonstrated greater rape myth acceptance than women who were embodied in other avatars.

Another explanation is that online sexual harassment does not happen in a vacuum. Some scholars have argued that online sexual harassment is symptomatic of a much larger anti-feminist and misogynist ideological movement, which is designed to intentionally harm women more generally. **Incels** (derived from the term *involuntary celibacy*) are typically groups of men who frequently express hostility towards women online usually because they have been rejected by them (Speckhard et al., 2021). Though not all incel group members are imminently violent, many members of these groups have carried out targeted social media harassment campaigns against women (Ging, 2019). Furthermore, Ging (2019) argues that incels are part of the broader *"manosphere"*, which refers to the loose collective of anti-feminist spaces online. Often referred to as an example collective campaign of targeted gender-based harassment and misogyny (Ging & Siapera, 2018; Massanari, 2017; Rubin, 2016), the #Gamergate scandal showed how intentionally targeted abuse can transfer from one digital space to another. During the #Gamergate scandal, several women in the video games industry reported experiencing violent abuse in online games, on social media, and in online public forums such as 4Chan, 8Chan, and Reddit. Some of the #Gamergate supporters were well-known social media figures who justified their involvement by changing the discourse of #Gamergate to be about ethics in journalism. Events such as #Gamergate demonstrate that abusers with collective power do not always have to rely on their anonymity when harassing their victims online.

Cyberstalking

Negative behaviour online can encompass cybercrime and criminal behaviour online which is covered more in Chapter 11. Cyberstalking is just like physically stalking a person but using the Internet or other forms of technology such as mobile phones to pursue and harass another. It follows the same characteristics of stalking behaviour such as persistently sending unwanted gifts or presents, threatening to damage the victim's property, and causing the victim's reputation to suffer by either spreading rumours or sharing personal information. In cyberstalking, unsolicited contact is made by email, instant messenger, social networking, or online chat rooms. The victim's inbox may be flooded with offensive messages or images. The stalker may have an obsessive interest in the victim's life and activities both online and offline. The stalker may even use spy software to track everything that happens on the victim's computer. In some cases, the stalker may assume the victim's identity and post material online which may or may not be false. The Internet can facilitate cyberstalking as it allows the stalker a perceived feeling of anonymity. The cyberstalker may threaten the victim by phone and can even approach the victim offline. There are many steps that a person can take to reduce the risk of being a victim of cyberstalking. It is important to check privacy settings on calendar apps and social media sites which may alert a person to your location. Using both good password management and updated security software will also help lessen your chance of being a victim. A recent scoping review of cyberstalking victimisation studies (Wilson et al., 2022) found that prevalence of victimisation rates could be as low as 0.7% and as high as 85.2% depending on the selected cyberstalking criteria. In the majority of these studies, most victims of cyberstalking tended to be women. Non-White victims more often than White victims did not report or seek help for cyberstalking. Victims often identified their perpetrators to be male acquaintances or complete strangers.

Griefing, Toxic Gamer Cultures, and Dark Participation

Negative behaviour happens in gaming contexts. Griefing is a term sometimes used in online gaming communities to describe general aggressive behaviour in video games. Warner and Raiter (2005, p. 47) have defined it as "the intentional harassment of other players which utilizes aspects of the game structure or physics in unintended ways to cause distress for other players". Some scholars have argued that general aggressive behaviour can look very different in video games compared to general aggressive behaviour in other digital or online spaces. Coyne et al. (2009) distinguished griefing from cyberbullying (see Chapter 17 for more details on cyberbullying) and described it as aggression towards an avatar, not a player. But sometimes this aggression can happen often and foster a toxic gamer culture affecting the avatar and the player.

Tang et al. (2020) argued that sexual harassment can be pervasive in unwelcoming and hostile gaming communities. The researchers explained how players can sometimes adopt a "gamer identity" which depersonalises and stereotypes a player so that they can carry out negative behaviours such as griefing, sexual harassment, and trolling. But not all gamer identities are problematic. Kaye and Pennington (2016) found that female players can combat some of the harms of stereotype threat affecting their gaming performance by identifying with a positive social identity. Although an increasing number of women and girls are playing video games nowadays, only 6% of them said they had any form of gamer identity (Pew Research Center, 2015). For these reasons, it is important to differentiate between "gamers" and "players" of video games, and to understand that video gaming can be a uniquely different experience for them. Despite this, digital games can be hostile places for female players. They sometimes adopt a variety of strategies to avoid harassment; these include not using feminine names or characters/avatars or any method that could identify their gender. Sometimes they hide their identities while playing games and interacting in gaming communities to avoid potential harassment from others (McLean & Griffiths, 2013).

Researchers, gamers, and players do not seem to agree on what "toxic" behaviour actually is in video games. Tang et al. (2020) stated that behaviours such as sexual harassment are toxic. Yet Kou (2020) found that some players of *League of Legends* consider the use of cheats to be a type of toxic behaviour because those players have an unfair advantage over others. Such distinctions led researcher Dr Rachel Kowert to catalogue all kinds of **dark participation** that can be found in video games (Kowert, 2020). Under dark participation, verbal (e.g. trash talking) and behavioural (e.g. swatting) actions in video games can be determined by how transient (i.e. in the moment) or strategic (i.e. taking time and planning) they are (Kowert, 2020). For example, a verbal transient action would be threats of violence because players can make threats in the moment using chat or voice features. Whereas a strategic behaviour would be "doxing" because it takes some degree of planning, research, and intention to search for a player's identifying information and post it online.

CYBERPSYCHOLOGY IN FOCUS: DOING SOMETHING ABOUT NEGATIVE BEHAVIOUR ONLINE

Negative behaviour online is likely less intriguing when it is us or others who are on the receiving end. It is arguably far more worrying to know that we or people we know and care about can experience it while we navigate our lives online. Many organisations and agencies such as Barnardos, Ofcom, and Ireland's National Advisory Council for Online Safety (NACOS) report figures often higher than 60% of people seeing others being cyberbullied online and many do nothing about it. If you see online abuse, screenshot as much evidence as you can and save it in case you need to show someone. Report and block the perpetrators on the social media site(s). If this is not handled well, consider reporting the abusive content to another trusted adult, the police, or the Ombudsman for Children. Do not assume online abuse will stop until something is done about it.

Conclusion

This chapter set out to provide an overview of some of the negative and disruptive behaviours that people may encounter online. It identified some of the more common negative behaviours such as trolling, flaming, online sexual harassment, and cyberstalking and across different online environments such as in digital games. It also described some of the effects of these behaviours on the victims. Some guidelines on how to reduce negative behaviours such as trolling, flaming, and online prejudice were offered in the chapter.

Activity

Devise an inclusive online safety programme for students that helps them notice negative behaviour online and suggest practical ways they could tackle online abuse if they encounter it. Consider vulnerable groups such as disabled students, LGBTI+ students, and ethnic minorities in your plan.

Discussion Questions

1. What practical advice would you give to your peers about how to tackle negative behaviour online?
2. What steps, if any, should social media and other online providers take to prevent trolling and sexual harassment online?
3. Which in your opinion better explains how/why individuals can carry out negative behaviour online – the choice to be anonymous or the power some individuals have over others?
4. How can we make the online world a more equal and inclusive place for women, ethnic minorities, LGBTI+ individuals, and other vulnerable groups?

Recommended Reading List

The following paper explores cyberhate victimisation and perpetration among young people across ten European counties. It applies routine activity and problem behaviour theory, which acts as part of a theoretical framework of an empirical study with a large sample:

Wachs, S., Mazzone, A., Milosevic, T., Wright, M. F., Blaya, C., Gámez-Guadix, M., & O'Higgins Norman, J. (2021). Online correlates of cyberhate involvement among young people from ten European countries: An application of the routine activity and problem behaviour theory. *Computers in Human Behavior, 123.* https://doi.org/10.1016/j.chb.2021.106872

These articles evaluate the behaviours, dark personality traits, and possible deterrence of trolls and trolling behaviour:

Buckels, E. E., Trapnell, P. D., & Paulhus, D. L. (2014). Trolls just want to have fun. *Personality and Individual Differences, 67,* 97–102. https://doi.org/10.1016/j.paid.2014.01.016

Gylfason, H. F., Sveinsdottir, A. H., Vésteinsdóttir, V., & Sigurvinsdottir, R. (2021). Haters gonna hate, trolls gonna troll: The personality profile of a Facebook troll. *International Journal of Environmental Research and Public Health, 18*(11). https://doi.org/10.3390/ijerph18115722

Sun, Q., & Shen, C. (2021). Who would respond to a troll? A social network analysis of reactions to trolls in online communities. *Computers in Human Behavior, 121.* https://doi.org/10.1016/j.chb.2021.106786

This paper is written by a feminist media scholar who draws from ideas in feminism and digital media theory in order to describe the "manosphere" and evaluate the role of incel groups within it:

> Ging, D. (2019). Alphas, betas, and incels: Theorizing the masculinities of the manosphere. *Men and Masculinities, 22*(4), 638–657. https://doi.org/10.1177/1097184X17706401

Glossary

Contact hypothesis: Allport's idea of how to reduce bias by encouraging contact as equals between two individuals or groups.
Dark participation: A set of behaviours that can be considered toxic, harmful, and anti-social in a digital gaming environment.
Deindividuation: The process by which you don't feel personally accountable for actions due to being part of a group.
Flaming: When personal insults are exchanged online.
Implicit association test (IAT): Allegedly measures attitudes that the person is unaware of or unwilling to admit to having.
Incels: Short for *involuntary celibates*. These are usually online groups of men who have been rejected by women or are unable to get a female romantic partner.
Online disinhibition: Suler's (2004) theory that argues the loosening or removal of social inhibitions when interacting online that would normally would be present in face-to-face communication.
Online social capital: Resources accumulated through the relationships and interactions we have with people online.
Ostracism: When one is excluded or isolated from a group.
Prejudice: General term for any negative attitude towards a social group.
Sexual harassment online: An umbrella term for all forms of sexual harassment that can occur online. Can be considered as a form of gender-based violence.
Social identity theory: Theory by Tajfel and Turner (1979) which seeks to explain intergroup discrimination and how we form in-groups/out-groups.
Trolling: Negative behaviours in online environments (such as social media and gaming) designed to provoke a reaction or sometimes cause harm.

References

Allport, G. (1954). *The nature of prejudice*. Addison-Wesley.
Ballard, M. E., & Welch, K. M. (2017). Virtual warfare: Cyberbullying and cyber-victimization in MMOG play. *Games and Culture, 12*(5), 466–491. https://doi.org/10.1177/1555412015592473
Batson, C. D., Chang, J., Orr, R., & Rowland, J. (2002). Empathy, attitudes, and action: Can feeling for a member of a stigmatized group motivate one to help the group? *Personality and Social Psychology Bulletin, 28*(12), 1656–1666. https://doi.org/10.1177/014616702237647

Branson, M., & March, E. (2021). Dangerous dating in the digital age: Jealousy, hostility, narcissism, and psychopathy as predictors of cyber dating abuse. *Computers in Human Behavior, 119.* https://doi.org/10.1016/j.chb.2021.106711

Buckels, E. E., Trapnell, P. D., & Paulhus, D. L. (2014). Trolls just want to have fun. *Personality and Individual Differences, 67,* 97–102. https://doi.org/10.1016/j.paid.2014.01.016

Coyne, L., Chesney, T., Logan, B., & Madden, N. (2009). Griefing in a virtual community: An exploratory survey of second life residents. *Journal of Psychology, 217*(4), 214–221. https://doi.org/10.1027/0044-3409.217.4.214

Craker, N., & March, E. (2016). The dark side of Facebook®: The Dark Tetrad, negative social potency, and trolling behaviours. *Personality and Individual Differences, 102,* 79–84. https://doi.org/10.1016/j.paid.2016.06.043

Doring, N. (2000). Feminist views of cybersex: Victimization, liberation, and empowerment. *Cyberpsychology and Behavior, 3*(5), 863–884. https://doi.org/10.1089/10949310050191845

Dotsch, R., & Wigboldus, D. H. J. (2008). Virtual prejudice. *Journal of Experimental Social Psychology, 44*(4), 1194–1198. https://doi.org/10.1016/j.jesp.2008.03.003

Fichman, P. (2022). The role of culture and collective intelligence in online global trolling: The case of trolling Trump's inauguration speech. *Information, Communication and Society, 25*(7), 1029–1044. https://doi.org/10.1080/1369118X.2020.1824006

Fox, J., Bailenson, J. N., & Tricase, L. (2013). The embodiment of sexualized virtual selves: The Proteus effect and experiences of self-objectification via avatars. *Computers in Human Behavior, 29*(3), 930–938. https://doi.org/10.1016/j.chb.2012.12.027

Fox, J., & Tang, W. Y. (2014). Sexism in online video games: The role of conformity to masculine norms and social dominance orientation. *Computers in Human Behavior, 33,* 314–320. https://doi.org/10.1016/j.chb.2013.07.014

Ging, D. (2019). Alphas, betas, and incels: Theorizing the masculinities of the manosphere. *Men and Masculinities, 22*(4), 638–657. https://doi.org/10.1177/1097184X17706401

Ging, D., & Siapera, E. (2018). Special issue on online misogyny. *Feminist Media Studies, 18*(4), 515–524. https://doi.org/10.1080/14680777.2018.1447345

Greenwald, A. G., McGhee, D. E., & Schwartz, J. L. K. (1998). Measuring individual differences in implicit cognition: The implicit association test. *Journal of Personality and Social Psychology, 74*(6), 1464–1480. https://doi.org/10.1037/0022-3514.74.6.1464

Gylfason, H. F., Sveinsdottir, A. H., Vésteinsdóttir, V., & Sigurvinsdottir, R. (2021). Haters gonna hate, trolls gonna troll: The personality profile of a Facebook troll. *International Journal of Environmental Research and Public Health, 18*(11). https://doi.org/10.3390/ijerph18115722

Hardaker, C. (2010). Trolling in asynchronous computer-mediated communication: From user discussions to academic definitions. *Journal of Politeness Research, 6*(2), 215–242. https://doi.org/10.1515/JPLR.2010.011

Herring, S. C. (2004). Slouching toward the ordinary: Current trends in computer-mediated communication. *New Media and Society, 6*(1), 26–36. https://doi.org/10.1177/1461444804039906

Hong, F. Y., & Cheng, K. T. (2018). Correlation between university students' online trolling behavior and online trolling victimization forms, current conditions, and personality traits. *Telematics and Informatics, 35*(2), 397–405. https://doi.org/10.1016/j.tele.2017.12.016

Hopkinson, C. (2013). Trolling in online discussions: From provocation to community-building. *Brno Studies in English, 39*(1), 5–25. https://doi.org/10.5817/BSE2013-1-1

Hundt, A., Agnew, W., Zeng, V., Kacianka, S., & Gombolay, M. (Eds.). (2022). Robots enact malignant stereotypes. In *ACM Conference on Fairness, Accountability, and Transparency*. ACM. https://dl.acm.org/doi/10.1145/3531146.3533138

Kafai, Y. B., Fields, D. A., & Cook, M. S. (Eds.). (2007). Your second selves: Resources, agency, and constraints in avatar designs and identity play in a tween virtual world. In *3rd digital games research association international conference: "Situated play"*. DiGRA.

Kaye, L. K., & Pennington, C. R. (2016). "Girls can't play": The effects of stereotype threat on females' gaming performance. *Computers in Human Behavior, 59*, 202–209. https://doi.org/10.1016/j.chb.2016.02.020

Kloess, J. A., & van der Bruggen, M. (2021). Trust and relationship development among users in Dark Web child sexual exploitation and abuse networks: A literature review from a psychological and criminological perspective. *Trauma, Violence, and Abuse*. Advanced online publication. https://doi.org/10.1177/15248380211057274

Kou, Y. (2020). Toxic behaviors in team-based competitive gaming: The case of League of Legends. In *Proceedings of the annual symposium on computer-human interaction in play* (pp. 81–92). https://doi.org/10.1145/3410404.3414243

Kowert, R. (2020). Dark participation in games. *Frontiers in Psychology, 11*. https://doi.org/10.3389/fpsyg.2020.598947

Kurdi, B., Ratliff, K. A., & Cunningham, W. A. (2021). Can the implicit association test serve as a valid measure of automatic cognition? A response to Schimmack (2021). *Perspectives on Psychological Science, 16*(2), 422–434. https://doi.org/10.1177/1745691620904080

Kuznekoff, J. H., & Rose, L. M. (2013). Communication in multiplayer gaming: Examining player responses to gender cues. *New Media and Society, 15*(4), 541–556. https://doi.org/10.1177/1461444812458271

Mantilla, K. (2013). Gendertrolling: Misogyny adapts to new media. *Feminist Studies, 39*(2), 563–570). https://doi.org/10.1353/fem.2013.0039

Massanari, A. (2017). #Gamergate and the Fappening: How Reddit's algorithm, governance, and culture support toxic technocultures. *New Media and Society, 19*(3), 329–346. https://doi.org/10.1177/1461444815608807

McLean, L., & Griffiths, M. (2013). The psychological effects of videogames on young people: A review. *Aloma, 31*(1), 119–133.

O'Sullivan, P. B., & Flanagin, A. J. (2003). Reconceptualizing "flaming" and other problematic messages. *New Media and Society, 5*(1), 69–94. https://doi.org/10.1177/1461444803005001908

Ortiz, S. M. (2020). Trolling as a collective form of harassment: An inductive study of how online users understand trolling. *Social Media and Society, 6*(2), 1–9. https://doi.org/10.1177/2056305120928512

Pew Research Center. (2015). *Who plays video games and identifies as a "gamer"*. https://www.pewresearch.org/internet/2015/12/15/who-plays-video-games-and-identifies-as-a-gamer/

Rubin, J. D. (2016). #Gendertrolling: A (new) virtual iteration of everyday misogyny. *Sex Roles, 74*(5–6), 266–267. https://doi.org/10.1007/s11199-016-0577-2

Schimmack, U. (2021). The implicit association test: A method in search of a construct. *Perspectives on Psychological Science, 16*(2), 396–414. https://doi.org/10.1177/1745691619863798

Shachaf, P., & Hara, N. (2010). Beyond vandalism: Wikipedia trolls. *Journal of Information Science, 36*(3), 357–370. https://doi.org/10.1177/0165551510365390

Speckhard, A., Ellenberg, M., Morton, J., & Ash, A. (2021). Involuntary celibates' experiences of and grievance over sexual exclusion and the potential threat of violence among those active in an online incel forum. *Journal of Strategic Security, 14*(2), 87–87. https://doi.org/10.5038/1944-0472.14.2.1910

Suler, J. (2004). The online disinhibition effect. *Cyberpsychology and Behavior, 7*(3), 321–326. https://doi.org/10.1089/1094931041291295

Sun, Q., & Shen, C. (2021). Who would respond to a troll? A social network analysis of reactions to trolls in online communities. *Computers in Human Behavior, 121.* https://doi.org/10.1016/j.chb.2021.106786

Tajfel, H., & Turner, J. C. (1979). An integrative theory of inter-group conflict. In W. G. Austin & S. Worchel (Eds.), *The social psychology of inter-group relations* (pp. 33–47). Brooks/Cole.

Tang, W. Y., Reer, F., & Quandt, T. (2020). Investigating sexual harassment in online video games: How personality and context factors are related to toxic sexual behaviors against fellow players. *Aggressive Behavior, 46*(1), 127–135. https://doi.org/10.1002/ab.21873

Thompson, J. D., & Cover, R. (2021). Digital hostility, internet pile-ons and shaming: A case study. *Convergence: The International Journal of Research into New Media Technologies,* 1–13. https://doi.org/10.1177/13548565211030461

Tynes, B. M., Giang, M. T., Williams, D. R., & Thompson, G. N. (2008). Online racial discrimination and psychological adjustment among adolescents. *Journal of Adolescent Health, 43*(6), 565–569. https://doi.org/10.1016/j.jadohealth.2008.08.021

Wachs, S., Mazzone, A., Milosevic, T., Wright, M. F., Blaya, C., Gámez-Guadix, M., & O'Higgins Norman, J. (2021). Online correlates of cyberhate involvement among young people from ten European countries: An application of the routine activity and problem behaviour theory. *Computers in Human Behavior, 123.* https://doi.org/10.1016/j.chb.2021.106872

Walther, J. B., Hoter, E., Ganayem, A., & Shonfeld, M. (2015). Computer-mediated communication and the reduction of prejudice: A controlled longitudinal field experiment among Jews and Arabs in Israel. *Computers in Human Behavior, 52,* 550–558. https://doi.org/10.1016/j.chb.2014.08.004

Warner, D. E., & Raiter, M. (2005). Social context in massively-multiplayer online games (MMOGs). *The International Review of Information Ethics, 4,* 46–52. https://doi.org/10.29173/irie172

Widyanto, L., & Griffiths, M. D. (2011). An empirical study of problematic internet use and self-esteem. *International Journal of Cyber Behavior, Psychology and Learning, 1*(1), 13–24. https://doi.org/10.4018/ijcbpl.2011010102

Williams, K. D., Cheung, C. K. T., & Choi, W. (2000). Cyberostracism: Effects of being ignored over the internet. *Journal of Personality and Social Psychology, 79*(5), 748–762. https://doi.org/10.1037/0022-3514.79.5.748

Wilson, C., Sheridan, L., & Garratt-Reed, D. (2022). Examining cyberstalking perpetration and victimization: A scoping review. *Trauma, Violence & Abuse.* Advanced online publication. https://doi.org/10.1177/15248380221082937

Yao, M. Z., Mahood, C., & Linz, D. (2010). Sexual priming, gender stereotyping, and likelihood to sexually harass: Examining the cognitive effects of playing a sexually-explicit video game. *Sex Roles, 62*(1), 77–88. https://doi.org/10.1007/s11199-009-9695-4

Yee, N., & Bailenson, J. N. (2006). Walk a mile in digital shoes: The impact of embodied perspective-taking on the reduction of negative stereotyping in immersive virtual environments. In *Proceedings of the presence 2006: The 9th annual international workshop on presence*. August 24–26.

Zadro, L., Williams, K. D., & Richardson, R. (2004). How low can you go? Ostracism by a computer is sufficient to lower self-reported levels of belonging, control, self-esteem, and meaningful existence. *Journal of Experimental Social Psychology*, *40*(4), 560–567. https://doi.org/10.1016/j.jesp.2003.11.006

Love and Relationships Online

Nicola Fox Hamilton

Chapter Overview

Technology has permeated every aspect of our lives, even to the core of our love lives. We expand our dating options and meet people we wouldn't otherwise know, ask each other on dates, investigate in depth the lives of our potential mates, profess our love, reassure each other of our affection, say hurtful and healing things in the heat of an argument, and even end our relationships. We use technology to both support and undermine our relationships, but there are few areas left untouched. This chapter will outline how we use technology in each of these areas, and help us understand the impact of computer-mediated communication (CMC) on a topic close to our hearts.

Key Terms

One of the key terms that will be addressed in this chapter is **self-presentation** in online dating. We will look at **uncertainty reduction** strategies, which are used at almost every stage in a relationship to reassure the dater about aspects of their partner or relationship. We will consider the effects of **computer-mediated communication (CMC)** and **hyperpersonal communication** on the various ways in which couples communicate with each other during relationship initiation, maintenance, and termination.

Seeking Love Online

Seeking help in finding a romantic partner is not a new phenomenon. Family, friends, matchmakers, and personal advertisements in newspapers are just some of the ways in which people have been brought together through the years. More recently, looking for love online has become increasingly common and acceptable. More and more people form relationships in cyberspace and successfully transition those relationships into their offline world. How we communicate online is different in several ways from our face-to-face interactions (see Chapter 3), and this impacts many aspects of our relationships.

DOI: 10.4324/9781003092513-10

Meeting Online: Where, Who, and Why?

There has been exponential growth in meeting new partners online over the last decades. It is now the most likely way for heterosexual couples to meet, superseding meeting through friends (Rosenfeld et al., 2019). Use among younger adults has grown substantially since the rise of mobile dating applications, with recent figures showing nearly half of those in the 18- to 29-year-old age group using them (Anderson et al., 2020). However, not everyone meets through online dating. Some meet through social networking sites, online communities such as discussion groups, virtual worlds, and multiplayer games (Hall, 2014).

It is interesting to note that CMC has not shifted the gender dynamic of asking someone on a date. Men send significantly more initiating messages on online dating platforms than women do (Kreager et al., 2014; Tyson et al., 2016; Zytko et al., 2014a). The gender of the person initiating contact affects how successful that connection will be, with messaging initiated by women twice as likely to result in a connection (Kreager et al., 2014).

CYBERPSYCHOLOGY IN FOCUS: MINORITY GROUPS AND ONLINE DATING

Same-sex couples have been meeting primarily online for quite some time, with 65% meeting this way since 2009 (Rosenfeld et al., 2019), and 55% of the LGBTQ+ community using online dating (Anderson et al., 2020). Other minority groups are also more likely to meet a partner online, for example, those who report having disabilities are twice as likely to (Lampard, 2020). Dating platforms can offer disabled people more opportunities to meet new partners and give them control over disclosing their disability. Some value the importance of getting to know someone without their disability becoming a factor that might hinder initial interactions, or they may not disclose to avoid attracting people with negative intentions (Mazur, 2022).

What Motivates People to Find Romance Online?

The majority of online dating site and app users are looking for romantic relationships, with a significant minority seeking short-term sexual encounters, though these can lead to long-term relationships too and don't impact negatively on the ensuing relationship (Timmermans & Courtois, 2018). However, there are many motivations for using dating apps beyond those mentioned. Many people download the apps out of curiosity because everyone else is doing so. It is also common to use Tinder and other dating apps to find friends and expand social networks, particularly for those who don't have access to an extensive group of people offline. Others use Tinder to pass the time and for alleviating boredom, while others see the interface design as game-like and find it fun to use. Apps can also be used to deliver an ego boost, sometimes in the wake of a breakup, providing users evidence that they are attractive when they match with others (LeFebvre, 2018; Timmermans & De Caluwé, 2017; Ward, 2017). Another reason for people to try online dating is to meet people who are similar to themselves (Hitsch et al., 2010). Going online can open a multitude of possibilities for those who share similar backgrounds, ethnicity, beliefs and values, and interests and hobbies.

Experiences and Outcomes

While the number of people trying dating online has increased, so too has the number of people who make a date to meet offline. In America, 77% of dating site or app users have gone on a date with someone they met on the platforms, and 39% of users have entered a marriage or committed relationship with someone they met (Anderson et al., 2020).

CYBERPSYCHOLOGY IN FOCUS: NEGATIVE EXPERIENCES OF ONLINE DATING

People's experience of online dating is positive for over half of daters; however, a substantial number of people have had negative experiences while dating. PEW Internet examined the experiences of a range of daters, including LGB members of the broader LGBTQ+ community. LGB daters, as well as young women, are substantially more likely to experience harassment and bullying, continued unwanted contact, being sent unsolicited sexual images or messages, and even threats of physical harm (Anderson et al., 2020). Additionally, many daters find dating apps and websites to be very frustrating and anxiety inducing to use (Anderson et al., 2020; Zytko et al., 2014a).

The stigma around meeting online has considerably reduced over time and it has become a more acceptable way for people to find a partner (Anderson et al., 2020). However, there are still some negative perceptions that people are dishonest on dating sites and that it has made meeting someone impersonal, and close to half of people think that they are not a safe way to meet people (Anderson et al., 2020). In addition, 10% of respondents feel that online dating keeps people from settling down because of the array of options available to them on the sites (Vogels & Anderson, 2020).

Several studies have looked at the long-term effects of a relationship having started online, two of which pre-date widespread dating app use. One found that those who meet online have relationships that are slightly less likely to end in divorce or separation (Cacioppo et al., 2013), while the other found that couples who meet online are more likely to break up (Paul, 2014). A more recent study by Rosenfeld (2017) found no difference in breakup rates between couples who met on- or offline since 1995, but couples who met online tended to get married more quickly than those who met offline. In particular, those who met through online dating were over three times more likely to transition into marriage, likely because online dating attracts those who are serious about finding a committed relationship and offers a wide pool of potential similar partners.

Online Dating Profiles

Dating profiles typically consist of one or more photographs, and one or more open text sections where the dater describes themselves and perhaps the kind of person they would like to meet. There may also be several fixed choice questions about surface characteristics such as height, body type, education, or relationship status, and potentially links to the dater's social media or music platforms. Levine (2000, p. 565) said "the beauty of the virtual medium is that flirting is based on words, charm, and seduction, not physical attraction and cues", and the "about me" text section of a profile is the second most important in determining the attractiveness and trustworthiness of a dater. However, physical attractiveness plays an important role in both offline and online dating. As such, the most important elements of a dating profile are the photographs. Photographs have what is known as a halo effect on the whole profile, where a photograph that is considered attractive influences the judgement of the profile in a positive way, or an unattractive photograph brings down the overall attractiveness rating of the whole profile (Fiore et al., 2008). Photographs also play an important part in daters validating their claims to enjoy certain hobbies or interests by showing images of themselves engaged in those activities. Walther and Parks's (2002) warranting principle posits that people are more likely to trust information online if it cannot be easily manipulated. Hence photographic evidence of a person's body type, physical fitness, or interest in a hobby is a better source of information than text, and this is evident in online dating (Sharabi & Dykstra-DeVette, 2019). Multiple images in a profile will increase the levels of perceived intimacy, social orientation, informality, composure, and other positive outcome values experienced by daters by reducing uncertainty (Ramirez et al., 2015). Tyson et al. (2016) found that Tinder profiles are far more likely to be viewed when photographs are included, and including multiple pictures increases the number of matches for male profiles in particular. During the initial stages of getting to know someone, social media is often used for uncertainty reduction, with daters delving into the profiles of their romantic Interest (Sharabi & Dykstra-DeVette, 2019). Here, photographs are again used to confirm behaviours, interests, and other aspects of the person's identity. This is generally seen as a positive approach, being able to take the time to learn more about who the person is, check friends in common, and look for deal-breaking information, such as a relationship status that is not set to single, or evidence that the person is not who they say they are (Fox et al., 2013; Sharabi & Dykstra-DeVette, 2019).

CMC and Its Effect on Online Romance

Because so much is being communicated about a dater through the medium of text in the "about me" section of the profile, and through initial messages exchanged with potential dates, it is important to look at how computer-mediated communication (CMC) affects the way we share and perceive information in the context of online dating (please see Chapter 3 for an overview of CMC research and theory and, in particular, hyperpersonal communication). For example, errors in spelling in a dating profile may be interpreted by different online daters in several ways, such as lack of education or not caring sufficiently about their profile, and even message length and the timing of a reply can be as important as the actual content of the message in forming impressions of the dater (Van Der Zanden et al., 2019).

In online dating, the speed at which communication becomes intimate can be faster than offline. Social penetration theory posits that relationships move from less intimate to more intimate involvement over time, with people disclosing deeper information about themselves as the relationship progresses (Altman & Taylor, 1973). In the initial stages of a relationship people act with caution, disclosing less intimate information, but gradually when they see signs of reciprocity, they begin to open up and share other aspects of themselves. In online dating this dynamic can shift, as dating profiles reveal a lot of the information that people would typically use for getting to know someone, removing the opportunity to gradually learn about each other. Additionally, because of the anonymity of online dating, the online environment can feel like a safer space in which to reveal core aspects of the self, so communications can become intimate very quickly. On the other hand, the information in a dating profile can also halt communication before it has even begun, as decisions about attraction are often made before any interaction has taken place (LeFebvre, 2018).

Antheunis et al. (2020) found that the hyperpersonal effect persisted in an online dating context when people moved from text-based CMC to meeting in person. Social attraction was higher for people who communicated via text than for those who communicated through video chat before meeting face to face, and that social attraction remained higher upon meeting for those in the texting condition, particularly for women. Romantic attraction, however, declined for both text and video groups on meeting in person. When lacking any physical cues to attraction, those who are texting may focus on uncovering similarities of attitudes and on uncertainty reduction, both of which have been linked to maintaining social attraction for online daters after meeting in person (Sharabi & Caughlin, 2017).

Self-Presentation and Deception in Online Dating

Self-presentation is how we strategically attempt to control the impressions others form of us. Online daters typically strive to present an image of themselves which is both accurate and positive; this is mediated by their fundamental wish to meet a potential partner face-to-face with the possibility of developing a relationship (Zytko et al., 2018). This results in a balance between the desire to self-market and truthful self-presentation, as they want to avoid disappointing a date with an exaggeratedly positive profile. Ellison et al. (2012) conceptualised this as the profile representing a promise or informal contract with others, that the person will not fundamentally differ from how they have presented themselves. Daters tend to be considered in how they present themselves, often analysing other profiles for unattractive or attractive elements, and then adapting their own (Ward, 2017).

Several studies have shown that deception is widespread in online dating profiles, and over 70% of people believe that others are being deceptive to make themselves more attractive (Anderson et al., 2020). Daters prefer profiles that they consider to be genuine and honest and are rarely forgiving of lies told by others. This illustrates a common bias that leads people to believe that others behave in less moral ways, like being deceptive online, than they would do themselves (Drouin et al., 2016). The amount by which people lie tends to be small, again mitigated by the desire to meet in real life, and most daters reframe it as exaggeration rather than blatant lying (Ellison et al., 2012; Toma et al., 2008). One of the reasons that online daters seek to quickly meet face-to-face after striking up communication with another dater is to ensure that the person matches the impression that they have created in their profile. Often this is not the case, and the dater has misrepresented themselves in some way (Anderson et al., 2020). When a dater perceives their partner to have been deceptive, romantic and social attraction and intention to meet again are reduced significantly (Sharabi & Caughlin, 2019).

What Makes a Dating Profile Attractive?

People tend to approach online dating as though shopping for a partner, complete with the requisite shopping list. They may start to view themselves and others as a commodity, and don't find this a positive aspect of online dating (Heino et al., 2010). Homophily, where people tend to like people who are similar to themselves, is evident in the choices people make when contacting others in online dating. Online daters seek homophily more than offline daters, perhaps because dating profiles highlight this information and make it more salient than it would be offline. Some of the most important qualities daters look for include shared similar hobbies and interests, attitudes and values, particularly around politics, and relationship goals (Anderson et al., 2020; Huber & Malhotra, 2017; Sharabi & Dykstra-DeVette, 2019). One area where daters prefer dissimilar others is attractiveness. All daters prefer others more attractive than themselves, but not excessively more so, as they might not expect a positive response from significantly more attractive others (Kreager et al., 2014; Lo et al., 2013). Men view more attractive profiles of women as less trustworthy, but still have a higher desire to date them (McGloin & Denes, 2018). Lo and colleagues (2013) found that people view very attractive photographs as being less authentic but will engage in more deceptive self-presentation to increase their chance of attracting the attention of the person photographed. It's possible that online dating makes this preference for very attractive others possible because of the low risk of contacting someone online and the reduced fear of rejection, as well as the greater access to attractive daters.

Shifting Modalities: Moving Offline

Online dating tends to move quickly to face-to-face contact, as daters don't want to waste time getting to know someone online before they have established if there is any physical chemistry present. The first date is often viewed as a final stage in the screening process rather than an actual date, though it can be reframed as a date in real-time if it goes well (Zytko et al., 2014b). People also want to ensure that the online persona matches the real person, and to be able to consider other profiles if a date doesn't work out. Meeting quickly in person is a successful strategy, as extended interactions result in more negative outcomes (Ramirez et al., 2015). We know that hyperpersonal communication is common to online dating, and can result in idealised impressions being created in the minds of daters about their prospective dates. Extended online communication amplifies this, as distortions may increase over longer periods of interaction. As a result, when the daters meet and are presented with a different person from their idealised mental construct, it can be difficult for them to accept, and the relationship is less likely to succeed. However, by meeting after a shorter interaction, people are more able to accept the discrepancies between their fantasy, which has not had too long to form, and reality. It is suggested that there is a tipping point somewhere between 17 and 23 days where further communication online brings negative results on meeting in real life (Ramirez et al., 2015). During the COVID-19 pandemic, people who were online dating during national lockdowns may have found themselves engaging in drawn-out courtship through texting and video with someone they had never met in person. It is quite likely that such situations would result in the idealisation of their communication partner, and possible disappointment on eventually meeting face-to-face. It is common even without extended online communication for potential partners to fail to live up to expectations formed during online communication, and most find their communication partners less attractive in person (Sharabi & Caughlin, 2017). The limitations of self-presentation in dating platforms mean that daters find it difficult to display the complexity of who they are and to perceive others accurately. This can lead to considerable frustration and anxiety with the process as well as a heightened fear of rejection (Zytko et al., 2014b).

Maintaining Relationships Online

Technology has impacted the way that couples maintain their relationships in both positive and negative ways (Vogels & Anderson, 2020). Some couples find that technology allows them to feel closer to their partner, to show love and affection towards them with small interactions throughout the day, or for long-distance couples to reconnect and focus on each other, and this can increase relationship satisfaction (Hertlein & Chan, 2020; Vogels & Anderson, 2020). The online disinhibition effect of CMC, particularly the effects of invisibility and asynchronicity, can make it easier for couples to open up and disclose intimate information that they may find it difficult to share face-to-face. For example, couples report finding it easier to resolve arguments through CMC because the asynchronicity of the communication allows them time to respond to their partner rather than responding immediately with heightened emotions (Houser et al., 2012; see Figure 6.1).

However, other couples feel that technology use introduces friction and conflict, and these experiences tend to be amplified for younger couples (Vogels & Anderson, 2020). Ignoring your partner in favour of interacting with others online, often called partner phubbing or technoference, can also result in decreasing relationship satisfaction. It can cause conflict over technology use and increase the perception of not being responsive to a partner's needs. It reduces the quality and quantity of time spent together resulting in less positive in-person interactions and more negative mood, all of which lead to dissatisfaction over time (Booth et al., 2021; McDaniel et al., 2021). This finding was exacerbated during the pandemic when couples experiencing lockdowns, worry, or boredom reported greater phone and social media use, resulting in increased conflict and lower relationship satisfaction (Zoppolat et al., 2022).

Jealousy, Surveillance, and Infidelity

The lack of cues, and the lack of context in social networks and online generally can sometimes lead to problems with the misinterpretation of communications (Walther, 1996). This can result in jealousy flaring up in response to communications posted online. About a quarter of older adults and over a third

Figure 6.1

Technology can bring couples together or create distance between them. Ben Rice McCarthy photographer.

of young adults have experienced feelings of insecurity or jealousy because of a partner's social media use (Vogels & Anderson, 2020). Lower self-esteem and being younger are both recurring predictors of jealousy activated by social media (Demirtaş-Madran, 2018).

Surveillance

Managing private relationships in a public forum can be tricky to accomplish. There is much discussion of the idea of social media stalking in popular media, and indeed there is an element of truth to the idea. People commonly engage in the surveillance of potential, current, and ex-partners online, but few reach the point where they cause fear in their targets. About half of all social media users have searched for information about a past partner, rising to 70% of younger users aged 18–29 (Vogels & Anderson, 2020). In fact, Joinson (2008) found that social surveillance is the second most likely thing to come to mind when thinking about social network sites. Partner surveillance through technology is not universally negative (Elphinston et al., 2013). It may be beneficial to those who are experiencing jealous thoughts if it is done without rumination and with positive self-talk, and a positive association was found between surveillance and relationship satisfaction. Rumination appears to be the mediator between jealousy, surveillance, and relationship satisfaction. Rumination is an unconstructive cognitive-emotional experience that is difficult to stop engaging in, and if people engage in surveillance while experiencing rumination, it leads to greater relationship dissatisfaction. Tokunaga (2011) found no connection between surveillance and previous infidelity and posited that surveillance may be a benign information-seeking strategy used in healthy relationships to reduce uncertainty.

Cyberstalking

However, online surveillance is not always benign, and while much of what people engage in online does not meet the legally required standard of stalking, some cross the line into criminal behaviour. There are three types of harassment observed on Facebook: covert provocation involves actions that may not be overtly obvious or damaging, but provokes the target of the harassment nonetheless; public harassment; and venting on Facebook about an ex-partner. Cyber obsessional pursuit (COP) involves using technology-based stalking behaviours to harass someone or demand intimacy from them; this becomes cyberstalking when the behaviour is repeated and severe and likely to cause fear in a reasonable person. Those who engage in Facebook harassment, both covert and overt, are more likely to commit COP, and this in turn is more likely to lead to offline stalking behaviour (Lyndon et al., 2011). Additional content on cyberstalking can be found in Chapters 5 and 11.

Infidelity and Cyber Cheating

Demirtaş-Madran (2018) found that men and women view online infidelity differently, with women more upset by emotional infidelity and men equally upset by sexual and emotional infidelity. The internet facilitates many types of infidelity, even when it is not deliberately sought out. Hyperpersonal communication can result in deeply connected relationships, and anonymity and online disinhibition can encourage people to act in ways they might not offline. The boundaries between what is or is not infidelity online can be blurred, but even when the definition is not clear, the behaviours can still cause significant distress and have serious negative consequences for relationships (Vossler & Moller, 2020). The fact that infidelity can occur through technology within the couple's home, even while sitting next to each other, can be particularly upsetting for the betrayed partner.

Breaking up

It is not only in the development and maintenance of relationships that technology has had an impact; increasingly relationships come to an end via CMC as well. Seventeen per cent of people have broken up with someone by text, email, or online message, and equally, 17% had it happen to them (Lenhart & Duggan, 2014). The online disinhibition that accompanies CMC use makes it easier for people to break up a relationship by these means. The invisibility of communication means that a partner's negative reaction is not experienced face-to-face, and it is easier for people to open up about their thoughts and feelings.

Ghosting, where all communication is cut off without any explanation, can also be facilitated by technology. This is an avoidance strategy for withdrawal from a relationship and is utilised for several reasons (Timmermans et al., 2020). These include convenience or avoiding conflict or intimacy, or a method of alleviating emotional distress with little effort. It can also be for safety reasons in situations perceived as potentially dangerous physically, or toxic mentally. People describe the lack of closure as difficult after being ghosted, not understanding why communication was ended, feeling self-criticism or doubt and anxiety over the discomfort of potentially encountering the ghoster in future.

Conclusion

This chapter has looked at how we use technology to find new partners, initiate contact, and begin to develop a relationship. CMC has been explored in the context of the impact that it has on our relationships, both to help people form connections and to avoid situations they find stressful or unpleasant such as asking someone out or breaking up with them. We have looked at how to utilise online tools to reduce uncertainty about situations, both in support of relationships, but also in unhealthy ways such as cyberstalking. Technology has touched upon almost every aspect of our personal lives and will only continue to do so as its reach expands.

Activity

Form groups. Each person should create an online dating profile "about me" text. It doesn't have to be truthful. Shuffle all of the profiles and swap them with another group. Take one profile each and answer the following questions, then discuss them within your group:

1. Think about the gender of the person who wrote this profile. What is it about the text that makes you pick that particular gender?
2. Describe three different cues you notice that give you extra information about the dater. These may be impressions that you form that don't come directly from what is written about in the text itself, for example, expressions that the dater uses, or paralanguage such as punctuation, emoticons, or spelling and grammar.

3. Explain how you think that other people might interpret those cues differently.

Discussion Questions

1. Would you be more comfortable asking someone out, or breaking up with a partner face-to-face or using CMC? Why? Would different channels of CMC make this more or less acceptable?
2. People have mentioned that technology can support or cause friction in relationships; do you think that technology is destroying our ability to form close relationships, or increasing our ability to create close connections?
3. Many people engage in the surveillance of potential, current, or ex-partners on Facebook and other social network sites. Think about your own experience. Do you think that this is socially acceptable or healthy behaviour? If you knew that someone was seeking information from your profile, would that raise concerns for you about your privacy?
4. If a person has an online relationship with someone other than his or her partner, but never meets them offline, is it really cheating?

Recommended Reading List

This book explores how technology impacts and interacts with our relationships, from online dating to technology in romantic relationships and its use in dissolving them, to technology-enhanced robot and augmented reality relationships.

> Papacharissi, Z. (Ed.). (2018). *A networked self and love* (pp. 208–218). Routledge.

Two of the chapters in *The Oxford Handbook of Cyberpsychology* are particularly relevant. Chapter 7 looks at how technology can interfere with and disrupt partner and family relationships.

> Drouin, M., & McDaniel, B. T. (2019). Technology interference in couple and family relationships. In A. Attrill-Smith, C. Fullwood, M. Keep, & D. J. Kuss (Eds.), *The Oxford handbook of cyberpsychology* (pp. 115–132). Oxford University Press.

Chapter 11 examines online romantic relationships and, in particular, delves into the psychological benefits and potential harms of dating online dating.

> Lloyd, J., Attril-Smith, A., & Fullwood, C. (2019). Online romantic relationships. In A. Attrill-Smith, C. Fullwood, M. Keep, & D. J. Kuss (Eds.), *The Oxford handbook of cyberpsychology* (pp. 195–215). Oxford University Press.

This Pew Research report examines how people are using technology both to find new romantic relationships and within their existing ones. It looks at how technology can distract and disrupt relationships, as well as how couples can use it more positively to connect with a partner.

Vogels, E. A., & Anderson, M. (2020, May). Dating and relationships in the digital age. *Pew Research Center : Internet & Technology.* https://www .pewresearch.org/internet/2020/05/08/dating-and-relationships-in-the -digital-age/

This study looks at the ways in which online daters go about attracting others, managing their own self-presentation, and interacting with potential dates.

Sharabi, L. L., & Dykstra-DeVette, T. A. (2019). From first email to first date: Strategies for initiating relationships in online dating. *Journal of Social and Personal Relationships, 36*(11–12), 3389–3407. https://doi.org/10 .1177/0265407518822780

Glossary

Computer-mediated communication (CMC): Human communication that relies on the medium of computer technology for messaging.
Cyber obsessional pursuit (COP): Using technology-based stalking behaviours to harass someone or demand intimacy from them.
Halo effect: A cognitive bias that occurs when one element of the dating profile, usually the photograph, influences the observer's impressions of the profile as a whole.
Homophily: The tendency for people to like others similar to themselves.
Online disinhibition: A loosing or removal of social inhibitions when interacting online, that would normally be present in face-to-face communication.
Paralanguage: The visual appearance of written language, such as punctuation, spelling, grammar, and keyboard characters.
Self-presentation: A strategic negotiation of how one presents one's self to audiences.
Social information processing theory (SIP): People encode and decode social information in the language they use in their text-based communications.
Uncertainty reduction: Strategies used at almost every stage in a relationship to reassure a person about aspects of their partner or relationship. Can include information seeking.
Warranting principle: People are more likely to trust information online if it cannot be easily manipulated.

References

Altman, I., & Taylor, D. A. (1973). *Social penetration: The development of interpersonal relationships.* Holt, Rinehart & Winston.

Anderson, M., Vogels, E. A., & Turner, E. (2020). *The virtues and downsides of online dating.* https://www.pewresearch.org/internet/2020/02/06/the-virtues-and-downsides-of-online-dating/

Antheunis, M. L., Schouten, A. P., & Walther, J. B. (2020). The hyperpersonal effect in online dating: Effects of text-based CMC vs. videoconferencing before meeting face-to-face. *Media Psychology, 23*(6), 820–839. https://doi.org/10.1080/15213269.2019.1648217

Booth, M. A., Coyne, S. M., Yorgason, J. B., & Dew, J. P. (2021). Domestic bliss, or technological diss? Problematic media use, partner responsiveness, and relationship outcomes. *Journal of Social and Personal Relationships, 38*(12), 3610–3632. https://doi.org/10.1177/02654075211031000

Cacioppo, J. T., Cacioppo, S., Gonzaga, G. C., Ogburn, E. L., & VanderWeele, T. J. (2013). Marital satisfaction and break-ups differ across on-line and off-line meeting venues. *PNAS Proceedings of the National Academy of Sciences of the United States of America, 110*(25), 10135–10140.

Demirtaş-Madran, H. A. (2018). Relationship among Facebook jealousy, aggression, and personal and relationship variables. *Behaviour and Information Technology, 37*(5), 462–472. https://doi.org/10.1080/0144929X.2018.1451919

Drouin, M., Miller, D., Wehle, S. M. J., & Hernandez, E. (2016). Why do people lie online? "Because everyone lies on the internet". *Computers in Human Behavior, 64*, 134–142. https://doi.org/10.1016/j.chb.2016.06.052

Ellison, N. B., Hancock, J. T., & Toma, C. L. (2012). Profile as promise: A framework for conceptualizing veracity in online dating self-presentations. *New Media & Society, 14*(1), 45–62. https://doi.org/10.1177/1461444811410395

Elphinston, R. A., Feeney, J. A., Noller, P., Connor, J. P., & Fitzgerald, J. (2013). Romantic jealousy and relationship satisfaction: The costs of rumination. *Western Journal of Communication, 77*(3), 293–304. https://doi.org/10.1080/10570314.2013.770161

Fiore, A. T., Shaw Taylor, L., Mendelsohn, G. A., & Hearst, M. (2008). Assessing attractiveness in online dating profiles. In *Proceeding of the twenty-sixth annual CHI conference on human factors in computing systems - CHI '08, 1992*, 797. https://doi.org/10.1145/1357054.1357181

Fox, J., Warber, K. M., & Makstaller, D. C. (2013). The role of Facebook in romantic relationship development. *Journal of Social and Personal Relationships, 30*(6). https://doi.org/10.1177/0265407512468370

Hall, J. A. (2014). First comes social networking, then comes marriage? Characteristics of Americans married 2005–2012 who met through social networking sites. *Cyberpsychology, Behavior, and Social Networking, 17*(5), 322–326. https://doi.org/10.1089/cyber.2013.0408

Heino, R. D., Ellison, N. B., & Gibbs, J. L. (2010). Relationshopping: Investigating the market metaphor in online dating. *Journal of Social and Personal Relationships, 27*(4), 427–447. https://doi.org/10.1177/0265407510361614

Hertlein, K. M., & Chan, D. (2020). The rationale behind texting, videoconferencing, and mobile phones in couple relationships. *Marriage and Family Review, 56*(8), 739–763. https://doi.org/10.1080/01494929.2020.1737624

Hitsch, G. J., Hortaçsu, A., & Ariely, D. (2010). Matching and sorting in online dating. *American Economic Review, 100*(1), 130–163. https://doi.org/10.1257/aer.100.1.130

Houser, M. L., Fleuriet, C., & Estrada, D. (2012). The cyber factor: An analysis of relational maintenance through the use of computer-mediated communication. *Communication Research Reports, 29*(1), 34–43. https://doi.org/10.1080/08824096.2011.639911

Huber, G. A., & Malhotra, N. (2017). Political homophily in social relationships: Evidence from online dating behavior. *Journal of Politics, 79*(1), 269–283.

Joinson, A. N. (2008). 'Looking at', 'looking up' or 'keeping up with' people? Motives and uses of Facebook. *CHI 2008 proceedings: Online social networks* (pp. 1027–1036). https://doi.org/978-1-60558-01101/08/04

Kreager, D. A., Cavanagh, S. E., Yen, J., & Yu, M. (2014). "Where have all the good men gone?" Gendered interactions in online dating. *Journal of Marriage and Family, 76*(2), 387–410. https://doi.org/10.1111/jomf.12072

Lampard, R. (2020). Meeting online or offline? Patterns and trends for co-resident couples in early 21st-century Britain. *Sociological Research Online, 25*(4), 589–608. https://doi.org/10.1177/1360780419895524

LeFebvre, L. E. (2018). Swiping me off my feet: Explicating relationship initiation on Tinder. *Journal of Social and Personal Relationships, 35*(9), 1205–1229. https://doi.org/10.1177/0265407517706419

Lenhart, A., & Duggan, M. (2014). Couples, the Internet and social media. *Pew Research.* https://www.pewresearch.org/internet/2014/02/11/couples-the-internet-and-social-media/

Levine, D. (2000). Virtual attraction: What rocks your boat. *Cyberpsychology and Behavior, 3*(4), 565–573. https://doi.org/10.1089/109493100420179

Lo, S. K., Hsieh, A. Y., & Chiu, Y. P. (2013). Contradictory deceptive behavior in online dating. *Computers in Human Behavior, 29*(4), 1755–1762. https://doi.org/10.1016/j.chb.2013.02.010

Lyndon, A., Bonds-Raacke, J., & Cratty, A. D. (2011). College students' Facebook stalking of ex-partners. *Cyberpsychology, Behavior, and Social Networking, 14*(12), 711–716. https://doi.org/10.1089/cyber.2010.0588

Mazur, E. (2022). Online dating experiences of LGBTQ+ emerging adults with disabilities. *Sexuality and Disability, 40*(2), 213–231. https://doi.org/10.1007/s11195-022-09726-2

McDaniel, B. T., Galovan, A. M., & Drouin, M. (2021). Daily technoference, technology use during couple leisure time, and relationship quality. *Media Psychology, 24*(5), 637–665. https://doi.org/10.1080/15213269.2020.1783561

McGloin, R., & Denes, A. (2018). Too hot to trust: Examining the relationship between attractiveness, trustworthiness, and desire to date in online dating. *New Media and Society, 20*(3), 919–936. https://doi.org/10.1177/1461444816675440

Paul, A. (2014). Is online better than offline for meeting partners? Depends: Are you looking to marry or to date? *Cyberpsychology, Behavior, and Social Networking, 17*(10), 664–667.

Ramirez, A., (Bryant) Sumner, E. M., Fleuriet, C., & Cole, M. (2015). When online dating partners meet offline: The effect of modality switching on relational communication between online daters. *Journal of Computer-Mediated Communication, 20*(1), 99–114. https://doi.org/10.1111/jcc4.12101

Rosenfeld, M. J. (2017). Marriage, choice, and couplehood in the age of the internet. *Sociological Science, 4*, 490–510. https://doi.org/10.15195/v4.a20

Rosenfeld, M. J., Thomas, R. J., & Hausen, S. (2019). Disintermediating your friends: How online dating in the United States displaces other ways of meeting. *Proceedings of the National Academy of Sciences of the United States of America, 116*(36), 17753–17758. https://doi.org/10.1073/pnas.1908630116

Sharabi, L. L., & Caughlin, J. P. (2017). What predicts first date success? A longitudinal study of modality switching in online dating. *Personal Relationships, 24*(2), 370–391.

Sharabi, L. L., & Caughlin, J. P. (2019). Deception in online dating: Significance and implications for the first offline date. *New Media and Society, 21*(1), 229–247. https://doi.org/10.1177/1461444818792425

Sharabi, L. L., & Dykstra-DeVette, T. A. (2019). From first email to first date: Strategies for initiating relationships in online dating. *Journal of Social and Personal Relationships, 36*(11–12), 3389–3407. https://doi.org/10.1177/0265407518822780

Timmermans, E., & Courtois, C. (2018). From swiping to casual sex and/or committed relationships: Exploring the experiences of Tinder users. *Information Society, 34*(2), 59–70. https://doi.org/10.1080/01972243.2017.1414093

Timmermans, E., & De Caluwé, E. (2017). Development and validation of the Tinder Motives Scale (TMS). *Computers in Human Behavior, 70,* 341–350. https://doi.org/10.1016/j.chb.2017.01.028

Timmermans, E., Hermans, A.-M., & Opree, S. J. (2020). Gone with the wind: Exploring mobile daters' ghosting experiences. *Journal of Social and Personal Relationships, 38*(2), 783–801. https://doi.org/10.1177/0265407520970287

Tokunaga, R. S. (2011). Social networking site or social surveillance site? Understanding the use of interpersonal electronic surveillance in romantic relationships. *Computers in Human Behavior, 27*(2), 705–713. https://doi.org/10.1016/j.chb.2010.08.014

Toma, C. L., Hancock, J. T., & Ellison, N. B. (2008). Separating fact from fiction: An examination of deceptive self-presentation in online dating profiles. *Personality and Social Psychology Bulletin, 34*(8), 1023–1036. https://doi.org/10.1177/0146167208318067

Tyson, G., Perta, V. C., Haddadi, H., & Seto, M. C. (2016). A first look at user activity on Tinder. In *Proceedings of the 2016 IEEE/ACM international conference on advances in social networks analysis and mining* (pp. 461–466). IEEE/ACM. https://qmro.qmul.ac.uk/xmlui/bitstream/handle/123456789/15759/Haddadi%20A%20First%20Look%20at%20User%202016%20Accepted.pdf?sequence=1&isAllowed=y

Van Der Zanden, T., Schouten, A., Mos, M., & Krahmer, E. (2019). Impression formation on online dating sites: Effects of language errors in profile texts on perceptions of profile owners' attractiveness. *Journal of Social and Personal Relationships, 37*(3), 758–778. https://doi.org/10.1177/0265407519878787

Vogels, E. A., & Anderson, M. (2020, May). Dating and relationships in the digital age. *Pew Research Center : Internet & Technology.* https://www.pewresearch.org/internet/2020/05/08/dating-and-relationships-in-the-digital-age/

Vossler, A., & Moller, N. P. (2020). Internet affairs: Partners' perceptions and experiences of Internet infidelity. *Journal of Sex and Marital Therapy, 46*(1), 67–77. https://doi.org/10.1080/0092623X.2019.1654577

Walther, J. B. (1996). Computer-mediated communication: Impersonal, interpersonal, and hyperpersonal interaction. *Communication Research, 23*(1), 3–43. https://collablab.northwestern.edu//CollabolabDistro/nucmc/Walther-CMCHyperpersonal-CommRes-1996.pdf

Walther, J. B., & Parks, M. R. (2002). Cues filtered out, cues filtered in Computer-mediated communication and relationships. In M. L. Knapp & J. A. Daly (Eds.), *Handbook of interpersonal communication* (3rd ed., pp. 529–563). Sage.

Ward, J. (2017). What are you doing on Tinder? Impression management on a matchmaking mobile app. *Information, Communication and Society, 20*(11), 1644–1659. https://doi.org/10.1080/1369118X.2016.1252412

Zoppolat, G., Righetti, F., Balzarini, R. N., Rodrigues, D. L., Debrot, A., Wiwattanapantuwong, J., Dharma, C., Chi, P., Karremans, J. C., & Schoebi, D. (2022). Relationship difficulties and "technoference" during the COVID-19 pandemic. *Journal of Social and Personal Relationships*, 1–24. https://doi.org /10.1177/02654075221093611

Zytko, D., Grandhi, S. A., & Jones, Q. (2014a). Impression management and formation in online dating systems. In *ECIS 2014 proceedings - 22nd European conference on information systems*, 1–10. https://aisel.aisnet.org/ecis2014/ proceedings/track12/9/

Zytko, D., Grandhi, S. A., & Jones, Q. (2014b). Impression management struggles in online dating. In *Proceedings of the group 2014*, 53–62. https://doi.org/10 .1145/2660398.2660410

Zytko, D., Grandhi, S. A., & Jones, Q. (2018). The (un)enjoyable user experience of online dating systems. In M. Blythe & A. Monk (Eds.), *Funology 2*. Springer. https://doi.org/10.1007/978-3-319-68213-6

7 Attention and Distraction Online

John Greaney and Emma Mathias

Chapter Overview

Many students now study in a multitasking environment, where the goal of study is one option amongst many: listening to music, responding to texts, watching videos, talking online. This chapter examines the prevalence and effects of such media multitasking with regard to the influence on attention, learning, and emotional states. The psychology of **attention**, **multitasking**, and self-control is brought to bear on the issue. Finally, some strategies for effectively managing technological distractions while learning are introduced.

Key Terms

Attention means directing the mind to any object of sense or thought. **Multitasking** involves doing more than one thing at once.

Studying in a Multitasking Environment

Many individuals now have access to a range of media devices with streams of input available at the touch at the button. Whether at home, work, school/college, or travelling, there is choice about what we attend to. This raises the question of the overall effect of such choice on attention, learning, and wellbeing. In particular, if we want to study and concentrate, what are the effects of **multitasking** and what strategies can students employ to manage information overload? According to Clifford Nass, the top 25% of Stanford students are using four or more media at one time whenever they're using media technology: "So when they're writing a paper, they're also Facebooking, listening to music, texting, Twittering, et cetera" (Nass, 2013).

Using Technology while Studying at Home

The question of the impact of media multitasking on learning has been the focus of a multitude of research. Students working in their home environments

DOI: 10.4324/9781003092513-11

were the focus of Rosen et al.'s (2013) research that looked at the impact of technological distractions on the learning of school and university students. They observed 263 students in their homes during 15-minute study periods. The average time on task was less than six minutes before participants switched their focus, most often to a technological distraction such as social media or texting. The tendency to switch task was associated with having more distractors available. Students who more consciously applied study strategies (such as self-testing to check their learning) were more likely to remain focused on-task than those who did not.

Using Technology during Class Time

Technology also presents a distraction during lecture and class time. Media multitasking has been associated with moderated effects of academic lectures and reduced academic performance (Abramova et al., 2017; Rosen et al., 2013). It has been found to have a negative impact on test performance, reading comprehension, note-taking, efficiency, and self-regulation amongst university students (May & Elder, 2018). In their 2017 study, Patterson and Patterson found that between 72% and 79% of students used laptops or other devices during lectures, an increase from the 57% reported in 2011 by Parker et al. This number is likely to have increased even further since the increase of online learning during the coronavirus pandemic. Research suggests that students may not be fully aware of the extent of their multitasking. For example, Abramova et al. (2017) measured self-awareness of media multitasking during an 80-minute undergraduate lecture using structured observations and self-report measures. They found that over 90% of students engaged in texting or browsing on their smartphones. Students accessed their smartphones an average of 8 times and heavier users an average of 21 times. Results also suggested that many participants had a lack of awareness around their multitasking habits: although approximately 40% of students correctly estimated, 21% overestimated and 41% underestimated the time they spent browsing or texting. Students also under-reported their frequency of email and instant messaging use in a similar study by Kraushaar and Novak (2010). The researchers found that students had applications unrelated to their course running about 42% of the time. Kraushaar and Novak (2010) also found that academic success was related to a greater proportion of time spent on "productive" (course-related) versus "unproductive" (unrelated to course work) multitasking.

These negative effects on learning can also extend to the habits of classmates. Hall et al. (2020), for example, reported detrimental effects to students' neighbours' learning when individuals used laptops for off-task activities. These studies are in line with the view that similar tasks do not add up to as high cognitive load as tasks that are very different (Rogers & Monsell, 1995).

Our brains are built to receive many stimuli at one time, but they're related stimuli. The problem with multitasking is not that we're writing a report of Abraham Lincoln and hear, see pictures of Abraham Lincoln and read words of Abraham Lincoln and see photos of Abraham ... The problem is we're doing a report on Abraham Lincoln and tweeting about last night and watching a YouTube video about cats playing the piano, et cetera.

(Nass, 2013)

For the student, this statement can relate to the experience of sitting down to complete an assignment and finding the attention wandering to other sources of information (all available at the click of a button) online.

How Do High Multitaskers Compare to Light Multitaskers?

As multitasking is very prevalent, researchers have looked at whether there are any advantages to this practice. For example, Orphir et al. (2009) divided student participants into two groups: those who reported they used several applications simultaneously ("most of the time") were designated as "high media multitaskers" (HMMs). These were compared to a group of students who were "low media multitaskers" (LMMs) in three computer-based tests.

Ability to Ignore Irrelevant Information

The first study by Orphir et al. (2009) measured how well the participants were able to ignore irrelevant information. Participants viewed pairs of red rectangles that were surrounded by different numbers of blue rectangles on a screen. Each configuration was glimpsed twice, and the participants had to decide whether the red rectangles moved position between the first and second trial. The LLMs were better able to ignore the blue rectangles to complete the task, but the HMMs were unable to ignore the distractions in the form of irrelevant blue shapes, suggesting HMMs have lower levels of cognitive control when it comes to filtering out irrelevant information. Van der Schuur et al. (2020) applied this to an academic setting with adolescents and found academic attention problems to be associated with high levels of media multitasking.

Working Memory Capacity

Working memory is the system for temporarily storing and managing the information required to carry out cognitive tasks such as learning and comprehension. Orphir et al. (2009) wondered whether the HMMs had better memories due to their inability to ignore information, so they measured participants' ability to organise items in their working memory in their second experiment. Results showed that HMMs performed badly compared to LMMs. Müller et al. found similar results in their 2021 study, with HMMs performing worse than LMMs on tests of working memory capacity and logical reasoning.

Skill in Switching from One Thing to Another

Orphir et al. (2009) questioned whether the HMMs in their study had developed superior ability in switching from one thing to another and they developed a third experiment to test this idea. Participants were shown letters and numbers simultaneously and had to either pay attention to the letters or the numbers. A category judgement was required: whether the digits were even or odd, whether letters were vowels or consonants. The LMMs did better than the HMMs in this measure of ability to switch focus, a somewhat surprising result given the role of task-switching in multitasking. Students who habitually multitasked could not easily separate relevant from irrelevant information: they were always drawn to the information in front of them. Thus, the availability of irrelevant information may slow down HMMs. This information may be related to the external world or the internal world of the individual.

Effects of Habitual Multitasking

The essence of Orphir et al.'s (2009) study is clear – HMMs fared worse on several measures of handling information. In essence they are worse at multitasking. LMMs were often better at ignoring irrelevant information, showed higher working memory capacity, and showed a better ability to switch focus. In a separate study, Abramova et al. (2017) found that students' visual and auditory attention was negatively affected by the number of times they looked at their smartphone, impacting on their ability to remember information presented visually and orally. The more time a student spent on their smartphone, the less auditory information they remembered. In addition, Edwards and Shin (2017) investigated differences in implicit learning for HMMs vs. LMMs. They found that HMMs fare worse when it comes to implicit learning, which the researchers theorised was due to their wider attentional scope.

Impact on Depth of Learning

Multitasking may also influence the *depth* of learning, a phenomenon investigated by Foerde et al. (2006). They conducted an experiment in which students learned on a computer while carrying out an additional task. Students who did both tasks simultaneously seemed to learn as much as those who did the first task alone. However, the group who multitasked were less able to apply their knowledge to new situations and possessed less flexibility in applying their knowledge, implying they had less depth of learning. Glass and Kang (2019) found that comprehension was not affected by media multitasking during a lecture, but that retention of information was impacted, as reflected in exam performance. Similarly, Wammes et al. (2019) found that media multitasking had a negative impact on learning outcomes in a university setting. A number of studies have found this negative relationship between media multitasking and academic achievement (e.g., Alghamdi et al., 2020; Demirbilek & Talan, 2018; Lau, 2017; Patterson, 2017).

Why Do People Multitask?

Given the evidence that multitasking appears to confer little benefit to performance, the question of *why* people multitask is relevant. Determining factors include age (with "digital natives" more likely to engage in media multitasking than "digital immigrants" [Carrier et al., 2015], gender (with women often more likely than men to multitask), and education level (with higher education levels associated with higher levels of media multitasking [Hwang et al., 2014; Seijn et al., 2017]). Although these descriptive factors may give some idea as to the general characteristics of those most likely to multitask, they are less adept at providing insights into *why* it is that individuals choose to do so.

To answer this question, Wang and Tchernev (2012) recruited 32 college students who agreed to report on media usage three times a day for a month. The students reported on whether they were multitasking and provided their motivations for each activity. Overall, multitasking occurred most often when students needed to study or work. Results showed that students who multitasked (e.g., watched TV while studying) reported feeling more emotionally satisfied compared to those who studied without additional media. While multitasking seemed to meet certain emotional needs (for fun/entertainment/relaxation), there was a negative impact on learning, so these students did not achieve their cognitive goals as well as those who did not multitask as much. The emotional boost from multitasking had not been something consciously sought by the students according to the research. However, this emotional lift may explain why multitasking is habit-forming. The results also suggest that multitasking is a habit that strengthens over time, so that if a student multitasks one day, it is more likely to happen the next.

Similarly, Stamenković et al. (2018) found that most of the university students in their study engaged in media multitasking out of habit and boredom, but also in the belief that they could obtain more knowledge and achieve as much as possible within a short time frame. Digital distractions offer easy but variable rewards that can promote an almost addictive checking (e.g., of social media). The emotional satisfaction that comes from multitasking may be short-lived when compared with the satisfaction derived from completing a difficult project or mastering a challenge. For such achievement it is necessary to hone certain abilities. In particular, the faculties of attention and self-control are vital for managing awareness and persistence.

Attention

To look more closely at what is going on when people attend to information online, we need to consider the psychology of attention. **Attention** is "the taking possession by the mind, in clear and vivid form, of one out of what seem several simultaneously possible objects or trains of thought", wrote psychologist and philosopher William James (James, 1890, pp. 403–4). "It implies withdrawal from some things in order to deal effectively with others and is a condition which has a real opposite in the confused, dazed, scatterbrained state which in French is called distraction".

Attention capacity has limits and we are regularly torn between a multitude of stimuli that require us to switch our attention from one item to another. People may feel they are taking in everything, but large changes can happen without being noticed. In the "invisible gorilla" experiment, participants watched a video that shows a group of people passing a basketball (Simons & Chabris, 1999). Participants were asked to count the number of passes made by people wearing white. Midway through the video a man wearing a gorilla suit walks past the throwers and does a dance. However, almost half of those watching failed to notice the gorilla when watching the video for the first time, indicating that many of the participants failed to switch their attention between the stimuli presented to them. According to neuroscientist Michael Posner, attention consists of distinct but overlapping systems – alerting, orienting, and executive control (Posner & Petersen, 1990) – a classification that was later supported by neuroimaging studies that examined which areas of the brain are active under different conditions.

Alerting and Orienting

The alerting system activates and maintains a wakeful state. This is related to a feeling of "readiness". The alert state may wane leading to "spacing out" and overlooking details. Consuming caffeine is one common method people employ to attempt maintain alertness. While orienting allows us to perceive something new and determine its importance. It focuses our senses on relevant information. In the case of looking at information online, we orient our attention by moving our eyes from place to place to take in details while attempting to ignore distractions. Shifting focus to changes in our environment is an important skill in evolutionary terms since it allows us to become aware of potential dangers. So, this offers one explanation for why technology distractions are so enticing – we have an attentional system that is tuned to respond to novel information.

Executive Control and Attention Network Test

The executive control system can be compared to air traffic control when managing multiple planes arriving and departing. The executive allocates attention in a flexible manner to our present voluntary goals, monitoring conflict between different desires. We may be presented with information such as advertisements that are often designed to attract attention (orienting) through colour and animation. As such, we have conflicting demands on our focus, and in order to stay on-task we need to apply effortful control to avoid distractions. Posner and others have put forward the idea that attention is trainable. Fan et al. (2002) developed the Attention Network Test (ANT), a computer-based measure of efficiency in each of these three networks (alerting, orienting, and executive control).

Training Attention Using Mindfulness and Meditation

Jha et al. (2007) investigated whether training in **mindfulness** had an impact on performance on the ANT for participants with different levels of experience of mindfulness training. Mindfulness training appeared to allow unexperienced participants to make significant improvements in terms of orienting, whereas the experienced participants made improvements in alerting. These results suggest that mindfulness training may enhance these subcomponents of attention and thus improve behavioural responses related to attention. In their study on the effect of meditation on attention, Kwak et al. (2020) found that participants' performance in relation to executive control (as measured by the ANT) improved significantly for those who engaged in a four-day intensive meditation retreat compared to a group who participated in a relaxation retreat.

A number of other researchers have flagged the utility of mindfulness and meditation of both short and long durations for improving elements of attention on both short- and long-term bases (e.g., Chen et al., 2020; Chin et al., 2021). Chin et al. (2021) theorised that those improvements in momentary and trait attentional control were driven by the present-focused monitoring skills fostered in mindfulness-based interventions.

Research suggests that it is possible to train attention skills even at a young age. Posner et al. (2013) developed exercises to help children develop executive attention skills such as self-control, planning, and observation. They found that after seven half-hour sessions, six-year-olds showed brain wave activity patterns similar to those of adults. They also had significant increases in executive attention.

CYBERPSYCHOLOGY IN FOCUS: ATTENTION DEFICIT DISORDER (ADD) AND ATTENTION DEFICIT HYPERACTIVITY DISORDER (ADHD)

Attention deficit disorder (ADD) and attention deficit hyperactivity disorder (ADHD) are conditions that significantly affect concentration in daily life. According to the ADHD Foundation, around 2–5% (around 1 in 30) of students at school are affected, with the experience of the world as "a constant stream of changing images and messages. It's difficult to focus on one thing at a time because something new is always coming". Students with these conditions will find independent study particularly challenging. These students will benefit from clear timelines and outlines to help with organising course materials. Other helpful strategies including highlighting key points and the use of summaries and colour coding, along with rest breaks to help absorb information. For further information see https://www.adhdfoundation.org.uk.

Developing Self-Control

Students are faced with the challenge of having to regulate their emotions and impulses if they want to master certain disciplines. For example, sustained concentration is needed to solve equations. Students will need to persist rather than opting for a more immediately satisfying activity (such as videos and social networking sites, which are all available at the click of a button). These skills of persistence, self-control, and delaying gratification can have far-reaching implications.

The Marshmallow Test: Self-Control and Delayed Gratification

In a well-known research project carried out in the 1970s, Mischel et al. (1972) conducted a study with preschool children who were given the option of eating a marshmallow or waiting 15 minutes to receive 2 marshmallows. When compared to those children who ate the first marshmallow straight away, children who delayed gratification went on to higher educational achievement and increased ability to cope with stress as adults. This marshmallow test has parallels with the online world that is replete with tempting distractions.

A Digital Marshmallow Test: The Academic Diligence Task

Galla et al. (2014) wanted to research the skill of self-control in a realistic scenario and were concerned with measuring how people behave rather than what they say or think they do (as measured through self-report). They devised a "digital marshmallow test" of sorts to use with school-going adolescents, which they called the Academic Diligence Task (ADT). The ADT has a split-screen that presents participants with a choice: on the left side, participants can do a series of maths problems; on the right side, they can watch short entertaining videos or play games. Participants were instructed to answer as many problems as they wanted as fast as they could and were allowed take a break at any time to watch videos or play games. They were told the maths problems would enhance their problem-solving skills in the long term. Participants spent on average half the time on the maths skills. Maths scores were correlated with participants' academic success and personality variables such as conscientiousness and grit. Unlike IQ, the researchers argued that self-control in schoolwork is a skill that can be nurtured and taught.

Strategies for Improving Focus and Handling Distraction

Research has uncovered the downsides to distraction, but what strategies can people employ to stay focused when faced with tempting options close at hand? There are several research-based approaches worth considering that will be discussed in turn.

Turning Study into a Game

When Galla et al. (2014) probed to see how the more focused students in their study had fared, they discovered some students resisted the distractions by turning the maths problem-solving into a game – e.g., seeing how many problems they could solve in a set period of time – instead of switching to the videos/games for a break. Such "gamification" of academic work (e.g., see Tsay et al., 2020) could thus present a fun and engaging way to encourage students to engage in "productive" as opposed to "unproductive" multitasking.

Technology Breaks

As previously mentioned, Rosen et al. (2012) examined the strategy of using "technology breaks". These are designed to address the "separation anxiety" that may be felt by someone used to routinely checking their smartphone or computer throughout the day. This procedure asks students to silence their smartphones for a study period and an alert informs them when they can check in next. Rosen et al. (2012) tested the effects of alternating a technology break of 1 minute followed by a 15-minute study period, which resulted in enhanced attention, focus, and learning.

Setting up an Intention to Wait to Check Technology

This strategy involves setting up an intention to wait until the end of a study period/lecture and ignore the marshmallow of incoming text messages. Rosen et al. (2011) found that students who delayed replying to a text message until the class was over did better than those who responded immediately. This intention to wait is an example of a metacognitive strategy or "plan of action" that a student could adopt in advance of a study session.

Using Technology to Block Distractions

In recent years, many programmes have been developed that allow a person to block the Internet (or specific websites or apps) for set periods of time and to track time spent on apps. Many smartphones now have these functions installed on them. For example, Android phones have a tool called "Digital Wellbeing" and iOS phones have a "Screen Time" function. Biedermann et al. (2021) conducted a systematic review of studies looking at digital self-control interventions. They categorised the interventions according to features such as those that used goal setting, visualisations of device usage, or blocking of Internet sites and apps. Positive outcomes were reported for each intervention type, but the effectiveness of each intervention varied. For example, interventions which relied on increasing awareness of usage (e.g., Whittaker et al., 2016) were not as effective as goal setting using prompts in leading to a reduction in device usage (e.g., Hiniker et al., 2016).

Listening to Music

Listening to familiar music while studying is one option that may not have the downsides of other technology choices. Lehmann and Seufert (2017) did not find any recall performance effects of background music for participants' learning outcomes or working memory capacities, but they did find an interaction effect in relation to comprehension: participants who had higher levels of working memory capacity appeared to learn *better* when listening to background music than those with lower working memory capacities. These results suggest there should be minimal interference between the study task and the listening to music task as music draws upon different sensory modalities from those involved in studying. Listening to background music may even have a positive impact on learning for some individuals.

Taking a Break from Media: Walking outside in Natural Environment

A break that involves switching to another technology source may not provide as many benefits as getting outside. Stenfors et al. (2019) conducted a meta-analysis of studies that tested the effects of interactions with nature vs. urban environments. They found significant positive cognitive effects of interacting with nature, especially in relation to attention. For example, Berman et al. (2008) found that participants who walked in nature made a 20% improvement in measures of attention and memory, while those who walked in an urban centre did not. Working on a computer requires directed attention and eventually leads to fatigue and the need for a break. Walking in nature allows this directed attention to rest in comparison to walking in urban areas, where you need to remain alert to dangers such as traffic.

Value of Time Unplugged

A more general strategy can be to recognise the value of time "unplugged", through getting outside, cooking a meal, or just daydreaming. Research has highlighted how taking breaks from online screen-based interaction may be more important than previously realised. A systematic review by Thomée (2018) examined many studies investigating the link between the use of mobile phones and mental health outcomes. The majority of these studies suggested that, for both children and adults, intensive mobile phones usage was associated with sleep problems, depression, and stress. Shin and Kemps (2020) found that media multitasking may provide a maladaptive coping strategy that individuals employ to avoid unpleasant emotions. This tendency has implications for how mental health issues such as anxiety and depression are managed. Researchers have started to probe the importance of the resting state of the brain and the value of free-form daydreaming and internal reflection. Immordino-Yang et al. (2012) emphasised the value of this resting state in terms of allowing space for internal reflection on memories and emotions. They further argue that pauses and rests from the input are important for the offline consolation of thinking, and social and emotional learning.

Conclusion

The typical student now has access to a proliferation of devices for connecting with new media and the Web at the click of a finger. The research on the effects of attention, distraction, and learning point to no discernible benefits for media multitasking. Although it can be trained, attention is a limited resource, and some tasks work together better than others. Certain strategies can be applied to enhance focus and reduce distractions. Successful strategies often have an element of enjoyment, either through scheduling breaks, or through transforming periods of focus into a game. Time unplugged from input can be important for learning, memory, and general wellbeing.

Activities

1. Try one or more of the activities described in the "Strategies" section when studying (e.g., technology breaks or meditation).
2. Experiment with software designed to block or track Internet usage. You can do this on your phone or computer. Many smartphones now have these functions installed on them. For example, Android phones have a tool called "Digital Wellbeing" and iOS phones have a "Screen Time" function. These allow you to track time on your apps and put in some usage restrictions.
3. Watch the "invisible gorilla" selective awareness test from Daniel Simons and Christopher Chabris: https://www.youtube.com/watch?v=vJG698U2Mvo.

Discussion Questions

1. William James thought that attention could not be highly trained "by any amount of drill or discipline". Posner would disagree. Do you think attention can be trained? Why?
2. We can no longer afford to indulge our automatic desires for mental distraction. Discuss.
3. Share your experiences of concentrating for a long time without distractions. Why do you think you were able to concentrate and what was your overall experience like? (For example, to what extent was the experience enjoyable? Challenging? Boring? Satisfying?) How do these experiences compare to those of multitasking or dividing attention?
4. Of the strategies outlined in the chapter, which of these approaches do you think would be most effective and why?
5. Do you think that having grown up with the Internet gives individuals multitasking skills? Explain.
6. "The bottom line is that our students are multitasking, and we cannot stop them without placing them in a boring, un-motivating environment. The trick is to develop educational models that allow for appropriate multitasking and that improve learning" (Rosen et al., 2010, p. 95). Do you agree with the statement? If so, why? What is meant by "appropriate multitasking"?

Recommended Reading List

This book puts forth the argument that our brains aren't naturally good at media multitasking and examines how we can learn to live with technology in a balanced way:

Gazzaley, A., & Rosen, L. D. (2016). *The distracted mind: Ancient brains in a high-tech world*. MIT Press.

This paper by Wood and Muñoz examines the effect of a "digital detox" on student learning:

> Wood, N. T., & Muñoz, C. (2021). Unplugged: Digital detox enhances student learning. *Marketing Education Review, 31*(1), 14–25. https://doi.org/10.1080/10528008.2020.1836973

This "digital detox" workbook provides a hands-on guide for de-stressing, cultivating mindfulness, improving mood and health, and finding balance in your daily life:

> Bowles, M., & Williams Rikard, E. (2019). *Life unplugged: A digital detox workbook*. Rock Point.

Headspace is a course of guided mindfulness meditations delivered via an app. Available from: https://www.headspace.com/

Glossary

Attention: Means directing the mind to any object of sense or thought.
Distraction: Is anything that prevents someone from concentrating on something else.
Media multitasking: Involves simultaneously engaging in more than one form of media or using media alongside non-media activities.
Mindfulness: Means paying attention in the present moment, on purpose and non-judgementally.
Multitasking: Involves doing more than one thing at once.
Working memory: Is the system for temporarily storing and managing the information required to carry out cognitive tasks such as learning and comprehension.

References

Abramova, O., Baumann, A., Krasnova, H., & Lessmann, S. (2017). To phub or not to phub: Understanding off-task smartphone usage and its consequences in the academic environment. In *Proceedings of the 25th European conference on information systems (ECIS)*, guimarães, portugal, June 5–10. https://doi.org/10.1016/j.chb.2019.08.018

Alghamdi, A., Karpinski, A. C., Lepp, A., & Barkley, J. (2020). Online and face-to-face classroom multitasking and academic performance: Moderated mediation with self-efficacy for self-regulated learning and gender. *Computers in Human Behavior, 102*, 214–222. https://doi.org/10.1016/j.chb.2019.08.018

Berman, M., Jonides, J., & Kaplan, S. (2008). The cognitive benefits of interacting with nature. *Psychological Science, 19*(12), 1207–1212. https://doi.org/10.1111/j.1467-9280.2008.02225.x

Biedermann, D., Schneider, J., & Drachsler, H. (2021). Digital self-control interventions for distracting media multitasking - A systematic review. *Journal of Computer Assisted Learning, 37*(5), 1217–1231. https://doi.org/10.1111/jcal.12581

Carrier, L. M., Rosen, L. D., Cheever, N. A., & Lim, A. F. (2015). Causes, effects, and practicalities of everyday multitasking. *Developmental Review, 35*, 64–78. https://doi.org/10.1016/j.dr.2014.12.005

Chen, R., Yang, Z., Li, J., Wu, M., Zhou, X., Xie, X., … Huang, L. (2020). State and short-term effects of mindfulness meditation training on attention. *Journal of Vision, 20*(11), 1815–1815. https://doi.org/10.1167/jov.20.11.1815

Chin, B., Lindsay, E. K., Greco, C. M., Brown, K. W., Smyth, J. M., Wright, A. G. C., & Creswell, J. D. (2021). Mindfulness interventions improve momentary and trait measures of attentional control: Evidence from a randomized controlled trial. *Journal of Experimental Psychology: General, 150*(4), 686–699. https://doi.org/10.1037/xge0000969

Demirbilek, M., & Talan, T. (2018). The effect of social media multitasking on classroom performance. *Active Learning in Higher Education, 19*(2), 117–129. https://doi.org/10.1177/1469787417721382

Edwards, K. S., & Shin, M. (2017). Media multitasking and implicit learning. *Attention, Perception, and Psychophysics, 79*(5), 1535–1549. https://doi.org/10.3758/s13414-017-1319-4

Fan, J., McCandliss, B. D., Sommer, T., Raz, A., & Posner, M. I. (2002). Testing the efficiency and independence of attentional networks. *Journal of Cognitive Neuroscience, 14*(3), 340–347. https://doi.org/ 10.1162/089892902317361886

Foerde, K., Knowlton, B. J., & Poldrack, R. A. (2006). Modulation of competing memory systems by distraction. *Proceedings of the National Academy of Sciences of United States of America, 103*, 11778–11783.

Galla, B. M., Plummer, B. D., White, R., Meketon, D., D'Mello, S. K., & Duckworth, A. L. (2014). The Academic Diligence Task (ADT): Assessing individual differences in effort on tedious but important schoolwork. *Contemporary Educational Psychology, 39*(4), 314–325. https://doi.org/10.1016/j.cedpsych.2014.08.001

Glass, A. L., & Kang, M. (2019). Dividing attention in the classroom reduces exam performance. *Educational Psychology, 39*(3), 395–408. https://doi.org/10.1080/01443410.2018.1489046

Hall, A. C., Lineweaver, T. T., Hogan, E. E., & O'Brien, S. W. (2020). On or off task: The negative influence of laptops on neighboring students' learning depends on how they are used. *Computers & Education, 153*, 103901. https://doi.org/10.1016/j.compedu.2020.103901

Hiniker, A., Hong, S., Kohno, T., & Kientz, J. A. (2016, May). MyTime: Designing and evaluating an intervention for smartphone non-use. In *Proceedings of the 2016 CHI conference on human factors in computing systems* (pp. 4746–4757). https://doi.org/10.1145/2858036.2858403

Hwang, Y., Kim, H., & Jeong, S. H. (2014). Why do media users multitask?: Motives for general, medium-specific, and content-specific types of multitasking. *Computers in Human Behavior, 36*, 542–548. https://doi.org/10.1016/j.chb.2014.04.040

Immordino-Yang, M. H., Christodoulou, J. A., & Singh, V. (2012). Rest is not idleness: Implications of the brain's default mode for human development and education. *Perspectives on Psychological Science, 7*(4), 352–364. https://doi.org/10.1177/1745691612447308

James, W. (1890). *The principles of psychology.* Holt.

Jha, A. P., Krompinger, J., & Baime, M. J. (2007). Mindfulness training modifies subsystems of attention. *Cognitive, Affective and Behavioral Neuroscience, 7*(2), 109–119. https://doi.org/10.3758/cabn.7.2.109

Kraushaar, J. M., & Novak, D. C. (2010). Examining the effects of student multitasking with laptops during the lecture. *Journal of Information Systems Education, 21*, 241–251.

Kwak, S., Kim, S. Y., Bae, D., Hwang, W. J., Cho, K. I. K., Lim, K. O., ... Kwon, J. S. (2020). Enhanced attentional network by short-term intensive meditation. *Frontiers in Psychology, 10*, 3073. https://doi.org/10.3389/fpsyg.2019.03073

Lau, W. W. (2017). Effects of social media usage and social media multitasking on the academic performance of university students. *Computers in Human Behavior, 68*, 286–291. https://doi.org/10.1016/j.chb.2016.11.043

Lehmann, J. A. M., & Seufert, T. (2017). The influence of background music on learning in the light of different theoretical perspectives and the role of working memory capacity. *Frontiers in Psychology, 8*, Article 1902. https://doi.org/10.3389/fpsyg.2017.01902

May, K. E., & Elder, A. D. (2018). Efficient, helpful, or distracting? A literature review of media multitasking in relation to academic performance. *International Journal of Educational Technology in Higher Education, 15*(1), 1–17. https://doi.org/10.1186/s41239-018-0096-z

Mischel, W., Ebbesen, E. B., & Zeiss, A. R. (1972). Cognitive and attentional mechanisms in delay of gratification. *Journal of Personality and Social Psychology, 21*(2), 204–218. https://doi.org/10.1037/h0032198

Müller, S. M., Schiebener, J., Brand, M., & Liebherr, M. (2021). Decision-making, cognitive functions, impulsivity, and media multitasking expectancies in high versus low media multitaskers. *Cognitive Processing*, 1–15. https://doi.org/10.1007/s10339-021-01029-2

Nass, C. (2013, May 10). *The myth of multitasking: Interview with Clifford Nass.* National Public Radio (NPR). http://www.npr.org/2013/05/10/182861382/the-myth-of-multitasking

Orphir, E., Naas, C., & Wagner, A. D. (2009). Cognitive control in media multitaskers. *Proceedings of the National Academy of Sciences of the United States of America, 106*(37), 11583–11587. https://doi.org/10.1073/pnas.0903620106

Patterson, R. W., & Patterson, R. M. (2017). Computers and productivity: Evidence from laptop use in the college classroom. *Economics of Education Review, 57*(C), 66–79.

Posner, M. I., & Petersen, S. E. (1990). The attention system of the human brain. *Annual Review of Neuroscience, 13*, 25–42. https://doi.org/10.1146/annurev.ne.13.030190.000325.

Posner, M. I., Rothbart, M. K., & Tang, Y. (2013). Developing self-regulation in early childhood. *Trends in Neuroscience and Education, 2*, 107–110.

Rogers, R., & Monsell, S. (1995). The costs of a predictable switch between simple cognitive tasks. *Journal of Experimental Psychology: General, 124*(2), 207–231. https://doi.org/10.1037/0096-3445.124.2.207

Rosen, L. D., Carrier, L. M., & Cheever, N. A. (2010). *Rewired: Understanding the iGeneration and the way they learn.* Palgrave Macmillan.

Rosen, L. D., Carrier, L. M., & Cheever, N. A. (2013). Facebook and texting made me do it: Media-induced task-switching while studying. *Computers in Human Behavior, 29*(3), 948–958. https://doi.org/10.1016/j.chb.2012.12.001

Rosen, L. D., Cheever, N. A., & Carrier, L. M. (2012). *iDisorder: Understanding our obsession with technology and overcoming its hold on us.* Palgrave Macmillan.

Rosen, L. D., Lim, A. F., Carrier, L. M., & Cheever, N. A. (2011). An empirical examination of the educational impact of text message-induced task switching in the classroom: Educational implications and strategies to enhance learning. *Psicologia Educativa*, *17*(2), 163–177. https://doi.org/10.5093/ed2011v17n2a4

Shin, M., & Kemps, E. (2020). Media multitasking as an avoidance coping strategy against emotionally negative stimuli. *Anxiety, Stress, and Coping*, *33*(4), 440–451. https://doi.org/10.1080/10615806.2020.1745194

Simons, D. J., & Chabris, C. F. (1999). Gorillas in our midst: Sustained inattentional blindness for dynamic events. *Perception*, *28*(9), 1059–1074. https://doi.org/10.1068/p281059

Stamenković, I., Đukić, T., & Aleksić, D. (2018). The phenomenon of media multitasking in the digital media era. *Facta Universitatis, Series: Teaching, Learning and Teacher Education*, 071–083. https://doi.org/10.22190/futlte1801071s

Stenfors, C. U., Van Hedger, S. C., Schertz, K. E., Meyer, F. A., Smith, K. E., Norman, G. J., … Berman, M. G. (2019). Positive effects of nature on cognitive performance across multiple experiments: Test order but not affect modulates the cognitive effects. *Frontiers in Psychology*, *10*, 1413. https://doi.org/10.3389/fpsyg.2019.01413

Thomée, S. (2018). Mobile phone use and mental health. A review of the research that takes a psychological perspective on exposure. *International Journal of Environmental Research and Public Health*, *15*(12), 2692. https://doi.org/10.3390/ijerph15122692.

Tsay, C. H. H., Kofinas, A. K., Trivedi, S. K., & Yang, Y. (2020). Overcoming the novelty effect in online gamified learning systems: An empirical evaluation of student engagement and performance. *Journal of Computer Assisted Learning*, *36*(2), 128–146. https://doi.org/10.1111/jcal.12385

van der Schuur, W. A., Baumgartner, S. E., Sumter, S. R., & Valkenburg, P. M. (2020). Exploring the long-term relationship between academic-media multitasking and adolescents' academic achievement. *New Media & Society*, *22*(1), 140–158. https://doi.org/10.1177/1461444819861956

Wammes, J. D., Ralph, B. C., Mills, C., Bosch, N., Duncan, T. L., & Smilek, D. (2019). Disengagement during lectures: Media multitasking and mind wandering in university classrooms. *Computers & Education*, *132*, 76–89. https://doi.org/10.1016/j.compedu.2018.12.007

Wang, Z., & Tcherney, J. (2012). The "myth" of media multitasking: Reciprocal dynamics of media multitasking, personal needs, and gratifications. *Journal of Communication*, *62*(3), 493–513. https://doi.org/10.1111/j.1460-2466.2012.01641

Whittaker, S., Kalnikaite, V., Hollis, V., & Guydish, A. (2016, May). 'Don't waste my time' use of time information improves focus. In *Proceedings of the 2016 CHI conference on human factors in computing systems* (pp. 1729–1738). https://doi.org/10.1145/2858036.2858193

The Dynamics of Groups Online

Olivia A. Hurley

Chapter Overview

This chapter details the dynamics of online groups, focusing on why online group membership is attractive for many people. It addresses topics such as how roles, norms, and group identity are expressed in online groups. Recent research that has examined: (i) the impact of online communications on individuals' mental well-being and social skills, when in-person group interactions were restricted during the COVID-19 pandemic, and (ii) phenomena such as group-think and social loafing related to online group interactions is also presented.

Key Terms

Group dynamics refers to the way individuals behave in groups, the factors thought to influence group behaviour, and the processes thought to change it. **Group norms** refer to rules that individuals are expected to obey as group members while **Group roles** refer to positions (formal or informal) that individuals fill within groups. **Groupthink** can occur when cohesive groups become overly concerned with group consolidation ("getting on" with each other, being similar to each other) and fail to critically evaluate individual performances, often resulting in under-performances and loss of individual flair (Moran & Toner, 2017). **Social loafing** describes a reduction in task effort by some people when performing as part of a group, compared to when they complete the same tasks alone.

Introduction

This chapter outlines how online groups form and regulate themselves. Questions of interest include: what is the psychological impact of online group membership, compared to group membership in physical work or sport settings? Are people more likely to join certain online groups compared to similar offline groups? Do individuals in online groups share characteristics compared to similar offline groups? In order to attempt to answer such questions, it is

125

DOI: 10.4324/9781003092513-12

important to first understand what a group is, how groups form, and why they form.

Groups: What, How, and Why

A group is a collection of people in a particular location or setting. Most people are members of many groups (e.g., their class or workgroup, and in today's digital age, a member of an online group, such as a social networking group). The question of how and why groups form has been investigated for decades. Maslow (1943) described human beings as having specific "needs". Physical and safety needs followed by love and belonging needs are prioritised. These needs relate to the human desire to be cared for, to form social bonds, to seek out contact with others (Pandey et al., 2021). These social needs are perhaps the greatest motivating factors for why individuals join groups, including online groups. During the COVID-19 pandemic, joining online groups enabled individuals to maintain a form of "connectedness and belonging" with family and friends, work colleagues, and communities. They helped many individuals cope with the loneliness of spending extended time apart from others. However, online group membership is determined by more than just social needs. It is influenced by individuals' access to and the usability of the technology that enables them to interact in online groups. So, knowing now what groups are and what may motivate individuals to join them, the specific reasons why individuals join online groups and how online group behaviours may differ from offline group behaviours will be discussed next.

As alluded to earlier, common reasons people join online groups appear to include: (i) the *need to alleviate loneliness* (whether temporary – moving to a new city – or more long-term – being housebound due to ill health or during a pandemic), and (ii) the *relative anonymity* that online group membership provides, which can be especially appealing for socially anxious individuals (Kirwan & Power, 2013), or those who wish to have greater control over the *amount and types of self-disclosures* they provide to other group members. People with social anxiety disorders who find it difficult to interact in real-life groups may feel safer and more at ease engaging online when they are not required to be physically present for such interactions. Similarly, such individuals' anxieties regarding other peoples' reactions in the real-world to *their "differences" or "special interests"* could result in them being, or feeling, ostracised and isolated from their offline, real-world peer groups, accounting perhaps for another of their motivations to join online groups, (iii) to *seek out like-minded individuals* to interact with online (Kirwan & Power, 2013). Support from peers in online groups designed to aid recovery from mental health difficulties has, for example, been recently reported (Strand et al., 2020). Joining online groups may also be attractive because: (iv) it offers individuals the ability to *communicate remotely* when meeting in person is not possible (due to time or location constraints, work/family commitments, or a pandemic). There is no need to be in the same location, or face-to-face (f2f) with group members to communicate online in such situations. However, many visual cues, such as full-body language signals, are often lost in online interactions (especially those that are text-based communications – posts or emails). Non-verbal cues in f2f exchanges often add richness to discourses that take place between group members. The loss of full f2f contact between online group members can mean a loss of discourse understanding, including tone and context, because only written words and perhaps emoticons are available on which to base interpretations of what individuals are attempting to communicate. However, online typed responses can also afford group members the luxury of re-reading their responses before posting or sending them to other group members which means responses can be "toned down" or rephrased in ways not reflective of what might be said if group members were engaged in f2f exchanges, where in-person un-checked responses could lead to conflict (Murgado-Armenteros et al., 2012). Group membership also presents another attraction: (v) a way for individuals to *present a "version"* of themselves to group members. Code and Zaparyniuk (2009) described how individuals often join online groups because they afford them the capacity to experiment with and develop their identities within such online groups, referred to as "impression management" (Kirwan & Power, 2013). Online group membership also provides individuals with: (vi) the possibility to form *multi-national networks*. This ability to communicate with individuals from other countries and cultures opens up a world of interesting exchanges between members. However, group members in such multi-cultural online settings may be less spontaneous and/or more guarded when communicating as there is a greater likelihood of communication misinterpretations happening in such settings (Murgado-Armenteros et al., 2012).

The online environment also removes environmental variables, such as room temperature, seating types and arrangements, and noise levels – in essence, the physical personal space preferences – which may be: (vii) another favourable feature of online group interactions for individuals who like having control of these variables as much as possible. The offline world also often places emphasis on individuals' physical appearance, which can be removed from interactions in some online settings that take place off-camera. This can result in individuals forming bonds with others they share common views and goals with, rather than being related to physical attraction. However, developing such online group relationships is not without risks. For example, can online group membership increase young people's risk-taking behaviours on- and offline? Today's young generation has grown up in an age where the Internet and advanced technologies have always been part of their lives, which is why they are referred to as the "digital generation" or "digital natives" (Jones et al., 2010). Research has also shown that teenagers engage in the most risk-taking behaviours of all age cohorts and DiClemente et al. (2013) predicted that adolescent risk-taking behaviour would become more problematic in the future. Why? As new forms of information technology and social media (SM) emerge they present additional challenges for young people in terms of their risk-taking behaviour, including greater exposure to cyberbullying and online content that could promote more "risky" activities (inappropriate sexual or violent behaviour, as well as illegal offline activities such as alcohol and tobacco use, and gambling – both on- and offline). Some recent research has suggested that strong online friendships may increase this risk-taking behaviour (Huang et al., 2014; Savolainen et al., 2019), while strong offline relationships may protect against it (Kaakinen et al., 2018).

So, while online group membership may benefit some people, including helping them to develop and maintain social relationships, as well as enhancing their well-being (Reinecke & Trepte, 2014), the impact of online group memberships is not entirely positive. Some SM use studies have reported associated links with higher levels of depression, lower self-esteem, decreased academic achievement, and poor sleep quality among some individuals (Lin et al., 2016; Woods & Scott, 2016). However, the ways users interact on SM platforms are important features to consider (Odgers & Jensen, 2020). For example, browsing passively through SM content has been negatively associated with well-being (Thorisdottir et al., 2019). However, the importance of considering who and what individuals are browsing is also important (Burnell et al., 2020). SM use has, for example, recently been associated with the amplification of gratitude and its benefits for well-being in f2f interactions.

SM network (SMN) use can also result in identity-driven online cliques, referred to as SM identity bubbles (Keipi et al., 2017). These bubbles are thought to develop as a result of SM interactions, based upon shared identity and a reliance on information from online networks which is often limited due to the selectivity and filtering technologies employed on SM platforms (Zollo et al., 2017). They can, therefore, impact individuals' attitudes, beliefs, and behaviours (Koivula et al., 2019). To illustrate, Savolainen et al. (2020) completed an international study of young individuals aged between 15 and 25 years from the United States (N = 1212), South Korea (N = 1192), Spain (N = 1212), and Finland (N = 1200) to determine if belonging to online/SM groups predicted problematic gambling in such cohorts. They reported that strong links to online communities, in addition to being part of SM identity bubbles, was associated with problematic gambling behaviour across three of the four countries' participants included in their study (with the participants from Finland being the exception). This study provides support for the view that online relationships can influence certain cohorts' risk-taking behaviours. Also, in an exploration of the effect of social contagion on behaviour change in online social networks, Graham et al. (2017) demonstrated that increased tie formation among online social networks' members, in their case for smoking cessation, was prospectively associated with abstinence. These recent research findings show how individuals' activities in online social networks can potentially predict their offline behaviours, positively or negatively. With this in mind then, how do online groups differ from offline groups?

Online Groups versus Offline Groups

People who use online SMNs such as Facebook and LinkedIn must typically request to connect with other users using a "friend/connection request" function. Therefore, online communities differ from offline groups because members may not know each other offline initially before "connecting" online. These communities sometimes result from shared interests in areas such as politics, sport, the arts, and health. In such virtual communities, group members typically engage in information sharing, as well as seeking or providing support to each other (Preece, 2001). Such online groups appear to have two primary functions: (i) bridging – connecting with people with different ideas and points of view, and (ii) bonding – bringing people with similar social and ideological profiles together (Norris, 2002). While many studies have examined how people behave as individuals in SM contexts, the specific social and communication characteristics of online groups remain somewhat unknown. Some research does appear to suggest that when people interact online they experience less inhibition, perhaps due to fewer social constraints being present in online contexts compared to f2f interactions (Voggeser et al., 2018). However, such conclusions require further investigation in order to be more generally supported. A contrasting hypothesis that, perhaps, the nature of online interactions may encourage some group members to be more conscious of each other and, as such, adhere to expected social norms more in the online world than they might do in the offline equivalent could actually be the supported position if such future investigations are more widely conducted.

CYBERPSYCHOLOGY IN FOCUS: LIFE SKILLS FOCUS

While online and offline interaction similarities and differences continue to be debated, what is apparent is that skills of diplomacy, including responsiveness and ambiguity, are important in group settings both online and offline in order to maintain group harmony and avoid conflicts. These skills allow individuals to move through disagreements, solidifying social relationships. Roos et al. (2020) suggested that socially regulating conversations online is more difficult compared to offline because the lack of synchronicity in online conversations means the interactions are less responsive, combined with the communications being more explicit and unambiguous because of subtle social cue limitations. In comparison, in f2f interactions, when people have differences of opinion they typically do not need to take an explicit stance. Instead, they can signal their disagreement in more subtle, implicit ways by frowning or pausing before commenting (using those important body language cues referred to earlier).

So, after a year of predominantly online interactions due to the pandemic, where many in-person body cues and signals may have been missing from many individuals' social communications, what risks could over-reliance on online group membership have presented for some individuals?

Reliance on Online Group Membership: Risks/Rewards

The suggestion that many people are "always" online and "connected" cannot be ignored in an SM-dominated world (Vorderer et al., 2016). While this may be beneficial in some ways, as alluded to already, *cyberostracism* may also be experienced by people using this online world (Williams et al., 2000). For example, Schneider et al. (2017) reported, when examining Facebook use, that being ostracised (not receiving "likes" or replies to messages or posts from "friends") resulted in some users experiencing feelings of exclusion by their peer groups. Negative implications of this included lower reported belonging and self-esteem levels, as well as some negative emotional well-being effects. Given that online ostracism is something most online users experience at some time, and knowing that it could have negative mood effects, appropriate emotion regulation and need restoration coping strategies are advised if using the SM world (Schneider et al., 2017). However, Kim et al. (2009) also reported that individuals who scored low on their ability to function in real-world social settings declared beneficial uses of online social groups in meeting their unfulfilled offline social needs. The group members they studied perceived their online groups as "safer" environments. However, the difficulties such individuals reported having in their offline social interactions, and how they felt about them, were not enhanced or solved by participating in online social groups. Therefore, relying on the online world for social support may result in individuals becoming more socially withdrawn from the offline world which could exacerbate their social anxiety even more.

So having addressed: (i) some of the reasons why individuals may be motivated to join online groups, and (ii) some advantages and risks of online group memberships, the issues of: (i) how people behave in groups online, compared to offline, and (ii) features of groups – such as identity, roles, norms, and social loafing in the online space – will now be considered.

How Do People Behave in Online Groups?

Does group behaviour online differ from group behaviour offline? To answer this question, the term group dynamics should be explained. Moran and Toner (2017) described group dynamics as the ways individuals act in groups, the factors thought to influence group behaviour, and the processes thought to change that behaviour. The main objective of online groups is often, as cited above, to provide members with a cyberspace in which to share experiences, seek advice, and communicate, with many similarities existing between online and offline groups (i.e., clubs, societies, political groups), such as the needs of both group type members for social connections and social support, as outlined earlier. However, some differences between online and offline groups have also been outlined (Howard, 2014). For example, group dynamics evident specifically in online discussion groups, that are often larger than those of traditional in-person, smaller, groups, include staggered participation and asynchronous communication. Tausczik and Huang (2019) reported that in online groups, where the profiles of individuals were hidden, individuals in medium-sized groups tended to share more information compared to smaller or larger sized groups. However, they appeared to face more difficulties than smaller groups when trying to resolve misunderstandings. The difficulties of building online communities stem from the unique nature of online social interactions, including the features of anonymity, high turnover, and computer-mediated communication (Kraut & Resnick, 2011). Online communities rely on social norms such as civility and collaborative filtering to counter some of these difficulties and to help create constructive online discussions. Considering this, can individuals learn to effectively problem-solve and positively cooperate in online groups, using digital game playing perhaps, compared to physical team-building activities? Hsu and Shih (2013) indicated this could be done and in 2018 they further explored such group dynamic benefits, specifically how a "group" could become a more effective "team", considering Tuckman's model of team formation: forming, storming, norming, performing, and adjusting (Tuckman & Jensen, 1977), by engaging in a digital game-based adventure education course. Lin and Shih (2018) reported that while the delivery of such courses using technology presented the usual difficulties of unstable networks and disruptions, their teenage participants liked the digital game approach utilised in their study, and that such courses involving digital tools could effectively develop cooperation and problem-solving social skills.

Guidi and Michienzi (2021) also sought to examine the dynamic features of online groups, specifically in online social groups' community structures. Focusing on the SMN Facebook, using 8 community detection algorithms to uncover the types of interactions among 17 chosen groups, they confirmed that interactions within such online communities were typically fragmented. This meant that several discussions could happen at the same time in these groups. Guidi and Michienzi (2021) suggested future research should seek to uncover the more specific dynamics of such online groups, including the impact of the communities' size, composition, and lifecycles on group members' behaviours. Some further interesting questions could be posed such as: do online groups serve different purposes in individuals' lives compared to their offline counterparts? How might cohesion, roles, and norms impact online group functioning? Do negative features of group behaviour offline exist online – such as groupthink and social loafing? These questions will be considered next.

Specific Features of Group Dynamics (Cohesion, Identity, Capital, Groupthink, Social Loafing)

Similar to the concept of team *cohesion* in sport and work-related environments (Moran & Toner, 2017), group survival in the online world likely relies on groups sharing some form of task and social cohesion. This means that a group must help individual members to fulfil certain desired objectives, while also meeting interpersonal (social) needs, if the individuals are to remain motivated to stay in the group. The extent to which the task, or social, element of this "bond" between group members remains a topic of interest for researchers, and similar to the sport and organisational psychology literature, the cyberpsychology literature seems to suggest that task needs are more important for maintaining online group environments than are social elements. For example, Lee and Park (2019) examined community attachment formation in a digital community to determine its influence on sustainable participation. They focused on the content and *social capital* of the online community. "Capital" refers to a resource with the potential ability to provide economic or non-economic benefits to individuals. When the source of that resource is human, it is known as human capital. When it is called social capital, it is based upon social relationships, including people and organisations. Lee and Park (2019) supported past research studies in this area, namely that, first, user satisfaction drives sustained group membership and involvement. They also reported that attachment to the community was important and the group members they examined reported feeling a stronger attachment to groups they could relate to more in terms of group objectives and characteristics, rather than those they had specifically close-knit social or attraction-based ties to.

With regard to group objectives and characteristics, the term *group identity* describes the common characteristics and goals, similar beliefs, and standards that often exist between group members (Chen & Li, 2009), with many groups, both on- and offline, establishing roles and norms to allow them to function effectively in this regard. A role within any group refers to the "position" a person fills within that group, such as a "leadership" role (similar to a "captain's role" within a team). Roles within groups can be described as formal or informal. A formal role could be a managerial or a captaincy role. These roles are explicitly stated and identified. An informal role could be the "joker" or the "peacemaker" role within a group. Norms, in contrast, refer to the "rules" groups put in place to regulate group members' behaviours. Groups often develop their norms by observing the "normal" or "accepted" behaviours of other groups (Borsari & Carey, 2003), such as arriving at the workplace on time. Penalties are often established to punish group members when they violate the group's norms. These measures often motivate members to conform to the agreed norms and help the group to exist harmoniously (Kirwan & Power, 2013). Depersonalisation can, however, also occur in such groups.

This phenomenon describes how people conform to a group prototype and behave only according to the group's norms (Code & Zaparyniuk, 2009). In such groups, individuals typically relinquish their individual views, beliefs, or needs, and instead accept the group's views. When individuals find themselves being influenced in this way by the members' opinions, *groupthink* can then occur. Groupthink refers to changes in group members' cognitions, especially when interacting with other group members. A reduction in personal judgement and rational thinking often occurs in such situations. Some conditions thought to contribute to groupthink occurring online include: (i) high levels of group cohesion and (ii) pressure to conform in the group, as well as (iii) feelings of isolation members may simultaneously be experiencing in their offline lives. Other negative group interactions can also exist in online groups, in the same way they may exist in offline groups. *Social loafing* is one such interaction. This term refers to individuals' decreased efforts when they work together on a task as part of a group, compared to working alone. In the offline world, this behaviour can have significant negative performance effects, especially within sport and organisational settings (Moran & Toner, 2017). Online, incidences of social loafing in groups have been linked to increased group size (Blair et al., 2005), similarly reported as a variable impacting large offline group performances (Moran & Toner, 2017). Ways to minimise the occurrence of these negative behaviours, while maximising the contributions of group members, remain a challenge for both online and offline group leaders.

So, having briefly presented some matters related to online group cohesion, identity, and capital as well as negative aspects of group behaviour, such as groupthink and social loafing, the debate surrounding the ability of the online world to either strengthen the bonds of groups or diminish offline interactions will now be considered, as some concern has been expressed in the past regarding online communication platforms' potential to dilute traditional human relations (Arora, 2011). Research findings from the early 2000s suggested that, rather than weakening social bonds between groups and communities, online communities could actually complement or solidify offline relationships enjoyed by group members (see Wellman et al., 2002). Considering this, Kaye and Quinn (2020) studied the psychosocial outcomes associated with engagement in the online group chat technology, WhatsApp. They aimed to assess how engaging in WhatsApp group chats, measured by reported usage (minutes per day and support motivations), related to reported feelings of loneliness, self-esteem, social competence, and psychological well-being. The mediators of online bonding, group identity, and quality of relationships with the WhatsApp partners were considered in the study. Kaye and Quinn (2020) reported that online bonding through WhatsApp was negatively related to loneliness, and positively related to psychological well-being, self-esteem, and social competence, while group identity through WhatsApp use was negatively related to loneliness, and positively related to two of the three psychosocial outcomes examined, self-esteem and social competence. However, Kaye and Quinn (2020) advised caution in drawing similar positive or negative psychological outcome assumptions about individuals spending time interacting in any online group and those reported for offline groups, especially if the online interactions are substituting rather than supplementing offline, already existing, relationships.

Future Directions for Research in Online Groups

Examinations of online groups and their behaviours, advantages, and risks for group members have undoubtedly uncovered some exciting areas of future research for many psychologists. Understanding the characteristics of individuals motivated to join different online groups over their offline counterparts is one such area. The role online group memberships play in enhancing the offline lives of individuals could also be a fruitful path of exploration, especially considering the well-being benefits of online group interactions. Future research on the impact that online community size, composition, and lifecycles may have on group members' behaviours is also worthy of more exploration, as suggested by Guidi and Michienzi (2021).

Conclusion

To conclude, this chapter has attempted to give an overview of groups online, what they are, and why they form. Some of the strengths and limitations of online group membership for group members, and how the continued study of features of online groups may contribute to a better understanding of group dynamics both in the online and offline world, have also been presented.

Activity

Examine a publicly available online social support network group focusing on a topical issue, such as climate change or mental health. Document all activities by the group's members which are viewable without logging in to the platform. This might include the material posted, the membership numbers, and an analysis of the comments posted within the group. This task could uncover interesting issues regarding group membership features in the online world, as Howard (2014) and Guidi and Michienzi (2021) encouraged.

Discussion Questions

1. Compare and contrast the behaviours of groups on- and offline.
2. Discuss Internet use as a source of individual social support.
3. Outline the potential dangers of over-relying on online SMNs over primary, physical social support interactions.

4. Consider if different online group types could be more, or less, susceptible to negative group features, such as depersonalisation, groupthink, and
social loafing.

Recommended Reading List

This peer-reviewed paper presents a study that explored the experiences, perceptions, and attitudes of patients and their care-givers using digital technologies as a way to remain connected during the COVID-19 pandemic.

> Pandey, V., Astha, A., Mishra, N., Greeshma, R., Lakshmana, G., Jeyavel,
> S., Rajkumar, E., & Prabhu, G. (2021). Do social connections and digital
> technologies act as social cure during COVID-19? *Frontiers in Psychology,
> 12*, 634621. https://doi.org/10.3389/fpsyg.2021.634621

> Amichai-Hamburger, Y. (2017). *Internet psychology: The basics*. Routledge.

Glossary

Group dynamics: The way individuals act in groups, the factors thought
to influence group behaviour and the processes thought to change group
behaviour.

Groupthink: "The tendency for cohesive groups to become so concerned
about group consolidation that they fail to critically and realistically evaluate their decisions and antecedent assumptions" (Park, 1990, p. 229).

Group norms: The rules individuals are expected to obey as members of a
particular group.

Group roles: The parts that individuals play within a group, or the positions
they fill within a group. Such positions may be formal or informal.

Social loafing: The reduction in effort exerted by some individuals when
they perform as part of a group.

References

Arora, P. (2011). Online social sites as virtual parks: An investigation into leisure
online and offline. *The Information Society, 27*(2), 113–120. https://doi.org/10
.1080/01972243.2011.548702

Blair, C. A., Thompson, L. F., & Wuensch, K. L. (2005). Electronic helping
behaviour: The virtual presence of others makes a difference. *Basic
and Applied Social Psychology, 27*(2), 171–178. https://doi.org/10.1207/
s15324834basp2702_8

Borsari, B., & Carey, K. B. (2003). Descriptive and injunctive norms in college
drinking: A meta-analytic integration. *Journal of Studies on Alcohol and Drugs,
64*(3), 331–341. https://doi.org/10.15288/jsa.2003.64.331

Burnell, K., George, M. J., & Underwood, M. K. (2020). Browsing different
Instagram profiles and associations with psychological well-being. *Frontiers
in Human Dynamics, 2*, 585518. https://doi.org/10.3389/fhumd.2020.585518

Chen, Y., & Li, X. (2009). Group identity and social preferences. *American Economic Review, 99*(1), 431–457. https://doi.org/10.1257/aer.99.1.431

Code, J. R., & Zaparyniuk, N. (2009). Social identities, group formation, and the analysis of online communities. In S. Hatzipanagos & S. Warburton (Eds.), *Handbook of Research on social software and developing communities ontologies* (pp. 86–101). Ideal Group Inc (IGC).

DiClemente, R. J., Hansen, W. B., & Ponton, L. E. (2013). *Handbook of adolescent health risk behaviour.* Springer Science & Business Media.

Graham, A. L., Zhao, K., Papandonatos, G. D., Erar, B., Wang, X., Amato, M. S., Cha, S., Cohn, A. M., & Pearson, J. L. (2017). A prospective examination of online social network dynamics and smoking cessation. *PLoS ONE, 12*(8), e0183655. https://doi.org/10.1371/journal.pone.0183655

Guidi, B., & Michienzi, A. (2021). Dynamic community structure in online social groups. *Information, 12*(3), 113. https://doi.org/10.3390/info12030113

Howard, M. C. (2014). An epidemiological assessment of online groups and typology: What are the (dis)similarities of the online group types? *Computers in Human Behaviour, 31*, 123–133. https://doi.org/10.1016/j.chb.2013.10.021

Hsu, Y. J., & Shih, J. L. (2013). Developing computer adventure education games on mobile devices for conducting cooperative problem-solving activities. *International Journal of Mobile Learning and Organisation, 7*(2), 81–98. https://doi.org/10.1504/IJMLO.2013.055616

Huang, G. C., Unger, J. B., Soto, D., Fujimoto, K., Pentz, M. A., Jordan-Marsh, M., & Valente, T. W. (2014). Peer influences: The impact of online and offline friendship networks on adolescent smoking and alcohol use. *Journal of Adolescent Health, 5*(5), 508–514. http://doi.org/10.1016/j.jadohealth.2013.07.001

Jones, C., Ramanau, R., Cross, S., & Healing, G. (2010). Net generation or digital natives: Is there a distinct new generation entering university? *Computers & Education, 3*(3), 722–732. https://doi.org/10.1016/j.compedu.2009.09.022

Kaakinen, M., Keipi, T., Räsänen, P., & Oksanen, A. (2018). Cybercrime victimization and subjective wellbeing: An examination of the buffering effect hypothesis among adolescents and young adults. *Cyberpsychology, Behaviour & Social Networking, 21*(2), 129–137. https://doi.org/10.1089/cyber.2016.0728

Kaye, L. K., & Quinn, S. (2020). Psychosocial outcomes associated with engagement with online chat systems. *International Journal of Human-Computer Interaction, 36*(2), 190–198. https://doi.org/10.1080/10447318.2019.1620524

Keipi, T., Näsi, M., Oksanen, A., & Räsänen, P. (2017). *Online hate and harmful content: Cross-national perspectives.* Taylor & Francis.

Kim, J., LaRose, R., & Peng, W. (2009). Loneliness as the cause and the effect of problematic Internet use: The relationship between Internet use and psychological well-being. *Cyberpsychology and Behavior, 12*(4), 451–455. https://doi.org/10.1089/cpb.2008.0327

Kirwan, G., & Power, A. (2013). What is cyberpsychology? In A. Power & G. Kirwan (Eds.), *Cyberpsychology and new media: A thematic reader* (pp. 3–14). Psychology Press.

Koivula, A., Kaakinen, M., Oksanen, A., & Räsänen, P. (2019). The role of political activity in the formation of online identity bubbles. *Policy and Internet, 4*(4), 396–417. https://doi.org/10.1002/poi3.211

Kraut, R. E., & Resnick, P. (2011). *Building online successful communities: Evidence-based social design.* The MIT Press.

Lee, S., & Park, D.-H. (2019). Community attachment formation and its influence on sustainable participation in a digitalized community: Focusing on content and social capital of an online community. *Sustainability, 11*(10), 2935. https://doi.org/10.3390/su11102935

Lin, C.-H., & Shih, J.-L. (2018). Analysing group dynamics of a digital game-based adventure education course. *Educational Technology & Society, 21*(4), 51–63. https://www.jstor.org/stable/26511537

Lin, L. Y., Sidani, J. E., Shensa, A., Radovic, A., Miller, E., Colditz, J. B., & Primack, B. A. (2016). Association between social media use and depression among US young adults. *Depression & Anxiety, 4*, 323–331. https://doi.org/10.1002/da.22466

Maslow, A. M. (1943). A theory of motivation. *Psychological Review, 50*, 370–396.

Moran, A. P., & Toner, J. (2017). *A critical introduction to sport and exercise psychology.* Routledge.

Murgado-Armenteros, E. M., Torres-Ruiz, F. J., & Vega-Zamora, M. (2012). Differences between online and face to face focus groups, viewed through two approaches. *Journal of Theoretical and Applied Electronic Commerce Research, 7*(2), 73–86. http://doi.org/10.4067/S0718-18762012000200008

Norris, P. (2002). The bridging and bonding role of online communities. *Harvard International Journal of Press/Politics, 7*(3), 3–13. https://doi.org/10.1177/1081180X0200700301

Odgers, C. L., & Jensen, M. R. (2020). Annual research review: Adolescent mental health in the digital age: Facts, fears, and future directions. *The Journal of Child Psychology & Psychiatry, 61*(3), 336–348. https://doi.org/10.1111/jcpp.13190

Pandey, V., Astha, A., Mishra, N., Greeshma, R., Lakshmana, G., Jeyavel, S., Rajkumar, E., & Prabhu, G. (2021). Do social connections and digital technologies act as social cure during COVID-19? *Frontiers in Psychology, 12*, 634621. https://doi.org/10.3389/fpsyg.2021.634621

Park, W. (1990). A review of research on groupthink. *Journal of Behavioural Decision Making, 3*(3), 229–245. https://doi.org/10.1002/bdm.3960030402

Preece, J. (2001). Sociability and usability in online communities: Determining and measuring success. *Behaviour & Information Technology, 20*(5), 347–356. https://doi.org/10.1080/01449290110084683

Reinecke, L., & Trepte, S. (2014). Authenticity and well-being on social network sites: A two-wave longitudinal study on the effects of online authenticity and the positivity bias in SNS communication. *Computers in Human Behaviour, 30*, 95–102. https://doi.org/10.1016/j.chb.2013.07.030

Roos, C. A., Koudenburg, N., & Postmes, T. (2020). Online social regulation: When everyday diplomatic skills for harmonious disagreement break down. *Journal of Computer-Mediated Communication, 25*(6), 382–401. https://doi.org/10.1093/jcmc/zmaa011

Savolainen, I., Kaakinen, M., Sirola, A., Koivula, A., Hagfors, H., Zych, I., Paek, H.-J., & Oksanen, A. (2020). Online relationships and social media interaction in youth problem gambling: A four-country study. *International Journal of Environmental Research and Public Health, 17*(21), 8133. https://doi.org/10.3390/ijerph17218133

Savolainen, I., Sirola, A., Kaakinen, M., & Oksanen, A. (2019). Peer group identification as determinant of youth behaviour and the role of perceived social support in problem gambling. *Journal of Gambling Studies, 1*(1), 15–30. https://doi.org/10.1007/s10899-018-9813-8.

Schneider, F. M., Zwillich, B., Bindl, M. J., Hopp, F. R., Reich, S., & Vorderer, P. (2017). Social media ostracism: The effects of being excluded online. *Computers in Human Behaviour, 73*, 385–393. https://doi.org/10.1016/j.chb.2017.03.052

Strand, M., Eng, L. S., & Gammon, D. (2020). Combining online and offline peer support groups in community mental health care settings: A qualitative study of users' experiences. *International Journal of Mental Health Systems, 39*. https://ijmhs.biomedcentral.com/articles/10.1186/s13033-020-00370-x

Tausczik, Y., & Huang, X. (2019). The impact of group size on the discovery of hidden profiles in online discussion groups. *ACM Transactions on Social Computing, 2*(3), 1–25. https://doi.org/10.1145/3359758

Thorisdottir, I. E., Sigurvinsdottir, R., Asgeirsdottir, B. B., Allegrante, J. P., & Sigfusdottir, I. D. (2019). Active and passive social media use and symptoms of anxiety and depressed mood among Icelandic adolescents. *Cyberpsychology, Behaviour & Social Networking, 22*(8), 535–542. https://doi.org/10.1089/cyber.2019.0079

Tuckman, B. W., & Jensen, M.-A. C. (1977). Stages of small-group development revisited. *Group & Organization Management, 2*(4), 419–427. https://doi.org/10.1177/105960117700200404

Voggeser, B. J., Singh, R. K., & Göritz, A. S. (2018). Self-control in online discussions: Disinhibited online behaviour as a failure to recognize social cues. *Frontiers in Psychology, 8*, 2372. https://doi.org/10.3389/fpsyg.2017.02372

Vorderer, P., Krömer, N., & Schneider, F. M. (2016). Permanently online – Permanently connected: Explorations into university students' use of social media and mobile smart devices. *Computers in Human Behaviour, 63*, 694–703. https://doi.org/10.1016/j.chb.2016.05.085

Wellman, B., Boase, J., & Chen, W. (2002). The networked nature of community: Online and offline. *IT & Society, 1*(1), 151–165.

Williams, K. D., Cheung, C. K. T., & Choi, W. (2000). Cyberostracism: Effects of beingignored over the Internet. *Journal of Personality and Social Psychology, 79*(5), 748–762. http://doi.org/10.1037/0022-3514.79.5.748

Woods, H. C., & Scott, H. (2016). #Sleepyteens: Social media use in adolescence is associated with poor sleep quality, anxiety, depression and low self-esteem. *Journal of Adolescents, 51*, 41–49. https://doi.org/10.1016/j.adolescence.2016.05.008

Zollo, F., Bessi, A., Del Vicario, M., Scala, A., Caldarelli, G., Shekhtman, L., & Quattrociocchi, W. (2017). Debunking in a world of tribes. *PLoS ONE, 7*, e018182. https://doi.org/10.1371/journal.pone.0181821

9 Persuasion and Compliance in Cyberspace

Hannah Barton

Chapter Overview

This chapter sets out to explain the concepts of compliance and conformity and will give examples of how social influence operates in the online environment. It will present how the models of persuasive communication are being used online. One example of how the principles of persuasion are being used through technology is in a field called **captology**. Examples of applications of social influence in advertising healthy habits and online trends will be described.

Key Terms

Social influence can be thought of as how we are affected by the real or imagined and even virtual presence of others. There are many types of social influence from **compliance** (public adherence to the requests of others) to **persuasion** (an attempt to bring about an attitude change). There is even a field of study called **captology** which looks at computers and apps as persuasive technologies.

What Is Social Influence?

Every day we face pressure to "fit in" and to "do the right thing". We are social beings and so we want to be just like the others in our group, despite the fact that we also like to see ourselves as unique individuals. **Social influence** is the way we respond to the real or imagined presence of others.

Social influence can be activated by the experience of playing with others in an online game, the number of likes on Facebook, and even by the presence of lurkers in a chat room online. Lurkers are those who do not actively participate or engage with others online, but just watch what is happening.

Deutsch and Gerard (1955) describe two different types of social influence. Informational influence occurs when information is accepted from another as

DOI: 10.4324/9781003092513-13

being right. It appeals to our reason. We are influenced because we agree with what they say. Normative influence on the other hand is when we accept it because we want to fit in and be accepted by the source of the information. We want approval from others or there is social pressure to conform. It appeals to our emotions. Some cues such as recommendations, reviews, and ratings on online retail sites may influence our purchasing decisions through normative influence.

There are three different processes of social influence that we will discuss in this chapter. These include:

1 **Compliance**: This is an external or obvious change in behaviour in response to a direct request. It can also happen when under the influence of an external party like a group. There is no change in the person's actual attitude, but their behaviour is amended.
2 **Obedience**: This involves compliance with the wishes of an authority figure.
3 **Conformity**: This is a change in attitudes as a result of pressure. This pressure can come from friends (**peer pressure**) or from belonging to a group (group norms).

Every day we are bombarded with messages through a variety of media such as television, newspapers, and the Internet (e.g. social media) telling us the best films to watch, the coolest music to listen to, and the "right" way to vote. These persuasive communications are deliberate attempts to influence our attitudes, thoughts, and behaviours. **Persuasion** works by either appealing to our emotions or to our reason. We face it every day online with spam or junk mail in our email. Pop-up advertisements used to be common before the use of blockers. Nowadays it is in-app advertisements or banner advisements that fill our screen as we try to watch online videos which are more frequently encountered. There is now the rise of influencers with their favourite brands and products cluttering social media telling us that these products will make us more popular.

Compliance

Cialdini and Goldstein (2004, p. 592) have described compliance as a particular kind of response (agreement) to a request. The request may be as direct as a request for help or money, or it may be implicit, as in a political advertisement that touts the qualities of a candidate without directly asking for a vote.

Cialdini (2021) has identified six principles which make it more likely for us to comply with a request from an external source. Some of these include:

1 **Reciprocity**: As humans we like to pay back any debt that we feel we owe to another; in fact, we feel obligated to repay any favour, present, card, or invite that we receive. This sense of indebtedness is universal in human culture. It is a powerful tool of social influence and so we will comply

willingly with a request from a person we feel indebted to. This works equally in online exchanges and has been shown to be a factor in why we treat computer agents the same as human agents as we often "mindlessly" apply social rules to online avatars and computers (Nass & Moon, 2000). This has been triggered by the Ethopoeia concept, which states that automatic social reactions are triggered by situations as soon as they include social cues (Nass & Moon, 2000).

2 **Liking**: We are more willing to comply with the request of someone we like. Liking can be in the form of someone we trust or someone we feel similar to or familiar with. This has recently been shown to work even with non-humans in a study by Cameron et al. (2021). This study showed that when a robot offered an apology for an error, this enhanced individuals' perceptions of its likability and in turn intentions to use the robot.

3 **Scarcity**: Things are more appealing or attractive to us if their availability is limited. This can be seen in shops which tell us "final offer" or "last ones remaining".

4 **Social proof**: This is how Cialdini (2001, p. 109) describes social proof: "We view a behaviour as correct in a given situation to the degree that we see others performing it". Basically, we look to others for guidance on how to behave in a given situation and take our cue on how to behave from them. We are more susceptible to this principle when we're feeling uncertain, and we're even more likely to be influenced if the people we see seem to be similar to us. This is one rationale for the power of online rating systems where you can see how many "likes" or "thumbs up" a video or film has received. It can also describe the retweeting of messages on Twitter/X which can take on greater influence if repeated frequently and spread widely to a large number of recipients (Kim et al., 2014). Retweets are powerful sources of influence.

5 **Commitment and consistency**: We like to appear consistent. If we say we are going to carry out a behaviour, we try to follow through and do it. We feel under pressure to behave consistently with that commitment. This is the most powerful of the principles and is the focus of several influence techniques that Cialdini (2001) has described.

6 **Authority**: We listen to those who we think are experts on the topic. We are socialised to place our trust in figures of authority. This nowadays extends to influencers and celebrities. In social media, audiences continue to place moderate to high levels of confidence in the recommendations of influencers and celebrities alike especially if they are giving us their "honest opinion" (Lee et al., 2021).

The **foot in the door technique** (FITD) is a two-step technique in which a requester first presents a participant with an extremely small request that is almost certain to be agreed to, such as signing an online petition. Then a larger request such as joining an online group or making a donation is made of the participant; this request is more likely to be met with compliance than if it had been presented by the same person as the first request. This technique works by activating self-perception theory (Bem, 1972). If the initial small request enables us to see ourselves as being a helpful person, we are more likely to exhibit the helpful behaviour of complying with the second request.

Another two-step compliance technique is the **door in the face** (DITF) technique. This is a person who is presented with an extremely large request that is almost certain to be declined. Then a more modest request is made of the participant; this request is more likely to be met with compliance than if it had been presented in the absence of the extremely large request. Teenagers might use this effectively when asking for a large sum of pocket money and later "backing down" to accept a more modest amount, which is the amount that they really wanted. It works on the norm of reciprocity (Cialdini & Goldstein, 2004). We are more likely to comply with the second request because we perceive that the requester has made a concession (backed down and made a lower request), and so we are more likely to make our own concession by moving to a position of compliance. The DITF technique is primarily an affiliative phenomenon (Cialdini & Goldstein, 2004). We agree to the second request because we feel some measure of obligation to help the requester.

Obedience and Authority

Another of Cialdini's (2001) principles is authority. This means that we are often influenced by the recommendations of those who we perceive to be an authority figure. As we are social beings, we have a tendency to categorise ourselves and others in terms of where we are in the social hierarchy. This can be done by using information such as social status. It can also be achieved using cues such as expertise (titles such as "doctor" or "professor") and authority (a position of power, such as a police officer) as part of the social evaluation. Sociometric popularity is another one of the social evaluations to determine position in the social hierarchy. It can be seen that sociometric popularity is associated with physical attractiveness – the more physically attractive one is, the more sociometrically popular they are perceived to be. This association takes place among both children and adults.

Research looking at the popularity of online contacts has shown that the number of Facebook friends of a profile owner generates positive impressions of that individual up to a point, but then it becomes a negative interaction (Tong et al., 2008). So we are influenced by popularity, expertise, and authority both offline and online.

Replication Online of Milgram's Electric Shock Experiments

Stanley Milgram (1974) set out in a series of experiments to investigate just how much we are influenced by authority and authority figures. He was interested in the extent to which people would follow orders from authority figures even if it meant going against their own beliefs and values. These infamous experiments ran from 1960 to 1963 and took place primarily in Yale University. There have been variations of the studies (for example, different locations, cultures, and using different authority figures, such as nurses) and a partial replication by Burger (2009) has shown that obedience to authority figures remains high.

Would it happen online? An interesting variation of the study investigating how people would respond to such a dilemma in a virtual environment was conducted using avatars by Slater et al. in 2006. This study showed how participants reacted strongly to and became stressed by an unknown female virtual person receiving electric shocks and displaying pain. Of the 34 participants, 23 saw and heard the virtual human, and 11 communicated with her only through a text interface. The results showed that in spite of the fact that all participants knew that neither the virtual person nor the shocks were real, the participants who saw and heard her tended to respond to the situation at the subjective, behavioural, and physiological (heart rate) levels as if it were real. This shows that we may react to similar situations online just as we would in real life and that we might treat avatars in pain exactly as we would treat a real human. This has been shown even if the virtual human is a representation of a stranger, but we feel more empathy towards a known virtual human (Bouchard et al., 2013). These findings have interesting repercussions for online gaming, where many games require users to hurt or kill the avatars of other players in order to progress. The gamer is aware that they are harming the avatar and can often speak directly to the player controlling that avatar using gaming headsets. However, there are notable differences between most gaming situations and that presented in the studies above – in most games the avatar does not demonstrate behaviours indicative of the pain which would be caused by the injuries inflicted. Second, most games allow the gamer's avatar to "respawn" relatively quickly after its virtual demise, and so permanent damage rarely occurs. Finally, the avatar is normally in a position where they have the possibility to defend themselves – they are usually armed in a similar manner to the perpetrator of an attack. It may also be that the infliction of electric shocks is relatively rare in gaming scenarios, with firearm wounds being a far more frequent occurrence, and so the use of the electric shock in the studies may represent a departure from online behaviour perceived by gamers to be normal.

Conformity

Conformity (or majority influence) refers to the change in opinions, perceptions, attitudes, and behaviour that can be observed when we want to think in the same way as those around us, or when we want people to believe that we have formed similar conclusions that they have. Experiments, such as that by Asch (1951), have shown that most people sometimes deny their own perceptions and yield to the influence of others. Participants and confederates of the experimenter were asked to identify lines which matched other lines in length.

Each person had to answer out loud and occasionally the confederates gave the wrong answer. Asch was interested in whether the real participants would conform and give the wrong answer or avoid conformity, giving the correct answer. The participants conformed by giving incorrect answers in 37 per cent of the trials where the majority answer in the group was incorrect (Asch, 1951). This demonstrates the strong pressure to fit in, and how we are motivated by normative influence to go along with the majority.

Asch's paradigm has been used to compare face-to-face conformity with "cyber-conformity" (Cinnirella & Green, 2007). The participants in the face-to-face condition were in a room with three confederates all sitting at computers. All answers to the task were given verbally. The computer-mediated communication (CMC) condition had no confederates but the computer that the participant sat at gave the same predetermined answers as the confederates in the face-to-face condition. In both conditions participant judgements were influenced by confederate answers. This means that we are prone to being influenced by the answers of others, regardless of the medium in which we receive those answers. And so social conformity can occur in CMC such as email and on social networking sites.

Online conformity can also be seen in the rise of "cyber-trends". One early example of this was the "ALS Ice Bucket Challenge", which spread across social media in the summer of 2014, where individuals were influenced by their friends to contribute to a social or good cause (i.e., advancing awareness of amyotrophic lateral sclerosis (ALS)) by engaging in the Ice Bucket Challenge, and which led to an increase in the donating of money to researching a cure for the illness. The challenge spread very quickly. The solicitation to contribute to the public good was frequently made in front of an audience of peers. Hong, Hu, and Burtch (2018) explained that its success was due to the potential benefit (damage) to the target's reputation and image from (not) responding. The social desire to conform to such a worthwhile cause was high as that was the thing to do in order to fit in. This is an example of normative influence.

Conformity is generally explained by the theory of normative influence – that is, we conform because we want to maintain harmony within the group. The simple fact of making the social norms prominent and obvious can influence the behaviour of individuals in the direction of these norms (Cialdini, 2001). This is done offline by group norms, by signs, or through the rules of the group. Online norms are sometimes made explicit through "Frequently Asked Questions" sections or pages. We also try to gauge the group opinion informally and this can affect us through social impact, a phenomenon in which people affect one another in social settings. This suggests that people will look at the collective opinion in social media environments such as Twitter/X (retweet button) and Facebook (number of likes as well as the sharing of photographs or items), and use this information to make judgements and decisions. People follow collective opinion because they see it as what is accepted as the norm. Under social impact theory (Latané, 1981) there are three factors that affect the degree of social impact: strength, immediacy, and number of people.

The online group that the person is a member of could be important to the individual, the group could feel close to the individual who is interested in the same information as the group, and the number of people in the group is often large (as represented by the number of likes or retweets that an item gets).

A very interesting cross-cultural effect was noted by Cinnirella and Green (2007) – in general, those from collectivistic cultures are expected to have a higher tendency to conform than those from individualistic cultures. But Cinirella and Green (2007) noted that this behaviour was mediated by CMC, with cultural tendencies to conform evident in face-to-face interactions, but less so when using CMC. However, the tendency to avoid conformity online may have changed as CMC has risen in popularity. Rosander and Eriksson (2012) found that over half of participants exposed to information about other individuals' responses in a web-based questionnaire demonstrated conformity to incorrect alternatives, with the proportion increasing with question difficulty level. They proposed several reasons for such conformity online, including the protection of self-esteem and the avoidance of social isolation.

CYBERPSYCHOLOGY IN FOCUS: CYBER-TRENDS – RAISING FUNDS FOR CHARITIES AROUND THE WORLD USING CONFORMITY

When the American Association for Amyotrophic Lateral Sclerosis (ALS) needed to raise money for and awareness of ALS in 2014, the organisation asked people to dump a bucket full of iced water over their heads or allow someone else to do it to them, thus creating the "Ice Bucket Challenge". It quickly went viral and, over that summer, more than 17 million people uploaded videos of themselves taking the challenge. Many celebrities such as Oprah Winfrey, Justin Timberlake, and Lady Gaga also took part. It brought in $100 million dollars in a 30-day period and $115 million over the summer. Charities in other countries followed the trend. MacMillian in the UK raised over 3 million pounds from the Ice Bucket Challenge. The big question is: are these short-term fads or can these cyber-trends have long-term benefits for charities? Cancer Research UK says it gained more than 200,000 new Facebook fans and tens of thousands of new Twitter/X followers following the no-makeup selfie viral campaign that ran in 2015. The Ice Bucket Challenge has been credited with funding the breakthrough research that found the genetic markers of ALS. This led to the Ice Bucket Challenge being hailed as a success by *Pulse* – a weekly health and science podcast – in August 2022.
https://whyy.org/segments/the-surprising-legacy-of-the-als-ice-bucket-challenge/

Persuasion

So far, we have looked at processes that have sought external agreement or change in behaviour rather than influence tactics that try to change private attitudes or beliefs. These influence tactics can be considered as **persuasion**.

CMC can be used to persuade in two ways: through mass media persuasion (for example, by broadcasting online advertisements or highlighting the number of likes or stars that a person or product has been given), or through interpersonal persuasion. The same models of persuasion can be applied to both online and offline environments. There are several models of persuasion which we can refer to, including the Yale model of persuasive communication and the elaboration likelihood model. Finally, we will examine the phenomenon of **captology**.

The Yale Model of Persuasive Communication

The Yale model of persuasive communication focuses on three components (Hovland et al., 1953), with the effectiveness of the persuasive communication depending on the combination of these. The three components are:

1 **Characteristics of the source or sender**: This can include many factors, including the personality and intelligence of the speaker and their attractiveness. In essence, this component asks if we trust the credibility of the source.
2 **Characteristics of the message itself**: This can include elements such as how factual it is, how strong the arguments are, and if it appeals to our emotions, such as fear.
3 **Characteristics of the audience**: Who is the target audience? What are their needs and concerns? Do they identify with the speaker? What about their personality traits?

The Elaboration Likelihood Model (ELM)

The elaboration likelihood model (ELM) develops the Yale model further by looking at what and how we pay attention to persuasive communications. It was developed by Petty and Cacioppo (see, for example, Petty & Cacioppo, 1986). The ELM takes the same variables as the Yale model, but also looks at how they interact with emotions, motivation, and cognition to determine how we will react to the communication.

There are two ways that a persuasive message can affect us – a central route and a peripheral route. Due to our personality, we may use one route more often than the other, but we are always able to access both routes. The central route is taken when people are motivated to examine in detail the content of the message – that is, we read the small print and are influenced by the quality of the argument or of the data being presented. We are motivated to pay attention to the content of the message. In the peripheral route, we pay attention to cues that are not important to the content of the message, such as the attractiveness of the source, the design of the website, and the photos on the website.

Another factor that is a key peripheral cue is source credibility. A source is deemed credible and more worthy of our trust if they are seen to be an expert and unbiased. If we perceive that the source is like us in some way (similar to us) then we are also more likely to trust them and deem them a credible source. For example, Lu and Eysenbach (2013) completed an experiment using online health blogs, and found that health-related similarities were particularly persuasive. Recently, research by Lee et al. (2021) examined how claims of being impartial affected influencer credibility. These non-sponsorship claims enhanced trustworthiness and expertise. According to Croes and Bartels (2021), influencers present themselves as "ordinary" people online and thus appear approachable, authentic, and friendly, all things that we would like to identify with.

Furthermore, in young adults in particular, perceived risk is significantly reduced when they make a purchase based on their admiration of and trust in an influencer as they "know" and trust them. This makes influencers very persuasive to young people who identify with them.

There are also individual differences in terms of how we process information. This tendency to engage with information has been called the need for cognition (Cacioppo & Petty, 1982). While this is a stable trait, it can by influenced by situational factors. Low need for cognition individuals do not enjoy exerting cognitive effort and prefer to use heuristics (short cuts), such as the opinion of others (ideally experts) or the attractiveness of the speaker or source of the communication. High need for cognition (HFC) individuals, on the other hand, will actively seek out knowledge and will engage with it. They like facts and will attend to the content of a message. Research by Kaynar and Amichai-Hamburger (2008) has shown that these differences in dealing with information extend to online behaviour. High NFC individuals believe that it is the information on a website that is more important and use the web for seeking out information or professional services rather than for social or leisure purposes. So individual differences such as the need for cognition, mood, and perceived similarity to us all can influence which route (central or peripheral) is taken. In addition, cognitive overload and stress can mean that we do not always have enough time or resources to attend to the message, and so even HFC individuals may use the peripheral route under those conditions (Petty & Cacioppo, 1979).

Captology

Captology (Computers As Persuasive Technologies) was first pioneered by the Stanford Persuasive Technology Lab, directed by B. J. Fogg. The focus is on software programmes and smart products that encourage or change behaviour in the fields of health, safety, environment, and personal management. There are numerous examples of captology described by Fogg (2009), including commerce sites, social networking, smartphone applications, commercial texting services, specialised consumer electronic devices such as "talking" pedometers, and personalised online recommendation systems found on some retail websites. Fogg also identified health-promoting video games as an example, and this has received some interest from researchers. For example, Khalil and Abdallah (2013) have examined the effectiveness of using personalised motivators and avatars to encourage people to exercise more, eat the right foods, and engage in more healthy lifestyles. Furthermore, Kang and Kim (2020) showed that creating a custom avatar which represents themselves allowed participants to process and be aware of positive and important aspects of the self. This led participants to feel better about themselves, thus reducing defensiveness against persuasive health messages. This shows how the use of such technologies can motivate behavioural change. More recently, the behaviour change support system (BCSS), which was first mentioned by Oinas-Kukkonen (2013) and defined as any "sociotechnical information system with psychological and behavioural outcomes designed to form, alter or reinforce attitudes, behaviours or an act of complying without using coercion or deception" by Cellina, Marzetti, and Gui (2021, p. 1), is being increasingly used. It works like the nudging approach described by Sunstein (2014). In fact, the techniques used here include providing feedback on the consequences of individual choices and inviting people to define personal goals for change either for personal good or for the collective good. For example, Cellina et al. (2021) detail a public transport and active mobility app launched in 2018 in Bellinzona (Switzerland) using app-based persuasive technologies. Other persuasive apps engage in individual or collective challenges (competition or collaboration) using leader boards and rewards through virtual elements (badges or notification messages) or tangible prizes (points or rankings). This is known as gamification (Hamari, 2017).

There are a number of persuasive technology tools identified by Fogg (2003) which are designed to change attitudes or behaviours by making the target behaviour easy to achieve. These include "reduction" and "tailoring". "Reduction" is when the target behaviour is made easy and effortless to do. "One-click shopping", where the user can purchase an item with a single mouse-click, is one example of reduction in action. "Tailoring" refers to personalising content. For example, when an email or message comes in and it is specifically addressed to you personally, rather than a generic message, this can be an effective strategy in changing attitudes or behaviours. While tailoring strategies may make us feel special and unique, the use of technology in this way can raise ethical concerns.

Conclusion

In this chapter we reviewed the concept of social influence and looked at some of the processes which underlie it such as compliance, conformity, and obedience. We saw examples of these processes at work in the online environment. The models of persuasion were described including examples of how they work online. Individual factors and situational factors influencing the route to persuasion were also discussed.

Activity

Select a number (three to four) of advertisements from the press (newspapers, magazines), television, and the Internet (banner advertisements or pop-up advertisements) and compare them in terms of the content/message of the advertisement, the target audience, and the source. How are they similar? How do they differ? Which route (central or peripheral) are they trying to activate?

Discussion Questions

1   What tactics do influencers use to persuade us to use their brands?
2   What individual factors make it more likely that a person will be susceptible to persuasive technologies such as tailoring and reduction?
3   Which of Cialdini's principles of compliance would be the most effective in an online environment?
4   Why do you think the participants became distressed when shocking an avatar? It is not a real person, so does it matter then to hurt them?

Recommended Reading List

A more detailed understanding of Cialdini's principles can be gathered by reading his book.

> Cialdini, R. B. (2021). *Influence: The psychology of persuasion* (7th ed.). Harper Business.

Fogg presents a comprehensive guide to captology, full of online examples of persuasive technology in action.

> Fogg, B. J. (2003). *Persuasive technology: Using computers to change what we think and do*. Morgan Kaufmann Publishers.

Petty, Brinol, and Priester's chapter provides a good historical account of persuasion in the media and applies the ELM model to media campaigns.

> Petty, R. E., Brinol, P., & Priester, J. R. (2009). Mass media attitude change: Implications of the elaboration likelihood model of persuasion. In J. Bryant & M. B. Oliver (Eds.), *Media effects: Advances in theory and research* (3rd ed., pp. 125–164). Routledge.

Rosander and Eriksson's study examines conformity in online communication, with a particular focus on gender and the difficulty of tasks.

Rosander, M., & Eriksson, O. (2012). Conformity on the Internet – The role of task difficulty and gender differences. *Computers in Human Behaviour, 28*(5), 1587–1595.

Glossary

Captology: The field of using computers as persuasive technologies.
Compliance: Public adherence to the requests of others.
Conformity: Change in our opinions, perceptions, attitudes, and behaviour that can be observed when we want others to believe that we agree with others around us.
Door in the face technique (DITF): Two-step compliance technique where a large request is initially made, which is then followed by a second, more modest, request.
Foot in the door technique (FITD): Two-step compliance technique where a small request is first made which is then followed up with a second, much larger, request.
Persuasion: An attempt to bring about a change in attitude or behaviour.
Peer pressure: Pressure to fit in with those we spend time with.
Social influence: How we are affected by the real or imagined presence of others.

References

Asch, S. E. (1951). Effects of group pressure upon the modification and distortion of judgments. In H. Guetzkow (Ed.), *Groups, leadership and men: Research in human relations* (pp. 177–190). Carnegie Press.

Bem, D. J. (1972). Self-perception theory. In L. Berkowitz (Ed.), *Advances in experimental social psychology* (Vol. 6, pp. 1–62). Academic Press.

Bouchard, S., Bernier, F., Boivin, E., Dumoulin, S., Laforest, M., Guitard, T., Robillard, G., Monthuy-Blanc, J. & Renaud, P. (2013). Empathy toward virtual humans depicting a known or unknown person expressing pain. *Cyberpsychology, Behaviour and Social Networking, 16*(1), 61–71.

Burger, J. (2009). Replicating Milgram: Would people still obey today? *American Psychologist, 64*(1), 1–11.

Cacioppo, J. T., & Petty, R. E. (1982). The need for cognition. *Journal of Personality and Social Psychology, 42*(1), 116–131.

Cameron, D., De Saille, S., Collins, E. & Aitken, J. (2021). The effect of social cognitive recovery strategies on likability, capability and trust in social robots. *Computers in Human Behaviour, 114*, 1–11. https://doi.org/10.1016/j.chb.2020.106561

Cellina, F., Marzetti, G. V., & Gui, M. (2021). Self-selection and attrition biases in app based persuasive technologies for mobility behaviour change; Evidence from a Swiss case study. *Computers in Human Behaviour, 125*, 1–12. https://doi.org/10.1016/j.chb.2021.106970

Cialdini, R. B. (2021). *Influence: The psychology of persuasion* (7th ed.). Harper Business.

Cialdini, R. B., & Goldstein, N. J. (2004). Social influence: Compliance and conformity. *Annual Review of Psychology, 55*, 591–621.

Cinnirella, M., & Green, B. (2007). Does 'cyber-conformity' vary cross-culturally? Exploring the effect of culture and communication medium on social conformity. *Computers in Human Behaviour, 23*(4), 2011–2025.

Croes, E., & Bartels, J. (2021). Young adults' motivations for following social influencers and their relationship to identification and buying behavior. *Computers in Human Behaviour, 124*, 1–10. https://doi.org/10.1016/j.chb.2021.106910

Deutsch, M., & Gerard, H. B. (1955). A study of normative and informational social influences upon individual judgment. *Journal of Abnormal and Social Psychology, 51*(3), 629–636.

Fogg, B. J. (2003). *Persuasive technology: Using computers to change what we think and do.* Morgan Kaufmann Publishers.

Fogg, B. J. (2009, April). Creating persuasive technologies: An eight-step design process. In *Persuasive '09: Proceedings of the 4th international conference on persuasive technology (Article No. 44).* ACM. http://ejournal.narotama.ac.id/files/an%20eight-step%20design%20process.pdf.

Hamari, J. (2017). Do badges increase user activity? A field experiment on the effects of gamification. *Computers in Human Behavior, 71*, 469–478. https://doi.org/10.1016/j.

Hong, Y., Hu, Y., & Burtch, G. (2018). Embeddedness, pro-sociality, and social influence: Evidence from online crowdfunding. *MIS Quarterly, 42*(4), 1211–1224. https://doi.org/10.25300/MISQ/2018/14105

Hovland, C. I., Janis, I. L., & Kelley, H. H. (1953). *Communication and persuasion: Psychological studies of opinion change.* Yale University Press.

Kang, H., & Kim, E. (2020). My Avatar and the affirmed self; Psychological and persuasive implications of avatar customization. *Computers in Human Behaviour, 112*, 1–9. https://doi.org/10.1016/j.chb.2020.106446

Kaynar, O., & Amichai-Hamburger, Y. (2008). The effects of need for cognition on Internet use revisited. *Computers in Human Behaviour, 24*(2), 361–371.

Khalil, A., & Abdallah, S. (2013). Harnessing social dynamics through persuasive technology to promote healthier lifestyle. *Computers in Human Behaviour, 29*(6), 2674–2681.

Kim, E., Sung, Y., & Kang, H. (2014). Brand followers' retweeting behaviour on Twitter: How brand relationships influence brand electronic word-of-mouth. *Computers in Human Behavour, 37*, 18–25.

Latané, B. (1981). The psychology of social impact. *American Psychologist, 36*(4), 343–356.

Lee, S., Vollmer, B., Yue, C. A., & Johnson, B. K. (2021). Impartial endorsements: Influencer and celebrity declarations of non – Sponsorship and honesty. *Computers in Human Behaviour, 122*, 1–9.

Lu, A. S., & Eysenbach, G. (2013). An experimental test of the persuasive effect of source similarity in narrative and nonnarrative health blogs. *Journal of Medical Internet Research, 15*(7), 1–11.

Milgram, S. (1974). *Obedience to authority: An experimental view.* Harper & Row.

Nass, C., & Moon, Y. (2000). Machines and mindlessness: Social responses to computers. *Journal of Social Issues, 56*(1), 81–103.

Oinas-Kukkonen, H. (2013). A foundation for the study of the behavioural change support services. *Personal and Ubiquitous Computing, 17*, 1223–1235.

Petty, R. E., & Cacioppo, J. T. (1979). Issue-involvement can increase or decrease persuasion by enhancing message relevant cognitive responses. *Journal of Personality and Social Psychology, 37*(10), 1915–1926.

Petty, R. E., & Cacioppo, J. T. (1986). The elaboration likelihood model of persuasion. *Advances in Experimental Social Psychology, 19*, 123–205.

Rosander, M., & Eriksson, O. (2012). Conformity on the Internet – The role of task difficulty and gender differences. *Computers in Human Behaviour, 28*(5), 1587–1595.

Slater, M., Antley, A., Davison, A., Swapp, D., Guger, C., Barker, C., Pistrang, N. & Sanchez-Vives, M. V. (2006). A virtual reprise of the Stanley Milgram obedience experiments. *PLoS ONE, 1*(1), e39.

Sunstein, C. R. (2014). Nudging: A very short guide. *Journal of Consumer Policy, 37*(4), 583–588. https://doi.org/10.1007/s10603-014-9273-1

Tong, S. T., Van Der Heide, B., Langwell, L., & Walther, J. B. (2008). Too much of a good thing? The relationship between number of friends and interpersonal impressions on Facebook. *Journal of Computer-Mediated Communication, 13*(3), 531–549.

Privacy and Trust Online

Gráinne Kirwan

Chapter Overview

In the earliest days of civilisation, humans lived in relatively small groups, often within the same room (or tent, or cave!) with very little privacy. Even today, in some small villages, inhabitants note that their activities and actions are known throughout the community, with such information being spread from person to person. On the other hand, those living in larger communities such as cities might find that they do not even know the names of their next-door neighbours. Nevertheless, they may find that this privacy is negated by the impact of the Internet as they disclose large amounts of information online. They may also have their information disclosed to others, sometimes without their consent. This chapter considers our concepts of online privacy and trust, the sacrifices we make to our privacy in order to make other perceived gains, and the important theories in the field that inform our understanding of privacy and security. It examines how we share information, what happens to our data online, how we decide what information to share, and how we go about reducing the available amount of online information about ourselves.

Key Terms

Research has long identified the tendencies of individuals to disclose considerable volumes of information online, particularly via online social networks (Gross & Acquisti, 2005). **Privacy** is a difficult concept to define clearly, to the extent that some researchers have suggested that the most effective definition instead involves the application of prototypes (Vasalou et al., 2015). For the purposes of clarity in this chapter, it will be used to describe the state or condition of not having personal information disclosed in public or semi-public settings. While many people appear to value privacy, many do not engage in behaviours that secure their information, a phenomenon sometimes referred to as the **knowing–doing gap**.

DOI: 10.4324/9781003092513-14

Sharing Information Online

Imagine living in a world where all of the inhabitants (including you) had telepathic abilities. Ambiguities and misunderstandings could be clearly resolved. But on the other hand, there would be no such thing as secrets and all information would be public knowledge. Many people would probably like to have telepathic abilities themselves – after all, it would give you an advantage in many business transactions and interpersonal relationships – but most individuals are also probably very grateful that everyone else does not have access to their most private thoughts. We like to have the ability to control what we share with others, and this is a core principle of privacy management.

If we had to choose a handful of individuals who could read our thoughts, who would they be? For some people these are likely to be their closest friends. But others might be happier if the potential telepaths were complete strangers who they would never meet. Perhaps we might be very comfortable with sharing the majority of our secrets with a small group of people who we know well, but when seeking advice about an embarrassing or deeply personal matter, we'd instead share our secrets with strangers who might be able to provide advice without being able to identify us by our face or name. The concept of privacy is complex, but we do share information online relatively readily. We will consider the concept of who we share what information with in more detail later in this chapter.

A considerable volume of research in cyberpsychology examines how we share our personal information online, and why we might choose to do so (or not to do so) depending on the circumstances. Some people carefully edit the information about themselves online, while others might find that they are of sufficient public interest that they cannot control what is said about them. Some eschew online contact with others entirely, or use the Internet solely to consume content, rather than sharing any of their own. However, this is not necessarily a reliable way of ensuring that our data is secure.

Think for a moment about how we share our personal and/or private information online. Some methods of doing so are easy to think of – we might post status messages or updates on social media, we might check in with our friends at a certain location, we might write online content about our lives or our opinions on current events. Thinking a little more, we might add our more private communications to that list – emails, instant messages, and text messaging. But we share other aspects of our lives unwittingly – our mobile phones can easily embed location data into photographs that are taken or messages that are sent. Data is accumulated about the websites that we visit, the information that we regularly type into online forms (including search engines), items that we browse in online stores, and where and when we access online information. Websites utilise **Internet cookies** to record information about user visits and compile information about user activity. Collectively, this information provides a substantial overview of our lives, and reduces our privacy considerably.

In addition to the concerns that might be raised by the information that any individual online service might hold about us, it is also worth considering what the accumulated data about us amounts to. Say, for example, that our social media account is listed under our real name, but contains relatively little profile data. However, we also have an online dating account, which does not include our real name, but has a lot more information, some of it deeply personal. We might feel relatively secure that these online accounts are separate, but we may not be aware that they could potentially be linked through a variety of means, including our log-on locations, a single smartphone being used for both accounts, or even the use of facial recognition and search software which could link both accounts to the same individual. Indeed, the combination of face recognition from photographs and social media information has important implications not only for privacy but also for other purposes such as commercial strategies, for example developing targeted and personalised advertising for previously anonymous shoppers in offline contexts based on their online profiles (Acquisti et al., 2014).

Another potential risk lies with the permanency of the information that we provide online. While a user might go to significant lengths to delete any posts and accounts that they have created in the past, sometimes this information is still held and can be accessed through applications as common as search engines. Situations such as this have led to individuals lodging complaints against agencies who store this information. The European Commission introduced regulations commonly referred to as the General Data Protection Regulation (GDPR), which restricts the data which organisations can collect and retain, and includes the "Right to be forgotten", which applies to both online and offline records (European Commission, 2016). There are similar rulings in many (but not all) other jurisdictions, which help to reduce the permanency of online information. However, many users do not go to such lengths to remove such data, or they may be unaware of the existence of it at all.

Finally, users may not consider who has access to their information before sharing it. When posting a status update on social media we may not consider who may be able to read it. Even if we restrict the comment to a relatively small group of people, such as our close friends and family, it is easy to forget that those individuals can share the information with others. Or if we comment on a friend's photograph, we may not realise that it is our friend's contacts that can see our message, rather than our own contacts. It is also very easy to forget how many people we are sharing information with, particularly if many of our contacts are generally silent "lurkers" who do not post themselves. As well as our contacts, others with potential access to our information include the company who provides the software (for example, the social media site), our Internet service provider, and anyone who they share the information with – potentially advertisers or government agencies. Finally, it is also possible that our information is divulged through other means, such as malicious hacking.

With so many ways that our information can be shared, it might be expected that users take care with their data before divulging it online. The next section considers how users decide what information to share, and describes some theories which are relevant to our understanding of information sharing.

Deciding What Information to Share

Given the amount of information that we share, it may be tempting to think that Internet users are not concerned about their privacy. However, this is not always the case, with several studies (e.g. Jozani et al., 2020) identifying various factors which are related to privacy concerns, such as perceived risk, perceived control over information, and user engagement with social media-enabled apps. It may simply be that users perceive more benefits in sharing such information than they perceive risks in such disclosure, and decide to share this data based on a perception that their data will be appropriately used and that they won't experience negative consequences based on this data sharing – a concept generally referred to as "privacy calculus" (Culnan & Armstrong, 1999). Conversely, there is research which suggests that even after high-profile news indicating that social media data is not as private as some might perceive (specifically, the Cambridge Analytica case, where information from approximately 87 million Facebook users was allegedly inappropriately collected), users may not make substantial changes to their privacy settings or delete online accounts (Hinds et al., 2020).

Accordingly, there may be many other, more subtle factors which determine our sharing of information online. This section considers various factors which may affect our decision to share what would otherwise be relatively private information in online settings. In particular, the section examines the role of cognitive psychology and decision making, Petronio's communication privacy management (CPM) theory, the concepts of social spheres and space, and the paradoxes and trade-offs that users might be susceptible to.

CYBERPSYCHOLOGY IN FOCUS: SHARING REALISTIC AND NON-REALISTIC PRESENTATIONS OF SELF ONLINE

Early online interactions with strangers were usually based only on text – no audio, no video, and no avatars. An early question when interacting with a stranger in an online chatroom was "A/S/L?" – short for "Age/Sex/Location?" – but the answers were generally not verifiable; someone who claimed to be an 18-year-old female from Kuala Lumpur might actually be a 56-year-old male from a rural British village. In some online interactions it is still possible to engage in this level of deception, but interesting research by Freeman and Maloney (2021) into presentation of the self in social virtual reality settings indicates that users generally (although not always) create avatars that resemble their physical selves, in terms of gender, ethnicity, and other factors. Several reasons were indicated for this, including a sense of the virtual self being an extension of the real self, but also because in many cases some characteristics of the individual could be disclosed through their voice as soon as they spoke. Even though some users described negative online interactions because of realistic depictions of their physical selves online (such as harassment, racism, and social stigma), the drive to depict their true selves online remained strong. A particular benefit of social virtual reality settings was indicated by two trans women who participated in the study. They indicated that the use of female avatars in social VR helped them to discover and affirm their gender identities, encouraging them to embark on and continue transgender procedures offline.

Cognitive Psychology and Decision Making

Cognitive psychology has examined how humans make decisions in considerable depth, and much of this can be applied to our decision making regarding privacy. For example, Kirwan (2015) considers the work of Nobel Prize winner Daniel Kahneman and its application to online decision making, particularly with regard to security and privacy. Kahneman (2011) describes two different types of thinking, which he called System 1 and System 2. When we make fast, almost instinctive decisions then we engage System 1 – these tend to be decisions that we make quickly and without much thought. An example could be when we are instant messaging a friend online – we don't tend to put too much thought into each individual word that we use, as otherwise the conversation would take a very long time and our friend would wonder why our responses are delayed. On the other hand, System 2 is a "slow" system, where we deliberate and consider a decision, expending a considerable amount of effort while doing so.

When we are thinking about purchasing a new car or laptop we are more likely to engage System 2, as it is an important and expensive decision. Applying this model to online privacy, it is easy to see how many of our decisions relating to online privacy might be managed under System 1, when really we should be considering the decision in more depth. For example, if we are installing a new game or other application onto our smartphone, we are likely to be excited by the prospect of using it, and we want to see what it can do. Therefore, when the application asks for access to information about us via social media or location-based services, we might favour System 1 over System 2, as it allows us quicker access to the software, as well as use of more features of that software. A very common example of this occurs when the user is asked to confirm that they have read the terms and conditions of use when downloading new software or completing an online form. The documents outlining these terms and conditions are often extremely long, and a user may be tempted to avoid reviewing the legal points in the document, in favour of achieving their current goal more quickly. However, these terms and conditions often include information regarding the sharing of user data, and so by agreeing to them without having read the document, users are often consenting to the sharing of their information without realising it. Another example of using the incorrect system occurs when posting status updates or other information online.

In these cases we may engage System 1 in our excitement of posting the message, especially if we are distracted by other factors such as being in an interesting environment. As we bypass System 2, we may make ourselves vulnerable by not considering the context of the information that we send or the potential recipients of this data.

Other aspects of cognitive psychology may also be relevant. For example, confirmation bias (Einhorn & Hogarth, 1978) describes how we tend to seek further information to support a tentatively held hypothesis, and we may avoid or ignore information that conflicts with this hypothesis. With regard to online privacy, we can consider an individual who has heard of the risks of online disclosure, but who has no direct evidence that their own information has ever been shared without their explicit consent. Without such explicit evidence they may believe that this has never happened to them, and they may feel that it is therefore safe to continue sharing information in the way that they have previously done without running the risk of their privacy being compromised.

On the other hand, if a person has recently experienced negative consequences from the disclosure of personal information, either through personal experience or through witnessing it occur to someone else, then the potential negative effects of unwanted disclosure are likely higher in their mind. In effect, because they have recent experience of it, they can visualise the consequences more clearly and it comes to mind more frequently. Tversky and Kahneman (1973) refer to this phenomenon as the availability heuristic, as the scenario is readily "available" to the individual and can be easily visualised. In this case, the individual may be more conscious of the potential risks of disclosure and may change their behaviours accordingly. However, if they have not experienced such events, then the thoughts regarding risks are less available to them, and they may engage in riskier behaviours.

The theories and biases outlined above are a small subset of the vast literature in cognitive psychology, and particularly decision making, which is relevant to our choice whether or not to disclose information, or to share it with third parties. As making decisions regarding privacy is subject to the same cognitive processes, biases, and heuristics (decision-making shortcuts) as making decisions regarding many other matters, their relevance to online privacy cannot be overstated. However, we will now consider several other theories which can help to inform our understanding of the online disclosure of information.

Communication Privacy Management

Sandra Petronio (Petronio, 2002, 2013; Petronio & Durham, 2015; Petronio & Child, 2020) has developed a theory regarding the sharing of private information, and this theory can be applied to online contexts. Her CPM theory includes several principles describing how individuals and groups view their information. One of these is that the individual or group believes that they own their private information and that they have the right to control the dissemination of the information. This includes the determination of how much information is shared and how it is shared. The individual or group also presumes that others who might hold this information will follow these rules. Relationship difficulties may occur if another individual or group shares the information without permission. As is evident, trust is a vital factor in choosing who an individual might disclose information to – the discloser is trusting their confidante to follow their rules when considering disclosure.

It is easy to see the applications of CPM theory in our offline communications – it is especially evident when the trust in a person is broken after the realisation that a secret has been shared. Confidantes may also face conflicts if someone discloses a secret to them, but the confidante feels that they must share that information with another party (for example, in a case where a child admits that they have been abused, but asks their confidante not to share this information with anyone).

Petronio's theory can also be applied to online settings. Users tend to hold beliefs about how a company or organisation will use their data, often expecting privacy and confidentiality. They may not realise the business model of companies who provide services to users without a fee but instead gain income by selling user data to third parties. In many of these cases users will have given the organisation the right to share their information by indicating their acceptance of the organisation's terms and conditions, but they are unaware of this as they may not have read that documentation in advance of accepting it. Users may also be surprised by the obligations of some organisations to share their information with government agencies without consulting the user in advance. Or the user may have unrealistic expectations regarding the ability of the organisation to protect their data from online intruders such as malicious hackers.

CPM theory is a very useful theory in understanding online disclosures by users, and its applications to various online settings have been examined, including communication topics as varied as celebrity gossip forums (McNealy & Mullis, 2019), "sharenting" (parents sharing information about their children online; see, for example, Walrave et al., 2022), and gender transitions (Coker, 2021), among many other topics.

Social Spheres and Space

As mentioned above, who we are comfortable disclosing private information to can vary greatly. It may be that we are only comfortable talking about our problems with close friends or family, or we may only trust one highly regarded other with our secret. But sometimes, if we feel that we are anonymous, we may be comfortable sharing our situation with a wider group of people, and perhaps even posting our experience and situation publicly. A brief perusal of online boards relating to pregnancy can quickly uncover many women who have recently discovered that they are pregnant, but who are not yet ready to disclose this to their family or friends as their pregnancy is in an early stage. Nevertheless, they may wish to compare their symptoms and situations with others in similar circumstances, and so groups of anonymous soon-to-be mothers form online to aid and support each other.

Such anonymous sharing of private information is only one of many examples of online sharing. The presence of privacy settings in social media results in circumstances where users may be selective about which of their acquaintances receive which information about them. Indeed, this selective inclusion of others in their social media circles can be an important method of enhancing privacy (Ellison et al., 2011). Problems may arise when there are "conflicting social spheres" (Marder et al., 2012, p. 859) as some communications may be perceived by some social spheres as negative, while to other spheres they are positive or neutral, depending on the members' social norms and standards. These multiple audiences can result in dilemmas for the user, and online self-presentation may veer towards the "ought self" – who the user feels that they ought to be, rather than who they actually are (Marder et al., 2015). A notable example of a privacy maintenance technique involving social spheres is the use of multiple social media accounts by the same individual, usually with at least one being carefully managed so that only a relatively small number of people can view it – when this occurs on the "Instagram" platform, the accounts are often referred to as "Finsta", or Fake Instagram (McGregor & Li, 2019). This strategy allows the individual to have a more general, public-facing account, as well as a more personal, hidden account which only a select group can access.

Paradoxes, Trade-offs, and Gaps

As previously mentioned, individuals are often aware of the risks of privacy disclosure, and they may even feel a sense of exposure or invasion when they feel that their privacy has not been sufficiently cared for (boyd, 2008). Even with the awareness of the vulnerability of our data online, we may still choose to engage in behaviours that increase the risk of unwanted disclosure. Such behaviours are examples of a phenomenon known as the **knowing–doing gap** (Cox, 2012). This describes a situation where the user knows what the most secure behaviour is, but fails to behave in a way which promotes such security. Similarly, Barnes (2006) described the privacy paradox, where users seemed concerned about their data but their behaviour seemed to conflict with this concern. These concepts are similar to the topic of "privacy calculus" previously discussed.

A possibility is that individuals utilise a variety of techniques to maintain privacy – these include privacy settings, but also the use of selective disclosures and selective inclusion of others in their social media circles (Ellison et al., 2011), as well as the maintenance of multiple social media accounts with varying audiences, as described above. It may be that users maintain a balance between these techniques when disclosing information. But it is also possible that many users do not take such care.

Here, the overlap between privacy and security must also be emphasised – one of the easiest ways in which a user can unwittingly disclose information is by failing to secure it effectively. As we accumulate highly personal data on portable devices such as smartphones, we increasingly put ourselves at risk of such data falling into the wrong hands through the theft or misplacement of such devices. The risks of disclosure can be minimised by including adequate security measures, such as complex passwords and passcodes for the device and each account on it, and not leaving these accounts logged in. However, such behaviours make accessing our accounts a relatively lengthy process, and the more secure the behaviours (for example, using different, complex passwords for each account), the more difficult they become for the user to complete. There are obvious rewards for the user in choosing less than safe behaviours – including quicker access to the applications and less likelihood of forgetting the passwords. Tam et al. (2009) noted this phenomenon, referring to it as the convenience–security trade-off, although it is often also referred to as a security–usability trade-off. For many users, unless a complex log-in process is a mandatory element of the interaction (such as, for example, online banking), then they will tend towards choosing the more convenient, and less secure, option. However there have been several attempts to identify how to encourage users to engage in more secure behaviours (e.g. Kaleta et al., 2019).

In the light of all of the above, it is possible that users' propensity to engage in secure behaviours is triggered by a complex collection of criteria. Rogers (1975, 1983) proposed **protection motivation theory** (PMT), which identified several factors which might trigger engagement in more secure behaviours. These include how severe the user perceives the threatened event to be, how likely they perceive the event to be, how effective the preventative measure is, the potential rewards if the threat is avoided, the potential costs of implementing the preventative measure, and whether the user believes that they can successfully implement the preventative measures (self-efficacy). It may be that it is a combination of these elements which results in a user taking or avoiding precautions with their privacy. However, with regard to online security, many studies have found that perceived self-efficacy is particularly important (see the meta-analysis by Hameed & Arachchilage, 2021). Unfortunately, given the role of various organisations in maintaining privacy and the potential for government agencies to request user data, it is possible that individuals may feel a lack of self-efficacy in protecting their own data as so many aspects of this task are beyond their control (Power & Kirwan, 2015).

Removing Our Data Online

Once our data has appeared online it is difficult to remove all traces of it. While the clarification of legislation regarding data management has resulted in the easier removal of data, including the deletion of online profiles, it is still difficult to erase all evidence of our online lives, once created. Partially, this is because of the easy replicability of digital information – should a person wish to make, keep, or distribute copies of an image or file it is extremely easy for them to complete this. In other cases the legal ownership of the data may exist with someone other than the individual, such as an organisation.

Nevertheless, it is important to consider why an individual might decide to remove information online. This may occur as a result of many factors; perhaps a user notices unwanted attention on their profile and fears cyberstalking activity. Or perhaps they change their mind regarding a message which was posted during an emotional time, or desire to remove a post which attracted negative comments or criticism. In other cases, a user may have been tagged in a photograph or post which they feel presents them in an unflattering light, and they may wish to remove evidence of this. The potential success of each of these can vary – for example, if a user wishes to distance themselves from undesirable photos on social media they have a variety of methods of managing such a situation, including untagging, which is often the preferred method (Lang & Barton, 2015). However, untagging does not remove the photo from the social media website entirely, and it may remain visible to other users.

A similar range of motivations, including "impression management triggers, personal safety identity triggers, relational triggers and legal/disciplinary triggers" (Child et al., 2011, p. 2017), can result in bloggers "scrubbing" their entries and altering protective behaviours. Other motives for the deletion of information can include employment security, fear of retribution, and relational cleansing (Child et al., 2012). Privacy concerns may even result in the complete removal of an online social networking profile, a phenomenon referred to as **virtual identity suicide** by Stieger et al. (2013).

Despite the behaviours above, many users do not engage in removal behaviours, instead leaving their information online and available. As social media platforms wax and wane in popularity, it is possible that individuals will leave a legacy of abandoned profiles, photographs, and posts in their wake. As mentioned earlier in this chapter, the accumulation of information across platforms may also be a risk factor in online privacy, and it is only as our online lives progress that we will become fully aware of the consequences of multiple online profiles.

Conclusion

There are many ways in which we share our information online, potentially threatening our privacy. The reasons why we share this information and how we decide who we share the information with are complex, involving aspects of cognitive psychology, social spheres, and communication theories. However, they are also vulnerable to paradoxes and trade-offs, and users may be unaware of the quantity and type of information that they are sharing. While it is becoming easier for users to remove their data from online settings, it is unknown how widespread such activities are, or what the consequences will be as private information accumulates across a variety of online settings.

Activity

Take a look at the profile set-up forms for one example of each of the following types of online accounts. What data do they ask users for? Is it essential or optional for users to provide each of these items of data? In your opinion, are there practical reasons for the company or organisation to ask for this information? Is it acceptable for certain organisations to require more information, and different types of information, than others?

a An online banking account.
b A social media account.
c An airline membership programme for the accumulation of airmiles.
d An online retailer selling groceries/electrical items/books/clothing/other small items.
e A mobile phone operator.
f An email service provider.

Discussion Questions

1 Do we give away our privacy too easily? Consider what sources we give information too, and what information they require of us.
2 Are users generally aware of how their data is shared? Would they act differently if they had a greater level of awareness of this?
3 Do you think that Petronio's CPM theory accurately explains how individuals think about their communications?
4 Do users take adequate security measures when using online services? How could their behaviours be changed to increase their security?

Recommended Reading List

Bruce Schneier has published widely in the areas of security and privacy. While all of his books are highly insightful readings in these areas, these two specifically consider data privacy and trust.

Schneier, B. (2015). *Data and goliath: The hidden battles to collect your data and control your world*. W.W. Norton & Company.

Schneier, B. (2012). *Liars and outliers: Enabling the trust that society needs to thrive*. John Wiley & Sons.

Edward Snowden, a former computer intelligence consultant, became famous when he revealed mass surveillance techniques being used by the United States government. His autobiography makes for fascinating reading.

> Snowden, E. (2019). *Permanent record.* Macmillan.

This paper by Vasalou, Joinson, and Houghton examines the complexity of the concept of privacy, describing methods of conceptualising it which may aid in both research and practice.

> Vasalou, A., Joinson, A. N., & Houghton, D. (2015). Privacy as a fuzzy concept: A new conceptualization of privacy for practitioners. *Journal of the American Society for Information Science and Technology, 66*(5), 918–929. https://doi.org/10.1002/asi.23220

The European Commission's GDPR has made significant changes to how organisations can use and maintain the data belonging to individuals.

> European Commission. (2016). Regulation (EU) 2016/679 of the European Parliament and of the Council of 27 April 2016 on the protection of natural persons with regard to the processing of personal data and on the free movement of such data, and repealing directive 95/46/EC (general data protection regulation). https://eur-lex.europa.eu/legal-content/EN/TXT/PDF/?uri=CELEX:32016R0679

Sandra Petronio and Jeffrey Child review research using communication privacy management concepts across a wide range of contexts.

> Petronio, S., & Child, J. T. (2020). Conceptualization and operationalization: Utility of communication privacy management theory. *Current Opinion in Psychology, 31*, 76–82. https://doi.org/10.1016/j.copsyc.2019.08.009

Glossary

Communication privacy management (CPM): A theory developed by Sandra Petronio (2002) describing how individuals view and share their private information.

Internet cookies: Data used by websites to record user activity.

Knowing–doing gap: A situation where the user knows what the most secure behaviour is, but fails to behave in a way which promotes such security.

Privacy: The state or condition of not having personal information disclosed in public or semi-public settings.

Protection motivation theory: A theory proposed by Rogers (1975, 1983) which identified several factors which might trigger engagement in protective behaviours.

Virtual identity suicide: The removal of an online profile, sometimes to increase privacy.

References

Acquisti, A., Gross, R., & Stutzman, F. (2014). Face recognition and privacy in the age of augmented reality. *Journal of Privacy and Confidentiality, 6*(2), 1–20. https://ssrn.com/abstract=3305312

Barnes, S. (2006, September). A privacy paradox: Social networking in the United States. *First Monday, 11*(9). https://doi.org/10.5210/fm.v11i9.1394

boyd, d. (2008). Facebook's privacy trainwreck. *Convergence: The International Journal of Research into New Media Technologies, 14*(1), 13–20. https://doi.org/10.1177/1354856507084416

Child, J. T., Haridakis, P. M., & Petronio, S. (2012). Blogging privacy rule orientations, privacy management and content deletion practices: The variability of online privacy management activity at different stages of social media use. *Computers in Human Behavior, 28*(5), 1859–1872. https://doi.org/10.1016/j.chb.2012.05.004

Child, J. T., Petronio, S., Agyeman-Budu, E. A., & Westermann, D. A. (2011). Blog scrubbing: Exploring triggers that change privacy rules. *Computers in Human Behavior, 27*(5), 2017–2027. https://doi.org/10.1016/j.chb.2011.05.009

Coker, M. C. (2021). What to withhold and when to disclose: Gender transitions and privacy management on social media. *Qualitative Research Reports in Communication, 23*(1), 39–45. https://doi.org/10.1080/17459435.2021.1929425

Cox, J. (2012). Information systems user security: A structured model of the knowing-doing gap. *Computers in Human Behavior, 28*(5), 1849–1858. https://doi.org/10.1016/j.chb.2012.05.003

Culnan, M. J., & Armstrong, P. K. (1999). Information privacy concerns, procedural fairness, and impersonal trust: An empirical investigation. *Organization Science, 10*(1), 104–115. https://doi.org/10.1287/orsc.10.1.104

Einhorn, H. J., & Hogarth, R. M. (1978). Confidence in judgement: Persistence of the illusion of validity. *Psychological Review, 85*(5), 395–416. https://doi.org/10.1037/0033-295X.85.5.395

Ellison, N. B., Vitak, J., Steinfield, C., Gray, R., & Lampe, C. (2011). Negotiating privacy concerns and social capital needs in a social media environment. In S. Trepte & L. Reinecke (Eds.), *Privacy online: Perspectives on privacy and self-disclosure in the social web* (pp. 19–32). Springer.

European Commission. (2016). Regulation (EU) 2016/679 of the European Parliament and of the Council of 27 April 2016 on the protection of natural persons with regard to the processing of personal data and on the free movement of such data, and repealing directive 95/46/EC (general data protection regulation). https://eur-lex.europa.eu/legal-content/EN/TXT/PDF/?uri=CELEX:32016R0679

Freeman, G., & Maloney, D. (2021). Body, avatar, and me: The presentation and perception of self in social virtual reality. *Proceedings of the ACM on Human-Computer Interaction, 4*(CSCW3), 1–27. https://doi.org/10.1145/3432938

Gross, R., & Acquisti, A. (2005). Information revelation and privacy in online social networks. In *Proceedings of the workshop on privacy in the electronic society, ACM, Alexandria*, 71–80.

Hameed, M. A., & Arachchilage, N. A. G. (2021). The role of self-efficacy on the adoption of information systems security innovations: A meta-analysis assessment. *Personal and Ubiquitous Computing, 25*(5), 911–925. https://doi.org/10.1007/s00779-021-01560-1

Hinds, J., Williams, E. J., & Joinson, A. N. (2020). "It wouldn't happen to me": Privacy concerns and perspectives following the Cambridge Analytica scandal. *International Journal of Human-Computer Studies, 143*, 102498. https://doi.org/10.1016/j.ijhcs.2020.102498

Joinson, A. N., Houghton, D. J., Vasalou, A., & Marder, B. L. (2011). Digital crowding: Privacy, self-disclosure, and technology. In S. Trepte and L. Reinecke, *Privacy online: Perspectives on privacy and self-disclosure in the social web* (pp. 33–45). Springer.

Jozani, M., Ayaburi, E., Ko, M., & Choo, K. K. R. (2020). Privacy concerns and benefits of engagement with social media-enabled apps: A privacy calculus perspective. *Computers in Human Behavior, 107*, 106260. https://doi.org/10.1016/j.chb.2020.106260

Kahneman, D. (2011). *Thinking, fast and slow*. Penguin.

Kaleta, J. P., Lee, J. S., & Yoo, S. (2019). Nudging with construal level theory to improve online password use and intended password choice: A security-usability tradeoff perspective. *Information Technology & People, 32*(4), 993–1020. https://doi.org/10.1108/ITP-01-2018-0001

Kirwan, G. (2015). Psychology and security: Utilising psychological and communication theories to promote safer cloud security behaviours. In R. Ko & K.-K. R. Choo (Eds.), *The cloud security ecosystem: Technical, legal, business and management issues* (pp. 269–281). Elsevier.

Lang, C., & Barton, H. (2015). Just untag it: Exploring the management of undesirable Facebook photos. *Computers in Human Behavior, 43*, 147–155. https://doi.org/10.1016/j.chb.2014.10.051

Marder, B., Joinson, A., & Shankar, A. (2012, January). Every post you make, every pic you take, I'll be watching you: Behind social spheres on Facebook. In *Proceedings of the 45th Hawaii international conference on system sciences* (pp. 859–868). IEEE.

Marder, B., Joinson, A., Shankar, A., & Archer-Brown (2015). Any user can be any self that they want so long as it is what they 'ought' to be: Exploring self-presentation in the presence of multiple audiences on social network sites. In L. Robinson Jr. (Ed.), *Marketing dynamism & sustainability: Things change, things stay the same … developments in marketing science. Proceedings of the academy of marketing science* (pp. 621–626). Academy of Marketing Science, Springer International Publishing.

McGregor, K. A., & Li, J. (2019). 73. Fake Instagrams for real conversation: A thematic analysis of the hidden social media life of teenagers. *Journal of Adolescent Health, 64*(2), S39–S40. https://doi.org/10.1016/j.jadohealth.2018.10.088

McNealy, J., & Mullis, M. D. (2019). Tea and turbulence: Communication privacy management theory and online celebrity gossip forums. *Computers in Human Behavior, 92*, 110–118. https://doi.org/10.1016/j.chb.2018.10.029

Petronio, S. (2002). *Boundaries of privacy: Dialectics of disclosure*. SUNY Press.

Petronio, S. (2013). Brief status report on communication privacy management theory. *Journal of Family Communication, 13*(1), 6–14. https://doi.org/10.1080/15267431.2013.743426

Petronio, S., & Child, J. T. (2020). Conceptualization and operationalization: Utility of communication privacy management theory. *Current Opinion in Psychology, 31*, 76–82. https://doi.org/10.1016/j.copsyc.2019.08.009

Petronio, S., & Durham, W. T. (2015). Communication privacy management theory: Significance for interpersonal communication. In D. O. Braithwaite & P. Schrodt (Eds.), *Engaging theories in interpersonal communication: Multiple perspectives* (2nd ed., pp. 335–347). Sage Publications.

Power, A., & Kirwan, G. (2015). Privacy and security risks online. In A. Attrill (Ed.), *Cyberpsychology* (pp. 233–248). Oxford University Press.

Rogers, R. W. (1975). A protection motivation theory of fear appeals and attitude change. *The Journal of Psychology, 91*(1), 93–114. https://doi.org/10.1080/00223980.1975.9915803

Rogers, R. W. (1983). Cognitive and physiological processes in fear appeals and attitude change: A revised theory of protection motivation. In J. Cacioppo & R. Petty (Eds.), *Social psychophysiology* (pp. 153–176). Guilford Press.

Stieger, S., Burger, C., Bohn, M., & Voracek, M. (2013). Who commits virtual identity suicide? Differences in privacy concerns, internet addiction and personality between Facebook users and quitters. *Cyberpsychology, Behavior and Social Networking, 16*(9), 629–634. https://doi.org/10.1089/cyber.2012.0323

Tam, L., Glassman, M., & Vandenwauver, M. (2009). The psychology of password management: A tradeoff between security and convenience. *Behaviour & Information Technology, 29*(3), 233–244. https://doi.org/10.1080/01449290903121386

Tversky, A., & Kahneman, D. (1973). Availability: A heuristic for judging frequency and probability. *Cognitive Psychology, 5*(1), 207–232. https://doi.org/10.1016/0010-0285(73)90033-9

Vasalou, A., Joinson, A. N., & Houghton, D. (2015). Privacy as a fuzzy concept: A new conceptualization of privacy for practitioners. *Journal of the American Society for Information Science and Technology, 66*(5), 918–929. https://doi.org/10.1002/asi.23220

Walrave, M., Verswijvel, K., Ouvrein, G., Staes, L., Hallam, L., & Hardies, K. (2022). The limits of sharenting: Exploring parents' and adolescents' sharenting boundaries through the lens of communication privacy management theory. *Frontiers in Education, 7*, 803393. https://doi.org/10.3389/feduc.2022.803393

PART 3

Applied Cyberpsychology

Cyberpsychology in Professional Practice

Interview 3

Fardus Sultan is a lecturer and programme co-ordinator in digital marketing

How does cyberpsychology relate to digital marketing?

Digital marketing relates to marketing efforts delivered through a variety of digital touchpoints where brands and consumers converge, leveraging consumer behaviour in the online environment. Typically, these touchpoints range from marketing on websites, search engines, social media, and newsletters to mobile apps and social media influencers' posts. This is where cyberpsychology provides a theoretical and empirical basis for understanding consumer behaviour online. It helps us to identify and appreciate how the online environment and technology mediate consumer behaviour and how various platforms offer different affordances and shape such behaviour.

Understanding what resonates with an online target market, what content type they are interested in, and how to engage them and create persuasive content to entice them to a call to action (CTA) is essential.

Given that much of our lives are now digital, having an insight into how consumers navigate websites, social media platforms, and apps can help address

171

DOI: 10.4324/9781003092513-16

potential pain points and improve how messages are communicated, and their overall consumer online experience. This impacts how consumers search for and discover products and services and the stages they go through in their online purchase journey. In picking up consumer cues and tailoring the marketing approach on each stage of this consumer journey, cyberpsychology aids in understanding how brands develop trust online, reduce cognitive as well as post-purchase dissonance, and consequently develop brand loyalty.

What are some of real-world applications of cyberpsychology in digital marketing?

Nowadays, it is accepted that technology has enormously changed the way we learn, work, socialise, and consume, and it continues to evolve at a massive speed. We are continuously having to learn new ways of making sense of the online environment, and how to leverage the power of technology to make our lives better, at a private, commercial, and societal level. While in the past we had limited access to information, products, and services, often due to geographical and political limitations, we now have access to an unprecedented amount of data and a wealth of information.

This has also brought about new challenges to whom we trust online, who has credible information, and how we navigate this array of choices and options. Through cyberpsychology research, we can identify key elements in building this trust and credibility online.

If we take a company's website as an example, research has identified that the look and feel of a company website, seen as a combination of fonts, colours, imagery, and the language used, together with clear navigation structure and technical backbone, impacts on the consumer trust in a website and, consequently, the reputability of the business itself. Frequently, such well-designed websites result in them being described as intuitive and seamless and can make a difference between a consumer making that final step and purchasing a product, or abandoning it altogether.

Moreover, when exploring what motivates consumers to shop online, while convenience has consistently been identified as one of the key drivers, cart abandonment has been found to be one of the leading challenges of online shopping.

Consequently, to address this issue, both Schwartz's paradox of choice and Cialdini's commitment and consistency are useful when exploring successful design and checkout processes. What this means for practical website design is that, through the Paradox of Choice, we understand that too many website options can lead to information overload, thus leading to decision paralysis and cart abandonment. Instead, to reduce this cognitive load and make the process smoother, clearly identifiable CTAs with a set number of available choices and clear navigation paths are recommended best practice approaches. Similarly, Cialdini's consistency and commitment principle suggests that if the initial commitment is easy and effortless, people are more likely to commit to a more demanding task that follows it. When applied in the website checkout process, instead of lengthy billing and shipping forms, which can overwhelm consumers, the initial commitment step (i.e. the form), should be short and effortless and, if needed, expanded in subsequent steps.

Social proof and liking, another two of Cialdini's principles of persuasive communication, suggest that people tend to observe the behaviour of others to inform their actions, especially if those others are similar to themselves. These principles have been found to be of immense use in the online environment, typically portrayed in the forms of consumer testimonials on websites as well as through social media influencers' posts. The research has indicated that such reviews, even when they are commercially motivated, as is regularly the case with social media influencers, have often been instrumental for consumers when making choices about an online product or a service. Such is the success of social media influencers' commercialised posts that they have even given rise to a dedicated marketing discipline, aptly named influencer marketing.

Evident then, from just a few examples above, is that successful digital marketers heavily rely on cyberpsychology research. In light of the evolving nature of the online environment, and in particular immersive technology and the much-publicised Metaverse, it is vital that research keeps pace with these changes and informs future evidence-based marketing practices.

Fardus Sultan
Dublin, Ireland

11 Forensic Cyberpsychology

Gráinne Kirwan

Chapter Overview

Forensic psychology holds huge potential in cybercriminal cases, including in work such as offender rehabilitation, victimology, offender profiling, and crime reduction strategies. It may also be used to help juries and police officers serving in cybercrime cases. This chapter begins with an introduction to the various types of cybercrime and proposed methods of classifying cybercrime. It then provides an overview of forensic psychology and how it can be applied to online crime. Key criminological and forensic psychological theories will be described and their application to cybercrime will be assessed. Finally, the difficulties in completing research in forensic cyberpsychology will be described.

Key Terms

Forensic psychology "is the application of psychology with people and organisations connected with the Court, Health or Justice systems" (British Psychological Society, n.d., "What Is Forensic Psychology?") and it is often a popular module in undergraduate psychology courses. According to Davies and Beech (2018), most aspects of forensic psychology can be classified as either **legal psychology** (which deals with the process of law, and particularly focuses on areas such as evidence, eyewitness memory, policing, and the courts) and **criminological psychology** (which deals mostly with understanding and reducing criminal behaviour). While **offender profiling** of suspects by forensic psychologists is a popular media portrayal of the field, relatively few forensic psychologists actually work within this area. **Cybercrime** encompasses a wide variety of different criminal behaviours and can broadly be considered as any unlawful act which is conducted using computing technologies. Most cybercrimes can be described as either **Internet-specific** or **Internet-enabled**, depending on whether or not the crime is specific to the Internet (and technology as a whole), or whether it can also occur in offline settings, but is enabled by advances in technology (Kirwan & Power, 2013).

DOI: 10.4324/9781003092513-17

Cybercrime

Cybercrime can refer to any criminal activity that is carried out using computers and computer networks. The term encompasses a wide variety of offences, and although much of the criminal act might occur online, in many cases the actions have offline consequences or implications. For example, consider the circumstances surrounding the use of Internet technologies to enable human trafficking or trade in illegal substances. In some other types of cybercrime there are fewer offline aspects, and sometimes the entirety of the offence is contained within computer networks.

One of the types of cybercrime which may be entirely contained online is malicious hacking. For many people, this is the first type of activity which springs to mind when the word "cybercrime" is mentioned, possibly due to the frequent portrayal of this activity in film and the interest the news media shows in high-profile cases. It should be remembered that the term "hacking" has varied usage in language – in popular media usage it regularly refers to the illegal infiltration of a computer network, but it originally had a much more positive connotation. Hacking initially referred to pushing the limits of a computer (or other device) so that it can achieve more or be used for a positive, and legal, goal. It should be remembered that many modern hackers use the term with this definition in mind, and that "hacking" does not even have to refer to computing technologies (for example, the term "life hacks" which is used to describe tips or tricks to complete tasks or achieve goals). Over the years, various attempts have been made to generate an alternative term which could be used to describe those involved in illegal or malicious hacking activities, with examples of such terms including "black-hat hackers" and "crackers". However, such alternatives are rarely employed in popular media, so many people only associate the term "hacking" with illegal and/or malicious activities. Hacking is often associated and/or confused with "hacktivism" – the use of hacking techniques in activism, especially involving online agencies. As with hacking for other goals, this behaviour may be legal and indeed beneficial to society as a whole, although again the term has frequently been used with purely negative connotations. Because of the confusion regarding this terminology, the phrase "malicious hacking" is used in this chapter to refer to incidences when hacking is conducted with the intent to cause harm or detriment.

Malware is a catch-all term for "malicious software" – including viruses, worms, Trojan horses, spyware, and many other types of code which may cause harm to our computers or networks. Early malware often specifically attacked the computer that it infiltrated, damaging files or corrupting data (see Kirwan & Power, 2013, pp. 79–86 for examples of different types of malware). More recent malware more commonly has the goal of spying on user activity (perhaps with the intent of identity theft or impersonation), or of gaining control of the computer to use it as part of a "botnet" – a network of infiltrated systems which can be used for a variety of purposes, but which are controlled by the cybercriminal. An increasingly common form of malware is "ransomware" – a type of malware which disables access to the user's files and makes a request for a "ransom" in order to access them again. This ransom is usually paid in a cryptocurrency, but it should be noted that the payment of a ransom does not always guarantee that the files will actually be accessible once paid.

Both malware and hacking have been associated with cyberterrorism. Researchers have varied in their definitions of cyberterrorism, mainly because of the wide variety of ways that terrorists can use the Internet in furthering their activities – such as recruitment, fundraising, operations, networking, communication, and the dissemination of propaganda. But many researchers (e.g. Conway, 2007; Denning, 2007) suggest that the term "cyberterrorism" should refer to use of the Internet to carry out an attack which results in severe violence and/or significant economic damage. This suggests that even high-profile website defacements or "denial of service" attacks would be unlikely to be classified as cyberterrorism. However, there is some evidence to indicate that exposure to news reports describing major cyber attacks can result in increased anger and stress in readers (Backhaus et al., 2020).

Many parents are concerned about the risks of technology for their children, with the greatest fear often being the presence of sexual predators who may be communicating with young people online. Considerable research has examined not only these offenders, but the risk factors for young people online, and there are many excellent resources for individuals who may be concerned by these risks. While such predators may also create and distribute explicit images of children being abused, these are frequently separate activities to predation. The literature regarding the former activity may refer to it as "child pornography", but many authors and researchers prefer the term "child exploitation material" or "child sexual exploitation material" as there are concerns that the term "pornography" implies consent. Individuals such as David Finkelhor and Ethel Quayle have been particularly prominent in psychological and criminological research regarding child-related offending online (see, for example, Finkelhor et al., 2021; Quayle, 2021).

Children, and adults, may also be at risk of cyberbullying and cyberstalking. While these are certainly disruptive online behaviours, they are not always criminal in nature. In many jurisdictions, unless there is a threat to the physical well-being of the victim, these are not considered illegal actions. That is not to say that these behaviours are not hurtful and do not have serious consequences, including suicides by victims. Other instances where cyberbullying and cyberstalking might be considered illegal can occur if hate speech forms part of the online communication, or if a "revenge porn" image of an underage victim is circulated.

Thankfully, the most frequent cybercrimes have much less severe consequences. Most Internet users have at some point received an email promising significant financial reward should they agree to what appear to be very minor requests (this is often an example of **advance fee fraud**). Similarly, most users have also received emails which appear to be from banks, revenue agencies, or online retailers asking them to click on a link embedded in the email so as to prevent a scam or confirm their details. Such **phishing** emails are attempts to engage in identity theft, where a cybercriminal seeks to obtain the user's login details in order to gain access to their financial affairs. Susceptibility to these emails can often be explained by many of the decision-making biases uncovered in research on cognitive psychology.

Many otherwise law-abiding Internet users engage in cybercrime through copyright infringement or digital piracy. The temptation to watch a film or television series without paying for the experience can be too much for many to resist, especially if that content would otherwise be unavailable for several days or weeks if it is legally available earlier in some countries than others. Films and television series are not the only media downloaded – software and music are also frequently illegally copied and distributed online. It should be remembered that copyright infringement occurred long before Internet technologies became popular, but the copying of analogue media such as that depicted in Figure 11.1 was more difficult to do, and remained a more geographically localised problem than what is evident today. There have been many proposed psychological and cultural factors which may increase a user's tendency to download copyrighted media, many of which are considered in Brown and Holt (2018).

Finally, it should also be remembered that crime may occur in online virtual worlds, such as those used for socialising and gaming. There have been several reported incidents of assaults on **avatars** within these worlds, with an early, and very famous, case being that of assaults conducted by an avatar called "Mr Bungle" on some of the other users of the text-based virtual

Figure 11.1
While copyright infringement is not a recent development, analogue media such as video cassettes, audio cassettes, and vinyl records were more difficult to copy than modern digital files (photograph by Liam Kirwan).

world "LambdaMoo" (Dibbell, 1993). Similar to cyberbullying and cyberstalking, many incidences of attacks within virtual worlds are not illegal acts, and indeed it would be extremely difficult to classify them as such as many online games require the killing and assault of other players' avatars to progress gameplay, and it is considered an acceptable part of the experience. Similarly, in some online virtual worlds, conducting property crimes against other players, through theft or piracy, is also part of normal gameplay. But in virtual worlds where such activities are not the norm, an assault on a person's avatar or a theft of their property might result in strong psychological responses in the victim (Kirwan, 2009). The potential of metaverse technologies may bring such issues to the fore in future years.

Categorising Cybercrime

Many attempts have been made to categorise the types of cybercrime above in order to provide a mechanism by which we can more carefully evaluate, understand, and combat them. Two of these taxonomies will be briefly described here – specifically those suggested by Wall (2001, 2007) and Kirwan and Power (2013), although there are several others (see Kirwan, 2019, for more examples).

David Wall (2001) suggested four areas of harmful activity online, specifically "cyber-trespass" (unauthorised passing of virtual boundaries), "cyber-deceptions/thefts" (such as identity theft and fraud), "cyber-pornography/obscenity" (such as publishing explicit materials), and "cyber-violence" (such as cyberstalking or hate speech). Later, Wall (2007) suggested that cybercrime has three main criminologies – computer integrity crimes (which attack network security, such as malicious hacking), computer-assisted crimes (which use networks to commit crimes, such as phishing scams), and computer-content crimes (considering illegal content on networks, such as the distribution of certain types of obscene materials).

In contrast, Kirwan and Power (2013) differentiate between three types of cybercrime. One type consists of crimes against the virtual person, including those which occur in online virtual worlds as described above. A second type identified by Kirwan and Power, Internet-enabled offences, includes types of crime which can and have occurred without the use of the Internet, but which are made easier or intensified because of Internet technologies. Examples of such offences include child predation and fraud. Much cybercrime literature utilises the term "old wine in new bottles" to describe this phenomenon see Figure 11.2. Internet-enabled offences are contrasted with the final type of cybercrime, Internet-specific offences, which require Internet technologies during their conduction and did not exist before these technologies were developed. An example of such an Internet-specific offence is malicious hacking. This distinction between Internet-enabled and Internet-specific offences is useful when considering the psychological aspects of cybercrime – previous research regarding the offline equivalents of Internet-enabled offences may be useful

Figure 11.2
Internet offences which have pre-existing offline equivalents have sometimes been referred to as "old wine in new bottles" (photograph by Liam Kirwan).

in understanding online offenders, while it may be that those who engage in Internet-specific offences would not otherwise conduct criminal activity, and therefore these might demonstrate psychological traits and mechanisms which are not usually found in other offenders. Because of this it is important that researchers of cybercriminal psychology also hold expertise in the broader field of forensic psychology as a whole. A brief synopsis of research and practice in this field is provided below.

Forensic Psychology: An Overview

Forensic psychology incorporates two subjects that many of the general public find fascinating – psychology and crime. Adding technology, such as the Internet, into this mix creates a combination that is difficult for television and movie producers to ignore. Unfortunately, as with the depictions of many professions online, the portrayal of the work of forensic psychologists in fictional media is often highly misleading (Kirwan, 2014). This is somewhat regrettable, as the actual work conducted by forensic psychologists and cybercrime investigators often involves much more scientific rigour and intricate consideration of minutiae than is seen in the media, and so a false impression of the professions involved may be formed in the minds of viewers. Forensic psychology is also much broader than media portrayals suggest – almost exclusively the psychologists depicted in such shows work with detectives in criminal cases, but the majority of forensic psychologists instead work in other settings, such as prisons, probation centres, hospitals, and universities. This section will continue by providing a very brief outline of some of the key research areas in forensic psychology with examples of how these are applicable to cybercrime.

CYBERPSYCHOLOGY IN FOCUS: THINKING CRITICALLY ABOUT FORENSIC PSYCHOLOGY IN FICTIONAL MEDIA

There are multiple successful movies and television programmes which depict a forensic psychologist working alongside law enforcement personnel to solve a case by creating a profile or persuading a suspect to confess to a crime. In many cases these depictions include multiple inaccuracies. Offender profiling does not magically direct law enforcement to a specific offender, deception detection is remarkably fallible (often occurring at barely above "chance" levels), and suspect interviewing techniques portrayed can result in confessions which are not admissible in courts. An over-reliance on offender profilers can also cause problems if real-life investigators put too much faith in these techniques. If you're interested in learning more about what real-life offender profiling involves, then consider reviewing the work by Professor David Canter, who has published numerous engaging books on the topic.

Research Topics in Forensic Psychology

Many lay people have come across the term "offender profiling", primarily because of the fictional portrayals mentioned above. In reality, there are several different approaches to offender profiling, such as clinical, typological, and statistical methodologies. Some researchers have attempted to investigate if profiling can be used to uncover the characteristics of cybercriminals, and Bada and Nurse (2021) provide a fascinating systematic review of the research in this area. Offender profiling can be considered an aspect of investigative psychology (see Canter & Youngs, 2009), which incorporates other ways in which psychologists can be of assistance to police investigations (such as linking cases, interviewing suspects, and advising on deception). For example, psychologists can advise on the accuracy of lie detection methods (see, for example, Vrij,

2019), the potential of a suspect to give a false confession (Gudjonsson, 2021), or the probable accuracy of eyewitness testimony (Loftus, 2019). A related area of police psychology involves research relating to policework, for example, Fortune et al. (2018) examined the stresses experienced by law enforcement personnel who work with distressing material online.

As mentioned, criminal psychology is an important aspect of forensic psychology. Much research attempts to determine what the risk factors of criminality are or to develop a greater understanding of specific types of offenders. Similarly, research has attempted to identify the characteristics of various cyber-criminal types. When conducting research regarding criminality and criminal psychology, attempts are often made to predict offending, to enhance understanding of the offender, and also to determine the most appropriate assessment and rehabilitation of these offenders. Forensic psychology also attempts to determine the most effective punishments for different types of offenders (for example, if a financial penalty is as much of a deterrent for an action as a prison sentence is, then it is a much more socially acceptable and economically viable alternative). Forensic psychologists working in prisons will frequently assess offenders to determine if the attempts at rehabilitation and punishment have resulted in a decreased likelihood of reoffending. The psychologist may also develop new rehabilitation programmes and psychological measures to determine if these are more effective than previously existing ones.

Forensic psychology also has a role to play within the courtroom, as it considers the decision-making strategies of jurors and judges (Peter-Hagene et al., 2019). It considers the role of victims – in terms of their experiences within the criminal justice system, the effects of the crime on them, and the impact that they can have on other individuals and groups (e.g. De Kimpe et al., 2020). Research in forensic psychology also examines how efforts can be made to reduce and prevent crime, through prevention and educational programmes, and also through less obvious methods, such as environmental design (for example, planning effective street layouts and lighting). It considers who is most fearful of cybercrime victimisation, while considering why others are not as afraid (Brands & Van Doorn, 2022).

As is evident from this section, forensic psychology is an extremely broad area, with conclusions based on a substantial body of empirical research. The interested reader should consider initially reviewing a forensic psychology textbook, such as that by Davies and Beech (2018) or Crighton and Towl (2021), before delving further into the plethora of excellent research articles in the field. Students interested in pursuing a career in forensic psychology should visit the website of their local psychological society (such as the British Psychological Society or the American Psychological Association) to identify the training and experience requirements in their region.

Theories of Crime

A society without crime would seem extremely strange, no matter how uto-pian it might be. Researchers and theorists from many different fields have attempted to form theories of crime that describe why crime occurs and who is most likely to become an offender. Some of these theories have a criminologi-cal focus, some psychological, some sociological, but most can give us some valuable insights. Here we will briefly consider a small selection of such theo-ries of crime and their applicability to cybercrime, although these are covered in much more depth elsewhere (see, for example, the recommended readings by Davies & Beech, 2018; and Crighton & Towl, 2021, mentioned below).

It is tempting to want to identify a single factor which differentiates crimi-nals from non-criminals, and many attempts have been made to do this. Researchers have searched for consistent differences between offenders and non-offenders in moral development, intelligence, empathy, social skills, cogni-tive skills, aggressiveness, extraversion, and many other traits. However, given the wide variety of types of offenders that there are, it is difficult to reliably find a single trait that provides a differentiating factor. For example, while some types of offenders might, on average, display a lower level of intelligence than the general population, this is frequently not the case for white-collar offenders or psychopaths. Similarly, there appears to be no personality structure indica-tive of terrorism (Horgan, 2019). There have also been attempts to uncover a genetic factor in offending, which does show some promise, but many who have the at-risk genetic structures never develop criminal tendencies.

Attempts have been made to apply learning theories to criminology, and the realisation that individuals often learn criminal behaviour by watching parents, siblings, or peers engage in criminal acts has led to the suggestion that Bandura's social learning theory (Bandura, 1962) might allow partial explana-tion of such trends. Both social learning and self-control seem to have strong links with digital piracy behaviours (e.g. Burruss et al., 2019). It has also been thought that other learning theories, such as classical and operant condition-ing, also have a role to play in criminality, with theories such as rational choice theory (RCT; see Oppenheimer, 2008, for a review of the development of this theory) attempting to explain crime in terms of criminal decision making given the possibilities of reward and punishment.

A popular theory which provides some explanation of crime is Robert Agnew's general strain theory (Agnew, 1992), which suggests that when indi-viduals are placed under strain criminality may occur (for example, if a person desires a certain goal, they may resort to criminal means to achieve it). Agnew has developed his theory significantly and adapted it to explain why certain individuals, such as younger males, are more likely to become offenders. Strain theory may provide insights into malicious hacking and malware, where cyber-criminals may see themselves as having an advantage that they are lacking in other aspects of their lives.

Other researchers have suggested that many offenders do not subscribe directly to deviant norms, but develop ways of rationalising their behaviour to reduce feelings of guilt. Sykes and Matza (1957) termed such techniques "neutralisations" – and these include various strategies such as denying any injury to the victim or denial of responsibility for their own offending. Other neutralisations have been identified by other researchers, such as "everybody's doing it", identified by Coleman (1987, p. 413). The presence of such neutralisations may mean that the offender does not actually consider themselves to be a "criminal", but rather is conducting a deviant behaviour for a specific purpose at a specific time, possibly because they do not perceive themselves as having an alternative. For example, much research in the area of child predators and collectors of explicit materials depicting children considers these offenders' use of "cognitive distortions" – distorted ways of thinking that are similar to the neutralisations proposed by Sykes and Matza (1957) – as they provide the offender with the perceived ability to justify their actions. The use of such cognitive distortions in online child sexual exploitation material offenders has been considered by many researchers (see, for example, the systematic review by Steel et al., 2020). Neutralisations have also been applied to many other types of cybercrime (for a review, see Brewer et al., 2020).

This relationship to identity perception is linked to "labelling theory", which considers how individuals label themselves and others, and the behaviours that this may result in. A risk with a juvenile who has begun to offend is that they perceive that society has labelled them as a "criminal", and they then begin to follow patterns of behaviour which they think are consistent with such a term. This may lead to an escalation of offending behaviour. Thankfully, many law enforcement agencies make significant efforts to avoid the introduction of such a label for first-time offenders with the intention of avoiding such a situation. Labelling theory is of particular interest when we consider the terminology issues regarding hacking outlined above – many individuals involved in various hacking activities appear to be highly concerned regarding the use of the term in the media.

Another popular theory of crime known as routine activity theory (RAT) considers how most criminal acts require the co-presence of three elements – a motivated offender, a suitable target, and an absence of guardians (Cohen & Felson, 1979). This theory allows us to consider how actions taken by offenders and potential victims might change the likelihood of a crime occurring, and provides insights into how to reduce crime rates. In cybercrime, the co-presence element is much easier to fulfil than for offline crimes, as geographical distance and boundaries are no longer a barrier to criminal activity. Almost any computer is a suitable target, as it either contains information which would be of use to a cybercriminal, or can be used as part of a "botnet" in other cybercriminal activity. So, the only element of RAT which remains, the absence of guardians, becomes particularly important. This theory provides insights into the importance of protective behaviours online, especially the use of antivirus and firewall technologies. However, it should be remembered that "no matter how well designed, security methods rely on individuals to implement and use them" (Huang et al., 2010, p. 221), and researchers such as Shappie et al. (2020) have identified certain personality variables (notably conscientiousness, agreeableness, and openness) which are related to self-reported cybersecurity behaviours.

Finally, it should also be remembered that crime itself tends to be socially constructed – in other words, an action is a crime because society creates laws and regulations regarding it. Because laws tend to be created by those with the most power or control in a society, they tend to reflect the values of those individuals and, in some regrettable circumstances, may be intentionally or unintentionally used by those individuals to ensure that other groups are marginalised. Some types of cybercrime were easily identified as criminal because of their similarity and overlaps with pre-existing offline offences (this is especially true of the Internet-enabled offences). However, for Internet-specific offences, it has been necessary to alter existing law, or create new laws, in order to ensure that they were reflected within criminal justice systems.

It should be noted that explanations of crime do not have to be considered as separate and discrete. Ideally, multiple theories can be integrated to provide a more cohesive model of offending. This has been attempted by some theorists, including Hans Eysenck (Eysenck & Eysenck, 1970), who have integrated various aspects into a single theory, although such models have not been without critique. Such composite theories may also be applied to cybercriminal cases, but the validity of these models is difficult to verify, partially because of the problematic nature of cybercriminal research.

CYBERPSYCHOLOGY IN FOCUS: RESEARCHING CYBERCRIME AND DISPELLING PSEUDOSCIENCE

It is tempting to say that cybercrime is fast-paced, and that waiting for empirical evidence to support a hypothesis is not feasible. But speculation in cybercrime can be as dangerous as speculation in other types of crime, and all crime is a serious issue that requires suitable research. Of course, technical solutions, such as software patches and updated malware lists, are extremely time-sensitive, but many of the psychological components of cybercrime have similar underlying aspects as are seen in offline crime, or in other aspects of psychology, such as cognitive or social theories.

Responding to cybercrime does require a certain amount of thinking on our feet, but this thinking needs to be based on existing literature and empirically supported theories – we must be cognisant of the threat of pseudopsychology in this field (Kirwan, 2018). Thankfully, psychologists working in this area do not need to generate their advice on pure speculation. However, it should also be remembered that any hypotheses proffered need to be empirically tested at the first opportunity. For this reason, empirically sound research with real cases and cybercriminals needs to be conducted.

There are problems with such research – for example, how can we contact such offenders? If an individual does respond to a call for research participants, how can we be sure that they are indeed the offender that they claim to be, as asking them to demonstrate their actions is at best an inconvenience and may potentially be a criminal act in itself? Even if they are a cyber-criminal, it is possible that those who volunteer as research participants are fundamentally and qualitatively different from those offenders who do not, so it may not be possible to ensure that our findings can be applied to the wider community. It is difficult to overcome these problems, and research in this field must be careful to consider such limitations when presenting find-ings and suggestions for policy. One potential approach to counter some of these problems involves analysis of public communications on relevant forums, as done by McAlaney et al. (2020) when they examined hacking-related threads on forums and subreddits. This technique provides the opportunity to analyse cybercriminals in ways which more traditional research methods don't allow, although there are still some methodological problems which research-ers need to be aware of (for example, the inability to ask participants questions directly, and a potential hesitance on their part to discuss certain matters in public forums).

Conclusion

Forensic psychology is an established field, with a significant quantity of high-quality research. The study of cybercrime can draw from this pre-existing knowledge and further it as it examines areas of crime and types of criminals which did not exist before recent advances in technology. There are many types of cybercrime, with a wide variety of offender types, but research in forensic psychology and theories of crime provide insights into how and why these offences occur, as well as how offenders might be rehabilitated and how future cybercrimes might be prevented.

Activity

Keep a log of any emails that you receive which include attempts at identity theft or fraud. For example, these might be emails that pretend to be from banks, online auction sites, other online retailers, or officials from other coun-tries. What is it about these emails that makes you think that they are fraudu-lent? What tactics do they use to try to persuade victims to provide information or click on links?

Discussion Questions

1. Consider any fictional film or television programme that portrays cyber-crime. How does the reality of cybercrime differ from that portrayed in the media? Why are they different?
2. Does it surprise you that forensic psychology is so much broader than offender profiling? Compare your perceptions of the field before and after reading this chapter.

3. Are some types of cybercrime really "old wine in new bottles", or are they fundamentally different types of offences?
4. Considering the online disinhibition effect and other aspects of online behaviour, would some people commit crime online who would never contemplate offending in offline environments?

Recommended Reading List

Readers who are interested in gaining a fuller insight into the complexity and breadth of forensic psychology will find the textbooks by Davies and Beech (2018) and/or Crighton and Towl (2021) helpful. These texts are approved by the British Psychological Society.

Davies, G., & Beech, A. (2018). *Forensic psychology: Crime, justice, law, interventions* (3rd ed.). BPS Wiley.

Crighton, D. A., & Towl, G. J. (2021). *Forensic psychology* (3rd ed.). BPS Wiley.

The current chapter, by necessity, provides only a very brief overview of the various types of cybercrime and the psychological research which furthers our understanding of it. Further detail can be found in this chapter in *The Oxford Handbook of Cyberpsychology*.

Kirwan, G. H. (2019). The rise of cybercrime. In A. Attrill-Smith, C. Fullwood, M. Keep, & K. J. Kuss (Eds.), *The Oxford handbook of cyberpsychology* (pp. 627–644). Oxford University Press.

Offender profiling is an aspect of forensic psychology which many find fascinating. Bada and Nurse's systematic review provides an excellent overview of how it has been applied to cybercrime.

Bada, M., & Nurse, J. R. (2021, June). Profiling the cybercriminal: A systematic review of research. In *2021 international conference on cyber situational awareness, data analytics and assessment (CyberSA)* (pp. 1–8). IEEE.

Most types of cybercrime are fascinating, but one of the types which is of greatest concern relates to online child sexual exploitation material. This paper by Steel et al. provides a systematic review of research relating to cognitive distortions in these offenders.

Steel, C. M., Newman, E., O'Rourke, S., & Quayle, E. (2020). A systematic review of cognitive distortions in online child sexual exploitation material offenders. *Aggression and Violent Behavior, 51*, 101375. https://doi.org/10.1016/j.avb.2020.101375

Glossary

Advance fee fraud: A type of online fraud where a user is promised a significant financial reward should they meet what initially appear to be minor demands and fees.

Avatar: An online representation of a user, especially in three-dimensional virtual worlds.

Criminological psychology: A branch of psychology which deals mostly with understanding and reducing criminal behaviour.

Cybercrime: Any unlawful act which is conducted using computing technologies.

Forensic psychology: "The application of psychology with people and organisations connected with the Court, Health or Justice systems" (British Psychological Society, n.d., "What Is Forensic Psychology?").

Internet-enabled cybercrime: Crimes for which offline equivalents exist, but which Internet technologies enable or extend.

Internet-specific cybercrime: Cybercrimes for which offline equivalents do not exist.

Legal psychology: A branch of psychology which deals with the process of law.

Offender profiling: The creation of profiles of criminal suspects, sometimes by forensic psychologists.

Phishing: Emails which appear to be from a reputable source which are designed to elicit sensitive information from a user, leaving them vulnerable to identity theft.

References

Agnew, R. (1992). Foundation for a general strain theory of crime and delinquency. *Criminology, 30*(1), 47–88. https://doi.org/10.1111/j.1745-9125.1992.tb01093.x

Backhaus, S., Gross, M. L., Waismel-Manor, I., Cohen, H., & Canetti, D. (2020). A cyberterrorism effect? Emotional reactions to lethal attacks on critical infrastructure. *Cyberpsychology, Behavior, and Social Networking, 23*(9), 595–603. http://doi.org/10.1089/cyber.2019.0692

Bada, M., & Nurse, J. R. (2021, June). Profiling the cybercriminal: A systematic review of research. In *2021 international conference on cyber situational awareness, data analytics and assessment (CyberSA)* (pp. 1–8). IEEE.

Bandura, A. (1962). Social learning through imitation. In M. R. Jones (Ed.), *Nebraska symposium on motivation* (pp. 211–274). University of Nebraska Press.

Brands, J., & Van Doorn, J. (2022). The measurement, intensity and determinants of fear of cybercrime: A systematic review. *Computers in Human Behavior, 127*, 107082. https://doi.org/10.1016/j.chb.2021.107082

Brewer, R., Fox, S., & Miller, C. (2020). Applying the techniques of neutralization to the study of cybercrime. In T. J. Holt & A. M. Bossler (Eds.), *The Palgrave handbook of international cybercrime and cyberdeviance* (pp. 547–565). Palgrave Macmillan.

British Psychological Society. (n.d.). *Division of forensic psychology*. Retrieved April 23, 2023 from https://www.bps.org.uk/member-networks/division-forensic-psychology

Brown, S. C., & Holt, T. J. (Eds.). (2018). *Digital piracy: A global, multidisciplinary account*. Routledge.

Burruss, G. W., Holt, T. J., & Bossler, A. (2019). Revisiting the suppression relationship between social learning and self-control on software piracy. *Social Science Computer Review, 37*(2), 178–195. https://doi.org/10.1177/0894439317753820

Canter, D., & Youngs, D. (2009). *Investigative psychology: Offender profiling and the analysis of criminal action*. John Wiley & Sons.

Cohen, L. E., & Felson, M. (1979). Social change and crime rate trends: A routine activity approach. *American Sociological Review, 44*(4), 588–608.

Coleman, J. W. (1987). Toward an integrated theory of white-collar crime. *American Journal of Sociology, 93*(2), 406–439. https://doi.org/10.1086/228750

Conway, M. (2007). Cyberterrorism: Hype and reality. In L. Armistead (Ed.), *Information warfare: Separating hype from reality* (pp. 73–93). Potomac Books.

Crighton, D. A., & Towl, G. J. (2021). *Forensic psychology* (3rd ed.). BPS Wiley.

Davies, G., & Beech, A. (2018). *Forensic psychology: Crime, justice, law, interventions* (3rd ed.). BPS Wiley.

De Kimpe, L., Ponnet, K., Walrave, M., Snaphaan, T., Pauwels, L., & Hardyns, W. (2020). Help, I need somebody: Examining the antecedents of social support seeking among cybercrime victims. *Computers in Human Behavior, 108*, 106310. https://doi.org/10.1016/j.chb.2020.106310

Denning, D. E. (2007). Cyberterrorism – Testimony before the special oversight panel on terrorism committee on armed services US House of Representatives. In E. V. Linden (Ed.), *Focus on terrorism, 9*, 71–76. Nova Science Publishers.

Dibbell, J. (1993). *A rape in cyberspace*. http://www.juliandibbell.com/articles/a-rape-in-cyberspace/

Eysenck, S. B. G., & Eysenck, H. J. (1970). Crime and personality: An empirical study of the three-factor theory. *The British Journal of Criminology, 10*(3), 225–239. http://www.jstor.org/stable/23635921

Finkelhor, D., Walsh, K., Jones, L., Mitchell, K., & Collier, A. (2021). Youth Internet safety eduction: Aligning programs with the evidence base. *Trauma, Violence, & Abuse, 22*(5), 1233–1247. https://doi.org/10.1177/1524838020916257

Fortune, N., Rooney, B., & Kirwan, G. H. (2018). Supporting law enforcement personnel working with distressing material online. *Cyberpsychology, Behavior, and Social Networking, 21*(2), 138–143. https://doi.org/10.1089/cyber.2016.0715

Gudjonsson, G. H. (2021). The science-based pathways to understanding false confessions and wrongful convictions. *Frontiers in Psychology, 12*, 308. https://doi.org/10.3389/fpsyg.2021.633936

Horgan, J. G. (2019). Psychological approaches to the study of terrorism. In E. Chenoweth, R. English, A. Gofas, & S. N. Kalyvas (Eds.), *The Oxford handbook of terrorism* (pp. 207–223). Oxford University Press.

Huang, D., Rau, P. P., & Salvendy, G. (2010). Perception of information security. *Behaviour & Information Technology, 29*(3), 221–232. https://doi.org/10.1080/01449290701679361

Kirwan, G. (2009). *Presence and the victims of crime in online virtual worlds*. Proceedings of Presence 2009 – the 12th Annual International Workshop on Presence, International Society for Presence Research, 11–13 November, Los Angeles, CA.

Kirwan, G. (2014). Scripts and sensationalism: The depiction of forensic psychology in fictional media. *The Irish Psychologist, 40*(8), 224–225.

Kirwan, G. H. (2018). Dispelling the pseudopsychology of cybercrime. *Cyberpsychology, Behavior, and Social Networking, 21*(2), 71–72. https://doi.org /10.1089/cyber.2017.29100.ghk

Kirwan, G. H. (2019). The rise of cybercrime. In A. Attrill-Smith, C. Fullwood, M. Keep, & K. J. Kuss (Eds.), *The Oxford handbook of cyberpsychology* (pp. 627–644). Oxford University Press.

Kirwan, G., & Power, A. (2013). *Cybercrime: The psychology of online offenders.* Cambridge University Press.

Loftus, E. F. (2019). Eyewitness testimony. *Applied Cognitive Psychology, 33*(4), 498–503. https://doi.org/10.1002/acp.3542

McAlaney, J., Hambidge, S., Kimpton, E., & Thackray, H. (2020, September). Knowledge is power: An analysis of discussions on hacking forums. In *2020 IEEE European symposium on security and privacy workshops (EuroS&PW)* (pp. 477–483). IEEE.

Oppenheimer, J. A. (2008). Rational choice theory. *The sage encyclopedia of political theory.* Sage Publications.

Peter-Hagene, L. C., Salerno, J. M., & Phalen, H. (2019). Jury decision making. In N. Brewer & A. B. Douglass (Eds.), *Psychological science and the law* (pp. 338–366). The Guilford Press.

Quayle, E. (2021). Online sexual deviance and pedophilia. In L. A. Craig (Ed.), *Sexual deviance: Understanding and managing deviant sexual interests and paraphilic disorders* (pp. 222–237). Wiley.

Shappie, A. T., Dawson, C. A., & Debb, S. M. (2020). Personality as a predictor of cybersecurity behavior. *Psychology of Popular Media, 9*(4), 475. https://doi .org/10.1037/ppm0000247

Steel, C. M., Newman, E., O'Rourke, S., & Quayle, E. (2020). A systematic review of cognitive distortions in online child sexual exploitation material offenders. *Aggression and Violent Behavior, 51*, 101375. https://doi.org/10.1016 /j.avb.2020.101375

Sykes, G. M., & Matza, D. (1957). Techniques of neutralization: A theory of delinquency. *American Sociological Review, 22*(6), 664–670. https://doi.org/10 .2307/2089195

Vrij, A. (2019). Deception and truth detection when analyzing nonverbal and verbal cues. *Applied Cognitive Psychology, 33*(2), 160–167. https://doi.org/10 .1002/acp.3457

Wall, D. S. (Ed.). (2001). *Crime and the Internet: Cybercrimes and cyberfears.* Routledge.

Wall, D. S. (2007). *Cybercrime: The transformation of crime in the information age.* Polity Press.

Cyberpsychology and Psychopathology

Cliona Flood and Audrey Stenson

Chapter Overview

Technology is a really important part of today's world and how we live our lives, enabling instant communication with friends and family. However, for some people, the Internet can be problematic. This chapter will look at how the Internet impacts mental health particularly in the arena of **pathological Internet usage.** It will also explore the topics of Internet addiction, social networking, online gaming, and mobile phone dependency and will look at therapeutic options.

Key Terms

Psychopathology is the study of mental health. This chapter will look at some of the mental health issues that relate to the overuse of technology. It considers **psychopathology**, which is the scientific study of **mental disorders.** One of the problems with the overuse of the Internet is that some people may become dependent on it. **Internet addiction** (IA) or **problematic Internet use** can be considered a **behavioural addiction** similar to problematic gambling. Excessive time playing **online games, online gambling**, or **social networking** can be considered problematic. Some people suffer anxiety when they are separated from their mobile phones or technologies. One word used to describe problems relating to mobile phones is **nomophobia.** This is a term that refers to the fear of being out of mobile phone contact. Different forms of technology-enhanced **cognitive behavioural therapy** and treatment in **virtual environments** have been found useful in the treatment of mental health problems, especially in children. **Online counselling** is another useful treatment for mental health sufferers.

What Is Psychopathology?

Pinning down a finite definition of what psychopathology is can be an elusive task. There is some agreement that there are certain shared features. Comer and Comer (2021) argue that these are often called **"the four D's",**

191

DOI: 10.4324/9781003092513-18

comprising **deviance** (being different, displaying extreme, bizarre, or extreme behaviours), **distress** (upsetting or unpleasant to the person or those around them), **dysfunction** (an inability to perform daily life tasks constructively), and **danger** (a danger to oneself, others, or society). It is also important to consider the cultural context in which the behaviour takes place. For example, the extreme behaviours of entertainers may be tolerated as a performance but not in society in general. In psychological terms, **psychopathology** refers to the issues that surround mental health.

The study of **mental health** embraces a broad field of psychological problems that may occur in people's lives. The scope of the issues covered in psychopathology includes problems relating to stress and anxiety, and problems of mood, mind, and body. It also studies psychosis and life span problems. As a scientific subject relating to clinical practice, it embraces strict research methods, explores different models of disorders, and looks at clinical assessment, diagnosis, and treatment options.

DSM-5-TR and How It Views the Internet

The fifth edition of the *Diagnostic and Statistical Manual of Mental Disorders* (DSM-5) was published by the American Psychiatric Association (APA) in 2013 but in March 2022, they published a text revision (DSM-5-TR). The DSM is considered to be the standard tool used to classify mental disorders. It uses a common language and standard criteria for the diagnosis of mental illness and is used by researchers, clinicians, policymakers, the legal system, and insurance companies as a benchmark.

The DSM-5 identified **internet gamers** as an at-risk population, who may develop dependence or an addiction to online gaming. Internet gaming disorder (IGD) was listed in section III of the DSM-5 and it is envisaged that further research will determine whether the condition should be included in the manual as a disorder. It outlines the proposed criteria for the inclusion of IGD in the manual. "Persistent and recurrent use of the Internet to engage in games, often with other players, leading to clinically significant impairment or distress" (DSM-5, p. 795). The criteria include preoccupation with Internet games, withdrawal symptoms when not playing, tolerance, unsuccessful attempts to control usage, loss of interest in previous hobbies, continued excessive use of Internet games despite knowing that it is causing problems, deception, escapism, and the loss or jeopardisation of a significant relationship, job, education, or career (American Psychiatric Association, n.d.). Initially, the APA considered that internet gaming may be similar to gambling as the reward systems of the brain are activated and can be considered a **behavioural addiction** (DSM-5). An alternative diagnostic tool is the International Statistical Classification of Diseases and Related Health Problems (ICD-11) published by the World Health Organization (WHO, 2019). The ICD-11 defines gaming disorder as "characterised by a pattern of persistent or recurring gaming behaviour ('digital-gaming' or 'video-gaming'), which may be online (i.e. over the internet) or offline"

(ICD-11, 2021). The above criterion for IGD diagnosis is the same in the DSM-5-TR, with the addition of using gaming to relieve negative emotions such as guilt or hopelessness. IGD is not classified as an addiction/mental disorder in either the DSM-5 or DSM-5-TR; instead the discussion continues as to whether IGD is a symptom of an underlying problem or if it is a disorder/addiction in its own right (Sherer, 2023).

There are many debates concerning IGD, such as the need for a clear differentiation between IGD and recreational gaming (Dong et al., 2020) and using games as escapism and as coping mechanisms to deal with mood states and negative feelings (Brand et al., 2020). Brand et al. (2020) argue that escapism is not used to diagnose alcoholism and question its pertinent in diagnosing IGD. A cautious approach to IGD diagnosis is encouraged concerning the need for more transparent research regarding the usefulness of focusing on gaming in particular when other "addictions" such as food, sex, and dancing, amongst others, are not identified in the DSM-5 and the ICD-11 (van Rooij et al., 2018). Generally, findings in the area of IGD are mixed; each study tends to use different methodologies and measurements and therefore further research is necessary using reliable and valid methods (Abendroth et al., 2020).

Considering the rapid development of online games, social media, and other digital platforms and the associated surrounding moral panic, psychological research can fall behind (Orben, 2020). Therefore, the positive role of psychology in new digital technologies may be stymied and this may influence the level of importance placed on IGD (van Rooij et al., 2018).

What Is the Range of Internet-Based Disorders?

There are many terms used when referring to problematic usage; these include **problematic Internet use (PIU)**, problematic computer use, IA, Internet dependency, and pathological Internet use (Morahan-Martin, 2007). A more recent term is problematic interactive media usage (PIMU) and describes behaviours relating to compulsive usage, increased tolerance, and negative reactions when removed from an interactive screen (Rich et al., 2017). Early research relating to IA draws on much of the addiction literature and the classic models of addiction, for example, Jellinek's classic model (Jellinek, 1960). In the classical models, addiction came to signify a "state" that limits voluntary control over a substance or behaviour. The issues of tolerance to the substance or behaviour, denial, and withdrawal symptoms were all part of the addiction (Clark, 2011). Early models of addiction were inclined to restrict the definition to dependence on substances. This has expanded to include exercise, sex, gambling, gaming, relationships, and shopping. Many of these activities have now migrated online. Griffiths (1997) introduced the concept of addiction to general Internet usage. So, although there are many forms of Internet use and misuse, we need to consider the negative as well as positive uses of the Internet.

There is a myriad of reasons why people use the Internet; much Internet use is linked to how we live our lives in today's world and it is impossible to work or attend college without accessing the Internet. Karacic and Oreskovic (2017) studied addiction rates in Germany and Croatia reporting a strong correlation between mental health, quality of life, and IA in teenagers. They argue that the better the health of adolescents then the less IA. Nevertheless, the term IA is prone to much debate. The term is overinclusive and the Internet cannot be separated from other overused media like gaming, gambling, and sexual activity, regardless of where these behaviours are performed (Starcevic & Aboujaoude, 2017). Additionally, there is a possibility that IA is a manifestation of multiple underlying mental health illnesses such as depression, anxiety, or loneliness that may contribute to the overuse of the Internet (Ryding & Kaye, 2018).

Internet Gaming

Internet gaming has attracted media and academic attention. Bueno et al. (2020) investigated motivations to use *Pokémon Go* and found that gamers identified eight main reasons for playing: enjoyment, fantasy, escapism, social interaction, social presence, achievement, self-presentation, and continuance intention. Virtual gaming worlds can be engaging and can be manipulated by gamers; players can gain status from other players, create resources, and gain power within the game. However, there can be a downside to excessive gaming; many hard-core players may suffer from low self-esteem which can predict problematic gaming (Wartberg et al., 2020). Gaming is considered in more detail in Chapter 20.

FEATURE BOX: ADOLESCENT MENTAL HEALTH – ONLINE GAMING INTERVENTIONS FROM AROUND THE WORLD

The cultural context of Internet gaming needs to be considered. In 2021, China implemented a social intervention to protect the mental health of under 18s, by minimising gaming time (Goh, 2021). The restrictions include reducing gameplay to one hour per day on Friday, Saturday, Sunday, and bank holidays. Meanwhile, in South Korea, the **shutdown law** (Cinderella Law), banning under 16s from playing between the hours of midnight and 6 am, was abolished in 2021, to respect children's rights and encourage at-home education (Hardawar, 2021). In 2021, the UK introduced the **Age Appropriate Design Code** that is designed to protect children's online data concerning gaming, social media, and other mobile phone apps. It means that service providers must ensure that only appropriate data is collected from children; age checks on the website/app are active; tracking services such as geolocation are switched off; nudge services that persuade children to share more data are switched off; and finally a default high level of security must be provided (Information Commissioners Office, n.d.).

Social Networking

What is it about the Internet that attracts users? Is it the content or the social connections? Social media such as WhatsApp, Facebook, Twitter/X, TikTok, and Instagram are part of everyday life for many people. Motivations behind using social media include social interaction, information seeking, affection seeking, and escape (Menon & Meghana, 2021). The area of adolescents' use of social media and the possible effect on wellbeing has gained traction over the last decade. Recent empirical findings suggest that the effect of adolescents' digital media engagement on mental health has not increased (Vuorre et al., 2021) and overall findings from a literature review suggest a negative small effect of social media use on well-being (Duadoni et al., 2020).

Nomophobia and Mobile Phone Usage

Nomophobia is a phobia shaped by the technological and digital advances of communication and defined by the irrational fear of being out of mobile phone contact (Bragazzi et al., 2014). The term is interchangeably used with other terms such as *mobile phone addiction*, *mobile phone overuse*, and *problematic mobile phone usage*. The question of why people use mobile phones considers motivations that include being able to chat to friends and playing online games (Hernández-Torrejón et al., 2020), to alleviate negative feelings such as loneliness (Zhen et al., 2019), and to relieve state anxiety (Shen et al., 2021). However, there is concern amongst researchers about the effects of phone use on adolescents' sleep and well-being. Foerster et al. (2019) found that nocturnal mobile phone usage was associated with awakenings during sleep and possibly other health-related problems for teenagers. However, they caution that the results coincide with adolescent development changes in circadian rhythm. Mixed findings in studies suggest that more research is needed to determine the association between sleep and digital usage amongst adolescents. For example, using self-report and time-diary measures of technology use, Orben and Przybylski (2020) found that digital use, including smartphones, before bedtime, was not substantively linked to the amount of sleep and late hours for adolescents. Other research suggests that digital use or mobile phone usage is not negatively associated with well-being (Vuorre et al., 2021).

Mixed findings in research imply that future research needs to consider areas such as definitions of digital terms that are used interchangeably in research, the wide array of self-report measurement scales, using objective measures such as usage data from apps on mobile phones, and considering when mobile phone usage benefits well-being (Kushlev & Leitao, 2020).

Pathological Internet Usage

The Possibility of Internet Addiction

Psychiatrist Ivan Goldberg introduced the concept of **"Internet addiction disorder"** in 1995 as a satirical hoax to parody how the DSM attempted to create medical explanations for excessive behaviours (Beato, 2010). One of the first papers on Internet addiction (Young, 1998) linked Internet addiction to impulse control disorder, which is considered the closest to pathological gambling of all the diagnoses referred to in the DSM. The problems that Young identified included dependents versus non-dependents, time distortion, personal and work-related, and academic problems (even though the Internet is a great place to do research!). Relationship issues were also evident; issues such as denial, hiding usage, and distrust were also evident. In addition, Young (1998) reported that users viewed online friendships and relationships as more exciting than face-to-face relationships. Dependents considered cybersex and romantic chat as harmless and yet neglected spouses over online "dates". Physical symptoms such as disrupted sleep patterns were identified and a sedentary lifestyle, carpal tunnel syndrome, eye strain, and back strain were often the physical consequences of overuse. Users had no desire to cut down or restrict their usage and were unable to live without the Internet.

Since then, the term **screen-time** was coined and refers to the time spent on any screen including mobile phones, laptops, and TV. However, research in the area is concerned with issues such as lack of definitions and inadequate self-report measurements (Kaye et al., 2020). Since March 2020, we have seen that online activity has become more prevalent because of the COVID-19 global pandemic (Paschke et al., 2021). However, a more complete picture of the social acceptance of the Internet, gaming, and social media since the pandemic is yet to be reported. In some cases, online forms of social interaction may have alleviated the damaging effects of social distancing, lockdowns, and quarantines for adolescents (Orben et al., 2020). Perhaps COVID-19 propelled us into a *next normal* (Sneader & Singhal, 2020) where society may become more accepting of online interactions as an integral part of everyday life.

FEATURE BOX: CRITICAL THINKING – IS IT POSSIBLE TO BE ADDICTED TO THE INTERNET?

There is a growing concern amongst researchers regarding the definition of the term "addiction" and the number of self-report measurements for social media addictions. Satchell et al. (2020) conducted a piece of research concerning "off-line friend addiction". The findings raised some pertinent questions concerning social connections as addictions and highlighted issues regarding the validation of the growing plethora of social media addiction scales. According to Ryding and Kaye (2018), without a firm definition of IA, there are difficulties in devising effective therapeutic methods. Griffiths (2018) argues that IA and smartphone addiction are misnomers, and that "smartphone addicts are no more addicted to the Internet or their smart phones than alcoholics are addicted to bottles" (Griffiths, 2018, p. 234).

Today there are numerous clinical detox programmes worldwide attempting to regulate the use of the Internet for problematic Internet users. Indeed, a growing number of people are taking voluntary **digital detox holidays** (DDH) to "unwire". Jiang and Balaji (2021) indicated that mindfulness, technostress, relaxation, and self-expression were among the reasons why DDH is attractive. The concept of digital detox is defined as "a periodic disconnection from social or online media, but advocates balance and awareness more than permanent disconnection" (Syvertsen & Enli, 2020 p. 1269). The fact that people feel the need to separate, even for a short time, from the Internet is insightful.

Treatment Options

Treatment options for addiction mainly suggest abstinence, but this isn't an option for someone who has a problem with Internet usage due to its ubiquitous nature. Interactive screen usage is part of everyday life (Rich et al., 2017); therefore, the treatment options available consist of some traditional treatments, such as variants of CBT. Young (2011) considered CBT to be effective as it helps clients to monitor their maladaptive thoughts and identify the triggers of addictive feelings. Clients can be taught coping skills to deal with their addiction. Young (2011) developed a new form of CBT called **cognitive behavioural therapy – Internet addiction (CBT-IA)** along with **harm reduction therapy (HRT).** The treatment plan consists of three phases – behaviour modification, which is aimed at gradually decreasing the amount of time the person spends online. The next phase is cognitive restructuring and identifies the thoughts that lead to the addiction and investigates the issues of why the addict spends so much time online. HRT is used to identify and treat any other issues, such as social isolation or depression, that could also be involved in the development of compulsive Internet use. Recent research emphasises the benefits of psychological interventions; these include CBT, counselling programmes, and group- and family-based interventions (Kim & Noh, 2019). The treatment of maladaptive Internet use is still in its infancy. New models of treatment will evolve from existing mental health treatments; this is a new area of research and practice. Agreement on terms and data collection will consolidate in the future and a clearer recovery path may emerge.

Using Technology to Support Recovery and the Treatment of Poor Mental Health

Reading the previous section may give a negative impression of Internet usage. But technology can be used to help recovery and the treatment of poor mental health. **Virtual reality** (VR) has been identified as a potentially useful treatment option in the field of clinical psychology. The usefulness of VR as a rehabilitative tool because it provides feedback in a controlled but motivating environment, which can enhance motor learning. This is particularly beneficial for patients with brain injuries and therapists showed positive attitudes towards VR (Glegg et al., 2013). Gainsford et al. (2020) indicate that there is promising evidence supporting the use of VR with people suffering from schizophrenia, particularly around social cognition. By combining VR with non-invasive brain stimulation, treatments can be powerful and there may be a positive lasting neuroplastic change. Gega et al. (2013) support the notion that **virtual environments** (VE) can support CBT interventions. Using a VE with video capture for a one-hour session mid-way through a 12-week CBC treatment, Gega et al. (2013) found significant improvement in outcomes relating to the role of safety behaviours and avoidance in the maintenance of social anxiety and paranoia. The participants were recovering from early psychosis, severe social anxiety, and moderate paranoia. By replaying the video capture the patients could discuss how the different situations made them feel and what thoughts were triggered. There was a significant improvement in outcomes. VR and its role in psychological therapy are considered in more detail in Chapter 21.

Interest in the topic of gamification in clinical and eHealth settings has increased in recent years and gaming can have positive impacts on mental health. Further empirical evidence to support mental health assessment and treatment is still needed. However, research to date has been positive (Rowntree & Feeney, 2019). The advantages of gamification have been embraced by business, marketing, and e-learning, but research in the area of eHealth is relatively new. Now there is a growing trend to include fun in mundane activities to motivate cognitive change and benefits (Sardi et al., 2017). Good design of eHealth computer applications is vital for them to be beneficial and van Dooren et al. (2019) recommend that the expectations of the stakeholder be aligned through framing, that the therapeutic aspects of the game are integrated into the game, and that there is a need for personalisation.

CBT, based on Aaron Beck's work (1991), has a long history as a psychological intervention for a range of mental health issues. In a literature review of how CBT transfers to a computer-based therapeutic tool, Twomey et al. (2013) outlined that, in the United Kingdom, technology has been used to increase access to psychological therapies. CBT was particularly evident, and this was given the term **computerised CBT (cCBT).** cCBT is an Internet-based self-help therapeutic intervention. They outline that cCBT has many advantages, as it can be either self-help or therapist based, and it can be relatively inexpensive and covers a wide range of health difficulties, such as depression, anxiety, stress, and alcoholism. In a more recent meta-analysis, Twomey et al. (2017) argue that cCBT programmes vary a great deal and there has been little evaluation of the studies carried out. However, they note that dropout rates from a Deprexis programme, an individually tailored cCBT programme (see Meyer et al., 2009), were low; subsequently, the findings support the effectiveness of Deprexis for depressive symptoms, indicating the strength of this form of therapy. The real value of cCBT programmes is that they are relatively low-cost and low-intensity interventions, which cover a wide range of psychological issues and are particularly useful in supporting primary care mental health services.

A team led by Professor Gary O'Reilly in University College Dublin developed a CBT intervention for children suffering from anxiety disorders called Pesky gNATS (see also Chapter 20). This computer-based treatment is an excellent example of a user-friendly, de-stigmatising form of therapy in which young people engage and have a positive experience. The game was developed in support of face-to-face CBT interventions for young people who were experiencing medium to severe mental health problems, especially relating to anxiety and depression. This computer-based game teaches children and adolescents about the concept of **negative automatic thoughts** (NATS). O'Reilly calls these thoughts gNATs and they have the potential to sting humans and produce negative thought patterns. The child-friendly gNAT trap game was devised so children can address their negative thoughts, such as "The Over-Generalising gNAT", "The Jumping to Conclusions gNAT", and "The Predicting the Future gNAT". Using an engaging computer game or app, children "swot" the gNATS and with their therapist explore alternative approaches to situations. A study of Pesky gNATs by Chapman et al. (2016) demonstrated that a brief intervention of seven sessions showed significant change. The retention rates were high, and all the participants completed the sessions with 4 of the 11 participants demonstrating excellent reductions in depression and anxiety.

Although gaming is a relatively new treatment intervention, **online counselling** has been an effective means of offering counselling to clients for several years. Psychological interventions can be provided over the Internet and this can be either synchronous, either by chat or webcam, or asynchronous by e-mail. Text-based counselling is by no means new; Freud conducted many of his analyses by letter, for example, the case study of "Little Hans" (Freud, 2001). It has taken some time for this mode of therapy to gain in popularity in the online arena and face-to-face counselling remains the favoured option (Dowling & Rickwood, 2014). The barrier to online therapy could be therapists' concerns that they would not be able to convey empathy online or build a proper client–therapist relationship (Roesler, 2017). Internet literacy and confidentiality issues are another concern, and many therapists may lack training and experience in providing online therapy. However, COVID-19 has accelerated change in this area. Psychotherapists and clients were unable to see each other in a face-to-face environment and had to use the Internet to conduct their therapy sessions regardless of their attitudes and experience of working in this environment (Békés & Aafjes-van Doorn, 2020). A somewhat positive attitude was taken to the online experience and therapists reported a likelihood of using the Internet in the future.

Conclusion

This chapter has discussed how the Internet impacts mental health. It identified several possible Internet addictions, such as gaming, social networking, and mobile phone addictions. The chapter has also identified treatment options for Internet overuse and how useful Internet applications such as gaming can be in the treatment of mental health issues.

Activity

Describe an approach you might choose if you were trying to change a friend's maladaptive social networking or online game usage.

ADDITIONAL READINGS/DOCUMENTS

The following book specifically focuses on the real-world application of human behaviour in relation to the use of the Internet. Specifically Chapter 6 explores the term **Internet addiction** from a clinical aspect.

- Attrill, A., & Fullwood, C. (Ed.). (2016). **Applied Cyberpsychology: Practical Applications of Cyberpsychological Theory and Research**. Palgrave MacMillan.

Understanding psychological theory in relation to online behaviour is core to cyberpsychology. In this book, areas such as technology interaction and interactivity, health, gaming, and cybercrime are addressed.

- Attrill-Smith, A., Fullwood, C., Keep, M., & Kuss, D. J. (Eds.). (2018). **The Oxford Handbook of Cyberpsychology**. Oxford University Press.

Technology itself is neither positive nor negative; how we use technology defines its positive and negative effects such as on well-being. Linda Kaye explores screen-time, gaming, and the effects of technology among other areas.

- Kaye, L. K. (2022). **Issues and Debates in Cyberpsychology**. McGraw Hill.

In this article Coyle, McGlade, Doherty, and O'Reilly (2011) explore the first adolescent therapeutic intervention to fully integrate a computer game into cognitive behavioural therapy.

- Coyle, D., McGlade, N., Doherty, G., & O'Reilly, G. (2011). Exploratory evaluations of a computer game supporting cognitive behavioural therapy for adolescents. In

Proceedings of the SIGCHI Conference on Human Factors in Computing Systems (pp. 2937–2946). ACM.

- http://www.davidcoyle.org/docs/Coyle%20et%20al%20CHI2011.pdf

The following two chapters from the book *Cyberpsychology* give an outline of the areas involved in online addiction and online counselling. Attrill, A. (Ed.). (2015). *Cyberpsychology*. Oxford University Press.

- Chapters 11: The Psychology of Online Addictive Behaviour – Mark D. Griffiths.
- Chapter 13: Online Therapies and Counselling – Melanie Nguyen.

The three chapters from *The Oxford Handbook of Cyberpsychology*, Oxford University Press by Attrill-Smith, A., Fullwood, C., Keep, M., & Kuss, D. J. (Eds.) (2019), may be of interest.

- Chapter 23: A Psychological Overview of Gaming Disorder – Daria J. Kuss, Halley Pontes, Orsolya Kiraly, and Zsolt Demetrovics.
- Chapter 25: The Therapeutic and Health Benefits of Playing Video Games – Mark Griffiths.
- Chapter 28: The Psychosocial Effects of Gaming – Michelle Colder Carras, Rachel Kowert, and Thornsten Quandt.

Discussion Questions

1. Evaluate the mental health information and treatments that are available online for sufferers and their families.
2. Social networking is how we communicate today; therefore, using the Internet is a way of life, not an addiction. Discuss.
3. How would you feel and behave if you were without access to the Internet for 48 hours?
4. Discuss the benefits of gaming. Do these outweigh the problems?

Recommended Reading List

The fundamentals of mental health can be found in a range of books relating to psychopathology. Ronald Comer's textbook is an example.

Comer, R. J., & Comer, J. S. (2021). *Abnormal psychology* (11th ed.). Palgrave Macmillan.

Adam Gazzaley and Larry Rosen's book addresses the concept that the human brain is not built for media multitasking or rapid switching between tasks.

Gazzaley, A., & Rosen, L. D. (2017). *The distracted mind: Ancient brains in a high-tech world*. The MIT Press.

Glossary

Addiction: The state of being enslaved to a habit or practice or to something that is psychologically or physically habit-forming.

Behavioural addictions: Involve a repeated compulsion to perform a particular behaviour.

CBT: Cognitive behavioural therapy – short-term psychotherapy developed by Aaron Beck and Albert Ellis.

cCBT: Computerised CBT.

CBT-IA: Cognitive behavioural therapy – Internet addiction.

DSM-5-TR: The *Diagnostic and Statistical Manual of Mental Disorders, Fifth Edition Text Revision* (DSM-5-TR).

Harm reduction therapy: Used to identify and treat any other issues, such as social isolation or depression, that could also be involved in the development of compulsive Internet use.

Internet addiction disorder: A disorder associated with the overuse of the Internet.

Internet gamers: Gamers who play online computer games.

Mental disorders: A wide range of mental health issues. These include anxiety, stress, mood disorders, and addiction.

Mental health: Defined as a state of well-being in which every individual realises his or her potential, can cope with the normal stresses of life, can work productively and fruitfully, and can contribute to her or his community.

Negative automatic thoughts: Thoughts that are unhelpful and negative.

Next normal: Economic and social reality after COVID-19.

Nomophobia: The fear of being out of mobile phone contact.

Online counselling: The delivery of therapeutic interventions over the Internet.

Online games: Games played over a computer network.

PIU: Problematic Internet use.

Psychopathology: The scientific study of mental disorders.

Social networking: Using websites and applications to interact with other people, or to find people with similar interests to yours.

Virtual environment (VE): A computer-generated 3D representation of a setting or situation.

Virtual reality (VR): A realistic simulation of an environment, which has a 3D effect.

References

Abendroth, A., Parry, D. A., le Roux, D. B., & Gundlach, J. (2020). An analysis of problematic media use and technology use addiction scales – What are they actually assessing? In M. Hattingh, M. Matthee, H. Smuts, I. Pappas, Y. K. Dwivedi, & M. Mäntymäki (Eds.), *Responsible design, implementation and use of information and communication technology.* I3E 2020. Lecture Notes in Computer Science, Vol. 12067. Springer. https://doi.org/10.1007/978-3-030-45002-1_18

American Psychiatric Association. (2013). *Diagnostic and statistical manual of mental disorders (DSM-5).* American Psychiatric Pub.

American Psychiatric Association. (n.d.). *Internet gaming disorder.* Retrieved September 2, 2021, from https://www.psychiatry.org/psychiatrists/practice/dsm/educational-resources/dsm-5-fact-sheets

Beato, G. (2010). *Internet addiction.* Retrieved September 3, 2021, from http://reason.com/archives/2010/07/26/internet-addiction

Beck, A. T. (1991). *Cognitive therapy and the emotional disorders.* Penguin Books.

Békés, V., & Aafjes-van Doorn, K. (2020). Psychotherapists' attitudes toward online therapy during the COVID-19 pandemic. *Journal of Psychotherapy Integration, 30*(2), 238–247. https://doi.org/10.1037/int0000214

Bragazzi, N. L., & Del Puente, G. (2014). A proposal for including nomophobia in the new DSM-IV. *Psychology Research and Behaviour Management, 7,* 155–160. https://doi.org/10.2147/PRBM.S41386

Brand, M., Rumpf, H.-J., King, D. L., Potenza, M. N., & Wegman, E. (2020). Clarifying terminologies in research on gaming disorder and other addictive behaviors: Distinctions between core symptoms and underlying psychological processes. *Current Opinion in Psychology, 36,* 49–54. https://doi.org/10.1016/j.copsyc.2020.04.006

Bueno, S., Gallego, M. D., & Noyes, J. (2020). Uses and gratifications on augmented reality games: An examination of Pokémon Go. *Applied Sciences, 10*(5). https://doi.org/10.3390/app10051644

Chapman, R., Loades, M., O'Reilly, G., Coyle, D., Patterson, M., & Salkovskis, P. (2016). 'Pesky gNATs': Investigating the feasibility of a novel computerized CBT intervention for adolescents with anxiety and/or depression in a Tier 3 CAMHS setting. *The Cognitive Behaviour Therapist, 9,* E35. https://doi.org/10.1017/S1754470X16000222

Clark, M. (2011). Conceptualising addiction: How useful is the construct? *International Journal of Humanities and Social Science, 1*(13), 55–64.

Comer, R. J., & Comer, J. S. (2021). *Abnormal psychology* (11th ed.). Palgrave Macmillan.

Dong, G., Wang, Z., Dong, H., Wang, M., Zheng, Y., Ye, S., Zhang, J., & Potenza, M. N. (2020). More stringent criteria are needed for diagnosing internet gaming disorder: Evidence from regional brain features and whole-brain functional connectivity multivariate pattern analyses. *Journal of Behavioral Addictions, 9*(3), 642–653. https://doi.org/10.1556/2006.2020.00065

Dowling, M. J., & Rickwood, D. J. (2014). Experiences of counsellors providing online chat counselling to young people. *Australian Journal of Guidance and Counselling, 24*(2), 183–196. https://doi.org/10.1017/jgc.2013.28

Duadoni, M., Innocenti, F., & Guazzini, A. (2020). Well-being and social media: A systematic review of Bergen addiction scales. *Future Internet, 12*(2), 24. https://doi.org/10.3390/fi1202002

Foerster, M., Henneke, A., Chetty-Mhlanga, S., & Röösli, M. (2019). Impact of adolescnets' screen time and nocturnal mobile phone-related awakenings on sleep and general health symptoms: A prospective cohort study. *International Journal of Environmental Research and Public Health, 16*(3), 518. https://doi.org/10.3390/ijerph16030518

Freud, S. (2001). *The standard edition of the complete psychological works of Sigmund Freud. Two case histories: 'Little Hans' and the 'Rat Man'* (Vol. X). Hogarth Press.

Gainsford, K., Fitzgibbon, B., Fitzgerald, P. B., & Hoy, K. E. (2020). Transforming treatments for schizophrenia: Virtual reality, brain stimulation and social cognition. *Psychiatry Research, 288,* 112974. https://doi.org/10.1016/j.psychres.2020.112974

Gega, L. W., White, R., Clarke, T., Turner, R., & Fowler, D. (2013). Virtual environments using video capture for social phobia and psychosis. *Cyberpsychology, Behavior, and Social Networking, 16*(6), 473–479.

Glegg, S. M. N., Holsti, L., Velikonja, D., Ansley, B., Brum, C., & Sartor, D. (2013). Factors influencing therapists' adopting of virtual reality for brain injury rehabiliation. *Cyberpsychology, Behaviour, and Social Networking, 16*(5), 385–401. https://doi.org/10.1089/cyber.2013.1506

Goh, B. (2021). Three hours a week: Play time's over for China's young video gamers. Retrieved September 2, 2021, from https://www.reuters.com/world/china/china-rolls-out-new-rules-minors-online-gaming-xinhua-2021-08-30/

Griffiths, M. D. (2018). Conceptual issues concerning internet addiction and internet gaming disorder: Further critique on Ryding and Kaye (2017). *International Journal of Mental Health and Addiction, 16*(1), 233–239. https://doi.org/10.1007/s11469-017-9818-z

Griffiths, P. E. (1997). *What emotions really are: The problem of psychological categories* (p. 114). University of Chicago Press.

Hardawar, D. (2021). *South Korea to end its controversial gaming curfew.* Retrieved September 2, 2021, from https://www.engadget.com/south-korea-gaming-shutdown-law-end-163212494.html?guccounter=1&guce_referrer=aHR0cHM6Ly93d3cuZ29vZ2xlLmNvbV88&guce_referrer_sig=AQAAAFagTzfY5JOYWnFlXNWXXTn5XTONp2jshONnE80QfeIKuAo9GR7KxI13ija1G5aRNcv8gDFFV6UYGMUjFzBS3HGp2uIUiGQy2lSQMElUEjDOS1_OFhLx929vLBsxlOKJBcsqTHyextyiob3so_xcEU3AAqvYA7Ss_IV16hIMu4LD

Hernández-Torrejón, M. V., Pastor-Molina, L., & Sosa-Manchego, L. (2020). Nomophobia in university students. *International Journal of Early Childhood Special Education, 12*(1), 488–495. https://doi.org/10.9756/INT-JECSE/V1211.201029

ICD-11. (2021, May). ICD-11 for mortality and morbidity statistics. Retrieved September 2, 2021, from https://icd.who.int/browse11/l-m/en#/http://id.who.int/icd/entity/1448597234

Information Commissioners Office. (n.d.). *Introduction to the age appropriate design code.* Retrieved September 3, 2021 from https://ico.org.uk/for-organisations/guide-to-data-protection/ico-codes-of-practice/age-appropriate-design-code/

Jellinek, E. (1960). *The disease concept of alcholism.* Hillhouse.

Jiang, Y., & Balaji, M. S. (2021). Getting unwired: What drives travellers to take a digital detox holiday? *Tourism Recreation Research,* 1–17. https://doi.org/10.1080/02508281.2021.1889801

Karacic, S., & Oreskovic, S. (2017). Internet addiction and mental health status of adolescents in Croatia and Germany. *Psychiatria Danubina, 29*(3), 313–321. https://doi.org/10.24869/psyd.2017.313

Kaye, L. K., Orben, A., Ellis, D. A., Hunter, S. C., & Houghton, S. (2020). The conceptual and methodological mayhem of "screen time". *International Journal of Environmental Research and Public Health, 17*(10). https://doi.org/10.3390/ijerph17103661

Kim, S., & Noh, D. (2019). The current status of psychological intervention research for internet addiction and internet gaming disorder. *Issues in Mental Health Nursing, 40*(4). https://doi.org/10.1080/01612840.2018.1534910

Kushlev, K., & Leitao, M. R. (2020). The effects of smartphones on well-being: Theoretical integration and research agenda. *Current Opinion in Psychology, 36*, 77–82. https://doi.org/10.1016/j.copsyc.2020.05.001

Kuss, D. J., Kristensen, A. M., & Lopez-Fernandez, O. (2021). Internet addictions outside of Europe: A systematic literature review. *Computers in Human Behaviour, 115.* https://doi.org/10.1016/j.chb.2020.106621

Menon, D., & Meghana, H. R. (2021). Unpacking the uses and gratifications of Facebook: A study among college teachers in India. *Computers in Human Behavior Reports, 3.* https://doi.org/10.1016/j.chbr.2021.100066

Meyer, B., Berger, T., Caspar, F., Beevers, C., Andersson, G., & Weiss, M. (2009). Effectiveness of a novel integrative online treatment for depression (Deprexis): Randomized controlled trial. *Journal of Medical Internet Research, 11*(2), e1151.

Morahan-Martin, J. (2007). Internet use and abuse and psychological problems. In A. M. Joinson & A. M. Joinson (Eds.), *The Oxford handbook of Internet psychology* (pp. 331–345). Oxford University Press.

Orben, A. (2020). The Sisyphean cycle of technology panics. *Perspectives on Psychological Science, 15*(5). https://doi.org/10.1177/1745691620919372

Orben, A., & Przybylski, A. K. (2020). Teenage sleep and technology engagement across the week. *PeerJ, 8.* https://doi.org/10.7717/peerj.8427

Orben, A., Tomova, L., & Blakemore, S.-J. (2020). The effects of social deprivation on adolescent development and mental health. *Viewpoint, 4*(8), 634–640. https://doi.org/10.1016/S2352-4642(20)30186-3

Paschke, K., Austermann, M. I., Simon-Kutscher, K., & Thomasius, R. (2021). Adolescent gaming and social media usage before and during the COVID-19 pandemic: Interim results of a longitudinal study. *Sucht, 67*(1), 13–22. https://doi.org/10.1024/0939-5911/a000694

Rich, M., Tsappis, M., & Kavanagh, J. R. (2017). Problematic media among children and adolescents: Addiction, compulsion or syndrome? In K. S. Kimberly & C. De Abreu (Eds.), *Internet addiction in children and adolescents: Risk factors, assessment, and treatment.* Springer.

Roesler, C. (2017). Tele-analysis: The use of media technology in psychotherapy and its impact on the therapeutic relationship. *Journal of Analytical Psychology, 62*(3), 372–394.

Rowntree, R., & Feeney, L. (2019). Smartphone and video game use and perceived effects in a community mental health service. *Irish Journal of Medical Science (1971–), 188*(4), 1337–1341.

Ryding, F. C., & Kaye, L. K. (2018). "Internet addiction": A conceptual minefield. *International Journal of Mental Health and Addiction, 16*(1), 225–232. https://doi.org/10.1007/s11469-017-9811-6

Sardi, L., Idri, A., & Fernández-Alemán, J. L. (2017). A systematic review of gamification in e-health. *Journal of Biomedical Informatics, 71*, 31–48.

Satchell, L., Fido, D., Harper, C., Shaw, H., Davidson, B., Ellis, D., Hart, C., Jalil, R., Jones Bartoli, A., Kaye, L., Lancaster, G., & Pavetich, M. (2020). Development of an offline-friend addiction questionnaire (O-FAQ): Are most people really social addicts? *Behavior Research Methods.* https://doi.org/10.3758/s13428-020-01462-9

Shen, X., Wang, H.-Z., Rost, D. H., Gaskin, J., & Wang, J.-L. (2021). Sate anxiety moderates the association between motivations and excessive smartphone use. *Current Psychology, 40*(4), 1937–1945. https://doi.org/10.1007/s12144-019-0127-5

Sherer, J. (2023). Internet gaming. American Psychiatric Association. Retrieved April 23, 2023, from https://www.psychiatry.org/patients-families/internet-gaming

Sneader, K., & Singhal, S. (2020). Beyond coronavirus: The path to the next normal. Retrieved September 12, 2021, from https://www.mckinsey.com/industries/healthcare-systems-and-services/our-insights/beyond-coronavirus-the-path-to-the-next-normal

Starcevic, V., & Aboujaoude, E. (2017). Internet addiction: Reappraisal of an increasingly inadequate concept. *CNS Spectrums, 22*(1), 7–13.

Syvertsen, T., & Enli, G. (2020). Digital detox: Media resistance and the promise of authenticity. *Convergence, 26*(5–6), 1269–1283.

Twomey, C., O'Reilly, G., & Byrne, M. (2013). Computerised cognitive behavioural therapy: Helping Ireland log on. *Irish Journal of Psychological Medicine, 30*(1), 29–56.

Twomey, C., O'Reilly, G., & Meyer, B. (2017). Effectiveness of an individually-tailored computerised CBT programme (Deprexis) for depression: A meta-analysis. *Psychiatry Research, 256*, 371–377.

van Dooren, M. M., Siriaraya, P., Visch, V., Spijkerman, R., & Bijkerk, L. (2019). Reflections on the design, implementation, and adoption of a gamified ehealth application in youth mental healthcare. *Entertainment Computing, 31*, 1–14. https://doi.org/10.1016/j.entcom.2019.100305

van Rooij, A. J., Ferguson, C. J., Colder Carras, M., Kardefelt-Winther, D., Shi, J., Aarseth, E., Bean, A. M., Bergmark, K. H., Brus, A., Coulson, M., Deleuze, J., Dullur, P., Dunkels, E., Edman, J., Elson, M., Etchells, P. J., Fiskaali, A., Granic, I., Jansz, J., ... Przybylski, A. K. (2018). A weak scientific basis for gaming disorder: Let us err on the side of caution. *Journal of Behavioral Addictions, 7*(1), 1–9. Retrieved September 1, 2021, from https://akjournals.com/view/journals/2006/7/1/article-p1.xml

Vuorre, M., Orben, A., & Przybylski, A. K. (2021). There is no evidence that associations between adolescents' digital technology engagement and mental health problems have increased. *Clinical Psychological Science.* https://doi.org/10.1177/2167702621994549

Wartberg, L., Zieglmeier, M., & Kammeri, R. (2020). An empirical exploration of longitudinal predictors for problematic internet use and problematic gaming behavior. *Psychological Reports, 124*(2), 543–554. https://doi.org/10.1177/0033294120913488

World Health Organization. (2019). *International statistical classification of diseases and related health problems* (11th rev.). World Health Organization.

Young, K. S. (1998). The emergence of a new clinical disorder. *CyberPsycholgoy & Behaviour, 1*(3), 237–244. https://doi.org/10.1089/cpb.1998.1.237

Young, K. S. (2011). CBT-IA: The first treatment model for Internet addiction. *Journal of Cognitive Psychotherapy: An International Quarterly, 25*(4), 304–312.

Zhen, R., Liu, R.-D., Hong, W., & Zhou, X. (2019). How do interpersonal relationships relieve adolescents' problematic mobile phone use? The roles of loneliness and motivation to use mobile phones. *International Journal of Environmental Research and Public Health, 16*(13). https://doi.org/10.3390/ijerph16132286

Sport and Health Cyberpsychology

Olivia A. Hurley

Chapter Overview

This chapter introduces readers to the impact of technology on behaviour in sport and health environments. It presents information on technologies used to assist athletes' performances [e.g., global positioning systems (GPS), virtual reality (VR), and wearable fitness devices]. Technology use in sport psychology consulting is also discussed, along with the influence of social media (e.g., Instagram, Twitter/X, Facebook, and LinkedIn) on sport environments. Similar technology uses in health contexts for remote support and encouraging engagement in physical activity (PA).

Key Terms

Mental preparation describes how athletes mentally "ready" themselves for their sport. Many technologies can impact this preparation including **social media (SM)** – online social communication platforms (Instagram, Twitter/X, Facebook, and LinkedIn, for example) that allow individuals to post short messages or images that others can read/"like"/repost. Technology that records training and competition activities, as well as health indicators, has also become popular in recent years. These technologies include wearable devices that record, for example, walking and running movements, as well as stress-related information linked to well-being (i.e., heart rate and sleep duration). These **wearables** are also used to help combat sedentary lifestyles which contribute to conditions such as obesity.

Introduction to Sport Cyberpsychology

Sport cyberpsychology refers to how individuals interact with technologies in sport settings, including how they may impact athletes' behaviours, performances, and well-being (Hurley, 2018, 2021). Several exciting avenues of research have emerged within this field in recent years including studies exploring the impact of wearable devices, SM use, and virtual/augmented reality technology

DOI: 10.4324/9781003092513-19

on athletes' performances, as well as the experiences of spectators, officials, and support personnel (i.e., doctors, dieticians, physiotherapists, coaches, and sport psychologists). Technology facilitating athletes' injury prevention and rehabilitation has also progressed (Earley, 2020a, 2020b), with virtual and augmented reality technologies refined for such purposes, as well as to enhance athletes' mental skills including their mental imagery skills (Bedir & Erhan, 2021), decision-making skills, concentration skills, and reaction times (Farley et al., 2020; Panchuk et al., 2018). Athletes' technology use to interact with the public has also risen, with most sports teams and competitors utilising various SM platforms. They can communicate directly with, and provide information to, their supporters about their sport and non-sport-related activities using these technologies (Hurley, 2018, 2021; Whales et al., 2020). Some of these technologies used to help athletes prepare for sport will be outlined below.

Athletes' Technology Use

Technologies used to help athletes prepare for competition have become commonplace in recent years. Sophisticated equipment that monitors athletes' performances and its impact on their bodies has emerged (Earley, 2020a, 2020b; Hurley, 2018). These technologies include advanced **GPS technology**, **virtual reality (VR), augmented reality (AR), and video analysis (VA).** GPS technology, commonly visible in the neck "pockets" of many athletes' jerseys, measures their movements as they train/compete (see Hennessy & Jeffreys, 2018, for a review of some features, strengths, and limitations of GPS technology used in soccer specifically). GPS technology allows athletes and their coaches to more objectively measure their work rate during training sessions/competitive performances than was previously possible using subjective self-report, perceived exertion rating tools (Borg, 1982; Williams, 2017). This data may also have psychological impacts on athletes as they can access their own and their teammates' statistics. In elite team sport environments where competition for places is typically high, athletes may feel they cannot afford to make any mistakes because their training and competition efforts are constantly monitored. They may also risk injury, straining themselves excessively in training/competition, for fear of being judged for exertion reductions (Kearney, 2020; O'Brien, 2020). This issue could also relate to VA, a common tool used in many sport arenas, not just for athlete performance monitoring but also for officiating personnel (Armenteros et al., 2019). Sport video technologies include Goal-Line Technology and Video Assistant Referees (soccer), Television Match Officials (rugby), Hawk-Eye (Gaelic games), and Hawk-Eye Live (tennis). These technologies can assist referees' decision-making during games when they are difficult to adjudicate in real-time due to human eye limitations. Video technology can also improve athletes' self-efficacy (self-belief) and mental imagery skills (Buck et al., 2016), as well as their pre-performance routine implementation (Cotterill, 2018) and decision-making skills (Pagé et al., 2019).

Gaming technology has also been applied for such purposes and will be outlined in the next section.

Gaming activities have also risen in recent years, perhaps due to the emergence of e-sports, where participants are often called "cognitive athletes" (Campbell et al., 2018). Companies creating the games these individuals play professionally also design games to help "traditional" athletes mentally and physically prepare. Gaming companies have developed products that mimic major sport events (i.e., the FIFA soccer World Cup, the Rugby World Cup, and Formula 1 motor car racing). These games can help athletes train desirable in-competition behaviours (Ciavarro et al., 2008). They may also enable spectators/fans to experience the "buzz" athletes often report feeling in competition. During 2020 when many athletes could not compete due to the pandemic, they referred to missing that "buzz". Some sport organisations developed fun ways for their athletes to experience that feeling. For example, in Formula 1, some top motor racing drivers engaged in virtual gaming competitions against each other when their F1 races were cancelled (Richards, 2020). Anecdotal evidence shows that such elite athletes continue to use gaming technology to prepare for their sport (Varley, 2018). In recent interviews, Formula 1 multiple World Champion British racing driver Lewis Hamilton stated that while in the past he had not used or liked training in a simulator (typically incorporating VR/gaming features), to prepare for his races, he has recently been using the technology more to help him and his team prepare for their races (Formula 1.com, 2021).

VR technology is also used to help athletes physically and mentally prepare for their sport. An appealing use of VR technology is its application in enhancing athletes' mental skills (e.g., their reaction times and spatial awareness skills), especially when returning from illness, injury, or suspension (Düking et al., 2018; Gokeler et al., 2014). In addition to sport settings, VR is used in military, education, and mental and physical health settings. It can include full, semi-, or non-immersive VR. Fully immersive VR involves the use of head-mounted displays (HMD) and computer-assisted virtual environments (CAVE), used to evaluate performances in ball sports such as rugby (Brault et al., 2012), soccer (Dessing & Craig, 2010), and basketball (Tsai et al., 2017). VR has also been used to help athletes practice their affective (emotional) and motor imagery skills (Akbaş et al., 2019). Building on the ball-sport research reviewed by Miles et al. (2012), Akbaş et al. (2019) included other sports in their review of VR technology use by athletes. Eighteen papers met their final inclusion criteria. Akbaş et al. (2019) concluded that VR can play a small, but beneficial, role in athletes' training. However, they stated that its real effectiveness requires more detailed analysis incorporating well-designed randomised control trials and more refined VR training programmes. Two years later Bedir and Erhan (2021) examined the effect of VR-based imagery (VRBI) training programmes on target-sport athletes' shot performance and imagery skills compared to visual motor behaviour rehearsal and video modelling use (VMBR + VM). Their participants, from the sports of curling, bowling, and archery, displayed statistically significant differences in their shot performance and imagery skills.

VRBI-trained athletes showed greater improvements in the four-week study than athletes in the VMBR + VM groups. The VRBI group also adapted to the imagery training earlier than the VMBR + VM groups. They showed faster shot performance development and appeared more efficient in their shot performance and imagery skills compared to the VMBR + VM groups.

So, in conclusion, VR technology does appear to be somewhat effective in helping some athletes' sport performance preparations. However, creating fully interactive VR technology, where athletes can influence their environments in a more "real" way, should remain a goal of VR designers.

Wearable Technologies: Activity, Sleep, and Psychological States

Many athletes now use fitness tracking technologies to monitor their activity, sleep, and stress levels. Research on activity-tracking app use in elite, and non-elite, populations has also become more "empirically" grounded (Peake et al., 2018), a welcome development, as the earlier research was often commissioned by the technology companies, where conflicts of interest could have occurred. Increased levels of autonomy, self-efficacy, and accountability are positive outcomes reported by individuals using fitness wearables. However, negative outcomes, such as feeling pressure to constantly compete with others and guilt if activity targets are not achieved, have also been reported (Kerner & Goodyear, 2017). Many activity-tracking features of wearables monitor individuals' daily step count. This can motivate some cohorts to stay active. However, the technology's limitations should also be acknowledged. Within elite sport settings, wearables that measure activity levels could result in athletes becoming "too" competitive with themselves and others. They may be tempted to constantly "beat" their personal bests (PBs). This could lead to injury, burnout, and psychological distress. Weekly activity "ranges" or "zoned" targets these individuals could aim to reach, not exceed, may be a more positive strategy to apply in such contexts (Hurley, 2021). Coaches' discussions with their athletes regarding the strengths and limitations of wearables, to help prevent the above issues from happening, should be prioritised.

Similar to physical activity (PA) monitoring, sleep monitoring has become a feature of interest for many athletes, given the importance of recovery for their performances. However, access to such data can also be unhelpful if the recorded data indicates the athletes are not obtaining the recommended sleep/rest to adequately recover from training/competing. They may become distressed by this data which could, paradoxically, lead to more sleep disturbance (Chen, 2019). The limitation accuracies of wearables should also be known. For example, many sleep monitoring wearables are negatively impacted by how much individuals wearing them move or turn during sleep (Lee et al., 2018). Wearable designers could aim to refine sleep monitoring features to address these limitations.

Psychological-state tracking, using wearables, has also become a feature of athlete screening in recent times. They can provide stress or body strain indicators (i.e., sleep duration and quality, as cited above), as well as other physiological responses including heart rate variability, resting heart rate, and respiration rate (Watters, 2020). These devices' stress indicators are often followed by recommendations to use other features of the device to positively adjust physical and mental states (i.e., engaging in relaxation and breathing focused exercises). Bush et al. (2019) reviewed some of the literature on psychological health monitoring, using various apps across different cohorts, considering specifically their use for self-management, supportive care, symptom tracking, and skill training. They reported that while the benefits of these digital options include their ease of access and cost-effectiveness, their more clinically targeted effectiveness is limited. The benefits of their use in helping to treat conditions such as depression (Watts et al., 2013) and anxiety (Grassi et al., 2011) have been indicated. However, Bush et al. (2019) again advised caution regarding the "overselling" of their benefits based on insufficient clinical trials, as well as data privacy issues.

CYBERPSYCHOLOGY IN FOCUS: MENTAL HEALTH AND WELL-BEING FOCUS

Regarding athlete wearables use, it is wise to remember that athletes are competitive people. Both they and their support personnel should closely monitor signs they could be preoccupied with their wearable "data" and discuss openly the above-cited benefits and dangers regarding their use. How accurately the technology gathers the "correct" or best data for athletes to have about their training and lifestyles remains empirically questionable (Bush et al., 2019; FITPRO, 2017; Nelson et al., 2020). It can often only offer a "guide" or estimate of fitness and well-being status. Athletes should not ignore their own bodies' biological signals that may be different to their wearable's data.

Sport Psychology Consultants' Technology Use

Technology used for remote consulting accelerated during the COVID-19 pandemic. It gave practitioners ways to support their clients when required to remain physically distant from them/work from home. Popular video technologies such as Zoom, Microsoft Teams, Skype, and Facetime were often used. The benefits and dangers of this technology for sport psychology consulting with athletes have been outlined (Hurley, 2021). A major advantage of delivering online sessions with athletes is obviously that they allow the individuals involved to overcome the obstacle of being in different physical locations. This was sometimes the case even pre-pandemic for athletes who travelled abroad to access training facilities, or compete, without their psychological support personnel joining them. Knowing their sport science support team, as well as their family members and friends, are easily accessible using the above technologies can be comforting for athletes. However, athlete access to consultants via this technology can result in a work-life balance erosion and burnout for consultants (McCormack et al., 2018). It can also present difficulties for consultants regarding professional boundaries, especially where SM use and security/data protection online issues are concerned. Many organisations, such as the British Psychological Society (2020) and the Psychological Society of Ireland (2020), provided advice to their members regarding these issues during the pandemic.

In today's SM world, practitioners should be mindful of their activities on SM platforms, and how information they share online may be viewed by their clients who access that information (if the profile of the practitioner is "public") and even if the client and psychologist are not "friends" or "mutual followers" on SM, which refers to "tools, platforms and applications that enable consumers to connect, communicate and collaborate with others" (Williams & Chinn, 2010, p. 422). Knowing how to manage the SM space can be challenging for sport psychologists. The American Counselling Association's (2014) code of ethics provides guidelines for distinguishing between professional and personal online identities. It also provides advice for ensuring client privacy when using electronic media, as well as suggesting that consultants include an SM policy in their informed consent documents/conversations with clients. Even with such SM guidelines being available, 60% of a sample of physicians, psychologists, and social workers expressed a desire for more guidance in navigating ethical issues related to SM networks (SMN) (Anderson & Guyton, 2013). If sport psychologists choose to have an SM presence, they should ensure they are comfortable with the information about them online being available to their clients. This topic should also be discussed with clients, ensuring open communication regarding SM interactions. This offers clients an opportunity to discuss SM matters they may otherwise avoid. Results from Knox et al. (2019) on Facebook use by consultants suggested that transparent communication is vital and may need to occur multiple times. While Knox et al. reported that the outcomes of most SM communication discussions were positive, this was not always true and some clients reported residual feelings of distress. Revisiting SM scenarios as often as is deemed necessary to help clients understand why a practitioner responded as s/he did may avoid such client feelings. Many psychologists may not have written SM policies and, as such, clients may be uncertain what is and is not appropriate SM contact. Including a clear statement of SM practices as part of informed consent information could avoid this. However, more empirical research on consultants' use of the online world to determine its specific advantages and disadvantages for them and their clients is warranted. Of course, issues arise from athlete SM use also and this will be addressed next.

Athletes' Social Media (SM) Use

Athletes often lead the way in embracing and capturing the attention of millions around the world via SM. Throughout the pandemic, athletes played important roles in communicating health-related messages to the public due to their vast SM "reach", as well as using SM to share aspects of their outside-sport lives (Sharpe et al., 2020; Tayech et al., 2020; Whales et al., 2020). In mid-2021, two of the top three most "followed" individuals on the SM platforms Instagram and Twitter/X were reportedly Cristiano Ronaldo (soccer) and Dwayne "The Rock" Johnson (athlete, movie star, and businessman; Wallach, 2021). Public interest in such professional athletes' lives has always been high and SM facilitates this curiosity by allowing spectators and fans to "follow" and communicate directly sometimes with their athlete heroes (Hambrick et al., 2010; Pegoraro, 2010). Sponsorship and investment opportunities are also more prevalent via SM and many athletes are "business people", as well as athletes. SM provide them with more ways to connect with their customers and business partners, brand themselves, and sell their products (Whales et al., 2020).

However, athletes are not immune to SM's negative features. Athletes are frequently cyberbullying targets, as evident during the Tokyo 2020 Olympic Games (Yan, 2021; Yip, 2021). Some athletes' posts have also resulted in them being fined and/or banned from competing by their clubs and governing sport organisations (ESPN, 2019). These negative features of athlete SM use have prompted teams, clubs, and governing bodies to devise SM use codes of practice for their athletes and those associated with them. SM use "black-outs" around competition time, which some clubs place upon their players, or athletes may self-impose due to the potential distractibility of SM use at those times, may then be justified.

So having discussed technology use by individuals in sport settings to: (i) assist them with their sport preparation, (iii) recover from time away from sport, and (iii) remain "connected" using their SMNs, an examination of technology used to assist individuals with more general health-related issues will now be considered under "health cyberpsychology".

Health Cyberpsychology

Health cyberpsychology, like sport cyberpsychology, has grown as an exciting research area over the past five years and, again, especially during the pandemic. Typical face-to-face health and medical consultations moved to mainly online delivery, or teleconsulting, when individuals were required to stay physically apart and away from their usual go-to medical facilities during 2020–1. The closure of schools also meant that physical education classes had to be delivered online. Many parents and teachers turned to celebrity trainers, such as Joe Wicks (popularly known as "The Body Coach"), for such lessons during the early stages of the pandemic (Bakare, 2020). Thankfully, the technological developments referred to earlier in this chapter enabled most health interventions to be delivered remotely. Individuals in today's society increasingly turn to the Internet and SM for their health-related information which, while understandable due to its ease of access, comes with risks if the sources of that health-related information are inaccurate or unreliable. Some benefits and risks of online health information searching and sharing, as well as intervention delivery, will be presented next.

Technology and Health

The promotion of health-related behaviours remains important, especially in a world where sedentary lifestyles continue to rise and obesity levels remain problematic. Statistics on disease prevalence, including some cancers, diabetes, and heart disease, associated with obesity and inactivity, especially among young children and teenagers, are alarming (WHO, 2021). Many individuals continue to fall short of the recommended daily physical activity (PA) levels which often leads to weight gain and increased disease risk. The health benefits of exercise and PA, both physically and mentally, are well documented (Gentile et al., 2020). They include and are not limited to positive effects on blood pressure, body weight, and cognitive functioning. During the pandemic, Antunes et al. (2021) reported that engaging in some consistent PA was positively associated with anxiety-buffering effects in 1,404 Portuguese individuals (aged 18 to 89 years). Social benefits are also derived from engaging in group PA. Given these well-supported reasons for why people should do some form of regular exercise or PA, questions continue to arise regarding why so many fail to do so. The most commonly cited reasons are a lack of time, resources, and/or facilities. Parental inactivity has also been indicated as an explanation (Silva et al., 2019). How then can and have technology advances, often indicated as culprits for sedentary behaviour too, be used to encourage people to engage in PA for its health and well-being benefits? How can psychologists and technologists continue to work together to improve the situation?

Research on the benefits and risks of using wearables has attempted to address aspects of the above-cited questions and barriers related to PA. Where exergames (e.g., WiiFit and Kinect games) to promote PA in various populations were popular a decade ago, they have broadly been replaced by wearables. Many health-related apps on these devices are also free to download, thus addressing one of the cited limitations for not doing PA (removing the need to join a gym, or club, to engage in PA). They also help individuals to manage their well-being via various stress management and motivational features as discussed earlier. Young populations have been the target groups for much of the PA research (Gentile et al., 2020), despite the importance of PA in ageing populations also, to protect against age-related illnesses. This area needs more research according to Kononova et al. (2019).

Health Information Searching Online: Benefits and Risks

Using the Internet alone for information gathering on health-related issues can pose risks. Many individuals searching for information online often accept that any "Googled" information is accurate and reliable when frequently the opposite is the case. This may lead to them refusing treatment offered by qualified medical professionals and scientists, which can be detrimental to their health. This was seen in the context of vaccination hesitancy and conspiracy theories that circulated during the COVID-19 pandemic (Bertin et al., 2020). Some individuals may resort to self-medicating by purchasing unregulated drugs online, for example. This can be life-threatening because a medical expert (doctor or healthcare professional) does not oversee such treatment and drugs purchased over the Internet may not contain the active ingredients they report containing. However, the online world can also be a positive source of support for individuals suffering from, recovering from, or managing various illnesses (Lu et al., 2021). Solberg (2014) reported some benefits of online health community membership including connecting with others with similar conditions, and receiving free medical advice from professionals regarding managing symptoms, as well as hearing about and becoming involved in research studies carried out on their conditions. Many health organisations continue to use social media platforms (e.g., Facebook, Twitter/X and Instagram) to grow their membership numbers in their quest to deliver helpful health information and social support to their patients while also recruiting them for research studies. Horrell et al. (2019) suggested this approach to healthcare could be beneficial for all. It is generally very cost-effective and, once used in an ethical way, it can continue to help many individuals cope with their medical diagnoses, while assisting them in their attempts to lead a life of high quality.

Conclusion

As is evident from the research cited in this chapter, developers continue to work with sport science teams, including sport psychologists, to create useful technologies for athletes to prepare more effectively, while also prioritising their well-being. New technologies are also being developed for general populations to help them engage in more positive health-related behaviours. The risks and dangers associated with using technologies and consulting the Internet as a source of health-related information have also been highlighted. Some exciting areas for future research in sport and health cyberpsychology could include: (i) detailed explorations of the impact of data availability and constant effort monitoring on athletes' psychological well-being which to date have continued to be more anecdotal than empirical, (ii) research on beneficial VR and SM use by athletes for their sport and overall well-being, (iii) evaluations of online consulting effectiveness, and (iv) empirical evaluations of wearables used by general populations to assist them in their desire to lead healthier lives.

Activity

Start by discussing the impact of some health-related conditions with your group/class/students/peers, e.g., the physical and psychological impact of being diagnosed with a condition such as concussion or asthma. Consider how designing a relevant "app" might help to improve the quality of life of individuals with such ailments.

Discussion Questions

1. What role can new technologies play in helping athletes to cope with the physical and psychological difficulties they experience when injured?
2. How has the sport psychology consulting process changed with the implementation of online communication technologies?
3. "VR technology can be positively applied in many sport and health settings". Discuss this statement in light of recent technological advances.
4. "New technologies can be used to combat health-related difficulties". Discuss this statement considering emerging technologies available to many individuals.

Recommended Reading List

Research studies in the areas discussed in this chapter are available in recommended peer-reviewed journals such as *Frontiers in Psychology* (open access), *Cyberpsychology, Behaviour and Social Networking*, and *The Sport Psychologist*.

This peer-reviewed paper provides a review of potential uses and impacts of various technologies on athletes and their support personnel during the COVID-19 pandemic.

> Hurley, O. A. (2021). Sport cyberpsychology in action during the COVID-19 pandemic (opportunities, challenges and future possibilities): A narrative review. *Frontiers in Psychology, 12*, 621283. https://doi.org/10.3389/fpsyg.2021.621283

Glossary

Social media: Websites and online social networks that individuals use to communicate and share information online.
Social networking: The use of websites and other online technologies that enable individuals to communicate with each other and share information.
Virtual reality: A realistic simulation of an environment, including three-dimensional graphics, by a computer system using interactive software and hardware.

Wearables: Electronic devices worn by a person (such as a watch/piece of clothing) that relay medical, biological, and exercise data to a database.

References

Akbaş, A., Marszałek, W., Kamieniarz, A., Polechoński, J., Słomka, K. J., & Juras, G. (2019). Application of virtual reality in competitive athletes – A review. *Journal of Human Kinetics, 69*, 5–16. https://doi.org/10.2478/hukin-2019-0023

American Counselling Association. (2014). *2014 ACA code of ethics*. https://www.counseling.org/resources/aca-code-of-ethics.pdf

Anderson, S. C., & Guyton, M. R. (2013). Ethics in an age of information seekers: A survey of licensed healthcare providers about online social networking. *Journal of Technology in Human Services, 31*(2), 112–128. https://doi.org/10.1080/15228835.2013.775901

Antunes, R., Rebelo-Gonçalves, R., Amaro, N., Salvador, R., Matos, R., Morouço, P., & Frontini, R. (2021). Higher physical activity levels may help buffer the negative psychological consequences of coronavirus disease 2019 pandemic. *Frontiers in Psychology, 12*, 672811. https://doi.org/10.3389/fpsyg.2021.672811

Armenteros, M., Benitez, A. J., & Betancor, A. Á. (2019). *The use of video technologies in refereeing football and other sports*. Routledge.

Bakare, L. (2020, March 23). A million people livestream Joe Wicks online PE lessons. *The Guardian*. https://www.theguardian.com/world/2020/mar/23/a-million-people-livestream-joe-wicks-online-pe-lesson

Bedir, D., & Erhan, S. E. (2021). The effect of virtual reality technology on the imagery skills and performance of target-based sports. *Frontiers in Psychology, 11*, 2073. https://doi.org/10.3389/fpsyg.2020.02073

Bertin, P., Nera, K., & Delouvée, S. (2020). Conspiracy beliefs, rejection of vaccination, and support for hydroxychloroquine: A conceptual replication-extension in the COVID-19 pandemic context. *Frontiers in Psychology, 11*, 565128. https://doi.org/10.3389/fpsyg.2020.565128

Borg, G. A. (1982). Psychophysical bases of perceived exertion. *Medicine and Science in Sports and Exercise, 14*(5), 377–381.

Brault, S., Bideau, B., Kulpa, R., & Craig, C. M. (2012). Detecting deception in movement: The case of the side-step in rugby. *PLOS ONE, 7*(6). https://doi.org/10.1371/journal.pone.0037494

British Psychological Society. (2020). *Guidance for psychological professionals during Covid-19 pandemic*. https://www.bps.org.uk/sites/www.bps.org.uk/files/Policy/Policy%20-%20Files/Guidance%20for%20psychological%20professionals%20during%20Covid-19.pdf

Buck, D. J. M., Hutchinson, J. C., Winter, C. R., & Thompson, B. A. (2016). The effects of mental imagery with video-modeling on self-efficacy and maximal front squat ability. *Sports, 4*(2), 23. https://doi.org/10.3390/sports4020023

Bush, N. E., Armstrong, C. M., & Hoyt, T. V. (2019). Smartphone apps for psychological health: A brief state of the science review. *Psychological Services, 16*(2), 188–195. https://doi.org/10.1037/ser0000286

Campbell, M. J., Toth, A. J., Moran, A. P., Kowal, M., & Exton, C. (2018). eSports: A new window on neurocognitive expertise? *Progress in Brain Research, 240*, 161–174. https://doi.org/10.1016/bs.pbr.2018.09.006.

Chen, B. (2019, July 28). Why sleep tracking devices are unlikely to help you to nod off. *The Irish Times*. https://www.irishtimes.com/life-and-style/health-family/why-sleep-tracking-devices-are-unlikely-to-help-you-nod-off-1.3963787

Ciavarro, C., Dobson, M., & Goodman, D. (2008). Implicit learning as a design strategy for learning games: Alert Hockey. *Computers in Human Behaviour, 24*(6), 2862–2872. https://doi.org/10.1016/j.chb.2008.04.011

Cotterill, S. (2018). Virtual reality and sport psychology: Implications for applied practice. *Case Studies in Sport and Exercise Psychology, 2*(1), 21–22. https://doi.org/10.1123/cssep.2018-0002

Dessing, J. C., & Craig, C. M. (2010). Bending it like Beckham: How to visually fool the goalkeeper. *PLOS ONE, 5*(10). https://doi.org/10.1371/journal.pone.0013161

Düking, P., Holmberg, H.-C., & Sperlich, B. (2018). The potential usefulness of virtual reality systems for athletes: A short SWOT analysis. *Frontiers in Physiology, 9*, 128. https://doi.org/10.3389/fphys.2018.00128

Earley, K. (2020a, August 31). Dublin's output sports has created a fitness wearable for elite athletes. *Silicon Republic*. https://www.siliconrepublic.com/start-ups/output-sports-dublin-wearable-elite-athletes

Earley, K. (2020b, April 16). Output Sports is using its technology to help athletes train remotely. *Silicon Republic*. https://www.siliconrepublic.com/start-ups/output-sports-is-using-its-tech-to-help-athletes-train-remotely#:~:text=UCD%20spin%2Dout%20Output%20Sports,optimise%20their%20remote%20training%20programmes

ESPN. (2019, November 4). Jermaine Whitehouse just the latest in long line of sports figures to run into trouble on social media. *ESPN*. https://www.espn.com/nfl/story/_/id/23660805/jermaine-whitehead-just-latest-long-line-sports-figures-run-trouble-social-media

Farley, O. R. L., Spencer, K., & Baudinet, L. (2020). Virtual reality in sports coaching, skill acquisition and application to surfing: A review. *Journal of Human Sport and Exercise, 15*(3), 535–548. https://doi.org/10.14198/jhse.2020.153.06

FITPRO. (2017, October 16). *The research value in wearable fitness tech*. FITPRO. www.fitpro.com/blog/index.php/the-research-value-in-wearable-fitness-tech/

Formula 1.com. (2021, July 1). *Hamilton reveals he's ramped up Mercedes simulator sessions as he seeks the edge over Red Bull*. https://www.formula1.com/en/latest/article.hamilton-reveals-hes-ramped-up-mercedes-simulator-sessions-as-he-seeks-edge.2PraKviJzLkaxPSblIXZiQ.html

Gentile, A., Boca, S., Demetriou, Y., Sturm, D., Pajaujiene, S., Zuoziene, I. J., Sahin, F. N., Güler, Ö., Gómez-López, M., Borrego, C. C., Matosic, D., Bianco, A., & Alesi, M. (2020). The Influence of an enriched sport program on children's sport motivation in the school context: The Esa Program. *Frontiers in Psychology, 11*, 601000. https://doi.org/10.3389/fpsyg.2020.601000

Gokeler, A., Bisschop, M., Myer, G. D., Benjaminse, A., Dijkstra, P. U., van Keeken, H. G., van Raay, J. J. A. M., Burgerhof, J. G. M., & Otten, E. (2014). Immersive virtual reality improves movement patterns in patients after ACL reconstruction: Implications for enhanced criteria based return-to-sport rehabilitation. *Knee Surgery, Sports Traumatology, Arthroscopy*. https://doi.org/10.1007/s00167-014-3374-x

Grassi, A., Gaggioli, A., & Riva, G. (2011). New technologies to manage exam anxiety. *Studies in Health Technology and Informatics, 167*, 57–62. https://doi.org/10.3233/978-1-60750-766-6-57

Hambrick, M. E., Simmons, J. M., Greenhalgh, G. P., & Greenwell, C. T. (2010). Understanding professional athletes' use of Twitter: A content analysis of athletes' tweets. *Journal of Sports Communication, 3*, 454–471. https://doi.org /10.1123/ijsc.3.4.454

Hennessy, L., & Jeffreys, I. (2018). The current use of GPS; its potential and limitations in soccer. *Strength and Conditioning Journal, 40*(3), 83–94. https:// doi.org/10.1519/SSC.0000000000000386

Horrell, L. N., Lazard, A. L., Bhowmick, A., Hayes, S., Mees, S., & Valle, C. G. (2019). Attracting users to online health communities: Analysis of LungCancer.net's Facebook advertisement campaign data. *Journal of Medical Internet Research, 21*(11), e14421. https://doi.org/10.2196/14421

Hurley, O. A. (2018). *Sport cyberpsychology*. Routledge.

Hurley, O. A. (2021). Sport cyberpsychology in action during the COVID-19 pandemic (opportunities, challenges and future possibilities): A narrative review. *Frontiers in Psychology, 12*, 621283. https://doi.org/10.3389/fpsyg .2021.621283

Kearney, R. (2020). *No hiding*. Reach Sport.

Kerner, C., & Goodyear, V. A. (2017). The motivational impact of wearable healthy lifestyle technologies: A self-determination perspective on fitbits with adolescents. *American Journal of Heath. Education, 48*(5), 287–297. https://doi.org/10.1080/19325037.2017.134316

Kirwan, G. (2016). Introduction to cyberpsychology. In I. Connolly, M. Palmer, H. Barton, & G. Kirwan (Eds.), *Introduction to cyberpsychology* (pp. 3–14). Routledge.

Knox, S., Connelly, J., Rochlen, A. B., Clinton, M., Butler, M., & Lineback, S. (2019). How therapists navigate Facebook with clients. *Training and Education in Professional Psychology, 14*(4), 265–276. http://doi.org/10.1037/tep0000267

Kononova, A., Li, L., Kamp, K. J., Bowen, M., Rikard, R. V., Cotton, S. R., & Peng, W. (2019). The use of wearable activity trackers among older adults: A focus group study of tracker perceptions, motivators, and barriers in different stages of behavior change. *JMIR mHealth and uHealth, 7*(4), e9832. https://doi .org/10.2196/mhealth.9832

Lee, J.-M., Byun, W., Keill, A., Dinkel, D., & Seo, Y. (2018). Comparison of wearable trackers' ability to estimate sleep. *International Journal of Environmental Research and Public Health, 15*(6), 1–13. https://doi.org/10.3390 /ijerph15061265

Lu, Y., Pan, T., Liu, J., & Wu, J. (2021). Does usage of online social media help users with depressed symptoms improve their mental health? Empirical evidence from an online depression community. *Frontiers in Public Health, 8*, 581088. https://doi.org/10.3389/fpubh.2020.581088

McCormack, H. M., MacIntyre, T. E., O'Shea, D., Herring, M. P., & Campbell, M. J. (2018). The prevalence and cause(s) of burnout among applied psychologists: A systematic review. *Frontiers in Psychology, 9*, 1897. https://doi .org/10.3389/fpsyg.2018.01897

Miles, H. C., Pop, S. R., Watt, S. J., Lawrence, G. P., & John, N. W. (2012). A review of virtual environments for training in ball sports. *Computers and Graphics, 36*(6), 714–726. https://doi.org/10.1016/j.cag.2012.04.007

Nelson, B. W., Low, C. A., Jacobson, N. E., Areán, P., Torous, J., & Allen, N. B. (2020). Guidelines for wrist-worn consumer wearable assessment of heart rate in biobehavioral research. *Nature Partner Journals: Digital Medicine, 3*, 90. https://doi.org/10.1038/s41746-020-0297-4

O'Brien, S. (2020). *Fuel*. Penguin.

Pagé, C., Bernier, P.-M., & Tremps, M. (2019). Using video simulations and virtual reality to improve decision-making in basketball. *Journal of Sports Sciences*, *37*(21), 2403–2410. https://doi.org/10.1080/02640414.2019.1638193

Panchuk, D., Klusemann, M. J., & Hadlow, S. M. (2018). Exploring the effectiveness of immersive video for training decision-making capability in elite, youth basketball players. *Frontiers in Psychology*, *9*, 2315. https://doi.org/10.3389/fpsyg.2018.02315

Peake, J. M., Kerr, G., & Sullivan, J. P. (2018). A critical review of consumer wearables, mobile applications and equipment for providing biofeedback, monitoring stress, and sleep in physically active populations. *Frontiers in Physiology*, *9*, 743. https://doi.org/10.3389/fphys.2018.00743

Pegoraro, A. (2010). Look who's talking: Athletes on Twitter: A case study. *International Journal of Sport Communication*, *3*(4), 501–514. https://doi.org/10.1123/ijsc.3.4.501

Psychological Society of Ireland. (2020). *Guidelines on the use of online or telephone therapy and assessments.* https://www.psychologicalsociety.ie/source/PSI%20Guidelines%20on%20use%20of%20Online%20or%20Telephone%20Therapy%20%26%20Assessment.pdf

Richards, G. (2020, March 20). F1 drivers prepare to face-off in virtual races following postponements. *The Guardian.* https://www.theguardian.com/sport/2020/mar/20/f1-drivers-virtual-races-following-postponements-bahrain-gp-codemasters-2019

Sharpe, S., Mountifield, C., & Filo, K. (2020). The social media response from athletes and sport organisation to Covid-19: An altruistic tone. *International Journal of Sport Communication*, *13*(3), 474–483. https://doi.org/10.1123/ijsc.2020.0220

Silva, D. R. P., Werneck, A. O., Collings, P., Fernandes, R. A., Ronque, E. R. V., Sardinha, L. B., & Cyrino, E. S. (2019). Identifying children who are susceptible to dropping out from physical activity and sport: A cross-sectional study. *Sao Paulo Medical Journal*, *137*(4), 329–335. https://doi.org/10.1590/1516-3180.2018.0333050719

Solberg, L. B. (2014). The benefits of online health communities. *American Medical Association Journal of Ethics*, *16*(4), 270–274. https://doi.org/10.1001/virtualmentor.2014.16.04.stas1-1404

Tayech, A., Arbi Mejri, M., Makhlouf, I., Mathlouthi, A., Behm, D. G., & Chaouach, A. (2020). Second wave of COVID-19 global pandemic and athletes' confinement: Recommendations to better manage and optimize the modified lifestyle. *International Journal of Environmental Research and Public Health*, *17*(22), 8385. https://doi.org/10.3390/ijerph17228385

Tsai, W.-L., Chung, M.-F., Pan, T.-Y., & Hu, M.-C. (2017). Train in virtual court: Basketball tactic training via virtual reality. In Proceedings of the 2017 ACM workshop on multimedia-based educational and knowledge technologies for personalized and social online training (pp. 3–10). https://doi.org/10.1145/3132390.3132394

Varley, C. (2018, November 22). *Can computer games make you better at sport in real life?* BBC. https://www.bbc.co.uk/bbcthree/article/008d2e50-81c9-4352-bfb8-c37379d8553a

Wallach, O. (2021, May 14). The world's top 50 influencers across social media platforms. Visual Capitalist. https://www.visualcapitalist.com/worlds-top-50-influencers-across-social-media-platforms/

Watters, E. (2020, October 7). *From Fitbit to Mindfit: The stress management score helps people recognise how their body reacts to stress.* https://blog.fitbit.com/fitbit-stress-management-approach/

Watts, S., Mackenzie, A., Thomas, C., Griskaitis, A., Mewton, L., Williams, A., & Andrews, G. (2013). CBT for depression: A pilot RCT comparing mobile phone vs. computer. *BMC Psychiatry, 13*, 49. http://doi.org/10.1186/1471 -244X-13-49

Whales, L., Frawley, S., Cohen, A., & Nikolova, N. (2020). Everyday things change: Australian athlete communication during the coronavirus lockdown. *International Journal of Sport Communication, 13*(3), 541–550. https://doi.org /10.1123/ijsc.2020-0219

Williams, J., & Chinn, S. J. (2010). Meeting relationship-marketing goals through social media: A conceptual model for sport marketers. *International Journal of Sport Communication, 3*(4), 422–437. https://doi.org/10.1123/ijsc.3 .4.422

Williams, N. (2017). The Borg rating of perceived exertion (RPE) scale. *Occupational Medicine, 67*(5), 404–405. https://doi.org/10.1093/occmed/ kqx06

World Health Organisation. (2021). *Obesity and overweight.* https://www.who.int /news-room/fact-sheets/detail/obesity-and-overweight

Yan, A. (2021, July 27). *Tokyo Olympics: Chinese athlete abused online after disappointing finish at Tokyo 2020.* SCMP. https://www.scmp.com/news/ people-culture/trending-china/article/3142605/tokyo-olympics-chinese -athlete-abused-online

Yip, W. (2021, August 3). *Tokyo Olympics: Chinese nationalists turn on their athletes.* BBC. https://www.bbc.com/news/world-asia-china-58024068

14 The Online Workplace

Cliona Flood and Audrey Stenson

Chapter Overview

The online workplace is constantly changing to meet the demands of a post-pandemic competitive business landscape and technology is driving this change. All manner of commercial and human transactions can now be conducted online through omnichannel communication. There is no need to speak to an individual or interact with a traditional organisation such as a shop, a bank, or an agency. Corporations will continue to seek globalised efficient solutions with diverse teams. The workplace today is different, as workers have had to adapt to the constant challenge of change, and flexible remote working may remain the norm in a post-pandemic world.

This chapter will outline the emerging challenges that technology poses to organisations, particularly in the workplace. It will address the transition to new working environments that embrace new technologies. The aim is to explore issues of working in a virtual environment, working with virtual teams, and team dynamics. The challenges and opportunities that technology poses will be explored and the future scope of work will be considered.

Key Terms

In the evolution of an online working environment, certain new organisational structures have emerged. Today many of us work in **boundaryless organisations,** where the walls of the institution are not physical. The boundaryless organisation has a wide scope, often global, and gives rise to the **virtual organisation (VO)** and **virtual teams (VT).** These organisations have a new type of organisational relationship (Priego-Roche et al., 2012) that involves a flexible network of independent groups, which can be linked together by information technology (Pang, 2001).

Virtual team members are drawn from diverse geographical backgrounds and may have different skill-sets to contribute to a project. They are liberated from traditional organisational boundaries and can develop a **boundaryless mindset** (Arthur & Rousseau, 1996), leading to flexible lifestyles, enhanced work satisfaction, and a better work–life balance. Workers have the opportunity to constantly develop skills and have greater adaptability within their careers. Many workers no longer work in a specific workspace or building and can be

DOI: 10.4324/9781003092513-20

considered **telecommuters** or **remote workers** who work independently from the "hub" and touch base only when necessary.

The online workplace can present behavioural challenges to management such as workers using company time and resources to pursue their interests online. This phenomenon has been termed **cyberslacking** and can be associated with **techno-invasion** and **digital intrusion** where work permeates home life and work–life balance suffers. Other **cyberdeviant** behaviours (O'Neill et al., 2014), such as **cyberbullying,** can also be an issue. **Constant connectedness** (or "always on") is an intrinsic part of today's work practices but can lead to difficulties for some workers. However, labour laws such as the **right to disconnect** allow workers to disconnect from work tasks outside of working hours without professional repercussions. In a post-pandemic world, the preference to partially work from home is prevalent (McCarthy et al., 2021). However, inadequate facilities at home have resulted in reports of **Zoom-fatigue,** neck pain, back pain, and eye strain. In addition, remote workers need to be educated on **cybersecurity** issues that may put companies at risk of data breaches.

Organisations Today: The Online Workplace

Where We Have Come from

Consider industries such as car manufacturing, pharmaceuticals, clothing, farming, or publishing. In the past, these industries employed hundreds of thousands of skilled workers, and goods were mass-produced. The process demanded a heavy human input for products to be made, distributed, and sold. These industries were the lifeblood of towns and cities. They offered secure and permanent employment. Work locations were fixed and the management style was autocratic. Organisations had clear boundaries, with layers of management and a "chain of command" mentality (Pang, 2001). They often lacked flexibility and were unable to adapt quickly enough to rapid change. In the past, this model worked as change was gentle and predictable. However, this is not the case today.

What about Today?

Today's organisational and commercial landscapes are very different. Smaller, flatter organisations reduce management layers and achieve greater organisational efficiency and effectiveness. In 1997, Christensen coined the term *"disruptive innovation"* where niche marketplaces came to the fore of commercial attention and smaller companies grew to oust the incumbents through new business models and the use of innovative technology. It became recognised that consumer demand was not always mainstream and niche products and services began to gain a foothold in the marketplace; this was referred to as *"The Long Tail"* (Anderson, 2006). For example, in the current era of converging e-commerce, digital marketplaces, and physical stores, *omnichannel* retailing is at the forefront of providing a seamless customer service and is a key driver of technology. It involves an immersive way of selling products or services across multiple connected channels such as social media, email, phone, and company websites, removing the need for face-to-face communication (Akter et al., 2019). With an increase in the use of online platforms to compete and survive in a competitive business environment, online retail platforms such as Amazon, which sell a large variety of niche and mainstream products (Amazon, 2021), reported a steep increase in profits since the COVID-19 pandemic began in March 2020 (Fortune, 2021). However, retail is not the only industry that is affected; consider Hollywood that produces mainstream movies where niche genres are generally overlooked. Over the last decade, we have seen a shift from broadcast TV and cinema to streaming services such as Netflix. Netflix began as a subscriber-based DVD rental company that serviced niche markets and used postal services to deliver and return rented DVDs (Anderson, 2006). In 2008, it began to stream movies online and subsequently began to produce movies and TV shows such as *House of Cards*, *Orange Is the New Black*, and *Stranger Things* (Shattuc, 2019). It is considered to be the leading force in the resurgence of independent TV and movie storytelling (Shattuc, 2019).

Over the last 60 years, technology has radically changed how people work. Indeed, as steam transformed transport and manufacturing in the 19th century, changes implemented to cope with the business challenges of the global pandemic have potentially radically changed how we work today. Not only have work processes and protocols changed, the speed of how things are done and how we communicate have also changed. The expectation that the Internet and technology can give us instant answers prevails. The tools for this change build on the types of information technologies already in use within the workplace. These include e-mail, Internet banking, messaging applications, video conferencing, and social media. Companies use Facebook, Twitter/X, and Instagram to communicate with their clients. Other platforms and tools, such as Yammer and Slack, are social networks specially designed for business and can be used to communicate internally and with virtual teams. Platforms such as Google Hangouts, Google Meet, Zoom, and Microsoft Teams are used to virtually meet with workplace colleagues, teams, and clients. The everyday dynamics of our working lives have changed, and technology is leading this change. Companies have a global focus because of the growth of virtual organisations and virtual teams. The operation of these virtual entities gives rise to some of the new and emerging challenges for today's workplace.

The Challenges Technology Poses for Today's Workplaces

The Challenge of Change

Today's workplace is fluid and adaptable to cope with economic trends and pressures to survive and thrive. Fast-paced technological environments demand that companies are interconnected and respond to environmental changes quickly to evolve and stay viable. Staff can be drawn from different countries and cultures and may not be domiciled in the home location of the organisation. Workers are no longer tied to one location or indeed one career throughout their working lives. Today's workers develop flexible job portfolios and transfer skills from one organisation or sector to another. Technology keeps workers and management constantly connected to their markets and clients whilst enabling diversity in job options and career development.

FEATURE BOX: NEURODIVERSITY

In today's world, where diversity is an essential for the success of businesses, it is important to include people with a diverse range of talents (Krzeminska & Hawse, 2020). Neurodiversity includes people with dyslexia, dyscalculia, autism, and ADHD, amongst other neurodiverse populations (Rosqvist et al., 2020). Traditionally, unemployment rates for people with disabilities has been high, particularly for people with autistic spectrum disorders. Many autistic people are skilled in STEM areas and can contribute to the development of technologies which can enhance not only their lives but the lives of non-neurodiverse population. In the past neurodiverse individuals have been classified as having a disability; however, today there is recognition that differences can be harnessed and the talents of a neurodiverse population can greatly enhance the modern workforce and the individual.

Over the past few years the digital workplace has changed. Remote working is an acceptable mode of work which can accommodate anxiousness and distance from a working hub and enable contribution and inclusion in the workforce. Digital transformations can provide opportunities for neurodiverse people to add value to modern organisations (Rosqvist et al., 2020). If you would like to read more about how autistic people can contribute to the digital economy, check out Specialisterne (the Danish word for "The Specialists"). Specialisterne is a social enterprise in Denmark providing employment and educational opportunities in the workplace for autistic people. The model has been acknowledged as a leading example of how autistic individuals can be included in society and make quality contributions to their organisations (Krzeminska & Hawse, 2020).

The efficiencies of the modern organisation were evident during the COVID-19 pandemic where the existence of many businesses was threatened. This led to a shift in business models and the adoption of innovative agile dynamic approaches to allow them to survive the sudden changes imposed upon them (Kurkertz et al., 2020; Seetharaman, 2020). Some technological companies utilised an agile *"fail fast"* approach supported by people and technology. Companies embrace quick failure as an opportunity to learn which can initiate faster learning and lead to innovative ways of improving products and services (Frankiewicz & Chamorro-Premuzic, 2020; Matson, 1991). For example, for several reasons, including lack of use, dated features, and software errors, Google often discontinues software development and support on products and services and subsequently invests time and resources into other aspects of the business (The Google Cemetery, n.d.).

Just as the Industrial Revolution, two world wars, the Internet, and a global depression changed the world, innovative business transformations accelerated by the COVID-19 pandemic mark the beginning of change.

It's a New World: The Virtual Environment

The Virtual Organisation

The virtual work environment is not a novel concept by any means. As far back as 2001, Pang outlined the aspects of a **virtual organisation** (VO). He argued that it is a flexible network of independent entities linked together by information technology to share skills, knowledge, and expertise. VOs are collaborative entities where people do not have to be in the same place or time zone. Skills and people can be geographically dispersed, and the VO can access a wider range of skills and only use, and indeed pay for these skills when they are needed. Employees who work as part of a VO are referred to as **telecommuters** or **remote workers.** The management of the virtual workplace has certain challenges that older organisations have not encountered. As a result, the remote management of teams who are geographically dispersed, diverse in nature and culture, calls for an entirely different skill-set than face-to-face management (Belling, 2021; Cascio, 2000; Parker et al., 2020). Not all jobs can translate into the virtual workspace; however those that do have a competitive edge. The roles better suited to remote working include graphic design, accountancy, digital marketing, software development, sales, and consultancy (Indeed, 2021).

Some caution is needed when considering the value of VOs. Cakula and Pratt (2021) posit that communication efficiency in VOs is not only dependent upon the system and processes in place but also on manager competency. In addition, VOs require well-designed websites, appropriate collaborative tools, a stable Internet connection, and tech-savvy individuals.

The **"boundaryless"** organisation challenges for management are to create more flexible organisations with horizontal networks rather than managerial hierarchies (Hirschorn & Gilmore, 1992). These organisations link functions and create strategic alliances with their clients and competitors. Although geographical boundaries can disappear, new boundaries are evident. These are more psychological than organisational and reflect the company's structure and culture. The move from a clear-cut management structure to one of independent entities contributing to a project is challenging and often ambiguous and, hence, traditional teams are giving way to virtual teams.

Virtual Teams

As the world gradually moves out of the COVID-19 pandemic, corporations and businesses are planning for the *"next-normal"* to remain innovative within a challenging business landscape. The continual striving towards competitive advantage and profit puts pressure on organisations to adapt quickly. This results in teams being formed, reformed, and disbanded quickly. Work teams are more fluid and dynamic in a complex digital environment, and many organisations operate **virtual teams (VT).** Teams are considered to be a temporary group of people brought together for a specific purpose to achieve a common goal through completing individual well-defined tasks (Salas et al., 1992, as cited in Tannenbaum et al., 2012). Tannenbaum et al. (2012) argue that VTs are different to face-to-face teams. The environment in which VTs operate is more dynamic, they use technology and remote working, they tend to have fewer managerial layers, and they may be more powerful. The advantage of VTs is that multiple skills and talents can be drawn into teams regardless of location and time zone. However, workers may encounter an increase in challenges that they did not face when working in an office. These challenges include physical space, equipment, Internet connectivity, and a good working relationship with their manager and team. All of these can impact work performance and hence affect the management style employed by their manager. Research suggests that trust and mutual respect between management and the team are pertinent to the success of the VT (Belling, 2021; Parker et al., 2020; Phillips, 2020).

In addition, **psychological safety** within teams is considered to be a group phenomenon that reduces interpersonal risk by removing repercussions for career, self-image, or status and results in feeling accepted and respected as a team member (Kahn, 1990). Feitosa and Salas (2021) claim that VTs can yield success through interpersonal processes such as establishing and maintaining trust within teams, by focussing on the benefits of VTs, by encouraging inclusion and diversity through psychological safety, and finally by frequently and consistently assessing teamwork using effective communications. Furthermore, challenges related to distance can relate to time zones, differences in work patterns, and fostering a social identity among workgroups (Morrison-Smith & Ruiz, 2020).

The Challenges That Technology Poses for Modern People

Career Planning

The workforce of today and tomorrow has many opportunities that were not open to previous generations. Stoltz et al. (2013) suggest that workers must be responsible for managing their own careers and continually developing their skills, which can be applied in different working environments and organisations. They draw on the work of Arthur and Rousseau (1996), who called for workers to develop a **"boundaryless mindset".** In other words, workers must be psychologically and environmentally responsive to change and learning that break free from traditional organisational boundaries. Constant change can lead to increased pressure and stress on employees and coping behaviour in response to these pressures can have an impact on the effect of stress on an individual or an organisation (Potgieter, 2021). Whilst some research found that remote working correlates positively with perceived worker well-being (Mostafa, 2021), other research suggests that companies need to continue to build a positive work environment that is conducive to work friendships, coping behaviour, and career adaptability (Potgieter, 2021). The **gig economy** has seen a rise in popularity over the last decade with individuals working remotely through online labour platforms such as fiverr.com and Amazon Turk where workers are paid for specific tasks. All requests, delivery, and payment occur online. Platforms such as these allow flexibility for workers but at the same time may be isolating (Glavin et al., 2021).

The Darker Side of Technology

The presence of the Internet at work gives people the opportunity to pursue goals that can be counterintuitive to the organisation that they work for. Current **cyberdeviant** behaviour typologies are restrictive in their application to new technologies and hybrid work and need to be considered in line with a perspective of "unacceptable outputs or behaviours, interpersonal deviance and misuse of resources" (Raza, St-Onge, & Ahmed, 2022, p. 14). Subsequently, cyberdeviant behaviour, such as **cyberslacking** and **cyberbullying,** may be present amongst remote workers and may increase due to the lack of supervision (O'Neill et al., 2014; Raza et al., 2022).

Cyberslacking refers to the use of workplace devices such as computers and phones for personal use during work hours. Given that most workplaces have moved partially if not fully online due to the COVID-19 pandemic, some workers may be constantly connected to work through technology where there are no boundaries around regular work hours; therefore **techno-invasion** (Tarafdar et al., 2011) can permeate home life and personal time (Gügerçin, 2019). Poor work–life balance may be the result of an inability to control workflow and establish boundaries between work and home life; this can impact well-being and work performance. Digital notifications for texts, email, and instant messaging may increase cognitive attention switching but simultaneously result in physiological effects of fatigue and hypervigilance (Uther et al., 2020). **Digital intrusion** can occur with work tasks where some tasks demand immediate attention and may distract from other tasks at hand. This could result in **cognitive overload** for the employee and, in turn, cause fatigue and lack of concentration. Cognitive load theory posits that information can only move into long-term memory when information has been processed by working memory (Sweller, 1988). The constant switching of attention from task to task due to digital disruption may interfere with this process.

Additionally, **Zoom fatigue** has gained traction throughout the COVID-19 pandemic and refers to the exhaustion that workers feel during and after attending online video conferencing calls. The feeling of fatigue may be related to having the camera on during video calls resulting in cognitive overload when trying to interpret social cues, looking at oneself, and feeling physically constrained due to situating oneself close to the camera (Bailenson, 2021). Leaving the camera on may impact meeting performance in addition to contributing to fatigue (Shockley et al., 2021). Moving into a post-pandemic world, video conferencing is likely here to stay considering that many workers would prefer the option to partially work from home (McCarthy et al., 2021). Management should consider developing and revising policies regarding the frequency of use and guidelines on how to minimise fatigue and lack of concentration. Furthermore, evidence from COVID-19 research suggests that eye strain increased during the pandemic especially for those with dry eye (Alabdulkader, 2021; Saldanha et al., 2021).

To address labour issues regarding transformed business practices, in January 2021 the EU parliament agreed on a law to protect workers concerning the **right to disconnect** from work tasks outside of designated working hours. France, Spain, and Italy had previously adopted labour laws that include the right to disconnect (Comunidad Autónoma de País Vasco, 2018; République Française, 2019; Senato della Repubblica, n.d.). In April 2021, the Irish government introduced the *Code of Practice on Right to Disconnect*. There are three main aspects covered by the code: (1) the right of an employee to not have to perform work tasks outside of work hours; (2) the right not to be penalised for not attending work matters outside of working hours; and (3) the duty to respect other workers' rights to disconnect (Workplace Relations Commission, 2021).

Poor workplace relations can lead to cyberdeviant behaviour, such as **cyberbullying.** D'Souza et al. (2020) suggest that corporate cyberbullying policies need to address the challenges of gender-based cyberbullying; other research also found that cyberbullying is a gender-based phenomenon with females reporting increased stress and job dissatisfaction (Loh & Snyman, 2020). In addition, corporate policymakers need to consider that cyberbullying can cross organisational boundaries and current policies may be ineffective (D'Souza et al., 2020) possibly due to the organisational climate and technology usage (Iftikhar et al., 2021). Social relationships in work are pertinent to the outcome of cyberbullying where bystanders would only intervene if the victim was a work friend rather than a work colleague (Madden & Loh, 2018). One of the challenges moving into a post-pandemic world will be to continue to develop social aspects of the workplace, even if virtually. Furthermore, there is a need for robust preventative and contingent organisational and social policies to address workplace relations issues. See Chapter 5 for more information on deviant online behaviours.

The Challenges for the Future of Work

Future Scope

Due to the competitive environment of the business landscape, organisations will continue to be driven by new technologies to rapidly adapt to a dynamic environment. This will potentially result in hybrid organisations. Reinvention to align with disruptive innovations and technologies seems to be the route that many companies need to embrace. However, many of tomorrow's jobs have not even been imagined yet. The PWC Report (n.d.) predicts rapid technological breakthroughs in artificial intelligence, robotics, and automation by 2030. It predicts that these breakthroughs may improve our lifestyles, but they need to be managed so that economic advantages are shared equally. Some of the factors driving this change will be a scarcity of natural resources and climate change, shifts in global economic power, demographic shifts, and continuing rapid urbanisation.

Some different organisational cultures and structures are already emerging. Employee rights are coming to the fore regarding the right to disconnect, and remote working options are more accessible to employees. Additionally, remote working and other efforts to control the COVID-19 pandemic are associated with positive effects on climate change concerning a reduction in fossil energy use although continuing global efforts to maintain this is necessary in a post-pandemic world, by nations meeting their emissions pledges (Reilly et al., 2021). Considering this move towards the preference to work from home, it is imperative to consider the cost implications whereby the expenses of working from home, such as additional office space and increased utility bills as well as Internet bills, have shifted from the employer to the employee (Lord, 2020) but these may be offset by travel expenses and the social costs of work. Additionally, Moretti et al. (2020) found that working remotely caused an increase in physical neck and back pain, and they suggest that the home environment is not adequate for remote work. Having said that, one of the potential advantages of remote working is that the personal lives of staff can be accommodated. Historically, the challenges of child-rearing and family responsibilities have fallen to women; evidence from studies on COVID-19 suggests that this continued to be the case. Research suggests that women bore the brunt of childcare and family responsibilities while working from home, which led, in some cases, to women leaving the workforce or changing their work hours (Collins et al., 2021; Poggi, 2021; Zamarro & Prados, 2021). Corporations need to devise remote work plans with employees to alleviate work-related stress in relation to equality, equity, and education (Bonacini et al., 2021; Como et al., 2021).

To address the sudden challenges of COVID-19, cybersecurity may have taken a backseat in the sudden move to online daily operations of businesses (Felding, 2021). The General Data Protection Regulation (GDPR) upholds the rights for individuals to have their personal data protected by organisations (Data Protection Commission, n.d.), and businesses are held liable for any data breaches. Businesses can be more vulnerable to hackers through phishing emails or insecurities in old versions of operating systems or firewalls when employees work from home. Considering the rise of the hybrid organisation, cybersecurity policies should be reviewed to ensure that remote workers have the technology, training, and skills to avoid potential data breaches (Felding, 2021).

Back to the Future?

Before the Industrial Revolution, the workforce was made up of artisans and agricultural workers, many of whom worked and networked from their own homes. It was the period that saw a transition from hand-made goods to machine manufacturing. Large factories and mills produced chemicals, iron, steel, and textiles. This major turning point in history was powered by harnessing the power of steam, improved transportation, and the move from wood and bio-fuels to coal. The impact on society was enormous. The populations in towns and cities grew exponentially as industry and jobs were located near ports and transport lines. As decades went by, the first mass-produced personal computers in the early 1980s (Knight, 2014) launched the start of an informational and technological revolution, to today's world of affordable personal technology. Now we find ourselves with more opportunities to socialise, communicate, learn, and work through digital devices.

History may be repeating itself albeit with a focus on technology. Global responses to COVID-19 forced businesses to rethink and innovate their daily operations and used technology to drive that change. In the same vein, as the steam engine catapulted the world into a new age of manufacturing, COVID-19 propels us into a new age of digital and technical opportunity that offers flexibility to the workforce to work from home. Rather than work in large organisations, factories, and corporations, small specialised companies, entrepreneurs, sole traders, and artists can work in a networked society powered by technology. Have we "gone back to the future"? Who knows? It has possibly taken us 300 years to rediscover that "small is beautiful". Roll on the future.

Conclusion

This chapter has considered the online workplace. We have looked at how traditional organisations have evolved, driven by the power of technology. We have considered the challenges that this change brings to organisations. We considered the virtual organisation that is "boundaryless" and the virtual teams that make up these organisations. We looked at the challenges that technology brings to 21st-century workplaces and the people who work in them. Issues of mental health and well-being are addressed in Chapter 12. Finally, we tried to predict the shape of future organisations, and although the future predictions may not be quite right (only time will tell), one thing is certain, in the words of the Greek philosopher, Heraclitus, "the only thing that is constant is change" (Graham, n.d.).

Activity

This activity can be done individually, in small groups, or as a class activity.

Consider the jobs/professions of your grandparents. What work were they involved in? What technological aspects were involved in their work? What do these jobs/professions look like today?

Discussion Questions

1. Outline your technological predictions for the next 25 years. How will these changes impact organisational life and the people who work within these new organisations?
2. What are the issues involved with staff using the Internet during working hours?
3. Discuss the advantages and disadvantages of working in a hybrid organisation.
4. How can the challenges of working in a virtual team be addressed?

Recommended Reading List

Anna Sutton's publication outlines the main issues in organisational psychology today. It is an excellent introduction to topics in work and organisational psychology.

Sutton, A. (2021). *Work psychology in action* (2nd ed.). Red Globe Press.

For the main issues in agile working today, this publication provides insights into new ways of working through utilising new technology to address business needs and goals.

Grant, C., & Russell, E. (Eds.). (2020). *Agile working and well-being in the digital age*. Springer. https://doi.org/10.1007/978-3-030-60283-3

For an insight into the literature surrounding VTs, this publication considers all of the factors affecting VTs and how management can address these.

> Morrison-Smith, S., & Ruiz, J. (2020). Challenges and barriers in virtual teams: A literature review. *SN Applied Sciences*, *2*(6). https://doi.org/10.1007/s42452-020-2801-5

Glossary

Boundaryless mindset: The mindset of staff that are not restrained by traditional organisational boundaries. They may work collaboratively across teams and as part of multi-disciplinary teams.

Boundaryless organizations: Organisations where barriers between internal and external functions have been reduced. Organisational layers are reduced in the hope of achieving greater organisational efficiency and effectiveness.

Constant connectedness ("always on"): An intrinsic part of work practices today involving an expectation of being available 24 hours a day.

Cyberbullying: Using technology to bully a person through hostile and/or threatening messages.

Cyberdeviant: A form of maladjusted Internet use at work that may be perpetuated by the lack of supervision in staff that work remotely.

Cyberslacking: Use of the Internet at work for personal reasons. Managers often fear that this can lead to loss of productivity and ultimately cost the organisation money.

Digital disruption: Alerts from devices signifying a new online message or email that disrupts the task at hand.

Gig economy: Workers work remotely on specific paid tasks through online labour platforms.

Right to disconnect: Workers' right to disconnect from work tasks outside of working hours.

Techno-invasion: When technology invades our personal and family time.

Telecommuters: Work independently from the "hub" and touch base only when necessary. They stay connected to the workplace by using a variety of digital technologies.

Virtual organisation: Where members work for the same company but are geographically distant from each other and communicate by information technology.

Virtual teams: A virtual team is made up of a number of different people who work together collaboratively using web-based technologies. They may never meet in person.

Zoom fatigue: A term used to encompass all video conferencing effects of exhaustion.

References

Akter, S., Hossain, M. I., Lu, S., Aditya, S., Hossain, T. M. T., & Kattiyapornpong, U. (2019). Does service quality perception in omnichannel retailing matter? A systematic review and agenda for future research. In W. Piotrowicz & R. Cuthbertson (Eds.), *Exploring omnichannel retailing*. Springer.

Alabdulkader, B. (2021). Effect of digital device use during COVID-19 on digital eye strain. *Clinical and Experimental Optometry, 104*(6), 698–704. https://doi .org/10.1080/08164622.2021.1878843

Amazon. (2021). *Amazon web services*. Retrieved August 21, 2021, from https:// www.aboutamazon.com/what-we-do/amazon-web-services

Anderson, C. (2006). *The long tail*. Hyperion.

Arthur, M. B., & Rousseau, D. M. (1996). A career lexicon for the 21st century. *Academy of Management Executive, 10*(4), 28–39.

Bailenson, J. N. (2021). Nonverbal overload: A theoretical argument for the causes of zoom fatigue. *Technology Mind and Behavior, 2*(1). https://doi.org/10 .1037/tmb0000030

Belling, S. (2021). *Remotely possible*. Apress. https://doi.org/10.1007/978-1-4842 -7008-0

Bonacini, L., Gallo, G., & Scicchitano, S. (2021). Working from home and income inequality: Risks of a 'new normal' with COVID-19. *Journal of Popular Economics, 34*(1), 303–360. https://doi.org/10.1007/s00148-020-00800-7

Cakula, S., & Pratt, M. (2021). Communication technologies in a remote workplace. *Baltic Journal of Modern Computing, 9*(2), 210–219. https://doi.org /10.22364/bjmc.2021.9.2.05

Cascio, W. F. (2000). Managing a virtual workplace. *Academy of Management Executive, 14*(3), 81–90. https://doi.org/10.5465/AME.2000.4468068

Christensen, C. (1997). *The innovators dilemma*. Harvard Business School Press.

Collins, C., Landivar, L. C., Ruppanner, L., & Scarborough, W. J. (2021). COVID-19 and the gender gap in work hours. *Gender, Work & Organisation, 28*(S1), 549–560. https://doi.org/10.1111/gwao.12506

Como, R., Hambley, L., & Domene, J. (2021). An Exploration of work-life wellness and remote work during and beyond COVID-19. *Canadian Journal of Career Development, 20*(1), 46–56. https://cjcd-rcdc.ceric.ca/index.php/cjcd /article/view/92

Comunidad Autónoma de País Vasco. (2018). *Ley Orgánica 3/2018, de 5 de diciembre, de Protección de Datos Personales y garantía de los derechos digitales*. https://datos .gob.es/en/catalogo/a16003011-ley-organica-3-2018-de-5-de-diciembre-de -proteccion-de-datos-personales-y-garantia-de-los-derechos-digitales1

Data Protection Commission. (n.d.). *The data protection commission*. https:// www.dataprotection.ie/

D'Souza, N., Forsyth, D. K., & Blackwood, K. (2020). Workplace cyber abuse: Challenges and implications for management. *Personnel Review*, ahead of print(ahead of print). https://doi.org/10.1108/PR-03-2020-0210

Feitosa, J., & Salas, E. (2021). Today's virtual teams: Adapting lessons learned to the pandemic context. *Organizational Dynamics, 50*(1). https://doi.org/10 .1016/j.orgdyn.2020.100777

Felding, J. (2021). The post-covid risk of hybrid workplaces. *Computer Fraud & Security, 20* 20.

Fortune. (2021). *Fortune 500: Amazon, rank 2*. Retrieved August 17, 2021, from https://fortune.com/company/amazon-com/fortune500/

Frankiewicz, B., & Chamorro-Premuzic, T. (2020). Digital transformation is about talent, not technology. *Harvard Business Review*. https://hbr.org/2020 /05/digital-transformation-is-about-talent-not-technology

Glavin, P., Bierman, A., & Schieman, S. (2021). Über-alienated: Powerless and alone in the gig economy. *Work and Occupations*. https://doi.org/10.1177 /07308884211024711

Graham, D. W. (n.d.). Heraclitus (fl.c. 500 B.C.E). *Internet encyclopaedia of philosophy*. Retrieved August 31, 2021, from www.iep.utm.edu/heraclit/

Gügerçin, U. (2019). Does techno-stress justify cyberslacking? An empirical study based on the neutralisation theory. *Behaviour & Information Technology, 39*(7), 824–836. https://doi.org/10.1080/0144929X.2019.1617350

Hirschorn, L., & Gilmore, T. (1992). The new boundaries of the "Boundaryless" company. *Harvard Business Review, 70*(3), 104–115.

Iftikhar, M., Qureshi, M. I., Qayyum, S., Fatima, I., Sriyanto, S., Indrianti, Y., Khan, A., & Dana, L.-P. (2021). Impact of multifaceted workplace bullying on the relationships between technology usage, organisational climate and employee physical and emotional health. *International Journal of Environmental Research and Public Health, 18*(6). https://doi.org/10.3390/ijerph18063207

Indeed. (2021, February 23). *15 great remote jobs that pay well.* https://www.indeed.com/career-advice/finding-a-job/best-remote-jobs

Kahn, W. A. (1990). Psychological conditions of personal engagement and disengagement at work. *Academy of Management Journal, 33*(4), 692–724. https://doi.org/10.5465/256287

Knight, D. (2014). Personal computer history: The first 25 years. *Low End Mac.* http://lowendmac.com/2014/personal-computer-history-the-first-25-years/

Krzeminska, A., & Hawse, S. (2020). Mainstreaming neurodiversity for an inclusive and sustainable future workforce: Autism-spectrum employees. In L. Wood, L. Tan, Y. Breyer, & S. Hawse (Eds.), *Industry and higher education.* Springer. https://doi.org/10.1007/978-981-15-0874-5_11

Kurkertz, A., Brändle, L., Gaudi, A., Hinderer, S., Reyes, C. A. M., Prochotta, A., Steinbrink, K. M., & Berger, E. S. C. (2020). Startups in times of crisis – A rapid response to the COVID-19 pandemic. *Journal of Business Venturing Insights, 13.* https://doi.org/10.1016/j.jbvi.2020.e00169

Loh, J., & Snyman, R. (2020). The tangled web: Consequences of workplace cyberbullying in adult male and female employees. *Gender in Management, 35*(6). https://doi.org/10.1108/GM-12-2019-0242

Lord, P. (2020). The social perils and promise of remote work. *Journal of Behavioral Economics for Policy, 4,* 63–67. https://doi.org/10.2139/ssrn.3613235

Madden, C., & Loh, J. (2018). Workplace cyberbullying and bystander helping behaviour. *The International Journal of Human Resource Management, 31*(19), 2434–2458. https://doi.org/10.1080/09585192.2018.1449130

Matson, J. V. (1991). *The art of innovation: Using intelligent fast failure.* Pennsylvania State University Press.

McCarthy, A., O'Connor, N., Ó Síocháin, T., & Frost, D. (2021). *Remote working: Ireland's national survey - Phase III report.* NUI Galway Whitaker Institute & Western Development Commission.

Moretti, A., Menna, F., Aulicino, M., Paoletta, M., Liguori, S., & Iolascon, G. (2020). Characterization of home working population during COVID-19 emergency: A cross-sectional analysis. *International Journal of Environmental Research and Public Health, 17*(17), 6284. https://doi.org/10.3390/ijerph17176284

Morrison-Smith, S., & Ruiz, J. (2020). Challenges and barriers in virtual teams: A literature review. *SN Applied Sciences, 2*(6). https://doi.org/10.1007/s42452-020-2801-5

Mostafa, B. A. (2021). The effect of remote working on employees wellbeing and work-life integration during pandemic in Egypt. *International Business Research, 14*(3), 41–52. https://doi.org/10.5539/ibr.v14n3p41

O'Neill, T. A., Hambley, L. A., & Bercovich, A. (2014). Prediction of cyberslacking when employees are working away from the office. *Computers in Human Behaviour, 34,* 291–298. https://doi.org/10.1016/j.chb.2014.02.015

Pang, L. (2001). Understanding virtual organizations. *Information Systems Control Journal*, *6*, 42–47.

Parker, S. K., Knight, C., & Keller, A. (2020). Remote managers are having trust issues. *Harvard Business Review*. https://hbr.org/2020/07/remote-managers -are-having-trust-issues

Phillips, S. (2020). Working through the pandemic: Accelerating the transition to remote working. *Business Information Review*, *37*(3), 129–134. https://doi .org/10.1177/0266382120953087

Poggi, J. (2021). Ad world looks to the future of work post-COVID. *Advertising Age*, *92*(3). https://adage.com/article/cmo-strategy/ad-world-looks-future -work-post-covid/2323281

Potgieter, I. L. (2021). Surviving the digital era: The link between positive coping, workplace friendships and career adaptability. In N. Ferreira, I. L. Potgieter, & M. Coetzee (Eds.), *Agile coping in the digital workplace: Emerging issues for research and practice* (pp. 57–78). Springer.

Priego-Roche, L. M., Thom, L. H., Rieu, D., & Mendling, J. (2012). Business process design from virtual organization intentional models. In *Advanced information systems engineering* (pp. 549–564). Springer. https://doi.org/10 .1007/978-3-642-31095-9_36

PWC Report. (n.d.). *Workforce of the future*. https://www.pwc.com/gx/en/services /people-organisation/publications/workforce-of-the-future.html

Raza, B., St-Onge, S., & Ahmed, A. (2022). A scoping review and qualitative investigations to develop A workplace deviance typology. *Deviant Behavior*, 1–19. https://doi.org/10.1080/01639625.2022.2106908

Reilly, J. M., Chen, Y.-H. H., & Jacoby, H. D. (2021). The COVID-19 effect on the Paris agreement. *Humanities and Social Sciences Communications*, *8*(16). https://doi.org/10.1057/s41599-020-00698-2

République française. (2019). *Code du travail*. https://www.legifrance.gouv.fr/ codes/article_lc/LEGIARTI000039785096/

Rosqvist, H., Chown, N., & Stenning, A. (Eds.). (2020). *Neurodiversity studies: A new critical paradigm* (1st ed.). Routledge. https://doi.org/10.4324 /9780429322297

Salas, E., Dickinson, T. L., Converse, S. A., & Tannenbaum, S. I. (1992). Toward an understanding of team performance and training. In R. W. Swezey & E. Salas (Eds.), *Teams: Their training and performance* (pp. 3–29). Ablex.

Saldanha, I. J., Petris, R., Makara, M., Channa, P., & Akpek, E. K. (2021). Impact of the COVID-19 pandemic on eye strain and dry eye symptoms. *The Ocular Surface*, *22*, 38–46. https://doi.org/10.1016/j.jtos.2021.06.004

Seetharaman, P. (2020). Business models shifts: Impact of Covid-19. *International Journal of Information Management*, *54*. https://doi.org/10.1016/j.ijinfomgt .2020.102173

Senato della Repubblica. (n.d.). *Misure per la tutela del lavoro autonomo non imprenditoriale e misure volte a favorire l'articolazione flessibile nei tempi e nei luoghi del lavoro subordinato*. http://www.senato.it/japp/bgt/showdoc/17 /DDLMESS/0/1022243/index.html?part=ddlmess_ddlmess1-articolato _articolato1

Shattuc, J. (2019). Netflix Inc. and online television. In *A companion to television* (pp. 145–164). https://doi.org/10.1002/9781119269465.ch7

Shockley, K. M., Gabriel, A. S., Robertson, D., Rosen, C. C., Chawla, N., Ganster, M. L., & Ezerins, M. E. (2021). The fatiguing effects of camera use in virtual meetings: A within-person field experiment. *Journal of Applied Psychology*, *106*(8), 1137–1155. https://doi.org/10.1037/apl0000948

Stoltz, K. B., Wolff, L. A., Monroe, A. E., Farris, H. R., & Mazahrea, L. G. (2013). Adlerian lifestyle, stress coping, and career adaptability: Relationships and dimensions. *Career Development Quarterly, 61*(3), 194–209. https://doi.org/10.1002/j.2161-0045.2013.00049.x

Sweller, J. (1988). Cognitive load during problem solving: Effects on learning. *Cognitive Science, 12*(2), 257–285. https://doi.org/10.1016/0364-0213(88)90023-7

Tannenbaum, S. I., Mathieu, J. E., Salas, E., & Cohen, D. (2012). Teams are changing: Are research and practice evolving fast enough? *Industrial and Organizational Psychology, 5*(1), 2–24. https://doi.org/10.1111/j.1754-9434.2011.01396.x

Tarafdar, M., Tu, Q., Ragu-Nathan, T. S., & Ragu-Nathan, B. S. (2011). Crossing to the dark side: Examining creators, outcomes, and inhibitors of technostress. *Communications of the ACM, 54*(9), 113–120. https://doi.org/10.1145/1995376.1995403

The Google Cemetery. (n.d.). *The Google Cemetery.* Retrieved August, 17, 2021, from https://gcemetery.co/

Uther, M., Cleveland, M., & Jones, R. (2020). Digital distractions: The effect and use of digital message alerts and their relationship with work-life balance. In C. Grant & E. Russell (Eds.), *Agile working and well-being in a digital age* (pp. 63–76). Palgrave Macmillan. https://doi.org/10.1007/978-3-030-60283-3

Workplace Relations Commission. (2021). *Code of practice for employers and employees on the right to disconnect.* https://workplacerelations.ie/wrc/en/what_you_should_know/codes_practice/code-of-practice-for-employers-and-employees-on-the-right-to-disconnect.pdf

Yammer. (2015). *The enterprise social network.* https://www.yammer.com/

Zamarro, G., & Prados, M. J. (2021). Gender differences in couples' division of childcare, work and mental health during COVID-19. *Review of Economics of the Household, 19*(1), 11–40. https://doi.org/10.1007/s11150-020-09534-7

The Internet as an Educational Space

Marion Palmer

Chapter Overview

The Internet is a significant educational space. It has content and many tools that engage and support learners. This chapter presents an overview of learning enabled by the Internet. It discusses informal and formal learning as well as the developments in open and online learning. It considers learning tools such as YouTube, Twitter/X, and VLEs. The interaction of learning and technology is explored and learning theories are considered. The impact of the COVID-19 global pandemic in 2020 and 2021 on education and learning is discussed. This chapter argues that learning is being transformed by the access to technology and the ability of learners to create and develop in the online world. The challenge is to fully use the Internet as an educational space.

Key Terms

Learning is the focus of this chapter as it considers the Internet as an educational space. Learning is considered a change in behaviour (Gagné et al., 1992). **Informal learning** is learning that people do as and when it suits them. **Formal learning** occurs when students take courses at schools, colleges, or the workplace (Selwyn, 2011). **Experiential learning** occurs when learners learn through and from their experiences. Learning is enabled by **instruction**. Gagné et al. (1992) consider this to be all the events that affect learning. **Teaching** is a key part of instruction; teachers (also called instructors) organise and plan the instruction for students and classes. **Assessment** is any process by which the learning is judged (Freeman & Lewis, 1998). **Educational technology** includes the artefacts and devices – that is, the technologies themselves, how the technologies are used in education and learning, and the context for their use (Selwyn, 2011). Learning using technology and electronic media has led to many associated terms often with similar meanings (Moore et al., 2011). The first of these terms is **elearning**, meaning learning with electronic technology. **Online learning** is generally taken to mean learning using the Web (Harasim, 2017). **Technology-enhanced learning** tends to emphasise the use of technology to support learning, often complementing face-to-face

DOI: 10.4324/9781003092513-21

classes. **Distance learning** takes place when the teachers and learners are in different physical spaces. It has been transformed by the Internet. **Multimedia** is any material that contains words and graphics. Words are **text** printed on a screen or spoken. **Graphics** are both static items such as illustrations, drawings, charts, maps, and photographs and dynamic items such as animation and video (Clark & Mayer, 2011). One of the key features of the Internet as an educational space is the access it provides to many multimedia resources. The Internet has led to the development of a range of learning environments and courses. Many colleges and schools have **VLEs,** Web-based electronic courses for students enrolled on specific courses or programmes. They are closed – that is, restricted to specific students. There are many online courses and finally, there are massive open online courses (MOOCs), courses accessible to all at little or no charge and taken by many students (Littlejohn, 2013).

The Internet and Its Impact on Learning

Learning is a key activity of human beings. It is a process that enables human beings to change behaviours and their capabilities (Gagné et al., 1992). Learning can be informal or unofficial. You can decide to learn something new and just look it up yourself or ask someone about it or you can learn formally by taking part in a course, doing the assessment, and possibly aiming for accreditation such as a degree or a certificate of achievement. Teachers, lecturers, and trainers take part in formal learning and design the instruction, teach, and manage the assessment. External and internal factors influence learning, the **conditions of learning** (Gagné et al., 1992). **Mastery** is achieved when learners are successful at learning tasks.

Before the Internet

Before the Internet, any kind of learning required movement. Looking something up required going to a library; talking to someone required a phone call or meeting them. Keeping up with an interest group required attending meetings and checking newsletters. Formal learning meant going to school or college, attending class, going to the library, and meeting fellow students and teachers/lecturers, essentially **face-to-face learning (f2f).** There was some technology in education but it had little impact on formal learning and some impact on informal learning.

The Internet

The Internet was developed to network computers and enable communication around the world. Different kinds of media, memory, and storage were developed and sharing media files, both audio and video, became much easier. YouTube and social media developed and social networking sites became commonplace. Harasim (2017) argues that the Internet is the fourth major paradigm of communication following speech, writing, and printing. She notes how quickly the Internet has had an impact on society and that the Internet represents a worldwide knowledge transformation on a global scale.

Tools and Content on the Internet

We have a range of digital technologies (Bower & Torrington, 2020) and access to them has become routine through devices such as mobile phones and tablets as well as traditional desktop and laptop computers. There is a lot of content for us to access. We have tools for designing, editing, and content creation (McWilliam & Haukka, 2008). It is argued and accepted that the Internet is an enabler of learning. The issue is often how to identify and select appropriate tools (and/or content) for learning (Bower & Torrington, 2020).

Informal and Formal Learning

The impact on informal learning has been considerable. Harasim (2017) considers online learning as the use of communication networks for educational purposes mediated by the Web. Hart (2014) argues that the Web enables "learning the new" – that is, keeping up to date with what is happening in a discipline or in a profession as well as finding out what is new to an individual. She argues that "learning the new involves being in the flow of new ideas and 'joining the dots' between unstructured pieces of knowledge that are encountered" (Hart, 2014). This informal learning takes place at an individual, group, or indeed system level. What is clear is that as technology is developed, how it is used for educational purposes and what contexts it is used in are surprising us all. It depends on people and how they behave and emerges through their experiences of the Internet, which can be considered a classic site of experiential learning. The impact on formal learning is more difficult to discern. This is now considered.

Learning in Schools, Colleges, and the Workplace

Workplaces have changed, as have schools and colleges. The role of the Internet in learning became both more accepted and more explicit. Effective online learning ranges from fully online to blended to **Web-enabled face-to-face** (Hodges et al., 2020). Key issues for formal learning such as the curriculum, the role of the teacher, the role of the student, and the control of the process, particularly assessment, are still contentious.

Emergency Remote Teaching and Learning

In the COVID-19 global pandemic of 2020, 2021, workplaces, schools, and colleges closed and people remained at home. Schools and colleges pivoted to using the Internet as an educational space and in a very short time, learning moved online. This pivot to emergency remote teaching (Hodges et al., 2020) and learning was a shock to students, learners, teachers, and trainers. It highlighted opportunities provided by the Internet for learning and shortcomings in the systems, particularly in terms of capabilities and access to digital technologies and the lack of digital skills in educators (European Commission, 2020). Even so, the Internet played a critical role in maintaining education during the COVID-19 pandemic (European Commission, 2020).

Learning Using the Internet

In this section learning using the Internet is considered starting with learning resources available on the Internet. Then we move to formal learning and the classroom, followed by closed Internet systems and open networks. **YouTube** and **Twitter/X** are reviewed, and this section concludes with a review of online courses. There is a shift from individual to group learning, and then learner networks.

Learning Resources on the Internet

The range of learning resources on the Internet is vast. They can be used by individuals, by groups, or by teachers in classrooms or online. Using these resources is often a case of experiential learning; learners use the resource (doing), reflect on how they use it, and develop their understanding through their experience of the resource. Parallel to the courses and content pages the Internet provides access to many tools. There is a technology tool for many educational tasks (Bower & Torrington, 2020).

Each year since 2007 Jane Hart has consulted learning development professionals to identify the Top 100 Tools for Learning. In 2007 the number one tool was Firefox, the Web browser; by 2009 it was Twitter/X, which remained at number one until 2015. In 2021 it is at number 4 for personal learning and number 21 for workplace learning and it does not feature in the top 100 tools for education (Hart, 2021c). Its place has been taken by YouTube (Hart, 2021a) which has been number one since 2016 and in 2021 is number one for personal learning and education and number five for workplace learning. The COVID-19 global pandemic is evident in the rapid rise of the Zoom video meeting and conference tool. It is number 2 on the overall 2021 list; it has jumped from number 66 in 2016 (Hart, 2021b).

YouTube and Twitter/X

YouTube (Hart, 2021a) is a video platform that enables access to video content. During the COVID-19 pandemic, YouTube was a key support for remote learning (YouTube, 2021). Educational videos have been used for many years in formal learning (Kohler & Dietrich, 2021). Mayer et al. (2020) have developed evidence-based guidelines for effective instructional videos as has Brame (2016). Noetel et al. (2021) identify many benefits of videos for student learning, especially when learning online. Rahmatika et al. (2021) considered the effectiveness of YouTube during the COVID-19 pandemic and identified how it supported teachers, students, and parents during school closures. It should be no surprise that YouTube is the top technology for learning (Hart, 2021c); there is clear evidence that learners find learning from video useful (Gedera & Zalipour, 2018), but it is how it is used that matters (Noetel et al., 2021).

Twitter (2021) (now X) is a microblogging tool. It enables an individual to access ideas and thoughts from around the world and is an example of "learning the new" (Hart, 2014), a way of keeping up-to-date with the leaders in a field or a discipline and of sharing such ideas with a personal network and it uses the Internet – the main network in the world – to do so. However, Twitter/X is not just a tool for individual or group informal learning; it can also be a resource for formal learning. Blessing et al. (2012) used Twitter/X to reinforce classroom concepts in an undergraduate psychology course and noted that students who received psychology-related tweets outperformed students who did not. Malik et al. (2019) find that despite limited research Twitter/X has a positive impact when it is integrated into formal teaching and learning. They echo Jane Hart (2014) in their summary of the value of Twitter/X for professional development and the development of networks.

The availability of resources and tools for learning on the Internet makes much of the argument for it as an educational space; however, it is how these resources are used in formal learning that makes the impact on education and learning. This is now considered.

Formal Learning Using the Internet

Classrooms are or were, until the COVID-19 pandemic, the key sites of formal learning. They are places that the teacher controls; teachers decide the content and activities for any particular session. It may be a lecture, a tutorial, or a seminar. The use of the Internet in the classroom is controlled by the teacher. Mobile phones and/or laptops may be permitted or banned. Classes may take place in computer labs. Data projectors and computers for teachers' use are provided in many classrooms and training rooms. These enable the use of **multimedia** by teachers. Once classrooms were connected to the Internet, teachers and learners had access to a wide range of tools and resources for learning; however, it is often the teacher/trainer who determines what is used.

One technology developed specifically for education is the VLE. These provide a closed Web-based system where teachers and students have access to a course. Students can access notes, contribute work, and do assignments and assessments depending on the design of the relevant course. Teachers may use VLEs to host presentations, and then give the presentations in class, but student access was mainly outside of class time. There may be labs that use the Internet for experiments or research. VLEs tend to support **Web-enabled face-to-face learning** (Hodges et al., 2020) although they can be used for both blended and online learning. VLEs are restricted to institutions. Dron (2021b) considers that we try to recreate classrooms online using VLEs.

It was clear that before the COVID-19 pandemic there was a shift from traditional learning, with its minimal technology use, to Web-enabled f2f learning (Hodges et al., 2020), but little of the class time was replaced by online work by students. Time in schools or colleges was set and online activities such as discussions or blogs were additions rather than replacements. The COVID-19 pandemic changed this when education moved online. The long-term impact of this shift, as classrooms and lecture halls reopen, is hard to tell. It may have enabled technology sceptics to experience how technology can support learning.

What are widely available are online courses. They can be non-profit, commercial, or run by academic institutions. They can be closed – the learner has to register and possibly pay. They can be open where the learner decides what to do and how to use the learning resource. **Instructional design** develops a course from a resource. This means that a teacher/instructor has planned the learning resource, set the learning goals/objectives, there is a beginning, middle and an end, and throughout the course, there may be readings, videos to watch, discussion questions to answer, and posts to be made. It has a pathway designed by the instructor and assessments. It may lead to accreditation.

There are many examples: TED talks and online videos (n.d.) provide learning about ideas and TED-Ed (n.d.) supports teachers to use these videos to create lessons and to share them for others to use. Khan Academy provides courses, practical exercises, and instructional videos free to learners, teachers, and parents on a range of subjects including maths, science, and history (Khan Academy, 2021). Alison (2021) provides free certified online learning and skills training. There are also MOOCs. The first MOOC was run in 2008 (Littlejohn, 2013). MOOCs aim to enable large numbers of students to participate in learning and to work together to learn (Littlejohn, 2013) for free.

All the examples are cited to show that the Internet is being used as an educational space. However, there seems to be a clear difference between using it as an educational resource – that is, as a source of learning content and skills – and using it as a learning environment – that is, as a space to connect with and work with other learners. Harasim (2017) noted how educators adapt traditional didactic teaching practices to the online world both in educational and workplace settings.

The COVID-19 pandemic has highlighted this difference as the Internet has been the space to connect teachers and learners, often through Zoom and other video conferencing platforms. Learning using the Internet poses challenges to our conceptions of learning and how we learn we now need to reflect on what has been learned and use it to benefit learners. This is explored in the next section.

Interrogating Learning and the Internet

There are two ways to interrogate learning and the Internet. One approach is to start with the technology and see how it can support and enable learning. The second is to start with what learning is and explore how learning is enabled by the Internet and the impact it has on teachers and learners.

The Impact of Technology

Technology, such as mobile phones or tablets, is now available to many. It can be used to access the Internet; it is interactive and meets the needs of individuals. This means that technology can be used in a range of contexts and educational settings and for different educational purposes (Selwyn, 2011). Dron (2021a) argues that education is a technological phenomenon, that pedagogies are technology like computers, and that any technology when combined with appropriate pedagogy can be used for learning. This certainly seems the case for the Internet. Learner activity is changed by access to the Internet and different learning activities are possible. Littlejohn (2013) identifies four learning behaviours in networks: we can *consume* – using knowledge; *connect* – with relevant knowledge, people, resources; *create* – make new knowledge through using it; and *contribute* back the new knowledge to the collective. Dron (2021a) summarises this by considering people in education as coparticipants with technology. However inequality of access to technology was a major issue during the COVID-19 pandemic (International Commission on the Future of Education, 2020).

CYBERPSYCHOLOGY IN FOCUS: THE DIGITAL DIVIDE – ACCESS TO LEARNING RESOURCES

COVID-19 and emergency remote teaching and learning widened inequality in education. It highlighted the gap in access to digital technologies and showed how important Internet access has become in learning (International Commission on the Future of Education, 2020). Yet, with appropriate support, learning using the Internet can play a key role in improving equality and inclusiveness in education (European Commission, 2020). One way in which to do so is to develop **open educational resources** for schools, teachers, and students (International Commission on the Future of Education, 2020).

Open educational resources are teaching and learning materials that are free to use and adapt as required (UNESCO, n.d).

Learning Theories

Views about how we learn with technology are informed by beliefs about "the psychological basis of learning and cognition" (Selwyn, 2011, p. 87). Traditional learning theories focus on the individual and the design of the instruction with the setting of goals and objectives (Gagné et al., 1992) starting with behaviourism and developing into more cognitive approaches. Mayer developed his cognitive theory of multimedia learning when learning with **text** and **graphics** (Mayer, 2014). Constructivist learning theories present a different view of how people learn (Harasim, 2017) by considering how learners make meaning.

Bransford et al. (2000) summarise research into learning theories. It is clear that learners come with preconceptions and this initial understanding has to be engaged if they are to grasp new concepts and information. Second, to develop competence, learners need the basic facts; they have to be able to understand the facts and ideas in the context of a conceptual framework, and they have to be able to use the knowledge in ways that facilitate retrieval and application. They argue that effective learning requires thoughtful activity and collaboration for learning with learners taking responsibility for learning and that learners need to learn about learning (Bransford et al., 2000).

More recent theories try to account for learning in a networked world such as the Internet. Downes (2012) developed a learning theory, connectivism, "the thesis that knowledge is distributed across a network of connections, and therefore that learning consists of the ability to construct and traverse those networks" (Downes, 2012), to reflect the network of the Internet and how it enables learning. Harasim (2017, 2021) developed collaborativism, previously online collaborative learning theory, to explain, study, and assess collaborative learning online.

Changing Roles of Teachers and Learners

Traditional approaches to teaching outlined by McWilliam (2007) are being challenged by the availability of technology, particularly mobile technology. McWilliam (2007) argues that we need to "unlearn pedagogy" if we are to take advantage of the digital world. Reviewing the role of the teacher and reflecting on learning theories, she argues that educators/teachers should move from providers of knowledge to co-creators of knowledge with students, from the "sage-on-the-stage and guide-on-the-side to meddler-in-the-middle" (McWilliam, 2007).

Learning from the COVID-19 Pandemic

The worldwide move to online learning and teaching during the COVID-19 pandemic has changed the experience of formal learning and assessment at all levels. It has enabled teachers and learners across the world to experience digital education (European Commission, 2020) and continue formal learning. It was "necessity as the mother of invention".

Recent pedagogical models, for example, the **flipped classroom** (Sharples et al., 2014), began to make sense. In the flipped classroom, learners have access to the content in their own time and the classroom (f2f or online via, for example, Zoom) became a space and time for discussion, collaboration, and argument. With their own devices, students can own their learning and their work. Both of these models challenge teachers to become managers of learning much as McWilliam (2007) argues. In many cases, the move online during the COVID-19 pandemic saw flipped learning with learners' own devices become a reality.

This experiential learning has highlighted the need for educators to be skilled in using digital technologies and the need to ensure that all children/learners can take part in digital education (European Commission, 2020). It has shown the strength and weaknesses of the Internet as an educational space.

Future Trends

It is difficult to predict the future. Pelletier et al. (2021) identify a range of scenarios for the future of postsecondary education including the possibility of transformation and access for all. Macgilchrist et al. (2020) imagine three possible futures for education and technology. Will learners of the 2020s become "smooth users" of technology as it exists now or "digital nomads" using technology or "collective agents" exploring institutions and experimenting with new ways of living (Macgilchrist et al., 2020, p. 6)? Dron's (2021a) coparticipant model for education and technology may help us imagine our future use of the Internet for learning.

Access to the Internet is a key issue worldwide. Pelletier et al. (2021) identify the widening of the digital divide as a social trend while noting the adoption of blended/hybrid learning where possible. Kukulska-Hulme et al. (2021) identify equity-oriented pedagogy as a key pedagogy for the future. Access to free and open-source technologies and the need to end inequality are identified by the International Commission on the Futures of Education (2020) as key issues in a post-COVID world. Policy and guiding principles for digital age education and training are part of the EU Action Plan for Digital Education (European Commission, 2020).

Learning is being transformed by the access to technology and the ability of learners to create and develop in the online world. Practical ideas (Sharples, 2019) and theoretical concepts such as collaborativism (Harasim, 2021) and the coparticipatory perspective on technology and education (Dron, 2021a) are needed for learning when the Internet is the educational space.

Strengths and Weaknesses of the Internet as an Educational Space

The strengths and weaknesses of the Internet are many. The strength is the access to knowledge, tools, and people. It is an amazing resource for learning. This means that access to knowledge and skills for all is possible and that teachers are no longer the gatekeepers.

One challenge and indeed weakness is the volume of information and ideas. Evaluating the information available and identifying its quality is a key issue for all. Teachers effectively are becoming curators of learning resources. Learners have to know where they get information and referencing and attribution is a key issue for all. A second challenge is using the tools and apps for learning. The ability to consume, connect, create, and contribute (Littlejohn, 2013) depends on the skills and knowledge of the users of the Internet as an educational space.

CYBERPSYCHOLOGY IN FOCUS: CRITICAL THINKING – TACKLING DISINFORMATION AND PROMOTING DIGITAL LITERACY

Using the Internet for learning demands critical thinking skills. Learners have to develop the skills to critically analyse information, identify **disinformation**, and manage the amount of information they meet. Guidelines for teachers that encourage **digital literacy** and help tackle disinformation (European Commission, 2020) support learning using the Internet.

Disinformation is false or misleading content that is spread with an intention to deceive or secure economic or political gain, and which may cause public harm (European Commission, 2022).

Digital literacy is the ability to work with information safely and appropriately through information technologies (European Commission, 2022).

Bower and Torrington (2020) note the limited use of technology tools. Harasim (2017) notes our tendency to integrate technology into traditional teaching and Harasim (2021) identifies the need for new learning theories for online learning. Essentially it seems that we use technology for learning but try to make it reflect our face-to-face classrooms (Dron, 2021b). Do we lack the imagination and skills to develop and adapt to the Internet as an educational space?

The Internet requires a rethink about how people learn and how to design learning. This linking of the opportunities for learning provided by the Internet with changing pedagogy is important and it means that learning can take advantage of the paradigm shift that Harasim (2017) argues it is. It enables individuals to achieve mastery through changed external conditions of learning (Gagné et al., 1992).

Conclusion

How the Internet as an educational space will develop is beyond our speculation. It now plays a role in all our learning. It is a key element of our informal learning, enabling us to find out, keeping us up to date. In many ways, it is part of our formal learning as much if not more so than a traditional library. It prompts and supports a wide range of informal learning both individually and in groups. Learning is being transformed by the access to technology and the ability of learners to create and develop in the online world.

The Internet has changed access to knowledge and skills, and this is changing the role of the teacher and how learning is organised, the external **conditions of learning** (Gagné et al., 1992). Access to technology enables learners to create and develop in the online world. Most of all it supports learners in achieving mastery in whatever they wish to learn. This makes learning available to all provided they have Internet access. It looks like the genie is out of the bottle and as the International Commission on the Futures of Education (2020, p. 6) argues, "we cannot return to the world as it was before". We need imagination and experience to fully explore what the Internet offers as an educational space.

Activity

1. Consider how you use technology in your everyday life. Take a day and over the day note what you do. How do communicate, get information, do your work? What technology do you use? What is essential? What is useful?
2. Audit your approach to learning. How do you find out information? How do you learn a new skill? Where do you learn? What tools do you use? How do you know that you have learned?
3. Explore the Top Tools for Learning at https://www.toptools4learning.com/. Select an application or tool from the list. Find out what it is, what it does. Do you use it? Would you use it?
4. Select something you might like to learn. Find an online resource/course. Learn from the resource and then assess your learning and evaluate the online course/resource.

Discussion Questions

1. There are many learning theories. What learning theories explain learning using the Internet and why?

2. What are the strengths and weaknesses of the Internet as an educational space? Is it a paradigm shift (Harasim, 2017)? Has it changed the external conditions of learning (Gagné et al., 1992)?
3. How can learners navigate the educational space of the Internet?
4. How can teachers support learning using the educational space of the Internet?

Recommended Reading List

Linda Harasim provides a coherent overview of learning theory and online technologies.

> Harasim, L. (2017). *Learning theories and online technologies* (2nd ed.). Routledge.

Multimedia is a key element of tools and content on the Web. Richard Mayer edits this handbook of research on how people learn from text and images in computer-based environments.

> Mayer, R. E. (Ed). (2014). *The Cambridge handbook of multimedia learning* (2nd edition). Cambridge: Cambridge University Press. HYPERLINK "https://doi.org/10.1017/CBO9781139547369"doi.org/10.1017/CBO9781139547369

Sharples explores a wide range of pedagogies for the digital age; they are organised into themes such as personalisation, reflection, and scale. Each pedagogy has a description, an account of how it is applied in practice with evidence of its success, and a discussion of the strengths and limitations.

> Sharples, M. (2019). *Practical pedagogy: 40 new ways to teach and learn.* Routledge.

Selwyn takes a critical, reflective view of how technology is used in formal education and challenges the reader to think critically about educational technology.

> Selwyn, N. (2011). *Education and technology: Key issues and debates.* Continuum International Publishing Group.

Glossary

Assessment: Any process by which learning is judged. It may lead to accreditation.
Blended (hybrid) learning: Learning through a combination of classroom-based (face-to-face) learning and online learning.

Bring your own devices (BYOD): Learners bring their own devices to the learning space.

Conditions of learning: The set of internal and external conditions that influence learning (Gagné et al., 1992).

Distance learning: Learning with teachers and learners are in different physical spaces.

Educational technology: The technological artefacts and devices used in education, how the technologies are used in education and learning, and the context for their use (Selwyn, 2011).

eLearning: Learning with electronic technology.

Experiential learning: Learning is through a cyclical process of doing, reflecting on action, identifying learning, and applying the new learning (Watkins et al., 2002).

Face-to-face learning (f2f): Teachers and learners are in the same physical space in classrooms, lecture theatres, labs, and studios.

Flipped classroom: Learners access concepts and ideas in their own time using video lectures and readings and the classroom (f2f or online) becomes a space for discussion and analysis enabling critical thinking and creativity.

Formal learning: Learning takes place in formal settings such as schools and colleges or through courses. It often leads to accreditation.

Graphics (pictures): Static items such as illustrations, drawings, charts, maps, and photographs and dynamic items such as animation and video.

Informal learning: Learning takes place when someone decides to learn something from a book, a video, or another person generally from interest or need.

Instruction: All the events that affect learning.

Instructional design: The systematic design of instruction to support learning (Gagné et al., 1992).

Learning: A change in behaviour.

Massive open online courses (MOOCs): These courses are available on the Internet and open to all who register at little or no charge and often taken by large numbers of students.

Mastery of learning: Achieved when learners are successful at learning tasks (Gagné et al., 1992).

Multimedia: Any material that contains words and graphics.

Online learning: Use of communication networks for educational purposes mediated by the Web.

Teaching: A key part of instruction, teachers (also called instructors) organise and plan the instruction for students and classes.

Technology-enhanced learning: The use of technology to support learning.

Text: Words printed on a screen or spoken.

Twitter/X: A microblogging tool and online social network, where individuals post short messages (tweets) of up to 280 characters that their "followers" can read, favour, and retweet.

Virtual learning environments (VLEs): Also called learning management systems (LMS) or course management systems (CMS) (Moore et al., 2011), these are Web-based courses that support formal learning in schools and colleges.

Web-enabled face-to-face learning: Learning in classrooms and at home with Web resources and tools including VLEs.

Web facilitated: Where learning is supported by online course materials and activities.

Wikis: Collaborative websites.

References

Alison. (2021). Alison, a power for good. https://alison.com/about/our-story

Blessing, S. B., Blessing, J. S., & Fleck, B. K. (2012). Using Twitter to reinforce classroom concepts. *Teaching of Psychology, 39*(4), 268–271. https://doi.org/10.1177/0098628312461484

Brame, C. J. (2016). Effective educational videos: Principles and guidelines for maximizing student learning from video content. *CBE Life Sciences Education, 15*(4). https://doi.org/10.1187/cbe.16-03-0125

Bransford, J. D., Brown, A. L., & Cocking, R. R. (2000). *How people learn, brain, mind, experience, and school.* National Academy Press. https://www.nap.edu/read/9853/chapter/1

Clark, R. C., & Mayer, R. E. (2011). *e-Learning and the science of instruction: Proven guidelines for consumers and designers of multimedia learning* (3rd ed.). Pfeiffer. https://doi.org/10.1002/9781118255971

Downes, S. (2012). *Connectivism and connected knowledge: Essays on meaning and learning networks.* Downes. https://www.downes.ca/me/mybooks.htm

Dron, J. (2021a). Educational technology: What it is and how it works. *AI & Society.* https://doi.org/10.1007/s00146-021-01195-z

Dron, J. (2021b). A few thoughts on learning management systems, and on integrated learning environments and their implementation. https://jondron.ca/a-few-thoughts-on-learning-management-systems-and-on-integrated-learning-environments-and-their-implementation/

European Commission. (2020). *Digital education action plan 2021–2027. Resetting education and training for a digital age.* European Commission.

European Commission. (2022). *Guidelines for teachers and educators on tackling disinformation and digital literacy through education and training.* European Union.

Freeman, R., & Lewis, R. (1998). *Planning and implementing assessment.* Kogan Page.

Gagné, R. M., Briggs, L. J., & Wager, W. W. (1992). *Principles of instructional design* (4th ed.). Wadsworth Thomson Learning.

Gedera, D. S. P., & Zalipour, A. (2018). Use of interactive video for teaching and learning. In *ASCILITE 2018 conference proceedings* (pp. 362–367). Deakin University, Geelong, Australia: Australasian Society for Computers in Learning in Tertiary Education.

Harasim, L. (2017). *Learning theories and online technologies* (2nd ed.). Routledge.

Harasim, L. (2021). Collaborativism aka online collaborative learning theory. https://www.lindaharasim.com/online-collaborative-learning/ocl-theory/

Hart, J. (2014). The web is 25 years old today – So how has it changed the way we learn? www.c4lpt.co.uk/blog/2014/03/12/the-web-is-25-years-old-today/

Hart, J. (2021a). 1 – YouTube. https://www.toptools4learning.com/youtube/

Hart, J. (2021b). 2 – Zoom. https://www.toptools4learning.com/zoom/

Hart, J. (2021c). 8 – Twitter. https://www.toptools4learning.com/twitter/

Hodges, C., Moore, S., Lockee, B., Trust, T., & Bond, A. (2020). The difference between emergency remote teaching and online learning. *Educause Review 2020.* https://er.educause.edu/articles/2020/3/the-difference-between-emergency-remote-teaching-and-online-learning

International Commission on the Futures of Education. (2020). *Education in a post-COVID world: Nine ideas for public action.* UNESCO.

Khan Academy. (2021). Khan academy about. www.khanacademy.org/about

Kohler, S., & Dietrich, T. C. (2021). Potentials and limitations of educational videos on YouTube for science communication. *Frontiers in Communication, 6*, 581302. https://doi.org/10.3389/fcomm.2021.581302

Kukulska-Hulme, A., Bossu, C., Coughlan, T., Ferguson, R., FitzGerald, E., Gaved, M., Herodotou, C., Rienties, B., Sargent, J., Scanlon, E., Tang, J., Wang, Q., Whitelock, D., & Zhang, S. (2021). *Innovating pedagogy 2021: Open University innovation Report 9*. The Open University.

Littlejohn, A. (2013). Understanding massive open online courses. CEMCA EdTech notes. https://www.cemca.org/ckfinder/userfiles/files/EdTech %20Notes%202_Littlejohn_final_1June2013.pdf

Macgilchrist, F., Allert, H., & Bruch, A. (2020). Students and society in the 2020s. Three future 'histories' of education and technology. *Learning, Media and Technology, 45*(1), 76–89. https://doi.org/10.1080/17439884.2019.1656235

Malik, A., Heyman-Schrum, C., & Johri, A. (2019). Use of Twitter across educational settings: A review of the literature. *International Journal of Educational Technology in Higher Education, 16*(1), 36. https://doi.org/10.1186/ s41239-019-0166-x

Mayer, R. E. (2014). Cognitive theory of multimedia learning. In R. E. Mayer (Ed.), *The Cambridge handbook of multimedia learning* (2nd ed., pp. 43–71). Cambridge University Press. https://doi.org/10.1017/CBO9781139547369 .005

Mayer, R. E., Fiorella, L., & Stulls, A. (2020). Five ways to increase the effectiveness of instructional video. *Education Technology Research and Development, 68*(3), 837–852. https://doi.org/10.1007/s11423-020-09749-6

McWilliam, E. (2007). Unlearning how to teach. Paper presented at creativity or conformity? Building cultures of creativity in higher education. http://www .creativityconference07.org/presented_papers/McWilliam_Unlearning.doc

McWilliam, E., & Haukka, S. (2008). Educating the creative workforce: New direction for twenty-first century schooling. *British Educational Research Journal, 34*(5), 651–666. https://doi.org/10.1080/01411920802224204

Moore, J. L., Dickson-Deane, C., & Galyen, K. (2011). e-Learning, online learning and distance learning environments: Are they the same? *Internet and Higher Education, 14*(2), 129–135. https://doi.org/10.1016/j.iheduc.2010 .10.001

Noetel, M., Griffith, S., Delaney, O., Sanders, T., Parker, P., del Pozo Cruz, B., & Lonsdale, C. (2021). Video improves learning in higher education: A systematic review. *Review of Educational Research, 91*(2), 204–236. https://doi .org/10.3102/0034654321990713

Pelletier, K., Brown, M., Brooks, D. C., McCormack, M., Reeves, J., Arbino, N., Bozkurt, A., Crawford, S., Czerniewicz, L., Gibson, R., Linder, K., Mason, J., & Mondelli, V. (2021). *2021 Educause horizon report, teaching and learning edition*. Educause.

Rahmatika, R., Yusuf, M., & Agung, L. (2021). The effectiveness of YouTube as an online learning media. *Journal of Education Technology, 5*(1), 152–158. https://doi.org/10.23887/jet.v5i1.33628

Selwyn, N. (2011). *Education and technology: Key issues and debates*. Continuum International Publishing Group.

Sharples, M. (2019). *Practical pedagogy: 40 new ways to teach and learn*. Routledge.

Sharples, M., Adams, A., Ferguson, R., Gaved, M., McAndrew, P., Rienties, B., Weller, M., & Whitelock, D. (2014). *Innovating pedagogy 2014: Open university innovation report 3*. The Open University.

Torrington, J. (2020). A typology of free web-based learning technologies (2020). https://library.educause.edu/-/media/files/library/2020/4/freeweb basedlearntech2020.pdf

Twitter. (2021). Using Twitter. https://help.twitter.com/en/using-twitter#tweets

UNESCO. (n.d.). *Open educational resources*. https://www.unesco.org/en/communication-information/open-solutions/open-educational-resources?hub=785

YouTube. (2021). How has YouTube responded to the global COVID-19 crisis? https://www.youtube.com/intl/ALL_ie/howyoutubeworks/our-commitments/covid-response/#remote-learning

Watkins, C., Carnell, E., Lodge, C., Wagner, P., & Whalley, C. (2002). *Effective learning. NSIN research matters No. 17*. Institute of Education.

Consumer Cyberpsychology and Online Marketing

Nicola Fox Hamilton

Chapter Overview

This chapter will provide an introduction to the psychology of online consumer behaviour. The types of customers who shop online and their characteristics will be explored, as well as the motivations and beliefs that influence their choice to engage in eCommerce. The consumer–brand relationship will be examined in the context of how the internet has profoundly changed the interaction between business and customers and the costs and benefits of increased choice and information will be discussed. Finally, the methods and effects of online persuasion will be explored.

Key Terms

One of the key terms that will be addressed in this chapter is **customer segmentation**, dividing a customer base into groups of individuals that are similar in specific ways useful to marketing. The **technology acceptance model (TAM)** and **theory of reasoned action (TRA)** are designed to explain why people do or do not use technology, and the intention to adopt certain behaviours. We will consider the effect of social media on the **consumer–brand relationship** and **brand awareness,** particularly in relation to **eLoyalty,** and the likelihood of the customer returning to purchase. Techniques of **persuasion** will also be examined.

Who Shops Online?

Researchers have attempted to profile or segment online shoppers according to their characteristics to understand different shopping behaviours, which can be then targeted by businesses seeking their custom. A typology of online consumers was developed by Huseynov and Özkan Yıldırım (2019) and looks not only at the psychographic characteristics of each group but also at their shopping

DOI: 10.4324/9781003092513-22

attitudes and behaviours. They examined a wide range of factors which help predict the use of online shopping to develop four segments: shopping lovers, direct purchasers, suspicious browsers, and incompetent consumers.

"Shopping lovers" are experienced and capable shoppers and find online shopping to be more convenient, with wider choices and better prices. They spend the most and are most likely to impulse buy because they enjoy browsing without any intention to purchase a specific product. They enjoy using social media and entertainment portals, making those platforms good advertising locations for this segment. "Direct purchasers" on the other hand mostly shop with purpose. They are also practised and adept online shoppers, but while they don't feel online shopping offers better prices or choice, they do find it meets their needs and they prefer it over shopping offline. They are not as active on social media and entertainment platforms, and improvements in the content or functionality of an eCommerce site are more likely to encourage them to shop more than advertising in those locations. "Suspicious browsers" are well described by the label they are given. While they are active online, engaging with entertainment platforms, social media, news, and other online spaces, they worry about the security and privacy of shopping online. They see the benefits of it, but they are distrustful and find some aspects, such as returns processes, too complex. As such, they tend to research products and trends online, but purchase offline. They can be reassured by increased privacy and security measures on the eCommerce site, as well as simple and free delivery and returns. Click and collect options can also be reassuring to fearful customers, because of the knowledge that a retailer has a physical location at which they can be reached if any problem arises. Similar measures can help reassure "incompetent consumers" too, along with measures to simplify the shopping process, such as recommender systems. This segment finds online shopping complex and difficult to use, and they worry about security and privacy. They shop very infrequently online and don't see any benefits to it (Huseynov & Özkan Yıldırım, 2019).

The Factors Affecting Online Shopping Acceptance

Increasing numbers of people are shifting to eCommerce for at least a portion of their purchases, but as we saw in the typology discussed, a sizable proportion of the population is still not comfortable with doing so. There are a number of psychological reasons explaining why people accept this use of technology or not. The theory of reasoned action (TRA; Fishbein & Ajzen, 2011) and the technology acceptance model (TAM; Bagozzi et al., 1992) have been examined by many researchers as a way to explain this resistance or acceptance of eCommerce, which can in turn help to attract consumers to shop online and to retain them as customers. The TRA examines people's intention to adopt certain behaviours, and that intention is determined by their attitude towards the behaviour, and by subjective norms about the behaviour. Huseynov and Özkan Yıldırım's (2019) findings regarding incompetent or suspicious consumers support this theory. They found that positive pressure from others around them who find online shopping useful or enjoyable is more likely to help people change a negative attitude about online shopping to a positive one. A positive attitude towards online shopping increases the intention to use it, because it is seen as useful and fitting with their lifestyle.

TAM was designed to explain why people do or do not use technology in the context of the workplace; however, because online shoppers are also technology users, it has also been used to explain people's inclination to adopt technology in online shopping. There are two main beliefs shaping attitudes towards online shopping technology that TAM examines, perceived usefulness and ease of use, and each of these influences the intention to use the technology. In addition to these, the other most common beliefs and factors examined in relation to online shopping adoption are trust, perceived risk, security and privacy concerns, previous shopping experience, self-efficacy, convenience, innovativeness of the user, enjoyment, and social influence (Zerbini et al., 2022). Again, we see how these support the typology developed by Huseynov and Özkan Yıldırım (2019). Those who do not trust online shopping, worry about privacy or security, find it too difficult to use, or do not see the benefits of it are less likely to shop online.

Many studies have been conducted using these variables in a variety of contexts with differing results (see Zerbini et al., 2022, for a full meta-analysis of the literature). Trust is typically measured in relation to the website, the retailer, or the online transaction process itself. Perceived risk examines the potential losses or negative outcomes that are present in all transactions, but are particularly salient in online shopping because of security and privacy issues. Self-efficacy indicates how much a person feels they are capable of carrying out the behaviour, while innovativeness indicates how open to new ideas and change a person is. Enjoyment is the extent to which the activity itself is enjoyable, and is sometimes connected to the experience of flow, where the user becomes fully immersed in the task and experiences a deep sense of enjoyment in it (Csikszentmihalyi, 1990). Social influence or norms examines the perception of an individual regarding the amount of online shopping that significant or important others believe that they should engage in.

Ingham et al. (2015) conducted a meta-analysis to examine the influence of these beliefs and created a strong model which explained 54% of the intention to use online shopping. They found that attitude towards shopping online was the most influential variable in predicting whether people intended to shop online or not. The beliefs that helped to shape people's attitude towards eCommerce were perceived usefulness, enjoyment, perceived risk, ease of use, and social intention.

A recent meta-analysis by Zerbini et al. (2022) incorporating the latest research in this well-explored field confirms many of these findings. In particular, attitude is still the strongest driver of intention, and intention predicts behaviour. Perceived usefulness, trust, and subjective norms are still important antecedents of intention to purchase online. However, it appears that consumers have developed more trust in eCommerce sites, and privacy and security concerns have decreased over time. Convenience has become a more significant driver of intention, where consumers feel that shopping online saves them time or energy, and consumer innovativeness also predicts how likely they are to shop online.

Unlike Ingham et al. (2015), Zerbini et al. (2022) did not find enjoyment to be a direct predictor of purchase intention in their meta-analysis. However, they found that the quality of web design and content on the eCommerce site significantly predicted intention to shop online (indicating the importance of UX research and design roles), and positive previous experiences shopping online also increased intention to buy again.

CYBERPSYCHOLOGY IN FOCUS: REAL-WORLD APPLICATIONS OF THE RESEARCH FOR ECOMMERCE DESIGNERS

Designers of eCommerce websites should aim to create enjoyable shopping experiences through the usability and content of the sites to fully activate their effect on purchase intention (Zerbini et al., 2022). Subjective norms are a significant driver of attitudes towards online shopping and, considering the popularity of social media for learning about brands and products, and increasingly for shopping, developing a strong social presence to encourage positive word of mouth could exploit the effect of social interaction on purchasing behaviour (Ingham et al., 2015).

Motivation for Shopping Online

In the typology developed by Huseynov and Özkan Yıldırım (2019), it is clear that hedonic and utilitarian motivations drive the behaviour of different consumer segments. Shopping lovers are motivated by the enjoyment of online shopping and spend time browsing with no specific product in mind. On the other hand, direct purchasers are driven by utilitarian motivations to shop online. They are goal-oriented, they focus on a specific product, and online shopping is convenient for them. Suspicious browsers are information seekers rather than online shoppers.

Bosnjak et al. (2007) found that emotional involvement is a strongly significant predictor of shopping intention, indicating that the decision to shop online is at least partly an emotional one. A conceptual and qualitative study by Pham and Sun (2020) examined the positive emotions of pride, excitement, and relaxation and found them to be common motivators and outcomes of consumer behaviour. Zerbini and colleagues found that social influence is a predictor of attitudes towards online shopping and purchase intention. Pride and excitement have the potential to be amplified by social media in sharing shopping experiences (Pham & Sun, 2020). For example, pride in finding a great deal or a perfect gift, or in the difficulty of achieving a goal such as purchasing an expensive product, when shared can lead to positive social feedback and an increase in perceived social status. Anticipatory or outcome excitement can be generated or amplified in online shopping through many means. For example, the use of scarcity to elevate the desirability of a product, such as a limited-edition piece, or through consumers overcoming obstacles like the levels you might find in a loyalty programme.

Bosnjak et al. (2007) found that need for cognition has a negative effect, and they suggest that perhaps online shoppers are cognitive misers seeking to minimise their efforts using shortcuts. The model arrived at in the study incorporating these factors was strongly predictive of willingness to shop online. This supports the findings of Zerbini et al. (2022) that convenience is one of the stronger motivators of online shopping adoption.

A complex web of factors affects online shopping acceptance including demographics, culture, motivations to shop, personality, and attitudes and beliefs about the technology involved. The research thus far has illuminated several areas that the designers of the shopping experience and marketers seeking customers can focus on to improve the experience and convenience of shopping, reduce risk, increase trust, and integrate social feedback.

Consumer–Brand Relationships

The internet has fundamentally changed the way that brands and customers interact. Where once brands almost exclusively communicated information to consumers, now the process has become a two-way channel where customers can express their excitement, satisfaction, apathy, frustration, or anger, as well as communicate their feedback, ideas, and knowledge to the business and other customers (Ibrahim et al., 2020). This can benefit companies who build strong brand social media pages and use effective social media marketing activities to engage customers. Social media marketing can lead to greater brand equity and this influences purchase intention because it encourages engagement and enhances customer experience (Ibrahim et al., 2020; Nardi et al., 2020). It can lead to greater brand awareness, brand satisfaction, stronger consumer–brand relationships, loyalty, and greater transmission of positive word-of-mouth (WOM) traffic, which in turn can have a significant effect on consumer choices and brand performance (Barreda et al., 2015; Nardi et al., 2020). A brand's interactive social media space should allow users to exchange rich, reliable, and up-to-date information in a timely manner. The quality of the system, the content, and the ability of consumers to engage in rewarding activities are all significant precursors of brand awareness (Barreda et al., 2015). Trust in the brand is important in this relationship; customers are unlikely to be engaged with a brand that they do not find trustworthy (Nardi et al., 2020).

To fully engage customers, it is vital to make them aware of the benefits they can expect from participation. Expected benefits drive enthusiasm for a brand and increase interaction (Nardi et al., 2020). The perceived benefits of a brand social media space influence the consumers' relationship, and a positive relationship leads to increased brand loyalty behaviour. Both experiential benefits, such as social interaction with others and enjoyment, and functional benefits, such as access to information and promotional deals, give a positive impression of the investment that the brand has made in the relationship with the customer. This leads to brand relationship quality and willingness to spread positive WOM about the brand by the consumer (Barreda et al., 2015; Nardi et al., 2020). Fans of brand pages can contribute to the community in numerous ways, such as being brand advocates, answering other customer questions, sharing positive experiences, or working out problems together, creating an interactive social experience that illustrates their commitment to the community. Active participation in the space rather than passively lurking is important in generating brand trust and commitment and strengthens the consumer–brand relationship. Brand social media spaces are an effective means of attracting customers and emotionally connecting them to the brand, leading to benefits for the business (Barreda et al., 2015; Dabbous et al., 2020).

A key aspect of customer engagement is word-of-mouth reviews and building positive WOM traffic is important to ensure the success of a retail business online. Over two-thirds of people read between one and six reviews online before making a purchase decision (Coppola, 2022). Research looking at the effect of product reviews on retail sales confirms that online product reviews have a significant effect on sales elasticity (Floyd et al., 2014). A large meta-analysis of the most helpful characteristics of product reviews for decision-making found that many factors are significant (Ismagilova et al., 2020). However, of most importance are the quality of arguments, the usefulness of the reviews, and the credibility of and trust in the reviews. The valence of the reviews is also key, with positive reviews having a marginally more positive impact on purchase intention than negative reviews do on reducing intention.

eLoyalty and Retention of Customers

Building and maintaining brand loyalty is essential to both online and offline businesses. Long-lasting customer relationships are considerably more valuable than once-off transactions. Reichheld and Sasser (1990) calculated that by retaining just 5% more of their customers, businesses could increase their profits by almost 100%, meaning that building customer relationships is an investment worthy of making. eLoyalty is generally conceived to be a favourable attitude towards an online business influencing the intention of the consumer to repurchase from a company, and the likelihood of them recommending the brand to someone else.

Online shopping has changed the landscape of the relationship between customers and brands in significant ways, such as the ease of switching brands and the access to information about available products from other retailers online. These changes affect the way in which businesses can encourage loyalty in their customers. Valvi and Fragkos (2012) broke down the factors involved in online retail loyalty into a conceptual framework with three broad categories centred on purchase: pre-purchase, during-purchase, and after-purchase. Pre-purchase involves the consumer recognising that they have a need to be satisfied, and their search for alternative solutions to meet their need. This category divides into two sub-categories: competitor attitudes and reputation, and customer characteristics. The competitor attitudes category consists of variables such as switching costs and barriers to the consumer, where higher costs and barriers make it more likely that the customer will remain loyal. Price and the reputation of the company also play a part in the competitive attitudes category. A strong reputation leads to loyalty through the development of trust. The second sub-category contains the characteristics of the customer profile such as demographics and the level of knowledge that the customer has. These are not characteristics that the business can change, but they can take them into account in their communications and actions involving the customer.

The during-purchase process includes evaluating the alternatives available and choosing the best fit, purchasing the chosen product or service, and finally using it to satisfy the need. The factors involved here are the quality of the web service, including the efficiency of the website itself, the purchase process, delivery, and service; and the enjoyment or entertainment of the customer during the process. Enjoyment is closely related to service, where poor service reduces enjoyment, and both high quality of service and high levels of enjoyment encourage customer repurchase intention.

After-purchase involves evaluating how well the need was met, feeding back that evaluation to others, and ending the purchase process. After-purchase factors include satisfaction, where contentment with the purchase translates into greater loyalty towards the brand; trust, which has a direct and positive relationship with loyalty; and perceived value, which is the overall appraisal of the benefit of the product. Consumers who feel that they are not getting value from a transaction are more likely to look elsewhere for their purchases (Valvi & Fragkos, 2012).

There is little longitudinal research on how loyalty develops over time in eCommerce. This is important because loyalty is a characteristic that can build cumulatively over multiple interactions or purchases in an online store, and most research focuses on a single large purchase like a car and retention of loyalty to that brand over time. Findings from a study by Pee et al. (2019) fit with the Valvi and Fragkos framework. They found that the perceived usefulness of an eCommerce site was most influential on loyalty with the first purchase, but that customer satisfaction became more important from that point onwards.

Decision-Making and Purchase Satisfaction

Consumers have been empowered by the internet in two distinct ways: the expansion of freedom of choice and the expansion of information. There are now an unprecedented number of products and services available to consumers regardless of their location, often with the possibility of customisation or personalisation. They also have unparalleled access to social knowledge about those products through review sites, social media, and user-generated content to make more informed and accurate decisions about those products (Dabbous et al., 2020). However, despite the benefits of this empowerment and the opportunities it offers for optimal decision-making, it is not without cost. The difficulty of decision-making has been increased by increasing task complexity, trade-off difficulty, and preference uncertainty (see Broniarczyk & Griffin, 2014, for a full review of the consumer decision-making literature).

Decision difficulty can develop from a multiplicity of variables, and these can be grouped into a framework of six concepts. Task complexity arises in the face of an excessive number of product alternatives or attributes, or in response to increasing uncertainty about product attributes. Information overload occurs when choice alternatives and attributes increase, and the decision becomes more demanding than our limited capacity to store and process information. The greater the information load the greater the cognitive resources required to process the task. WOM in particular is known to increase the cognitive burden on decision-makers when the quality of the reviews is low, resulting in greater decision difficulty and lower satisfaction with decisions, particularly for those with less knowledge about the product (Hu & Krishen, 2019). Trade-off difficulty occurs when a consumer must sacrifice one goal for another, for example, price for quality, and is cognitively taxing. Trade-offs can evoke emotional difficulty as well as cognitive demand, from anticipatory emotions such as anxiety and despair, to loss at having to relinquish a desired product or attribute when choosing another. Preference uncertainty arises when the preference for a product is not clearly defined or is unstable. Constructing preferences while shopping further increases the burden of choice (Broniarczyk & Griffin, 2014). Consumers are faced with a number of outcomes in the event of decision difficulty online, and most of those outcomes involve poor choice-making. Many experience choice paralysis when faced with over-choice, particularly if they are maximisers who exert effort to try to make the best possible choice (Manolică et al., 2021). Others engage in choice simplification where they only engage with easily comparable attributes or choose the product that has been best described, and all these decisions may lead to sub-optimal purchases (Broniarczyk & Griffin, 2014).

There are also consequences after the decision has been made when the effect of excessive choice can lead to post-purchase regret and diminished satisfaction (Broniarczyk & Griffin, 2014; Manolică et al., 2021). This is particularly the case where considerable cognitive effort was expended in evaluating a product and when a difficult decision cannot be easily justified, leading to regret at the wasted effort (Park & Hill, 2018). Dissatisfaction can lead the consumer to shop elsewhere, and so businesses need to ensure that they assist the consumer in the decision-making process in a way that reduces the cognitive load and simplifies the process. While, on the one hand, the internet creates the sources of difficulty, it can also provide decision-making aids which can help in resolving them. For example, a simple star rating system, with no further detailed information on each alternative, can reduce perceived task difficulty and increase decision satisfaction among consumers with low knowledge of the product (Morrin et al., 2012). Other useful tools include product filtering, comparison tools, and collaborative filtering-based recommendations. Providing a range of tools is useful, as these are used in different ways across the choice process, and are used more by satisficers than maximisers (Virdi et al., 2020).

One area where decision-making has an impact on the spending patterns of consumers is in-app purchases. Soroush et al. (2014) found that frustration with being unable to progress within a game (*Candy Crush Saga*), and decision difficulty about whether to purchase something within the game to make progression easier, leads to ego depletion, in particular for those with low self-control. In addition, resistance to in-app purchasing can be caused by a perception of aggressive monetisation. While the decision to spend on in-app purchases is related to time spent playing, willingness to pay, and the size of the payment, where smaller transactions generate higher willingness (Salehudin & Alpert, 2021).

Persuasion

The internet is permeated with persuasion across areas such as education, fitness, healthcare, and activism, but it is particularly salient in the area of online marketing and online shopping. Fogg and colleagues (2007), at the Persuasive Technology Lab at Stanford University, posit that creating successful human–computer interactions requires skills in the motivation and persuasion of people through the design of the interfaces people use.

There are four ways in which computers, or technology, are used as tools for persuasion. First, increasing self-efficacy, which helps people feel more efficient, productive, and in control, contributes in an important way to the behaviour change process. Second, providing tailored information relevant to the specific needs of the consumer can help achieve a persuasive outcome, and with the level of data tracking that businesses can now access to monitor their customers' preferences, this is a common persuasive tactic in eCommerce. Third, interfaces can be used to trigger decision-making; tools such as product recommenders and comparison tools encourage consumers to engage in choice-making in online shopping. Finally, simplifying or guiding people through a process can remove barriers to the desired behaviour. For example, an online store may have a facility to remember customer details such as delivery and billing address, as well as credit card details, thus speeding up and simplifying the checkout process (Fogg et al., 2007). More information on persuasion online can be found in Chapter 9.

The Impact of Design on Persuasion

There is also a direct relationship between the credibility of a website and its ability to persuade users to adopt a specific attitude or behaviour (Fogg et al., 2003). The website design aesthetic is key for influencing perceived credibility. There are two types of aesthetic design, classical and expressive. Classical aesthetics are simple, clear, orderly, clean, and pleasant, while expressive aesthetics are complex, rich, novel, and with special effects. Classical aesthetics applied to eCommerce websites are perceived by users as more credible than expressive aesthetics (Oyibo et al., 2018). Yoo and Kim (2014) found that image-oriented homepage designs increased visual fluency, the ease with which visual stimuli can be processed. Given that first impressions of a website are instantaneous and that those impressions last (Lindgaard et al., 2006), it is important that the storefront of an eCommerce site gives users a visually fluent first response. This is even more the case for people who value aesthetics highly. Visually fluent homepages also lead to a greater preference for the site, and importantly, higher browsing and revisit intentions. The design of the page is even more important for visual fluency than brand familiarity (Yoo & Kim, 2014).

Persuasive strategies are often built into the design of eCommerce websites as well as social commerce. Cialdini (2001) outlined a number of strategies that are commonly used to persuade consumers to purchase, and that sometimes encourage impulse buying in an eCommerce setting (Iyer et al., 2020). For example, scarcity and urgency are often activated through limited-time offers, rare or exclusive products, or low stock warnings, and these trigger a fear of missing out on deals or products in consumers, increasing consumers' likelihood of purchasing, particularly impulse purchasing (Hodkinson, 2019; Iyer et al., 2020). Social proof, or consensus, is used to indicate that a product or brand is desirable because others like it or have purchased it, particularly other people similar to the consumer. This has a strong influence on sales in online shopping through the use of word-of-mouth reviews incorporated into the online shopping experience (Amblee & Bui, 2011).

Dark patterns in user experience design are often used to unethically persuade or coerce users into taking action that they didn't want or intend to take (Karagoel & Nathan-Roberts, 2021). These might include hidden costs or subscriptions that are hard to cancel, countdown timers, or visual interference misdirecting a user to click on something they didn't intend.

User experience (UX) research and design play a key role in creating credible, persuasive, and attractive eCommerce websites and mobile apps. Chapter 19 reviews UX research and design processes in greater depth.

As the adoption of smartphones has increased, consumers are increasingly willing to use mobile payment methods because of their simplicity and convenience (Smith et al., 2012). In fact, in Europe, India, and China, mobile payment options like PayPal and Alipay are the most used payment methods, while credit and debit cards are still more common in America (Coppola, 2022). Soman (2003) found that payments via cash, rather than credit or pre-paid cards, were more immediate and transparent, increasing the pain felt in payment. As a result, people paying by card were more likely to spend more than those paying with cash. This has been found in subsequent studies, indicating that overspending is more likely with the use of mobile wallets, particularly for those with low financial knowledge (Ahn & Nam, 2022).

Conclusion

This chapter has provided an overview of consumer cyberpsychology and online marketing, looking at who shops online, how they can be grouped according to behaviour or motivations, and the beliefs and attitudes that influence their enthusiastic adoption of online shopping or resistance to it. The Internet has fundamentally changed the consumer–brand relationship, and the results of that have been increased consumer empowerment, changes in how loyalty is gained by brands, and also decision difficulty for consumers in the face of expansive choice and information. Finally, the means of persuading online customers have been explored, along with consumers' contribution to persuading others through word of mouth.

Activity

Choose a product (for example, a smartphone, a book, or an item of clothing). Find three online retail websites which sell this item, and identify the techniques used by each website to encourage sales.

Which techniques do you think are the most effective? Which website do you think will have the lowest number of sales? Is this because of the marketing techniques used, or for a different reason? Which types of shoppers would be most likely to purchase this product online?

Discussion Questions

1. Think about your own online shopping experiences. Do you often buy more online than your intended purchase? What are the tactics employed by online retailers that encourage you to do this?
2. What persuasion strategies do you think are most and least effective in convincing consumers to purchase online?
3. Which online shopping companies do you trust, or not trust? In your own experience what were the factors that gained or lost your trust?

4. Have you ever engaged in positive or negative word of mouth about a company, through reviews, feedback, complaints, etc.? What were your motivations for engaging with the company publicly in this way?

Recommended Reading List

This book focuses on the interaction of social media with consumer behaviour, including word of mouth, branding and promotion, and consumer engagement. It also looks at big data research, and consumer welfare.

> Dimofte, C. V., Haugtvedt, C. P., & Yalch, R. F. (Eds.). (2016). *Consumer psychology in a social media world*. Routledge.

This book presents scholarly theory and research to help explain consumer behaviour with examples from many European countries. It examines consumer needs, attitudes, and values, as well as their decision-making processes and purchasing behaviour.

> Bartosik-Purgat, M., & Filimon, N. (Eds.). (2022). *European consumers in the digital era: Implications of technology, media and culture on consumer behavior*. Taylor & Francis.

A meta-analysis examining the many internal and external factors and stimuli that lead to impulse buying, including individual differences, motives, resources, and marketing stimuli.

> Iyer, G. R., Blut, M., Xiao, S. H., & Grewal, D. (2020). Impulse buying: A meta-analytic review. *Journal of the Academy of Marketing Science*, *48*(3), 384–404. https://doi.org/10.1007/s11747-019-00670-w

This meta-analysis identifies the particular characteristics that make word-of-mouth communications more or less successful, including argument quality, usefulness, trust, volume, and credibility.

> Ismagilova, E., Slade, E. L., Rana, N. P., & Dwivedi, Y. K. (2020). The effect of electronic word of mouth communications on intention to buy: A meta-analysis. In *Information Systems Frontiers* (Vol. 22, Issue 5, pp. 1203–1226). https://doi.org/10.1007/s10796-019-09924-y

Glossary

Brand awareness: The ability to recognise and recall the brand from a relevant cue.
Consumer–brand relationship: What consumers think and feel about a brand and experience with a brand.

Customer segmentation: Dividing a customer base into groups of individuals who are similar in specific ways such as by demographics, lifestyle, and values, or by psychological factors such as personality and motivations.

eLoyalty: A favourable attitude towards an online business influencing the intention of the consumer to repurchase from a company and the likelihood of them recommending the brand to someone else.

Persuasion: An attempt to bring about a change in attitude or behaviour.

Technology acceptance model (TAM): Designed to explain why people do or do not use technology in the context of the workplace; however, because online shoppers are also technology users, it has also been used to explain people's inclination to adopt technology in online shopping.

Theory of reasoned action (TRA): The TRA examines people's intention to adopt certain behaviours, and that intention is determined by their attitude towards the behaviour and by subjective norms about the behaviour.

Word of mouth (WOM): Communication by a consumer to others actively influenced or encouraged by an organisation.

References

Ahn, S. Y., & Nam, Y. (2022). Does mobile payment use lead to overspending? The moderating role of financial knowledge. *Computers in Human Behavior*, *134*(February), 107319. https://doi.org/10.1016/j.chb.2022.107319

Amblee, N., & Bui, T. (2011). Harnessing the influence of social proof in online shopping: The effect of electronic word of mouth on sales of digital microproducts. *International Journal of Electronic Commerce*, *16*(2), 91–114. https://doi.org/10.2753/JEC1086-4415160205

Bagozzi, R. P., Davis, F. D. D., & Warshaw, P. R. (1992). Development and test of a theory of technological learning and usage. In *Human Relations*, *45*(7), 659–686. https://doi.org/10.1177/001872679204500702

Barreda, A. A., Bilgihan, A., Nusair, K., & Okumus, F. (2015). Generating brand awareness in Online Social Networks. *Computers in Human Behavior, 50*, 600–609. https://doi.org/10.1016/j.chb.2015.03.023

Bosnjak, M., Galesic, M., & Tuten, T. (2007). Personality determinants of online shopping: Explaining online purchase intentions using a hierarchical approach. *Journal of Business Research, 60*(6), 597–605. https://doi.org/10.1016/j.jbusres.2006.06.008

Broniarczyk, S. M., & Griffin, J. G. (2014). Decision difficulty in the age of consumer empowerment. *Journal of Consumer Psychology, 24*(4), 608–625. https://doi.org/10.1016/j.jcps.2014.05.003

Cialdini, R. B. (2001). Harnessing the science of persuasion A conversation with mark morris. *Harvard Business Review, R0109D*, 72–79.

Coppola, D. (2022). *E-commerce worldwide - Statistics & facts*. www.statista.com. https://www.statista.com/markets/413/topic/544/key-figures-of-e-commerce/#overview

Csikszentmihalyi, M. (1990). *Flow: The psychology of optimal experience* (1st ed.). Harper & Row.

Dabbous, A., Aoun Barakat, K., & Merhej Sayegh, M. (2020). Social commerce success: Antecedents of purchase intention and the mediating role of trust. *Journal of Internet Commerce, 19*(3), 262–297. https://doi.org/10.1080/15332861.2020.1756190

Fishbein, M., & Ajzen, I. (2011). *Predicting and changing behavior: The reasoned action approach.* Psychology Press. https://doi.org/10.4324/9780203838020

Floyd, K., Freling, R., Alhoqail, S., Cho, H. Y., & Freling, T. (2014). How online product reviews affect retail sales: A meta-analysis. *Journal of Retailing, 90*(2), 217–232. https://doi.org/10.1016/j.jretai.2014.04.004

Fogg, B. J., Ph, D., Soohoo, C., Danielson, D., Marable, L., Stanford, J., & Tauber, E. R. (2003). How do people evaluate the credibility of web sites? A study with over 2,500 participants. In *Proceedings of the 2003 conference on designing for user experiences*, 1–15. https://doi.org/10.1.1.125.8137

Fogg, B. J., Cuellar, G., & Danielson, D. (2007). Motivating, influencing, and persuading users: An introduction to captology. In A. Sears & J. A. Jacko (Eds.), *The human-computer interaction handbook* (2nd ed., pp. 133–146). CRC Press. https://doi.org/10.1201/9781410615862

Hodkinson, C. (2019). 'Fear of missing out' (FOMO) marketing appeals: A conceptual model. *Journal of Marketing Communications, 25*(1), 65–88. https://doi.org/10.1080/13527266.2016.1234504

Hu, H., & Krishen, A. S. (2019). When is enough, enough? Investigating product reviews and information overload from a consumer empowerment perspective. *Journal of Business Research, 100*(October 2018), 27–37. https://doi.org/10.1016/j.jbusres.2019.03.011

Huseynov, F., & Özkan Yıldırım, S. (2019). Online consumer typologies and their shopping behaviors in B2C e-commerce platforms. *SAGE Open, 9*(2). https://doi.org/10.1177/2158244019854639

Ibrahim, B., Aljarah, A., & Ababneh, B. (2020). Do social media marketing activities enhance consumer perception of brands? A meta-analytic examination. *Journal of Promotion Management, 26*(4), 544–568. https://doi.org/10.1080/10496491.2020.1719956

Ingham, J., Cadieux, J., & Mekki Berrada, A. (2015). E-Shopping acceptance: A qualitative and meta-analytic review. *Information and Management, 52*(1), 44–60. https://doi.org/10.1016/j.im.2014.10.002

Ismagilova, E., Slade, E. L., Rana, N. P., & Dwivedi, Y. K. (2020). The effect of electronic word of mouth communications on intention to buy: A meta-analysis. In *Information Systems Frontiers, 22*(5), 1203–1226. https://doi.org/10.1007/s10796-019-09924-y

Iyer, G. R., Blut, M., Xiao, S. H., & Grewal, D. (2020). Impulse buying: A meta-analytic review. *Journal of the Academy of Marketing Science, 48*(3), 384–404. https://doi.org/10.1007/s11747-019-00670-w

Karagoel, I., & Nathan-Roberts, D. (2021). Dark patterns: Social media, gaming, and e-commerce. *Proceedings of the Human Factors and Ergonomics Society Annual Meeting, 65*(1), 752–756. https://doi.org/10.1177/1071181321651317

Lindgaard, G., Fernandes, G., Dudek, C., & Browñ, J. (2006). Attention web designers: You have 50 milliseconds to make a good first impression! *Behaviour and Information Technology, 25*(2), 115–126. https://doi.org/10.1080/01449290500330448

Manolică, A., Guță, A. S., Roman, T., & Dragăn, L. M. (2021). Is consumer overchoice a reason for decision paralysis? In *Sustainability (Switzerland)* (Vol. 13, Issue 11). https://doi.org/10.3390/su13115920

Morrin, M., Broniarczyk, S. M., & Inman, J. J. (2012). Plan format and participation in 401(k) Plans: The moderating role of investor knowledge. *Journal of Public Policy and Marketing, 31*(2), 254–268. https://doi.org/10.1509/jppm.10.122

Nardi, V. A. M., Jardim, W. C., Ladeira, W. J., & Santini, F. (2020). A meta-analysis of the relationship between customer participation and brand outcomes. *Journal of Business Research, 117*(October 2019), 450–460. https://doi.org/10.1016/j.jbusres.2020.06.017

Oyibo, K., Adaji, I., & Vassileva, J. (2018). What drives the perceived credibility of health apps: Classical or expressive aesthetics? *CEUR Workshop proceedings, 2216*(1), 30–35.

Park, J., & Hill, W. T. (2018). Exploring the role of justification and cognitive effort exertion on post-purchase regret in online shopping. *Computers in Human Behavior, 83*, 235–242. https://doi.org/10.1016/j.chb.2018.01.036

Pee, L., Jiang, J., & Klein, G. (2019). E-store loyalty: Longitudinal comparison of website usefulness and satisfaction. *International Journal of Market Research, 61*(2), 178–194. https://doi.org/10.1177/1470785317752045

Pham, M. T., & Sun, J. J. (2020). On the experience and engineering of consumer pride, consumer excitement, and consumer relaxation in the marketplace. *Journal of Retailing, 96*(1), 101–127. https://doi.org/10.1016/j.jretai.2019.11.003

Reichheld, F. F., & Sasser Jr., W. E. (1990). Zero defections: Quality comes to services. *Harvard Business Review, 68*(5), 105–111.

Salehudin, I., & Alpert, F. (2021). To pay or not to pay: Understanding mobile game app users' unwillingness to pay for in-app purchases. *Journal of Research in Interactive Marketing*. https://doi.org/10.1108/JRIM-02-2021-0053

Smith, A., Project, A. L., & Anderson, J. Q. (2012). The future of money: Smartphone swiping in the mobile age. *Pew Research Center's Internet & American Life Project*.

Soman, D. (2003). The effect of payment transparency on consumption: Quasi-experiments from the field. *Marketing Letters, 14*(3), 173–183. https://doi.org/10.1023/A:1027444717586

Soroush, M., Hancock, M., & Bonns, V. K. (2014). Self-control in casual games: The relationship between Candy Crush Saga players' in-app purchases and self-control. *2014 IEEE Games Media Entertainment*, 1–6. https://doi.org/10.1109/GEM.2014.7048099

Valvi, A. C., & Fragkos, K. C. (2012). Critical review of the e-loyalty literature: A purchase-centred framework. *Electronic Commerce Research, 12*(3), 331–378. https://doi.org/10.1007/s10660-012-9097-5

Virdi, P., Kalro, A. D., & Sharma, D. (2020). Online decision aids: The role of decision-making styles and decision-making stages. *International Journal of Retail and Distribution Management, 48*(6), 555–574. https://doi.org/10.1108/IJRDM-02-2019-0068

Yoo, J., & Kim, M. (2014). The effects of home page design on consumer responses: Moderating role of centrality of visual product aesthetics. *Computers in Human Behavior, 38*, 240–247. https://doi.org/10.1016/j.chb.2014.05.030

Zerbini, C., Bijmolt, T. H. A., Maestripieri, S., & Luceri, B. (2022). Drivers of consumer adoption of e-commerce: A meta-analysis. *International Journal of Research in Marketing*. https://doi.org/10.1016/j.ijresmar.2022.04.003

Young People and the Internet

17

Irene Connolly

Chapter Overview

Developmental psychology examines the areas of cognitive, physical, and language development, alongside social and emotional development in young people. This chapter presents these developmental areas concerning a young person's interaction with the Internet. Technology offers entertainment and communication while cognitively and educationally providing an outlet for critical thinking and creativity; however it also exposes young people to some risks. This chapter will focus on the risk of cyberbullying, while other risks are examined in Chapters 5, 10, and 11.

Key Terms

Embracing technology as part of young people's development is a natural progression in today's society. At no other time in our history has this been more apparent than during the COVID-19 pandemic. Technology acted as a tool for communication between educators and young people and a means of socialising with peers during a time when physical interaction was inadvisable. As a result, the debate over whether technology plays a **negative** or **positive** role in young people's lives has taken a different turn.

In developed countries, pre-schoolers are also going online, with babies under the age of two having an **online presence**, often through their parents' devices. Research has shown that young people's preferred method of accessing the Internet is through using a smartphone; less than 50% use desktops or notebooks, 3–15% access through a wearable device, and 1–18% connect using a toy (EU kids online, 2020). In the United Kingdom, figures show that 52% of three- to four-year-olds and 82% of five- to seven-year-olds are online (Ofcom, 2019), reinforcing the idea proposed by Prensky in 2001 of young people as **digital natives** (Prensky, 2001).

DOI: 10.4324/9781003092513-23

The Positive Role of Technology

Young people's interaction with technology focuses on social media, apps, and gaming. On an individual level, social media allows young people to connect or socialise with others, hence developing social skills and interests, or simply providing entertainment. It can be used to share knowledge such as class assignments/homework or group work with one another. It can build communities, as physical boundaries are no longer an issue in the virtual world (Akram & Kumar, 2017).

Past research has emphasised the importance of technology in the classroom, where it was recognised as a fundamental tool, stimulating the language, cognitive, and social development of young children (Couse & Chen, 2010). It exposes them to an environment of activities and information that would be impossible without technology. Furthermore, adolescents use the Internet when seeking information about health and sex, particularly when it is not available from personal face-to-face sources like friends or family (Ngo et al., 2008). Technology connects children to the world, by providing access to

Figure 17.1
Time on technology.

people and resources throughout the world. The positive role of technology during the pandemic has been acknowledged widely. Socially, it made a difficult time more bearable for young people, while allowing them to pursue their education remotely. Online learning during the pandemic is discussed further in Chapter 15.

During adolescence, identity formation is paramount, where young people reassess their childhood identifications as their awareness of societal values increases (Erikson, 1968). Changes to one's identity during this period are influenced dually by societal practices and cognitive changes. Now operating within the formal operations level of cognitive development (Piaget, 1981) permits the young person to begin to form an identity of themselves, encapsulating their role within society. The ability to adopt new and varied social roles magnifies the possibilities available to them as they form their self-theory.

Today, the Internet provides individuals with even more options for identity experimentation, with young people using social media as platforms for self-expression, self-construction, and identity exploration (Patchin & Hinduja, 2017). Social media plays a role in identity-building and self-expression (Eleuteri et al., 2017), including sexual identity and gender (Crocetti, 2017). Socialising and relationship-building habits through various social media platforms imitate the same methods of offline behaviour, with the numerous tools allowing them to manage a variety of different types of relationships online. Wang and Simon (2016) found that, rather than intentionally trying to harm others, there was a great effort by young people to protect and support one another, allowing friendships to develop online.

Social media keeps young people up-to-date concerning the important things happening to their friends. Although offline interactions remain very important for young people, they have been complemented and partially replaced by interactions via social media. Modes of young people's social media interactions can be characterised as mixed modalities (Decieux, Heinen, & Willems, 2019). They can exchange news instantaneously with their friends without having to wait to meet up, while visual content adds to the richness of interactions and increases their social presence (Thulin, 2017). Young people view social media activities as a way to support existing friendships (Awan & Gauntlett, 2013).

Young people use social media to obtain emotional support or to educate themselves about mental health issues. Furthermore, individuals use social media to develop a sense of belonging with online digital communities. Communicating with others who share similar characteristics or ideals can be extremely empowering, allowing minority groups (such as those with disabilities, those from ethnic minority groups, or people who identify as LGBTQI+) to become "global citizens" which can prevent a sense of isolation, help the development of a personal identity, and increase resilience in young people who might not have that presence in their real-life communities (Farnham et al., 2013).

CYBERPSYCHOLOGY IN FOCUS: YOUNG PEOPLE USE OF SOCIAL MEDIA FOR SUPPORT

With young people turning to social media for online support when they are going through difficult times, work has begun by clinicians and researchers to explore the potential of online support to reach young people in distress (Gibson & Trnka, 2020). This includes developing and investigating the value of mental health information available online (Gowen, 2013), text-based counselling support (Gibson & Cartwright, 2014), digital computer games (Merry et al., 2012), and social media interventions that aim to identify those with high levels of distress or suicidality so that they can receive targeted support (Robinson et al., 2015). Providing young people with quality support from trusted sources is key here.

There is a plethora of research examining whether or not technology is beneficial or detrimental to young people, with the research examining the socio-emotional, psychological, and physical impacts of technology, which in turn has led to systematic analyses (Dickson et al., 2018; Orben, 2020) of the work being carried out, with the outcome suggesting that, despite all of the studies conducted, there is no scientific consensus on the impact of social media/technology engagement on young people's mental health (Frith, 2017). Recent analyses and reviews have shown a trend whereby individuals who report greater technology engagement tend to also report higher levels of mental health problems, but the factors underlying these cross-sectional relationships remain poorly understood (Appel et al., 2020). Much of this research is restricted by its use of self-reports of technology use, which can be biased and not true reflections of online engagement (Johannes et al., 2020; Parry et al., 2020; Scharkow, 2016; Shaw et al., 2020). Orben's (2020) systematic review and data analyses suggest that research on the effects of young people's use of technology and social media on their well-being reveals inconsistent results – the lack of quality of the studies causes the production of much conflicting evidence. Orben suggests that research focused on the area of young people's interaction with technology should increase in clarity, uniformity, and proficiency.

Gaming

There has been much debate over the past few years regarding the potential mental health effects of video gaming or online gaming for the players. While the *Diagnostic and Statistical Manual of Mental Disorders* (DSM-5) did not classify any psychiatric conditions it does recommend that Internet gaming disorder should be researched in more detail (Kardefelt-Winther, 2015). The World Health Organization adopted a more definitive approach and included gaming disorder in the International Classification of Diseases (ICD-11), accentuating extreme amounts of time spent gaming as an essential element (Aarsett et al., 2017).

The potential influence of video games on the social behaviour of young people has drawn much attention. As this group's leisure has increasingly moved away from public spaces, home media use has increased, with young people spending more time on media than any other activity (Coyne et al., 2013). Compared to the video games of the past, modern video games have become increasingly social in nature (Olson, 2010). Many games require social and emotional skills to play the game at the maximum level; these skills are also necessary to succeed in the workplace and adult life (Hromek & Roffey, 2009). Prosocial skills include controlling negative emotions, taking turns, and sharing, and also support orientations to others that are reasonable and respectful. Furthermore, massively multiplayer online games encourage social links among players, creating a community constructed on cooperation (Cole & Griffiths, 2007). Gaming can be cooperative (working together to achieve an objective) or competitive (a distinct win or lose outcome), where cooperative gaming may promote prosocial behaviour (Dolgov et al., 2014) and may curb aggressive behaviours (Velez et al., 2014).

The amount of time young people spend gaming and the consequences of this are a source of much research. Eklund and Roman (2019) investigated how time spent on digital gaming influenced how teenagers made friends during the first year of high school, using interview data to explore the subjective experiences of young people. They found no indication that high-use players made fewer friends during their first year of upper-secondary school than non- or infrequent players. Results indicated that similar usage of digital gaming enabled social relationships, but did not support the idea that this similar use determined friendship creation. In interviews, young people discussed how they actively managed their schedule to include gaming, social life, and school. This suggests that gaming is seen as part of their socialisation with others, rather than something distinct from it.

In a study of six-year-olds in Norway, Hygen et al. (2020) examined gaming patterns in relation to their social development. This was followed up at ages 8, 10, and 12 while controlling for body mass index, socioeconomic status, and time spent gaming together with their friends. The results found that greater social competence at ages eight and ten years predicted less gaming two years later. They also reported that higher levels of gaming at age 10 predicted less social competence at age 12, but only found this in females. This led the authors to question that perhaps children with less social competence spend longer times gaming and hence questioned whether they should be allowed to game for such long periods.

Furthermore, a large-scale, cross-sectional study among Canadian adolescents indicated that video gameplay was positively associated with symptoms of depression and anxiety (Maras et al., 2015). These problems seem to emerge as a result of the diversion; problematic gamers seem attracted to gaming as a way to avoid their problems. This escapism may offer fleeting digression, but without addressing real-world difficulties, extreme gaming may only aggravate the struggles. The cross-sectional nature of previous studies continues to query whether individuals with internalising problems retreat to video games as an escape, or whether gaming acts as a predecessor to these problems. Spending time online can be very rewarding but there are also some risks associated with it.

Recent research which examined children's perceived life satisfaction, while accounting for gender, age, socio-economic status (SES), emotional problems, country of origin, and family environmental factors, found that, in 11,200 children (aged 9–16 years) surveyed across Europe, time spent online appeared to have no negative effect on their self-reported life satisfaction (SRLS). Furthermore, the positive effects of children's family environment and their socioeconomic status accounted for 43% of the overall 50% of the variance in SRLS scores (Milosevic et al., 2022).

Cyberbullying

Although technology presents risks such as cyberbullying and associated well-being, George and Odgers (2015) found that most behaviours and risks that occur online can often be predicted by offline behaviours and personal characteristics. Young people are aware of the risks online and feel that they are prepared to handle them, but this is not always the case (Gazzard & Stone, 2019).

Cyberbullying has been defined as "an aggressive, intentional act carried out by a group or individual, using electronic forms of contact, repeatedly and overtime against a victim who cannot easily defend him or herself" (Smith et al., 2008, p. 376). Unlike traditional bullying, cyberbullying does not involve face-to-face or physical confrontation. It does not require any close proximity to the cybervictim and can be conducted from any location. There is little escape from it: cyberbullying can occur at any time as long as the cybervictim is accessing technology.

Figure 17.2
Gaming in action.

Under closer examination, it becomes apparent that many of the online behaviours may be variations of offline behaviour now being carried out online. The following are methods used by cyberbullies in the execution of cyberbullying. Firstly, *flaming* is an online fight with one person or a group, where the exchange is usually vulgar and explicit. This is similar to an offline argument. *Denigration* involves sending or posting gossip or rumours about a person to damage his or her reputation or friendships. The equivalent real-world action is gossiping. *Social exclusion* is similar to the traditional form of exclusionary bullying, where one person is left out of the social group. In the cyberbullying context, this occurs by being deleted or completely omitted from social media groups.

In addition, there are also cyberbullying methods that are solely techno-logically based, such as *outing and trickery*: tricking someone into giving embar-rassing information and either posting it online or sending it on to others. *Masquerading/impersonation* is pretending to be someone else by obtaining access to their social media page/mobile phone; they can alter information about that person's status or send damaging messages to other people (Willard, 2004). *Cyberstalking* is repeated, intense harassment that includes threats or cre-ates significant fear. An example of this is a young person receiving a multitude of messages/posts from the same person with whom they don't wish to have a conversation. It may continue despite a lack of response from the cybervictim.

Another concern is the issue of *sexting*. Sexting is defined as the "send-ing or receiving of sexually explicit or sexually suggestive nude or semi-nude images or video", usually via mobile devices (Hinduja & Patchin, 2012, p. 50; Patchin & Hinduja, 2019a). Sexting is relatively common among young people as a method of starting a romantic relationship with another person (Bianchi et al., 2016). Foody et al. (2021) carried out research on a sample of adolescents from the age of 15 to 18 years, where they found that receiving sexts is more common (9.4%) than sending them (4.3%). Only a small proportion of adoles-cents reported that they were two-way sexters (12.6%), with most sexts sent or received by a romantic partner.

While these rates are relatively low, it is important to educate young peo-ple about the permanence of those images online. While they are exchanging images with romantic partners, relationships don't always last, which leaves the images in the hands of someone with whom they may no longer be on good terms. The issue of distributing intimate images (also known as *revenge porn*) has become something of concern for many countries, with several introduc-ing laws to combat the issue. One example is Ireland, where provisions regard-ing the distribution of intimate images (also unofficially known as Coco's law in honour of Nicole "Coco" Fox) were added to the Harassment, Harmful Communications, and Related Offences Bill in 2020, to deal with the growing issue of intimate images being released online without the person's knowledge or their permission.

Another issue contributing to cyberbullying is anonymity, which seems to embolden the cyberbully; the belief that they cannot be identified seems to remove social inhibition and norms (Hinduja & Patchin, 2006a), resulting in **disinhibition** (Suler, 2004), where young people say and do things online that they might never do face to face. Dooley, Pyzalksi, and Cross (2009) put forward an argument that a further power imbalance exists within cyberbullying which is the permanency of materials in the cyber world and the difficulties associated with attempting to remove them, hence contributing to the powerlessness of the cybervictim.

Psychological Effects of Cybervictimisation

Research has begun to investigate the consequences of cybervictimisation where the magnitude of the effect on the cybervictims could be related to the potential audience to their harassment (Slonje, 2011). Early research by Beran and Li (2005) on 432 Canadian students in grades 7–9 found the following psycho-social outcomes of being the victim of cyberbullying. The cybervictims reported anger, anxiety, and feeling sad, but the cybervictims also reported that they found it difficult to concentrate in school, affecting both their learning ability and their consequent success at school. In addition, Hinduja and Patchin (2009) in a study of almost 2,000 middle school students in the US also found that the cybervictims reported similar effects of anger and sadness, but also being frustrated and even scared following a cyberbullying episode. This research revealed that the self-esteem of both the cyberbullies and cybervictims was lower than their counterparts who were not involved in bullying. In terms of consequences, research has regularly found that experiences with both school bullying and cyberbullying contribute to a host of maladaptive emotional, psychological, behavioural, and even physical problems. These include, but are not limited to, anger, self-pity, depression, anxiety, eating disorders, and chronic illness (Bauman et al., 2013). Minor and moderate forms of school misbehaviour and violence have also been associated with cyberbullying (Nixon, 2014).

Tackling Cyberbullying

To counter this, a whole-school approach is required, where parents and schools work together to counter cyberbullying. Anti-bullying programmes vary across the world, with many educating young people about the role of being a bystander and developing a positive school climate while encouraging parents to speak with their children regularly about online safety. The KiVa approach (kivaprogram.net) in Finland is an example of an empirically based anti-bullying programme (Salmivalli et al., 2012).The KiVa programme offers a range of tools and materials for schools to tackle bullying. Analysis of KiVa shows that it has reduced bullying and victimisation, while it increases empathy towards victimised peers and self-efficacy to defend them. Furthermore, the programme produced reductions in the reinforcement of the bullies' behaviour. A further finding was that students participating in KiVa had an increase in school liking and school motivation, while it has led to significant reductions in anxiety, depression, and negative peer perceptions among children and youth (Salmivalli et al., 2013). Gaffney et al. (2021), in a systematic review of school-based anti-bullying programmes, found that they were effective in reducing bullying perpetration outcomes by roughly 18–19% and bullying victimisation by roughly 15–16%. The findings implied that numerous intervention elements, such as a whole-school approach, the existence of an anti-bullying policy in schools, classroom rules, information for parents, unofficial peer involvement, and working with victims, were significantly correlated with larger effect sizes for school-bullying perpetration consequences. The occurrence of unofficial peer involvement and information for parents were correlated with larger effect sizes for school-bullying victimisation outcomes. Schools often have to deal with the consequences of cyberbullying, although it takes place off school grounds. Therefore, it is vital to include cyberbullying in a school's anti-bullying policy in an attempt to counter bullying as a whole. Technology and young people are now intrinsically linked, so it's important to educate each child from a very young age about the appropriate way to behave online, so that anonymity and disinhibition are not excuses for inappropriate behaviour. Education is key here, and programmes need to be implemented in schools across the world to keep our young people safe in all online interactions. It is also important to provide a strong roadmap of how and where to seek help, should they require it.

Conclusion

Technology has become an integral part of young people's lives. Parents and teachers need to guide them from a very early age, with regard to acceptable online behaviour and also the dangers that exist. The positive aspects of technology use are vast and increasing steadily. Cognitive, social, and emotional development, alongside linguistic development, all occur through the use of technology. Further enhancement can occur through increased student motivation to learn and the exploration of one's identity. Establishing ways to stay safe online and educating young people about the potential risks online are vitally important. Specific attention for "at risk" children is required as a result of increasing evidence that those low in self-esteem, or without satisfying friendships or relations with parents, are at risk through online social networking communication (Livingstone & Helsper, 2007) and that those at risk may also be those who then perpetuate harm towards others. Finally, the "online" world and the "offline" are not seen as two distinct worlds by young people. They are simply different elements of the same world that they occupy. There is the idea that switching off the technology and reverting to the real world will solve problems, but this is rarely the case. As a consequence, we as educators and researchers need to ensure that when young people access technology they are safe and their rights as young people extend into the digital world.

Activity

Technology offers wonderful opportunities for learning, working, sharing, and having fun. It is a big part of young people's lives and their future. Design a board game (old-fashioned approach) highlighting the positives and negatives of technology. Then explore how this game could be implemented online, highlighting safety and responsibility online.

Discussion Questions

1. What are the psychological impacts of experiencing being cyberbullied?
2. Technology is part of a young person's social development. Do you think it is possible to live without technology in our society today? Support your answer.
3. Why do children and young people enjoy online gaming? Give examples using games that you play.
4. Should parents have access to a young person's online world? Or is this a breach of their privacy?

Recommended Reading List

Sonia Livingstone and Alicia Blum-Ross have written extensively in the area. This book focuses on parenting in the digital age and insights relevant to parents, policymakers, educators, and researchers everywhere.

> Livingstone, S., & Blum-Ross, A. (2020). *Parenting for a digital age: How hopes and fears about technology shape children's lives.* Oxford University Press.

EU Kids Online is a multinational research network. It seeks to enhance knowledge of European children's online opportunities, risks, and safety (2020). http://www.lse.ac.uk/media@lse/research/EUKidsOnline/Home.aspx

> Smahel, D., Machackova, H., Mascheroni, G., Dedkova, L., Staksrud, E., Ólafsson, K., Livingstone, S., & Hasebrink, U. (2020). *EU kids online 2020: Survey results from 19 countries.* EU Kids Online. https://doi.org/10.21953/lse.47fdeqj01ofo

Cheryl Olson writes about whether children should play video games and how to maximise potential benefits and identify and minimise potential harms.

Olson, C. K. (2010). Children's motivations for video game play in the context of normal development. *Review of General Psychology, 14*(2), 180. https://doi.org/10.1037/a0018984

Sameer Hinduja and Justin Patchin have produced a great deal of research on cyberbullying in the United States. This book provides the tools to prevent and respond to cyberbullying.

Hinduja, S., & Patchin, J. W. (2015). *Bullying beyond the schoolyard: Preventing and responding to cyberbullying* (2nd Ed.). Sage Publications.

KiVa is an anti-bullying programme that is evidence-based which means that the effectiveness of KiVa has been proven scientifically. KiVa offers a wide range of concrete tools and materials for schools to tackle bullying.

KiVa Anti Bullying Program (2021). https://www.kivaprogram.net/

Glossary

Anonymity: Nobody can identify you online.
Cyberbullying: Various types of bullying that occur using technology.
Disinhibition: Behaving differently in the online world than in the real world.
Online gaming: Computer or console/video games that can be played over the Internet with other players.

References

Akram, W., & Kumar, R. (2017). A study on positive and negative effects of social media on society. *International Journal of Computer Sciences and Engineering, 5*(10), 351–354. https://doi.org/10.26438/ijcse/v5i10.351354

Appel, M., Marker, C., & Gnambs, T. (2020). Are social media ruining our lives? A review of meta-analytic evidence. *Review of General Psychology, 24*(1), 60–74. https://doi.org/10.1177/1089268019880891

Awan, F., & Gauntlett, D. (2013). Young people's uses and understandings of online social networks in their everyday lives. *Young, 21*(2), 111–132. https://doi.org/10.1177/1103308813477463

Bauman, S., Toomey, R., & Walker, J. (2013). Associations among bullying, cyberbullying, and suicide in high school students. *Journal of Adolescence, 36*(2), 341–350. https://doi.org/10.1016/j.adolescence.2012.12.001

Beran, T., & Li, Q. (2005). Cyber-harassment: A study of a new method for an old behaviour. *Journal of Educational Computing Research, 32*(3), 265–277. https://doi.org/10.2190/8YQM-BO4H-PG4D-BLLH.

Bianchi, D., Morelli, M., Baiocco, R., & Chirumbolo, A. (2016). Psychometric properties of the Sexting Motivations Questionnaire for adolescents and young adults. *Rassegna di Psicologia, 35*(3), 5–18. https://doi.org/10.4558/8067.

Cole, H., & Griffiths, M. (2007). Social interaction in massively multiplayer online role-playing games. *Cyberpsychology and Behaviour, 10*(4), 575–583. https://doi.org/10.1089/cpb.2007.9988.

Couse, L. J., & Chen, D. W. (2010). A tablet computer for young children? Exploring its viability for early childhood education. *Journal of Research on Technology in Education, 43*(1), 75–89. https://doi.org/10.1111/j.1083-6101 .2007.00380.x

Coyne, S. M., Padilla-Walker, L. M., & Howard, E. (2013). Emerging in a digital world: A decade review of media use, effects, and gratifications in emerging adulthood. *Emerging Adulthood, 1*(2), 2. https://doi.org/10.1177 /2167696813479782

Crocetti, E. (2017). Identity formation in adolescence: The dynamic of forming and consolidating identity commitments. *Child Development Perspectives, 11*(2), 145–150. https://doi.org/10.1111/cdep.12226.

Décieux, J. P., Heinen, A., & Willems, H. (2019). Social media and its role in friendship-driven interactions among young people: A mixed methods study. *Young, 27*(1), 18–31. https://doi.org/10.1177/1103308818755516.

Dickson, K., Richardson, M., Kwan, I., Macdowall, W., Burchett, H.,, & Stansfield, C. (2018). *Screen-based activities and children and young people's mental health and psychosocial wellbeing: A systematic map of reviews.* EPPI-Centre, Social Science Research Unit, UCL Institute of Education, University College London.

Dolgov, I., Graves, W. J., Nearents, M. R., Schwark, J. D., & Brooks Volkman, C. (2014). Effects of cooperative gaming and avatar customization on subsequent spontaneous helping behavior. *Computers in Human Behavior, 33,* 49–55. https://doi.org/10.1016/j.chb.2013.12.028

Dooley, J. J., Pyzalksi, J., & Cross, D. (2009). Cyberbullying versus face to face bullying. A theoretical and conceptual review. *Journal of Psychology, 217*(4), 182–188. https://doi.org/10.1027/0044-3409.217.4.182

Eklund, L., & Roman, S. (2019). Digital gaming and young People's friendships: A mixed methods study of time use and gaming in school. *Young, 27*(1), 32–47. https://doi.org/10.1177/1103308818754990.

Eleuteri, S., Saladino, V., & Verrastro, V. (2017). Identity, relationships, sexuality, and risky behaviors of adolescents in the context of social media. *Sexual and Relationship Therapy, 32*(3–4), 354–365. https://doi.org/10.1080/14681994 .2017.1397953

Erikson, E. (1968). *Identity: Youth and crisis.* WW Norton & Company.

Farnham, J. M., Sulmasy, L. S., Worster, B. K., Chaudhry, H. J., Rhyne, J. A., & Arora, V. M. (2013). Online medical professionalism: Patient and public relationships. Policy statement from the American College of physicians and federation of state boards. *Annals of Internal Medicine, 158,* 620–627. https:// doi.org/10.7326/0003-4819-158-8-201304160-00100.

Foody, M., Mazzone, A., Laffan, D. A., Loftsson, M., & O'Higgins Norman, J. (2021). "It's not just sexy pics": An investigation into sexting behaviour and behavioural problems in adolescents. *Computers in Human Behavior, 117,* 106662. https://doi.org/10.1016/j.chb.2020.106662.

Frith, E. (2017). *Social media and children's mental health: A review of the evidence.* Education Policy Institute. Retrieved June 10, 2021, from https://epi.org.uk /wp-content/uploads/2018/01/Social-Media_Mental-Health_EPI-Report.pdf

Gaffney, H., Ttofi, M. M., & Farrington, D. P. (2021). Effectiveness of school-based programs to reduce bullying perpetration and victimization: An updated systematic review and meta-analysis. *Campbell Systematic Review, 17*(2), e1143. https://doi.org/10.1002/cl2.1143

Gazzard, J., & Stone, S. (2019). Social media and young people's health. In S. Stone, J. Gazzard, & M. R. Muzio (Eds.), *Selected topic in child and adolescent mental health* (pp. 7–21). InTechOpen. https://doi.org/10.5772/intechopen .88569

George, M., & Odgers, C. (2015). Seven fears and the science of how mobile technologies may be influencing adolescents in the digital age. *Perspectives on Psychological Science, 10*(6), 832–851. http://doi.org/10.1177 /1745691615596788

Gibson, K., & Cartwright, C. (2014). Young people's experiences of mobile phone text counselling: Balancing connection and control. *Children and Youth Services Review, 43*, 96–104. https://doi.org/10.1016/j.childyouth.2014 .05.010

Gibson, K., & Trnka, S. (2020). Young people's priorities for support on social media: "It takes trust to talk about these issues". *Computers in Human Behavior, 102*, 238–247. https://doi.org/10.1016/j.chb.2019.08.030

Gowen, L. K. (2013). Online mental health information seeking in young adults with mental health challenges. *Journal of Technology in Human Services, 31*(2), 97–111. https://doi.org/10.1080/15228835.2013.765533

Hinduja, S., & Patchin, J. W. (2006a). Bullies move beyond the schoolyard: A preliminary look at cyberbullying. *Youth Violence and Juvenile Justice, 4*(2), 148–169.

Hinduja, S., & Patchin, J. W. (2009). *Bullying beyond the schoolyard: Preventing and responding to cyberbullying.* Sage Publications.

Hinduja, S., & Patchin, J. W. (2012). *School climate 2.0: Preventing cyberbullying and sexting, one classroom at a time.* Sage Publications.

Hromek, R., & Roffey, S. (2009). Promoting social and emotional learning with games: Its fun and we learn things. *Simulation & Gaming, 40*(5), 626–644. https://doi.org/10.1016/j.sbspro.2014.07.696

Hygen, B., Belsky, J., Stenseng, F., Skalicka, V., Kvande, M., Zahl-Thanem, T., & Wichstrøm, L. (2020). Time spent gaming and social competence in children: Reciprocal effects across childhood. *Child Development, 91*(3), 861–875. http://doi.org/10.1111/cdev.13243

Johannes, N., Vuorre, M., & Przybylski, A. K. (2020). Video game play is positively correlated with well-being. *PsyArXiv.* https://doi.org/10.31234/osf .io/qrjza

Kardefelt-Winther, D. (2015). A critical account of DSM-5 criteria for Internet gaming disorder. *Addiction Research and Theory, 23*(2), 93–98. https://doi.org /10.3109/16066359.2014.935350

Livingstone, S., & Blum-Ross, A. (2020). *Parenting for a digital age: How hopes and fears about technology shape children's lives.* Oxford University Press.

Livingstone, S., & Helsper, E. (2007). Graduations in digital inclusion: Children, young people and the digital divide. *New Media and Society, 9*(4), 671–696. https://doi.org/10.1177/146144807080335.

Maras, D., Flament, M. F., Murray, M., Buchholz, A., Henderson, K. A., Obeid, N., & Goldfield, G. S. (2015). Screen time is associated with depression and anxiety in Canadian youth. *Preventive Medicine, 73*, 133–138. https://doi.org /10.1016/j.ypmed.2015.01.029

Merry, S. N., Stasiak, K., Shepherd, M., Framptom, C., Fleming, T., & Lucassen, M. F. (2012). The effectiveness of SPARX, a computerised self-help intervention for adolescents seeking help for depression: Randomised controlled non-inferiority trial. *BMJ, 344*, e2598. https://doi.org/10.1136/bmj.e2598

Milosevic, T., Kuldas, S., Sargioti, A., Laffan, D. A., & O'Higgins Norman, J. (2022). Children's Internet use, self-reported life satisfaction, and parental mediation in Europe: An analysis of the EU kids online dataset. *Frontiers in Psychology, 12,* 698176. https://doi.org/10.3389/fpsyg.2021.698176

Ngo, A. D., Ross, M. W., & Ratliff, E. A. (2008). Internet influences on sexual practices among young people in Hanoi, Vietnam. *Culture, Health and Sexuality, 10,* S201–S213. https://doi.org/10.1080/13691050701749873

Nixon, C. L. (2014). Current perspectives: The impact of Cyberbullying on Adolescent health. *Adolescent Health, Medicine and Therapeutics, 5,* 143. https://doi.org/10.2147/AHMT.S36456

Ofcom (2019). *Children and parents: Media use and attitudes report 2018.* Retrieved June 8, 2021, from https://www.ofcom.org.uk/research-and-data/media-literacy-research/childrens/children-and-parents-media-use-and-attitudes-report-2018

Harassment, harmful communications and related offences bill (2017). Retrieved April 26, 2021, from https://data.oireachtas.ie/ie/oireachtas/bill/2017/63/eng/ver_a/b63a17d.pdf

Olson, C. K. (2010). Children's motivations for video game play in the context of normal development. *Review of General Psychology, 14*(2), 180. https://doi.org/10.1037/a0018984

Orben, A. (2020). Teenagers, screens and social media: A narrative review of reviews and key studies. *Social Psychiatry and Psychiatric Epidemiology, 55*(4), 407–414.https://doi.org/10.1007/s00127-019-01825-4

Parry, D. A., Davidson, B. I., Sewall, C., Fisher, J. T., Mieczkowski, H., & Quintana, D. (2020). *Measurement discrepancies between logged and self-reported digital media use: A systematic review and meta-analysis.* PsyArXiV. https://doi.org/10.31234/osf.io/f6xvz

Patchin, J. W., & Hinduja, S. (2017). Digital self-harm among adolescents. *Journal of Adolescent Health, 61*(6), 761–766. https://doi.org/10.1016/j.jadohealth.2017.06.012

Patchin, J. W., & Hinduja, S. (2019a). It is time to teach safe sexting. *Journal of Adolescent Health, 66*(2), 140–143. https://doi.org/10.1016/j.jadohealth.2019.10.010

Piaget, J. (1981). *Intelligence and affectivity: Their relationship during child development.* Annual Reviews.

Prensky, M. (2001). Digital natives, digital immigrants, Part 1. *On The Horizon, 9,* 3–6. http://doi.org/10.1108/10748120110424816

Robinson, J., Cox, G., Bailey, E., Hetrick, S., & Rodriguez, M. (2015). Social media and suicide prevention: A systematic review. *Early Intervention in Psychiatry, 10*(2), 103–121. https://doi.org/10.1111/eip.12229

Salmivalli, C., Garandeau, C. F., & Veenstra, R. (2012). KiVa anti-bullying program: Implications for school adjustment. In A. M. Ryan & G. W. Ladd (Eds.), *Adolescence and education: Peer relationships and adjustment at school* (pp. 279–305). IAP Information Age Publishing.

Salmivalli, C., Poskiparta, E., Ahtola, A., & Haataja, A. (2013). The implementation and effectiveness of the Kiva Antibullying Program in Finland. *European Psychologist, 18*(2), 79–88. https://doi.org/10.1027/1016-9040/a000140

Scharkow, M. (2016). The accuracy of self-reported Internet use—A validation study using client log data. *Communication Methods and Measures, 10*(1), 13–27. https://doi.org/10.1080/19312458.2015.1118446

Shaw, H., Ellis, D. A., Geyer, K., Davidson, B. I., Ziegler, F. V., & Smith, A. (2020). Quantifying smartphone 'use': Choice of measurement impacts relationships between 'usage' and health. PsyArXiv. https://doi.org/10.31234/osf.io/mpxra

Slonje, R. (2011). *The nature of cyberbullying in Swedish schools: Processes, feelings of remorse by bullies, impact on victims and age and gender differences.* Unpublished PhD thesis, Goldsmiths, University of London.

Smahel, D., Machackova, H., Mascheroni, G., Dedkova, L., Staksrud, E., Ólafsson, K., Livingstone, S., & Hasebrink, U. (2020). *EU kids online 2020: Survey results from 19 countries.* EU Kids Online. https://doi.org/10.21953/lse.47fdeqj01ofo

Smith, P. K., Mahdavi, J., Carvalho, M., Fisher, S., Russell, S., & Tippett, N. (2008). Cyberbullying: Its nature and impact in secondary school pupils. *Journal of Child Psychology and Psychiatry, 49*(4), 376–385. https://doi.org/10.1111/j.1469-7610.2007.01846.x

Suler, J. (2004). The online disinhibition effect. *Cyberpsychology and Behavior, 7*(3), 321–326. https://doi.org/10.1089/1094931041291295.

Thulin, E. (2017). Always on my mind: How smartphones are transforming social contact among young. *Young, 26*(5), 1–19. https://doi.org/10.1177/1103308817734512

Velez, J. A., Greitemeyer, T., Whitaker, J. L., Ewoldsen, D. R., & Bushman, B. J. (2014). Violent video games and reciprocity: The attenuating effects of cooperative game play on subsequent aggression. *Communication Research, 43,* 1–21. https://doi.org/10.1177/0093650214552519

Wang, V., & Simon, E. (2016). Strangers are friends I haven't met yet: A positive approach to young people's use of social media. *Journal of Youth Studies, 19*(9), 1204–1219. https://doi.org/10.1080/13676261.2016.1154933

Willard, N. (2004). *Educator's guide to cyberbullying: Addressing the harm caused by online social cruelty.* Retrieved April 28, 2021, from http://clubtnt.org/safeOnline/printResources/EducatorsGuideToCyberbullyingAddressingTheHarm.pdf

18 Older Adults in the Digital Age

Liam Challenor

Chapter Overview

Research on the use of technology by older adults is diverse, ranging from how technology may support them to age in place by improving their ability to live and age independently (Baldassar et al., 2017), to increasing the ability of older adults with age-related cognitive decline to interpret conversation semantics through the use of emojis (Garcia et al., 2022). However older adults may also face negative impacts as a result of their technology use such as isolation (Ward et al., 2020, Power et al., 2019) and cybersecurity threats (Morrison et al., 2020). This chapter will discuss the relationship between older adults and technology, the barriers to technology use, as well as the positive and negative impacts resulting from their interactions with technology.

Key Terms

Cybersecurity is the process of protecting computer-based devices and systems from digital attacks from an unauthorised third party. **Digital inclusion** is the process of creating equitable access to and of digital technologies with socially excluded groups. **Social isolation** is the lack of social contacts or having reduced social interactions with others which has a detrimental impact on the individual.

Technology Adoption

Technology adoption is a common theme in cyberpsychology research and aging populations as there is a preconception that older adults are unwilling or less able to operate emergent digital devices. Adoption continues to grow as digital technologies become more readily available in line with reductions in cost, with younger adults adopting technology faster than older adults. Vaportizis et al. (2017) discuss how this adoption varies in speed depending on how useful the technology is perceived to be by the user to improve their quality of life. One of the main challenges in an older adult's use of technology are their

DOI: 10.4324/9781003092513-24

own attitudes and beliefs towards technology and their use of it. Research by Xi et al. (2022) discussed the implications of these beliefs, finding that older adults may hold negative stereotypes of their own capabilities to use technology which may contribute to opposition to technology adoption. These negative stereotypes can be reduced, promoting ease of use and through training.

CYBERPSYCHOLOGY IN FOCUS: BARRIERS TO TECHNOLOGY ADOPTION

Is technology adoption a wider societal problem as it doesn't impact the majority of society? The real-world application to these barriers directly impacts on the digital exclusion of older adults either by design or by the support, or lack of supports, to aid this transition. Xi et al. (2022) examined the barriers to their adoption of technology and the impact on ability. Several barriers were identified to the adoption of technology including self-perception of their own aging, technophobia, ease of use, and newness of technology. Interestingly the authors identified that while attitudes towards technology are important for adoption, the newness and ease of use of technology impacted a participant's perceptions of aging, with unfamiliar and newer technologies negatively impacting on their own perceptions of aging but also significantly increasing their opposition to technology use. These findings provide insight into how technology adoption opposition may be mitigated through the use of education and training programmes to reduce the impact of perceptions of aging due to a lack of knowledge and skills around technology use.

Vaportizis et al. (2017) focused their research on older adults' perceptions of technology and barriers to interacting with tablet computers using a sample of 65–76-year-olds. The main focus of their research was to identify attitudes towards tablet and technology use while identifying potential barriers to their adoption. Barriers to use including a lack of knowledge, confidence, and cost reduced adoption while feelings of low digital self-efficacy also hindered use. However, technology adoption for information seeking was a positive indicator for use. While older adults may seek to adopt technology, knowledge, skills, and technological literacy are needed to increase the digital self-efficacy of older adults (Age Action Ireland, 2020).

As various traditional services continue to alter their business structures such as the reduction in banking branches and traditional "bricks and mortar" businesses migrating to an online transactional model, how does this impact an older adult who may not have the same digital skills training or trust in online media?

Research by Alvarez-Dardet et al. (2020) aims to address these misconceptions, investigating the use of and attitudes towards computers among older Spanish participants (N = 212, aged 60+). Rationales for device use were consistent with other research, the main purpose being information seeking followed by communication with others. Results identified that a willingness to use and positive attitude towards device use were positively associated with device use. The authors further emphasise that if users can be provided with a sense of control over the device they are using then they will be more likely to adopt the device for long-term use. Importantly Alvarez-Dardet et al. (2020) indicate that their findings did not identify technophobia in their sample which is often reported as a rationale for opposing technology adoption; instead a lack of ICT knowledge was the main barrier to adoption. This leads to an important reflection point: are emergent digital technologies designed for older users or do older users require additional training in comparison to a conventional younger user? Broady et al. (2010) suggested that older users engage with technology for a specific purpose rather than rejecting it outright, which may support adoption.

Website design has been the focus of many usability research studies, often examining how older adults use websites in comparison to younger populations, as design may influence how older adults specifically use websites (Bergstom et al., 2013). Research which may impact the design of commerce websites which use digital assistants for older adults was conducted by Chattaraman et al. (2019), investigating the role of digital assistants in shopping websites. The research implemented two different forms of digital assistant, one task-oriented in its interaction, aimed at reducing the cognitive load of the older consumer, and the other social-oriented, engaging in small talk and encouragement during the task. In addition to the digital assistant manipulation, the internet competency of participants was also recorded to identify its relationship with the interaction. The researchers aimed to investigate the relationship between the digital assistant and internet competency levels to identify outcomes on social, cognitive, functional, and behaviour intent variables in the transaction process. The findings suggest that digital assistants that have a social-orientated interaction style with an older consumer lead to better social outcomes and interaction leading to greater trust in the website but only for those with high internet competency. Older consumers with lower internet competency require a digital assistant that is more orientated to the task to provide a positive outcome. This is a challenge for user experience designers focused on older adults as it may be difficult to assess users' internet competency during the transaction process.

Technology for Communication

Research focused on the use of smartphones by older Norwegian adults examined the rationales for smartphone use in the older population. The researchers aimed to identify if problematic smartphone use was prevalent among older adults, a finding which was not supported. Busch et al. (2021) also hypothesised that loneliness, social influence, and habit would be associated with emotional gain, all of which were supported. The researchers identified that loneliness was the strongest predictor of emotional gain in older adult smartphone users with social media being the most prevalent behaviour on their devices (23% of daily usage) to reduce feelings of loneliness.

Researchers have focused on how older adults' use of computer-mediated communication compares to that of younger adults. Garcia et al. (2022) focused on the use of emojis to facilitate the semantics of written sarcasm to better understand the meaning of conversation using older adults. Utilising a between groups method, the findings identified that older adults had increased difficulty in interpreting sarcastic content when compared to younger adults. However, the implementation of emojis in the same content, specifically the winking face emoji, was found to increase older adults' ability to interpret messages. Garcia et al. (2022) suggested that emoji use when having conversations with older adults with and without age-related cognitive deficits may improve the clarity of intergenerational conversation.

Digital inclusion

The digital inclusion of older adults may be fostered through digital skills training, Baldassar et al. (2017) recommend that, to promote the digital inclusion of older adults and increase their ability to stay in touch with relatives, digital literacy programmes for the elderly are needed. Research by Hill et al. (2015) focused on the qualitative experiences of 17 older adults, aged 70 and above. The researchers sought to identify the ways in which technology can be used to enhance the lives of older adults and increase their well-being in addition to their technology use and attitudes. Results support other researchers who advocate for digital inclusion, as older adults who perceive that they lack knowledge and skills to use digital technologies are less likely to engage in their use. Participants further support the need for digital inclusion, stating that as society moves further into a digital space for everyday tasks their own participation as a result becomes limited and a digital divide continues to grow. However, contrasting findings for older adults provide support for the benefits of digital skills training. Those with digital skills felt a sense of power and control over simple tasks and used devices to complete simplistic tasks. These tasks may become more difficult with age such as shopping or accessing digital services in addition to digital socialisation (Hill et al., 2015).

The above results provide support not only for the positive and empowering characteristics digital technologies can provide older adults with but also for the potential to disempower and create digital inequality if older adults are not provided with support, training, and guidance in emergent digital technologies (Lissitsa et al., 2022). Without this additional support the digital divide may further ostracise older adults and reduce their ability to access essential business services as they further increase their digital presence and move human-operated tasks into an online setting.

Positive Impacts of Technology on Older Adults

The adoption and integration of technology in the daily lives of older adults may have a number of positive and negative impacts on older adults. Positive impacts may include a reduction in **social isolation** (Baldassar et al., 2017), increased autonomy (Kim & Choudhyry, 2021), empowerment (Hill et al., 2015), increased social capital (Zhang & Kaufman, 2015), increased social inclusion (Cortellessa et al., 2018), improving executive function (McCord et al., 2020), and increasing resilience (Paul et al., 2022).

CYBERPSYCHOLOGY IN FOCUS: POSITIVE IMPACTS OF TECHNOLOGY FOR OLDER ADULTS

Older adults' use of technology can also have positive impacts on their well-being as a result of increased social capital. Social capital is a widely researched concept as it investigates the networks which are built and maintained by an individual over time. Social capital is increasingly relevant to older adults as both forms, whether the network of weak ties (bridging social capital) or the close-knit network of strong personal connections (bonding social capital), have been identified to have positive impacts for younger and older generations (Ellison et al., 2007; Cho, 2015).

Research by Cho (2015) focused on the effects of smartphone applications on social capital using a comparison of younger and older participants. The research expected that communication and social networking apps would positively predict bonding and bridging social capital while both forms of social capital would reduce participant feelings of **social isolation**. A positive relationship was identified between communication apps and bonding social capital. Social networking apps were found to have an association with bonding social capital. While there were no differences between older and younger participants, the use of communication and social networking applications was found to reduce the social isolation of all participants.

Bonding and bridging social capital may not only be increased by smartphone applications but also by other digital environments such as gaming. Research by Zhang and Kaufman (2015) focused further on social capital, investigating the impact of social interactions in massively multiplayer online role-playing games (MMORPGs). Research which focused on the MMORPG *World of Warcraft* identified the impact of in-game communication and relationships on bonding and bridging social capital. The research identified that older adult participants developed higher levels of bridging social capital in *World of Warcraft* but their levels of bonding social capital were lower than those not playing the game. However the engagement and enjoyment of participants while playing the game were related to higher levels of bonding and bridging social capital, mediated by who they interacted with more than the time spent playing. Zhang and Kaufman (2015) supports the suggestion that gaming can have positive impacts on social capital for older adults, but their enjoyment and interactions in game are important to increase both forms.

While technology continues to be integrated in many homes, the use of voice-assisted, artificially intelligent technologies may have a number of positive impacts on the lives of older adults. Some of these conversational agents and voice assistant-based artificial intelligence devices such as Amazon Alexa and Google Home systems are becoming increasingly common. Kim and Choudhury (2021) investigated the perceptions of older adults of adopting and using voice-based AI assistants to support their lives. While voice-based virtual assistants grow in popularity it is important to not only investigate how they may be used by older adults, but also how they could be improved to support adults as they age and support independence. Kim and Choudhury (2021) focused on the rationales for why older adults use voice assistants: their perceived benefits from use but also the challenges in their use.

While voice assistants may provide convenience and provide users with an opportunity to derive a sense of companionship, limitations for older adults may include common physical and cognitive challenges to their use such as hearing or cognitive impairments which may prevent their use. Kim and Choudhury (2021) conducted a longitudinal study in the homes of 12 older adults (65+) with various physical and cognitive impairments (wheelchair users, arthritis, or memory deficits). Interestingly the research identified the varying use of virtual voice assistants, including playing music, searching for general information, making conversation with the agent, or performing tasks such as setting reminders or finding weather forecasts. The results support the findings of other research on the technology adoption of older adults, primarily the ease of use of the device and its set up, operation without the need for physical interaction, and the consequences of making a mistake during the device's use. On the basis of Kim and Choudhury's (2021) research, further investigation into the application of virtual assistants as digital companions (similar to social robots) is needed as, while the virtual assistants may have humanlike qualities, the boundaries of this companionship have yet to be fully identified.

In addition to technology in the home for companionship or entertainment, technology can be used to support older adults to maintain their independence as they age. Assisted living traditionally would involve varying levels of home help and can be financially taxing on an older person or their family. However, active and assisted living technologies can provide and supplement the support given to older adults by their families. Research by Bieg et al. (2022) focused on evaluating the implementation of assisted living technologies with older adults (N = 150, 70+), focusing on the participants' feelings of self-determination, social participation, and perceived safety in their homes. Assisted living devices range in their scope and capabilities from cameras and voice-assisted devices to wearable technology and sensors. As such there are varying results in the field and, as Bieg et al. (2022) discuss, few consistent findings for their application, which is supported by Kaye (2017) who argued that further research is needed in the space of health-related assistive technology to justify the funding to support older adults in remaining independent.

Bieg et al. (2022) focused their research on the WAALTeR system, an integrated home assistive technology with a smart watch component. The system has typical at-home voice-assisted AI features for common requests in addition to emergency calling, GPS tracking, health information, and other commercial applications. While participants reported increases in their autonomy, competence, relatedness, social participation, and perceived safety there was no statistically significant difference. An interesting and consistent theme identified by Bieg et al. (2022) in other research which focuses on older adults' use of technology was the need for digital literacy to utilise the assisted living devices (Xi et al., 2022). While the results of the above study provide support for the use of assisted technology, further training and support in their use ahead of research may provide a long-lasting benefit to older adults.

Digital technologies can have a number of positive impacts on the physical and mental health of older adults. Gaming is a technology which is often subject to research with younger samples or focused on problematic use. However gaming can have positive impacts on older adults, improving executive function. Research by McCord et al. (2020) with 80–97-year-olds in residential care settings used an action first-person-shooter game, *Star Wars Battlefront*, to identify if there was a positive relationship between executive function which declines with age and participants' gameplay. The results identified that 6 individual sessions consisting of 30 minutes of gameplay could provide significant increases in working memory and visual attention compared to those who didn't participate in gameplay.

Further to the positive impacts gaming may have on executive function, virtual environments may also increase the psychological resilience of older adults. Research by Paul et al. (2022) focused on the role social virtual worlds can have in increasing psychological resilience with younger and older people during the COVID-19 pandemic. The authors investigated the psychological distress caused by the pandemic, identifying a coping strategy to support individuals, specifically, creating an avatar representing the participant in a social virtual environment where the pandemic did not exist or pose a risk to them; the authors state that this may be connected to the proteus effect. The proteus effect is a phenomenon where a person is impacted by a digital representation of themselves, where their behaviour follows the behaviour of their online self. Paul et al. (2022) state that social virtual worlds provided an outer body experience for participants to alleviate stress and anxiety and build resilience towards psychological harm. The findings of Paul et al. (2022) provide some insights into how avatars in social virtual environments may provide an opportunity for older adults to explore and create experiences which would traditionally place them under physical or psychological strain, instead allowing a safe space for new experiences.

Research in cyberpsychology on **social isolation** among older adults has often focused on the use of social robots as a support to mitigate the negative impacts of such isolation by encouraging social inclusion in home (Cortellessa et al., 2018) and supporting healthcare settings to engage with older patients (Breazeal, 2017). Cortellessa et al. (2018) suggest that the use of a telepresence robot, Robin, can provide support and monitor the health of older adults and promote psychological and physical well-being as it was perceived by older users to be usable and pleasant to interact with, promoting positive interactions and fostering its adoption.

Telepresence robots such as Robin have the potential to support older adults in the home by providing practical and emotional support to an aging population (Liu et al., 2021). These social robots vary in their own capability and have become more common in assisting an aging population. Liu et al. (2021) conducted research on the challenges which social robots may address using a sample of older Chinese adults (N = 1,480). They aimed to identify if the perceived warmth or competence of a social robot could reduce the concerns of older adults regarding their use. They identified that older adults perceived smaller, animal-like robots to be high in warmth in comparison to machine-like robots, which were perceived to be higher in competence. This perceived competence in social robots among older adults was related to concerns around privacy.

Negative Impacts of Technology on Older Adults

While there are many positive impacts of technology for older adults, digital environments may pose increased risk for users who have less digital literacy and experience online. These older adults may be more likely to experience **cybersecurity** risks such as misinformation (Wylie et al., 2014; Choudrie et al., 2021) and online scams such as phishing (Paek & Nalla, 2015; Leng et al., 2020). However, research has identified that older adults (50 and above) may also have higher information security awareness than younger populations, identifying they were more risk adverse and more sceptical about online content (McCormac et al., 2017).

Research on fake news, disinformation, and misinformation continues to grow in cyberpsychology on older adults (Wylie et al., 2014); however, there is still a lack of research focusing on the impact of misinformation on older adults and its long-term impact on the individual. Wylie et al. (2014) conducted a meta-analysis on the research on older adults and misinformation; of the 39 studies reviewed, 31 identified a significant relationship between older adults and misinformation, finding they were more susceptible than younger adults. Research which focused on the way older adults process information and misinformation in relation to health information on COVID-19 was conducted by Choudrie et al. (2021). Utilising a qualitative approach, 20 older adults were interviewed about their willingness to trust traditional media and new media sources. Participants conveyed confusion and a lack of understanding due to the amount of contrasting information online. Chourdrie et al. (2021) referred to this phenomenon as the COVID-19 infodemic, as older adults may be susceptible to the varying information online and likely to fall for false or misleading content. Results identified that participants were unaware of how to verify information online when from a source that was unknown to them; this included valid sources designed to correct misinformation. The results provide support for the inclusion of misinformation awareness training and guidance on fact checking content online to evaluate the source and content of online content.

The COVID-19 pandemic highlighted these concerns among researchers, particularly the relationship between privacy behaviour and **cybersecurity** risks. Leng et al. (2020) aimed to understand the mindset of older adults when considering cybersecurity risks using a qualitative approach. They identified that older adults, while aware of cybersecurity threats, are uncertain of how to tackle common risks such as phishing and malware but continue to use technology where risks may occur, such as online transactions and social networking, as they are limited in other options.

There are differences in information-seeking behaviour by older adults identified by Nicolson et al. (2019). Older adults chose to prioritise social resources in their own network they identified as having cybersecurity knowledge rather than seeking out a cybersecurity expert for support resulting in poor-quality information and potentially increased vulnerability to cyberattacks. Research by Morrison et al. (2020) identified the transition from middle to older age/retirement as having a number of areas where changes in daily life may contribute to cybersecurity risk. These are reductions in social interaction, financial well-being, feelings of competency, and technological support, as these are seen to be protective factors to build cyber-resilience.

Online Scams

Cybersecurity risks include online scams such as phishing. Researchers such as Gavette et al. (2017) and Grilli et al. (2021) have raised concerns about older adults being victims of phishing emails, where another person aims to manipulate them and steal information for financial gain. In their research, Grilli et al. (2021) investigated the ability of older adults to identify real or phishing emails according to their perceived safety. They identified that older adults perceived the risk of phishing emails to be lower and were less accurate when evaluating genuine and phishing-based content within an email, advocating further cybersecurity training. Research from South Korea investigating the relationship between receiving a phishing attempt and identify theft across older and younger participants identified a relationship between age and victimisation;

specifically, as participants increased in age victimisation increased (Paek & Nalla, 2015).

The susceptibility of older adults to cybersecurity risks such as phishing scams may be due to changes in executive function as a result of aging. Gavett et al. (2017) aimed to identify the variance in susceptibility due to differences in executive function comparing younger and older adults, assessing executive function and controlling for other variables such as education and prior phishing knowledge. The results identified that older adults had more knowledge of phishing, and more experience of victimisation than younger adults, and could not identify that older adults were more vulnerable than younger ones. The authors instead suggest that further and more robust measures of cognitive function are needed to investigate older adults' vulnerability to phishing but emphasise the need, similarly to Grilli et al. (2021), for educational interventions.

Conclusion

This chapter provided an overview of the relationship between older adults and technology use. The research suggests that different forms of technology may have either positive effects (such as assistive technologies to combat social isolation and increase independent living) or negative effects (such as cybersecurity threats' impact on the lives of older adults in the digital age). However these positive changes can be fostered and negative impacts prevented using digital literacy training. Further research is still required to support and foster the positive digital experiences of older adults.

Activity

Identify an app and/or a website you use frequently. Consider the platform, its purpose, and how you currently use it. How could this app/website be adapted to encourage use by older adults? Reviewing this chapter and the challenges faced by older adults, such as lower internet competency and digital access, how can you support its use? How can features of the platform be improved for an older adult to use them? What about the app's design: could aspects such as colour or font be improved?

Discussion Questions

1 Are older adults excluded from technology adoption? Consider who specific technologies are designed and marketed to.
2 Consider the social isolation of older adults and the role of technology; are there any current technologies that are not currently implemented with older adults?

3 Older adults may be more susceptible to cybersecurity risks; how could we reduce the risks for older adults online?

4 Are older adults marginalised as a social group online? Do we hold misconceptions about their technological abilities? Consider the misconceptions around their technology use (e.g., older adults not being as skilled as a younger group).

Recommended Reading List

"Older Adults and Digital Technologies" by Lovarini et al. (2019) is a chapter in *The Handbook of Cyberpsychology* by Atrill, Fullwood, Keep, and Kuss (2019). It provides a concise focus on the interactions between older adults and wider society.

> Lovarini, M., O'Loughlin, K., & Clemson, L. (2019). Older adults and digital technologyes. In A. Atrill, C. Fullwood, M. Keep, & D. J. Kuss (Eds.), *Oxford handbook of cyberpsychology* (pp. 133–148). Oxford University Press.

"Older Adults and Technology Use" by the Pew Research Centre (2014) provides an introduction to older adults' technology use. The author, Aaron Smith, provides a high-level introduction to older adults' attitudes, impacts, and barriers to technology adoption.

> Smith, A. (2014). *Older adults and technology use.* Pew Research Centre. https://www.pewresearch.org/internet/2014/04/03/older-adults-and -technology-use/

Vaportzi, Clausen, and Gow (2017) conducted research on older adults' perceptions of technology. This is a focus group study on tablet use. It provides good insights into some of the barriers to technology and perceptions of older adults including attitudinal and skill-based barriers.

> Vaportzi, E., Clausen, M. G., & Gow, A. J. (2017). Older adults' perceptions of technology and barriers to interacting with table computers: A focus group study. *Frontiers in Psychology, 8.* https://doi.org/10.3389/fpsyg.2017 .01687

DeAngelis (2021) provided a concise overview of the considerations that are needed to design and adapt technologies to make them understandable for older adults. The authors provide a human–computer interaction and user experience perspective focusing on technology at home, safer driving, and technology adoption.

> DeAngelis, T. (2021). *Optimizing tech for older adults.* American Psychological Association. https://www.apa.org/monitor/2021/07/tech-older-adults

Busch, Hausvik, Ropstad, and Pettersen (2021) conducted research investigating smartphone use among older adults. To date there has been little research on older adults' smartphone use when compared with other age groups. They identified habitual and social influences on the social and non-social use of devices.

> Busch, P. A., Hausvik, G. I., Ropstad, O. K., & Pettersen, D. (2021). Smartphone usage among older adults. *Computers in Human Behavior, 121*, Article 106783. https://doi.org/10.1016/j.chb.2021.106783

Glossary

Cybersecurity: Cybersecurity is the process of protecting computer-based devices and systems from digital attacks from an unauthorised third party.
Digital inclusion: The process of creating equitable access to and of digital technologies with socially excluded groups.
MMORPG: A massively multiplayer online role-playing game is an online game hosted on an online server where players play in a remote environment with each other.
Social isolation: A lack of social contacts or having reduced social interactions with others which has a detrimental impact on the individual.

References

Age Action. (2020). Supporting digital literacy among older people. https://www.ageaction.ie/sites/default/files/supporting_older_peoples_digital_literacy_briefing_paper_6_january_2020_update_of_paper_5_first_published_march_2018.pdf

Alvarez-Dardet, A. M., Lara, B. L., & Perez-Padilla, J. (2020). Older adults and ICT adoption: Analysis of the use and attitudes toward computers in elderly Spanish people. *Computers in Human Behavior, 110*, Article 106377. https://doi.org/10.1016/j.chb.2020.106377

Baldassar,, L., Wilding, R., Boccagni, P., & Merla, L. (2017). Aging in place in a mobile world: New media and older peoples support networks. *Transnational Social Review, 7*, (1), 2–9. DOI:10.1080/21931674.2016.12778645

Bieg, T., Gerdenitsch, C., Schwaninger, I., Kern, B. M. J., & Frauenberger, C. (2022). Evaluating Active and Assisted Living technologies: Critical methodological reflections based on a longitudinal randomized controlled trial. *Computers in Human Behavior, 133*, Article 107249. https://doi.org/10.1016/j.chb.2022.107249

Breazeal, C. (2017). Social robots: From research to commercialization. *Proceedings of the 2017 ACM/IEEE international conference on human-robot interaction 1-1.* https://doi.org/10.1145/2909824.3020258

Broady, T., Chan, A., & Caputi, P. (2010). Comparison of older and younger adults' attitudes towards and abilities with computers: Implications for training and learning. *British Journal of Educational Technology, 41*(3), 473–485. https://doi.org/10.111/j.1467-8535.2008.00914.x

Busch, P. A., Hausvik, G. I., Ropstad, O. K., & Pettersen, D. (2021). Smartphone usage among older adults. *Computers in Human Behavior, 121*. https://doi.org /10.1016/j.chb.2021.106783

Chattaraman, V., Kwon, W., Gilbert, J. E., & Ross, K. (2019). Should AI-based, conversational digital assistants employ social- or task- oriented interaction style? A task-competency and reciprocity perspective for older adults. *Computers in Human Behavior, 90*, 315–330. https://doi.org/10.1016/j.chb .2018.08.048

Cho, J. (2015). Roles of smartphone app use in improving social capital and reducing social isolation. *Cyberpsychology, Behavior, and Social Networking, 18*(6). https://doi-org.dcu.idm.oclc.org/10.1089/cyber.2014.0657

Choudrie, J., Banerjee, S., Kotecha, K., Walambe, R., Karende, H., & Ameta, J. (2021). Machine learning techniques and older adults processing of online information: A Covid 19 study. *Computers in Human Behavior, 119*. https://doi .org/10.1016/j.chb.2021.106716

Cortellesa, G., Fracasso, F., Sorrentino, A., Orlandini, A., Bernardi, G., Coraci, L., De Benedictis, R., & Cesta, A. (2018). ROBIN, a telepresence robot to support older users monitoring and social inclusion: Development and evaluation. *Telemedicine and E-Health, 24*(2), 145–154. https://doi.org/10.1089/tmj.2016 .0258

Ellison, N. B., Steinfield, C., & Lampe, C. (2007). The benefits of Facebook "friends:" Social capital and college students' use of online social networking sites. *Journal of Computer-Mediated Communication, 12*(4), 1143–1168. https:// doi.org/10.1111/j.1083-6101.2007.00367.x

Garcia, C., Turcan, A., Howman, H., & Filik, R. (2022). Emoji as a tool to aid the comprehension of written sarcasm:evidence from younger and older adults. *Computers in Human Behavior, 126*. https://doi.org/10.1016/j.chb.2021.106971

Gavette, B. E., Zhao, R., John, S. E., Bussell, C. A., Roberts, J. R., & Yue, C. (2017). Phising suspiciousness in older and younger adults: The role of executive functioning. *PLOS ONE, 12*(2). https://doi.org/10.1371/journal.pone.0171620

Grilli, M. D., McVeigh, K. S., Hakim, A. M., Wank, A. A., Getz, S. J., Levin, B. E., Ebner, N. C, & Wilson, R. C. (2021). Is this Phishing? Older age is associated with greater difficulty discriminating between safe and malicious Emails. *Journals of Gerontology: Psychological Sciences, 76*(9), 1711–1715. https://doi.org /10.1093/geronb/gbaa228

Hill, R., Betts, L. R., & Gardner, S. E. (2015). Older adults' experiences and perceptions of digital technology: (Dis)empowerment, wellbeing, and inclusion. *Computers in Human Behavior, 48*, 415–423. http://doi.org/10.1016 /j.chb.2015.01.062

Kaye, J. (2017). Making pervasive computing technology pervasive for health and wellness in aging. *Public Policy and Aging Report, 27*(2), 53–61. https://doi .org/10.1093/ppar/prx005

Kim, S., & Choudhury, A. (2021). Exploring older adults' perception and use of smart speaker-based voice assistants: A longitudinal study. *Computers in Human Behavior, 124*. https://doi.org/10.1016/j.chb.2021.106914

Leng, O. T. S., Vergara, R. G., Khan, N., & Khan, S. (2020). Cybersecurity and privacy impact on older persons amid COVID-19: A Socio-Legal study in Malaysia. *Asian Journal of Research in Education and Social Sciences, 2*(2), 72–76.

Lissitsa, S., Zychlinski, E., & Kagan, M. (2022). The silent generation vs baby boomers: Socio-demographic and psychological predictors of the "gray" digital inequalities. *Computers in Human Behavior, 128*. https://doi.org/10 .1016/j.chb.2021.107098

Liu, S. X., Shen, Q., & Hancock, J. (2021). Can a social robot be too warm or too competent? Older Chinese adults' perceptions of social robotos and vulnerabilities. *Computers in Human Behavior, 125.* https://doi.org/10.1016/j .chb.2021.106942

McCord, A., Cocks, B., Barreiros, A. R., & Bizo, L. A. (2020). Short video game play improves executive function in the oldest old living in residential care. *Computers in Human Behavior, 108.* http://doi.org/10.1016/j.chb.2015.01.062

McCormac, A., Zwaans, T., Parsons, K., Calic, D., Butavicius, M., & Pattinson, M. (2017). Individual differences and informational security awareness. *Computers in Human Behavior, 69.* http://doi.org/10.1016/j.chb.2016.11.065

Morrison, B. A., Coventry, L., & Briggs, P. (2020). Technological change in the retirement transition and the implications for cybersecurity vulnerability in older adults. *Frontiers in Psychology, 11.* https://doi.org/10.3389/fpsyg.2020 .00623

Nicolson, J., Coventry, L., & Briggs, P. (2019). If It's important it will be a headline: Cybersecutiyy information seeking in older adults. *CHI 2019 Paper,* Glasgow, Scotland. https://doi.org/10.1145/3290605.3300579

Paek, S. Y., & Nalla, M. K. (2015). The relationship between receiving phishing attempt and identify theft victimization in South Korea. *International Journal of Law, Crime and Justice, 43*(4), 626–642. http://doi.org/10.1016/j.ijlcj.2015.02.003

Paul, I., Mohanty, S., & Sengupta, R. (2022). The role of social virtual world in increasing psychological resilience during the on-going Covid-19 pandemic. *Computers in Human Behavior, 127.* https://doi.org/10.1016/j.chb.2021.107036

Power, J., Sjöberg, L., Kee, F., Kenny, R. A., & Lawlor, B. (2019). Comparisons of the discrepancy between loneliness and social isolation across Ireland and Sweden: Findings from TILDA and SNAC-K. *Social Psychiatry and Psychiatric Epidemiology, 54*(9), 1079–1088. https://doi.org/10.1007/s00127-019-01679-w

Romano Bergstom, J. C., Olmsted-Hawala, E. L., & Jans, M. E. (2013). Age-related differences in eye tracking and usability performance: Website usability for older adults. *International Journal of Human-Computer Interaction, 29*(8), 541–548. https://doi.org/10.1080/10447318.2012.728493

Vaportzis, E., Clausen, M. G., & Gow, A. J. (2017). Older adults perceptions of technology and barriers to interacting with tablet computers: A focus group study. *Frontiers in Psychology, 8,* 1687. https://doi.org/10.3389/fpsyg.2017 .01687

Ward, M., Layte, R., & Kenny, R. A. (2019). *Loneliness, social isolation, and their discordance among older adults Findings from the Irish Longitudinal Study on Aging (TILDA).* https://tilda.tcd.ie/publications/reports/pdf/Report_Loneliness.pdf

Ward, M., McGarrigle, C., Hever, A., O'Mahoney, P., Moynihan, S., Loughran, G., & Kenny, R. A., (2020). *Loneliness and social isolation in the Covid-19 pandemic among the over 70s: Data from the Irish longitudinal study on ageing (TILDA) and alone.* https://www.doi.org/10.38018/TildaRe.2020-07

Wylie, L. E., Patihis, L., McCuller, L. L., Davis, D., Brank, E. M., Loftus, E. F., & Bornstein, B. H. (2014). Misinformation effects in older *versus* younger adults: A meta-analysis and review. In M. P. Toglia, D. F. Ross, J. Pozzulo, & E. Pica (Eds.), *The elderly eyewitness in court.* Psychology Press.

Xi, W., Zhang, X., & Ayalon, L. (2022). When less intergenerational closeness helps: The influence of intergenerational physical proximity and technology attributes on technophobia among older adults. *Computers in Human Behavior, 131.* https://doi.org/10.1016/j.chb.2022.107234

Zhang, F., & Kaufman, D. (2015). The impacts of social interactions in MMORPGs on older adults' social capital. *Computers in Human Behavior, 51,* 495–503. http://doi.org/10.1016/j.chb.2015.05.034

PART 4

Psychology and Technology

Cyberpsychology in Professional Practice

Interview 4

Phelim May has been working as a Head of Human Factors for three years.

What are your main responsibilities and/or daily activities?

Leading human factors activity related to the development of applications that will be used in clinical trials, to support clinical diagnosis, and as companion devices to existing treatments.

When did you first become interested in cyberpsychology, and how did you develop this interest into part of your career path?

While working in telecommunications it became clear that more and more of our daily interactions were moving to and mediated by the internet. I did the MSc in Cyberpsychology in the Dun Laoghaire Institute of Art, Design, and Technology in 2012, so the last ten years have seen a massive expansion in connectivity and capability. In healthcare especially, the need to understand the differing needs and capabilities of the user and the context of use has never been more critical. Cyberpsychology offers key insights and approaches to

DOI: 10.4324/9781003092513-26

better understand the patient/user interaction with technology and how that will impact the problem that is to be solved or the job that needs to be done.

What cyberpsychological knowledge is of most relevance to your current role?

On the surface human–computer interaction is fundamental to my current role but beneath that the awareness that our own assumptions need to be tested and the capability to validate those assumptions are critical elements in the development of applications and services that are both safe and effective for users.

Are there any theories in cyberpsychology which you find applicable to your work? If so, which one(s), and how are they relevant to your responsibilities in your role?

The importance of the use environment, design affordances, and the user's working memory, attention, or cognitive load would be key concepts I would come back to over and over again.

What do you think are the most important real-world applications of cyberpsychology?

In the life sciences sector it would be the application of the myriad tools that support the creation of applications that are safe and effective to use. For example heuristic evaluation, interview, contextual inquiry, and simulated use testing.

Is there anything else that you'd like to add about cyberpsychology in your professional life?

Not really, just to acknowledge the significant benefit of having a greater understanding of human capabilities, motivation, and behaviour in the context of the development of products and services.

Phelim May
Dublin, Ireland

Human–Computer Interaction

Andrew Errity

Chapter Overview

This chapter commences with brief coverage of the history of human–computer interaction (HCI) and the current state of the field, addressing key terminology used and the variety of disciplinary perspectives involved. It will then look at how HCI principles are applied in practice and provide appropriate examples. There will then be a discussion on the relationship between HCI and cyberpsychology, noting the key contributions each field can make.

Key Terms

The field of HCI is concerned with the study, design, and testing of interactive computer systems that exist at the point where humans and computers meet. This point, the **interface**, is typically a **graphical user interface** (GUI) that uses elements including text, icons, buttons, and windows to communicate information to the user and allows the user to interact with the interface using devices such as a mouse, keyboard, touchscreen, etc. It is vital to consider both the **usability** and **user experience** (UX) of an interface. Usability refers to the extent to which users can achieve specified goals with effectiveness, efficiency, and satisfaction using an interface, while UX refers to how a user feels when interacting with an interface.

Introduction

What Is Human–Computer Interaction?

The goal of HCI is to create interactive computer-mediated experiences that are satisfying, effective, efficient, and useful. Those working in the field study the ways humans interact with computers to develop new and better interaction paradigms, models, and theories.

The use and meaning of the term human–computer interaction have evolved over its history. It is rooted in the more general terms "human–machine

DOI: 10.4324/9781003092513-27

interaction" and "man–machine interaction" that refer to the interaction of humans and some form of physical machine – for example, in a manufacturing plant. With the growth of computing, the more specific term human–Computer interaction emerged. The following is a classic and helpful definition of the term: "Human-computer interaction is a discipline concerned with the design, evaluation and implementation of interactive computing systems for human use and with the study of major phenomena surrounding them" (ACM SIGCHI, 1992, p. 5).

As someone reading a cyberpsychology textbook, this will likely sound somewhat familiar. The fields of cyberpsychology and HCI have much in common. Both involve studying interactions involving humans and technology; however, with cyberpsychology the focus is on the human, rather than the technology, whereas in HCI this balance may be more heavily weighted towards the computer (Norman, 2008).

To provide some context, it is worth considering some typical HCI projects. One example would be the design, implementation, and testing of the **interface** of a mobile app for an online social network. Three key factors are vital to consider in this, and any other, HCI project:

1. The user: who will be using this interface? What are their characteristics, capabilities, and limitations?
2. The computer: what computer system will the user be interacting with, what affordances does it provide (e.g. input and output devices), and what constraints does it impose (e.g. small screen size)?
3. The task: what does the user need from the system? What functionality should it provide?

Not paying sufficient attention to any one of these factors may result in an interface that fails to be *useful* (allows the user to perform a required task), *usable* (the user can efficiently perform the task, e.g. without error, delay, etc.), and *used* (provides an experience that users will want to use, e.g. be satisfying, fun, etc.) (Dix et al., 2004). These three factors could be evaluated during the HCI process to gauge the success of the mobile app interface design.

HCI projects can also be more research-focused and experimental. For example, a HCI research project could involve designing, implementing, and testing multiple **prototype** keyboard layouts for text entry on a touchscreen display. Again, the user, computer, and task must all be considered in this process. The associated evaluation could involve measuring the number of words typed per minute or the number of spelling errors made per minute to determine which of the prototypes was best or to develop some model of human typing performance on a touchscreen display.

The ramifications of producing a poor human–computer interface can be significant. Take the social networking app discussed above as an example. If this app provides an unsatisfactory, frustrating experience the network's customers may move to a competitor, costing the company money. Similarly, if the app is not usable and causes users to make errors – e.g. sharing photos publicly rather than with selected friends – it may have negative consequences for the user. These hypothetical damages may be significant but the cost of bad HCI can be even more extreme. One classic example of catastrophic consequences resulting from a poor interface is the partial meltdown that occurred at the Three Mile Island nuclear power plant on 28 March 1979. User interface problems were found to be among the factors contributing to the cause of this event (Stone et al., 2005). For example, Norman (1983) points out that an important instrument that needed to be monitored was mounted on the rear of a control panel. Further examples of the impact of bad product design are detailed by Shariat and Saucier (2016).

Who Is Involved?

HCI is a multidisciplinary field involving various areas such as human factors, computer science, cognitive psychology, sociology, communication, design, engineering, information science, and – as highlighted above – cyberpsychology. This mix of disciplines makes HCI an extremely interesting, if at times complex, field to work in. When working on HCI projects, one often has to read and conduct research in an area outside of one's specialism. Similarly, such projects often involve working with interdisciplinary teams – e.g. consisting of a software engineer, psychologist, graphic designer, and sociologist. Collaborating with individuals from varying backgrounds and viewpoints can prove a challenge but can also be a gratifying and educational experience.

There are likely to be significant and expanding opportunities for collaboration between the fields of cyberpsychology and HCI. The knowledge of the human mind and behaviour in the context of human–technology interaction brought to the table by cyberpsychologists will be a valuable complement to the skills and knowledge of those working on human–computer interfaces. Cyberpsychologists can provide an insight into the psychological effects of interface design decisions on the users of these interfaces.

The Origins of Human–Computer Interaction

Naturally, the emergence of the HCI field is closely linked to the invention and exponential growth of computers. To understand how the HCI field developed and provide some context for its current state it is helpful to consider some of the milestones in the history of HCI.

Vannevar Bush: As We May Think

The roots of the field of HCI can be traced back as far as Vannevar Bush's seminal 1945 article "As We May Think" (Bush, 1945). This article was written at a time before the invention of personal computers, when only a small number of early computers existed, each of which was the size of entire rooms. In "As We May Think" Bush presents a prescient vision of a future in which computers augment the intellectual ability of humans.

J.C.R. Licklider: Man–Computer Symbiosis

The year 1960 saw the publication of one of the most influential papers in the history of HCI and computer science, Joseph Carl Robnett Licklider's "Man-Computer Symbiosis" (Licklider, 1960). In this paper Licklider, a psychologist and computer scientist, stressed the importance of a close, interactive relationship between humans and computer systems. His view was that, rather than computers replacing human intelligence, computers could be used to amplify human intellect and free us from mundane tasks. Licklider's ideas would appear much later in the shape of modern GUIs and spoken language systems such as Apple's Siri, a technology that allows users to interact with their computing devices using natural speech.

Ivan Sutherland: Sketchpad

One of the critical concepts of the GUIs we are familiar with today is that the user's input is performed directly on the system's output. This is known as direct manipulation and makes the interface much easier to use. This innovation was first implemented by Ivan Sutherland (1963) in his Sketchpad system. Sketchpad allowed a user to draw directly on an oscilloscope display with a light pen. The graphical objects on the oscilloscope display could also be directly manipulated using the light pen input device. This feature would later make its way into more modern user interfaces where a mouse would be used rather than a light pen.

Douglas Engelbart: The Mother of All Demos

The ideas of Bush and Licklider were later pursued by inventor and engineer Douglas Engelbart. In 1968 Engelbart gave a lecture at the Fall Joint Computer Conference in San Francisco that has been retroactively named "The Mother of All Demos". In this lecture, Engelbart gave a live demonstration of a computer system called the oN-Line System (NLS) that contained many of the fundamental elements of modern computer systems and interfaces, including bitmapped screens, windows, the mouse, collaborative editors, and video conferencing. This demonstration had a massive influence on computing and inspired many similar projects in the future.

Alan Kay and Xerox PARC: Dynabook and Xerox Star

In 1972, Alan Kay proposed (Kay, 1972) a portable personal computing device, named Dynabook, to act as an educational aid to children. This device built on the ideas of Engelbart and early cardboard prototypes of the Dynabook were developed in a tablet form factor that was unachievable in practice using the technologies of the time. Working at Xerox Paulo Alto Research Center (PARC), Kay and others developed this idea over several years. This work culminated in 1981 with the release of the Xerox Star, the first commercial system to incorporate elements such as icons, folders, windows, the mouse, Ethernet networking, file and print servers, and email.

Birth of the Field

With the advent of the personal computer era in the late 1970s and early 1980s, computers became more readily available and spread beyond commercial research labs and university campuses into peoples' homes and businesses. Computers and humans were beginning to interact on a scale and in a manner that had never been seen before. Thus, the need for the field of HCI became extremely important. This period saw the release of one of the first books on the topic, Ben Shneiderman's (1980) *Software Psychology*, and saw the first conference on human factors in computing systems take place in the US in 1982 (this would later become the annual **ACM SIGCHI** conference) marking what some consider the formal foundation of the HCI field (Lazar et al., 2017). A more detailed account of the history of HCI is provided by Grudin (2012).

The Current State of the Field

Technological Shifts

The field has evolved dramatically since the early days described in the previous section. Advances in computing power and the associated emergence of technologies such as the web, touchscreens, gestural interfaces, speech recognition and synthesis, virtual and augmented reality, wearables, blockchain, etc., presented new questions and avenues for HCI research and design.

Two of the more interesting potential areas of future HCI research are artificial intelligence (AI) and brain–computer interfaces (BCI). AI has the potential to be transformative in HCI with applications including autonomous vehicles, computer vision, robotics, automated design (even of HCI products themselves), etc. It will be essential to combine HCI and AI in an appropriate manner (Li & Hilliges, 2021).

A BCI is a direct communication pathway between an external device – e.g. robotic limb or computer – and a brain. Applications of BCIs include rehabilitation, gaming, neuroscience, telepresence, and affective computing. The field of BCI could effect a fundamental change in the relationship between humans and computers. Saha et al. (2021) provide a thorough review of the state-of-the-art in BCI.

As new technologies emerge, it is incumbent on HCI researchers and practitioners to work ethically and responsibly to ensure technologies benefit society and do so without disadvantaging any specific subgroup of users over another.

Philosophical Shifts

Initially, HCI focused on the **usability** of computer applications, defined by ISO9241-11 (1998) as the "extent to which a product can be used by specified users to achieve specified goals with effectiveness, efficiency and satisfaction in a specified context of use". However, in the mid-1990s, there was a growing consideration of the broader UX of a product, incorporating the range of feelings and emotions a human has when interacting with the product. This change in focus saw the emergence of a new field, **interaction design** (IxD), defined by Sharp et al. (2019, p. xvii) as "designing interactive products to support the way people communicate and interact in their everyday and working lives". This new field is broader in scope than traditional HCI, encompassing the design of any interactive experience.

Human–Computer Interaction in Practice

The Process of Designing Interactive Experiences

As discussed above, the field of HCI is ever-changing: new technologies emerge (changing the "computer"); users' attitudes, knowledge, experience, expectations, etc., shift (changing the "user"); and new functionalities and activities are required to be modelled (changing the "task"). As a result, there is no single, universally applicable model for HCI. However, most HCI design projects involve four fundamental activities (Sharp et al., 2019):

1. Gathering requirements.
2. Designing a solution(s).
3. Constructing a prototype(s).
4. Evaluating.

These activities are commonplace throughout HCI research and industry but may be referred to using different terminology and wrapped in bespoke process models.

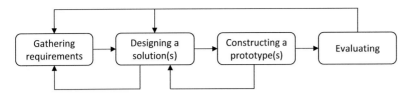

Figure 19.1
A process for designing interactive experiences. Adapted from Sharp et al. (2019).

One key characteristic of this process is that it is iterative. For example, following evaluation, a flaw may be identified in the interface. This may require returning to the design stage and continuing from there, or if necessary returning to the requirements gathering stage and continuing through all four stages again. Another important feature of the process is that each stage provides input to the next. For example, a prototype constructed at step 3 will be evaluated in step 4. A visual representation of this process is shown in Figure 19.1.

HCI projects often apply a **user-centred design** (UCD) approach. UCD involves placing the user at the heart of the design thinking and ensuring that the designed system will fit the needs of the user, rather than the user having to adapt to fit the system's needs. The nature of this user-centredness varies with each step and will depend on the techniques used. The following sections outline each of the four steps.

Gathering Requirements

Before attempting to design the interface, it is essential to understand each of the three key factors in any HCI project – user, computer, and task. Thus, the project's initial phase typically involves gathering data about these factors and using this to inform the subsequent activities.

Task

Before proceeding with the design of an interface, we must clearly establish what the interface should do. There may be an obvious need that the interface is addressing or it may require some work to elicit the users' needs. Sharp et al. (2019) and Baxter et al. (2015) present a range of techniques for establishing requirements, including interviews, questionnaires, focus groups, direct observation, indirect observation (e.g. getting users to keep diaries), and researching similar products (also called competitor analysis). For example, to elicit the user requirements for an online dating app, one might run a focus group with users to understand their needs when it comes to tasks such as creating a profile, searching for a suitable partner, accepting or declining requests for dates, controlling who can see a user's profile and what data can be seen, etc.

When designing an interface to allow the user to perform tasks, one must also understand the characteristics of these tasks. Who performs this task? When do they perform it? How frequently is the task performed? What tasks occur before/after this task? Is this task made up of subtasks? If so, how are these subtasks organised? Answers to these questions should be elicited using the techniques listed above. Having established the requirements and these task characteristics it is useful to summarise and clearly present them. Common approaches to this include writing an "informal narrative description" called a scenario (Carroll, 2000, p. 41), constructing a storyboard (Krause, 2018), or using the "Jobs to Be Done" framework (Ulwick & Osterwalder, 2016).

User

Taking a user-centred approach we must gain an understanding of the characteristics of our target users to make optimal design decisions for these users. A pivotal mantra to remember is: "you are not the user; design for the user not for yourself". Mayhew (1999) identifies four types of characteristics that should be considered: psychological characteristics (e.g. attitude and motivation), knowledge and experience (e.g. computer proficiency and task experience), job and task characteristics (e.g. frequency of use and task structure), and physical characteristics (e.g. physical impairments). Data relating to these characteristics is typically gathered using questionnaires distributed to users, interviews with users, interviews with people knowledgeable about the user population (e.g. subject matter experts), or ethnographic research.

Once this user profile data has been gathered it must be analysed to draw high-level conclusions. In some cases, it may be evident from the data that there are distinct subgroups within the user population and each may need to be considered separately – e.g. in a hospital doctors, nurses, and administrative staff may display significantly different characteristics. One popular approach to summarising the data for each user group is constructing **user personas**. A user persona is a hypothetical user with the same features, motivations, and goals as the actual user population (Laubheimer, 2020). By giving personas names and photographs, our minds can extrapolate to create a coherent picture of a whole person that can be used in our thinking when making design decisions. For example, one hypothetical user persona for an online dating app could be: "35-year-old Jack, whose busy job in the financial sector makes it difficult for him to find time to meet new people…" A real persona would flesh out these details to provide a more complete view of this type of user.

Computer

Having built a picture of the human, it is necessary to consider the computing **platform** they will be interacting with – i.e. the computer hardware and software that the interface being developed must run on. Both the capabilities and constraints (Mayhew, 1999) of the computing platform should be analysed. For example, if developing a mobile app for a smartphone, the capabilities may include a high-resolution multi-touch screen, microphone, speaker, haptic feedback (vibration), accelerometer, etc. Whereas the constraints of this platform could include a five-inch screen size, eight-hour battery life, limited multi-tasking, etc. These characteristics of the computing platform have a fundamental impact on the interface that can be implemented.

Designing and Prototyping

Once the characteristics of the user, computer, and tasks have been established the iterative interface design and prototyping process can begin. However, these activities are not isolated away from the previous phase. While designing the interface it may become apparent that some requirements have not been adequately captured and it may be necessary to gather more data.

Design Guidelines and Heuristics

Interfaces are not designed in an intellectual vacuum. The wealth of knowledge generated in the HCI field over decades of research studies and commercial interface development projects should be considered when designing any new interface. Thankfully, work has been done to examine this large pool of knowledge and derive a set of usability principles, known as **heuristics**, that can be used as "rules of thumb" (Nielsen, 1995) for interface design. One commonly used set of heuristics was developed by Nielsen (1993) based on an analysis of 249 usability problems and later revised to the following (Nielsen, 1995):

1. Visibility of system status.
2. Match between system and the real world.
3. User control and freedom.
4. Consistency and standards.
5. Error prevention.
6. Recognition rather than recall.
7. Flexibility and efficiency of use.
8. Aesthetic and minimalist design.
9. Help users recognise, diagnose, and recover from errors.
10. Help and documentation.

In addition to these general usability principles, specific design guidelines may apply to the platform the interface will run on. For example, both Google (2022b) and Apple (2022) provide interface design guidelines that should be followed when designing for Android and iOS, their respective mobile platforms. Designing an interface that does not follow these platform guidelines risks breaking the "consistency and standards" heuristic. Work has also been done to develop guidelines for more niche application areas – e.g. augmented reality (Google, 2022a) and mobile augmented reality (Dirin & Laine, 2018)

CYBERPSYCHOLOGY IN FOCUS: INCLUSIVE DESIGN

When designing interactions between humans and technology, it is crucial to understand the people using the product to address the potentially wide variety of needs they will have. An inclusive design approach allows one to consider aspects such as "accessibility, age, culture, economic situation, education, gender, geographic location, language, and race" (Joyce, 2022). The goal is to be non-exclusionary – this can open a product to a broader audience. For example, when designing drop-down menus for gender, radio buttons for "male" and "female" would exclude gender-diverse users. Another way inclusive design can be applied is in the choice of visuals for a project – do the icons used have the same meaning for all users, e.g. across cultures? Are the people pictured on your website representative of the diversity of your users or just one subset? Is the text legible to users with less-than-perfect vision? There is a multitude of similar issues to consider – following an inclusive design approach helps to ensure these are not overlooked.

Prototyping

The design and prototyping tasks go hand-in-hand. Initially, only a **conceptual model** of the interface will be designed. This conceptual model incorporates high-level design decisions such as the overall structure of the interface and the fundamental interaction paradigm to be used. Once this has been evaluated and validated, as described in the next section, the design can proceed to consider more low-level details such as icons, fonts, menus, and sound.

At each stage of this iterative design process, it is vital to construct a manifestation of the design to allow the designer to get a real sense of the interface and, arguably more importantly, they can be presented to users for evaluation throughout the HCI process. The manifestation, or prototype, can take many forms – e.g. simple sketch on paper, cardboard mock-up, **low-fidelity** prototype (see example in Figure 19.2), **high-fidelity** prototype. It is common to see a range of different prototypes produced. These often start with a low-fidelity prototype that doesn't closely resemble the final product, usually built using a different material or technology, as shown in Figure 19.2. Gradually the process will move to higher-fidelity prototypes that more closely resemble the final interface. The advantages of starting out with low-fidelity prototypes is that they are quicker to construct, promote exploration, and facilitate rapid

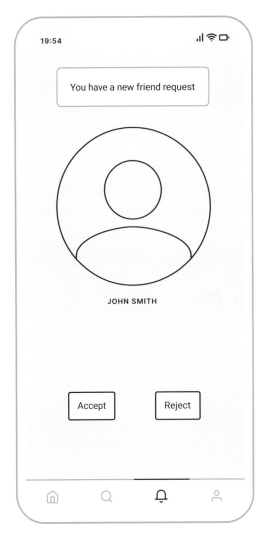

Figure 19.2
An example of a low-fidelity prototype for a mobile social networking app. (Created
with Balsamiq Mockups: http://balsamiq.com/products/mockups.)

redevelopment. Having users interact with simple low-fidelity paper mock-ups,
known as paper prototyping (Gordon, 2021), is a valuable technique.

Evaluation

Following the construction of an interface, it is time to test its usability and
the UX it provides. The testing goals will vary from project to project but will
typically be defined in advance. Goals can be categorised as usability goals (e.g.

can users perform tasks quickly, without making errors?) and UX goals (e.g. do users find the interface fun and enjoyable to use?).

Sharp et al. (2019, p. 500) define three categories of evaluation techniques:

1. *Controlled settings involving users*, for example:

Usability testing: tests are conducted in a laboratory-style setting. Users are typically given test tasks to perform and data is collected using various methods – e.g. questionnaires, observations, and interviews. This is a fundamental approach in HCI and many authors have described ways to conduct such tests (Barnum, 2020; Sharp et al., 2019; Baxter et al., 2015, Dix et al., 2004; Mayhew, 1999). The controlled nature of the environment also provides the opportunity for additional data collection methods such as eye tracking and physiological measurements (e.g. heart and respiration rates).

2. *Natural settings involving users*, for example:

Diary studies: users are asked to log their activities in a diary periodically (Baxter et al., 2015). Diaries can take a variety of formats and entries may include positive and negative reactions to elements of the interface.

Field studies: users are observed performing tasks in the real use context. An investigator will take notes and possibly also make video recordings (Baxter et al., 2015).

Online field studies: similar to the above; however, users are observed in virtual/online worlds, message boards, etc. (Fielding et al., 2016).

3. *Any settings not involving users*, for example:

Heuristic evaluations: the interface's adherence to a set of usability principles – e.g. Nielsen's (1995) ten heuristics – is measured by one or more expert evaluators.

Models: primarily used to test alternative interfaces for the same system – e.g. the optimal arrangement of user interface elements on-screen – by predicting user behaviour. One classic predictive model is Fitts's law (1954), which predicts how long a user will take to reach a particular on-screen target using a pointing device, based on the size of the object and the distance to it. More recently, techniques such as combinatorial optimisation have been used to computationally generate or adapt user interfaces (Oulasvirta et al., 2022).

Cyberpsychology and Human–Computer Interaction

Psychology has played a crucial role in the field of HCI, beginning with classic work by Norman (1983) and Card et al. (1983), and continued through to present-day literature. In a review of the psychological aspects of HCI, Olson and Olson (2003) explain that psychology has attempted to provide an understanding of "the involvement of cognitive, perceptual and motor components in the moment-by-moment interaction a person encounters when working at a computer". Understanding a person's ability to multi-task, maintain attention, recognise and recall information, learn, reason, perceive their environment, etc., helps inform the design of an interface that will take advantage of a person's abilities while compensating for their limitations (Weinschenk, 2020; Evans, 2017). Models and theories from cognitive psychology have been used in HCI, including distributed cognition, information processing, and mental models. An exploration of these is beyond the scope of this chapter; however, a thorough explanation of these models and theories is provided by Carroll (2003).

The emergence and growth of the field of cyberpsychology is closely linked to these previous crossovers between psychology and HCI. As the interactions between humans and technology became more intimate, frequent, and immersive there was a need for a field – cyberpsychology – to study the psychological phenomena surrounding these interactions. As previously mentioned, HCI and cyberpsychology have much in common, both involving the study of humans and technology, but cyberpsychology places a greater emphasis on the human (Norman, 2008). Given this strong link between the two fields, there is great potential for collaboration and sharing of knowledge.

HCI can contribute decades of theory relating to the usability and UX of user interfaces. Practical elements of HCI such as design and prototyping may also be useful when constructing interactive experiences to test cyberpsychology theories or to attempt to apply lessons from cyberpsychology in real systems. The range of evaluation techniques used in HCI may be applicable in areas of cyberpsychology research and practice. For example, the online field studies mentioned in the "Evaluation" section above are highly relevant to cyberpsychology.

Similarly, cyberpsychology can make significant contributions to HCI. While HCI is not necessarily explicitly concerned with the psychological effects of an interface on a human, cyberpsychologists may have a role in providing input into the HCI design process – e.g. to ensure interfaces result in the desired psychological effect and avoid an undesirable effect. Further, cyberpsychologists may have a role in performing interface evaluations and experiments to build theories of the psychological phenomena surrounding human–computer interactions. This will be particularly relevant when it comes to new and emerging technologies.

Conclusion

As computers become increasingly involved in all aspects of our lives the importance of creating satisfying, efficient, and effective interactive experiences between humans and computers increases. Similarly, as these interactions become more intimate and mediate more of our social interactions, it is becoming more and more important to understand the effects of such interactions on our psyche and to incorporate knowledge from the field of cyberpsychology into HCI research and practice. In the future, as new technologies emerge, the fields of HCI and cyberpsychology will have a vital, collaborative role to play in ensuring that these new developments improve our quality of life and sense of well-being, augment our intellect, and help us achieve our goals.

Activity

Imagine you are tasked with the design of a mobile app that aims to teach the user about some facet of cyberpsychology.

- Produce a low-fidelity paper prototype of your app.
- Observe a number of people using the prototype and encourage them to comment.
- How would users rate the usability and UX of the app?
- Based on their feedback, how could you improve the app in the next design iteration?

Discussion Questions

1. Do you think J.C.R. Licklider's (1960) dream of "Man-Computer Symbiosis" has been achieved? If so, what examples can you provide to support your view? If not, what developments need to take place to reach this fabled symbiosis?
2. In recent years the concerns of HCI have moved beyond usability to issues of UX such as emotion. Can you think of some interfaces that are particularly fun and enjoyable to use? What do these interfaces have in common?
3. The decisions made when designing a human–computer interface could have a significant psychological impact on its users. Can you think of any examples where such design decisions have had a negative psychological impact? How could this have been avoided?
4. Discuss the various ways in which cyberpsychologists could work with people from other disciplines to contribute to a project involving the design, implementation, and evaluation of a human–computer interface.

Recommended Reading List

This is a comprehensive and practical introduction to the field of interaction design.

Sharp, H., Rogers, Y., & Preece, J. (2019). *Interaction design* (5th ed.). Wiley.

Helpful introduction to UX for those from a non-UX background.

> Stull, E. (2018). *UX fundamentals for non-UX professionals: User experience principles for managers, writers, designers, and developers.* Apress.

A comprehensive introduction to the field of HCI, expanding on many of the topics outlined in this chapter.

> Shneiderman, B., Plaisant, C., Cohen, M., Jacobs, S., & Elmqvist, N. (2018). *Designing the user interface: Strategies for effective human-computer interaction* (6th ed.). Pearson.

A classic work that presents vivid, relatable examples of good and bad design and provides some fundamental principles of use when designing for people.

> Norman, D. (2013). *The design of everyday things* (Rev. and expanded ed.). Basic Books.

Glossary

ACM SIGCHI: Association for Computing Machinery's Special Interest Group on Computer–Human Interaction.

Conceptual model: Developed early in the interface design process, the conceptual model incorporates high-level design decisions such as the overall structure of the interface and the basic interaction paradigm to be used.

Graphical user interface (GUI): This is the layer between the human and the computer. The graphical user interface may consist of icons, buttons, text, windows, and other visual indicators.

Heuristics: A set of guidelines or rules of thumb used to guide the design and/ or evaluation of an interface.

High-fidelity prototype: Similar in look and behaviour to the desired finished product. Typically computer-based, allowing the user to interact with the prototype using a mouse, touchscreen, etc.

Human–computer interaction (HCI): Refers to the field that studies the design and testing of interactive computer systems that exist at the point where humans and computers meet.

Interaction design (IxD): A field similar to HCI, but wider in scope, incorporating any interactive experience.

Interface: The boundary between the human and the computer through which the two parties exchange information. Most commonly, this is represented on screen via a graphical user interface and the human provides commands by clicking or touching on screen interface elements such as icons or buttons.

Low-fidelity prototype: Often used early in the interaction design process, these prototypes are far from the finished product and may be developed using simple materials such as paper, offering no real user interaction.

Platform: The combination of hardware and software making up a computer system.

Prototype: A sample or model constructed to test an interface concept.

Usability: The extent to which users can achieve specified goals with effectiveness, efficiency, and satisfaction using a product.

User-centred design (UCD): A design philosophy that focuses on the needs, desires, and capabilities of the actual users of the product, rather than focusing on business goals, technologies, or other aspects.

User experience (UX): Involves a user's emotions and attitudes about interacting with a product.

User persona: A description of a hypothetical user with the same characteristics, motivations, and goals as the target user.

References

ACM SIGCHI. (1992). Curricula for human-computer interaction. http://sigchi.org/cdg

Apple. (2022). Human interface guidelines. https://developer.apple.com/design/human-interface-guidelines/guidelines/overview/

Barnum, C. (2020). *Usability testing essentials: Ready, set ...test!* (3rd ed.). Morgan Kaufmann.

Baxter, K., Courage, C., & Caine, K. (2015). *Understanding your users: A practical guide to user research methods* (2nd ed.). Morgan Kaufmann.

Bush, V. (1945). As we may think. *Atlantic Monthly, 176*, 101–108. http://www.theatlantic.com/magazine/archive/1945/07/as-we-may-think/303881/

Card, S., Moran, T., & Newell, A. (1983). *The psychology of human-computer interaction*. L. Erlbaum Associates.

Carroll, J. M. (2000). Introduction to the special issue on scenario-based systems development. *Interacting with Computers, 13*(1), 41–42.

Carroll, J. M. (Ed.) (2003). *HCI models, theories, and frameworks toward a multidisciplinary science*. Morgan Kaufmann.

Dirin, A., & Laine, T. (2018). User experience in mobile augmented reality: Emotions, challenges, opportunities and best practices. *Computers, 7*(2), 33. https://doi.org/10.3390/computers7020033

Dix, A. J., Finlay, J. E., Abowd, G. D., & Beale, R. (2004). *Human-computer interaction* (3rd ed.). Pearson Education.

Evans, D. C. (2017). *Bottlenecks: Aligning Ux design with user psychology*. Apress.

Fielding, N. G., Lee, R. M., & Blank, G. (2016). *The sage handbook of online research methods*. Sage Reference.

Fitts, P. M. (1954). The information capacity of the human motor system in controlling the amplitude of movement. *Journal of Experimental Psychology, 47*(6), 381–391.

Google. (2022a). Android design guidelines. https://developer.android.com/design/index.html

Google. (2022b). Augmented reality design guidelines. https://developers.google.com/ar/design

Gordon, K. (2021). Paper prototyping: A cutout kit. Nielsen Norman Group. https://www.nngroup.com/articles/paper-prototyping-cutout-kit/

Grudin, J. (2012). A moving target: The evolution of human-computer interaction. In J. Jacko (Ed.), *Human-computer interaction handbook: Fundamentals, evolving technologies, and emerging applications* (3rd ed.). CRC Press.

ISO9241-11. (1998). *Ergonomic requirements for office work with visual display terminals (VDTs) -Part 11: Guidance on usability*. ISO.

Joyce, A. (2022). Inclusive design. Nielsen Norman Group. https://www.nngroup.com/articles/inclusive-design

Kay, A. C. (1972). A personal computer for children of all ages. In *Proceedings of the ACM annual conference (ACM '72)*. ACM.

Krause, R. (2018). Storyboards help visualise UX ideas. Nielsen Norman Group. https://www.nngroup.com/articles/storyboards-visualize-ideas/

Laubheimer, P. (2020). 3 persona types: Lightweight, qualitative, and statistical. Nielsen Norman Group. https://www.nngroup.com/articles/persona-types/

Lazar, J., Feng, J., & Hochheiser, H. (2017). *Research methods in human computer interaction* (2nd ed.). Morgan Kaufmann.

Li, Y., & Hilliges, O. (2021). *Artificial Intelligence for human computer interaction: A modern approach*. Springer.

Licklider, J. (1960). Man-computer symbiosis. *IRE Transactions on Human Factors in Electronics HFE-1, 1*, 4–11.

Mayhew, D. (1999). *The usability engineering lifecycle: A practitioner's handbook for user interface design*. Morgan Kaufmann.

Nielsen, J. (1993). *Usability engineering*. Academic Press.

Nielsen, J. (1995). 10 usability heuristics for user interface design. Nielsen Norman Group. http://www.nngroup.com/articles/ten-usability-heuristics/

Norman, D. (1983). Some observations on mental models. *Mental Models, 7*(112), 7–14.

Norman, K. (2008). *Cyberpsychology: An introduction to human-computer interaction*. Cambridge University Press.

Olson, G. M., & Olson, J. S. (2003). Human-computer interaction: Psychological aspects of the human use of computing. *Annual Review of Psychology, 54*, 491–516.

Oulasvirta, A., Dayama, N. R., Shiripour, M., John, M., & Karrenbauer, A. (2020). Combinatorial optimization of graphical user interface designs. *Proceedings of the IEEE, 108*(3), 434–464. https://doi.org/10.1109/JPROC.2020.2969687

Saha, S., Mamun, K. A., Ahmed, K., Mostafa, R., Naik, G. R., Darvishi, S., Khandoker, A. H., & Baumert, M. (2021). Progress in brain computer interface: Challenges and opportunities. *Frontiers in Systems Neuroscience, 15*. https://doi.org/10.3389/fnsys.2021.578875

Shariat, J., & Saucier, C. S. (2016). *Tragic design: The impact of bad product design and how to fix it*. O'Reilly Media.

Sharp, H., Rogers, Y., & Preece, J. (2019). *Interaction design* (5th ed.). Wiley.

Shneiderman, B. (1980). *Software psychology: Human factors in computer and information systems*. Winthrop.

Stone, D., Jarrett, C., Woodroffe, M., & Minocha, S. (2005). *User interface design and evaluation*. Elsevier.

Sutherland, I. (1963). *Sketchpad: A man-machine graphical communication system* (Doctoral dissertation). http://www.cl.cam.ac.uk/techreports/UCAM-CL-TR-574.pdf

Ulwick, A. W., & Osterwalder, A. (2016). *Jobs to be done: Theory to practice*. Idea Bite Press.

Weinschenk, S. (2020). *100 things every designer needs to know about people*. Peachpit Press/New Riders.

Gaming

20

David Hayes, Andrew Errity, Brendan Rooney, and Conall Tunney

Chapter Overview

Gaming has developed from a relatively niche activity to a pastime engaged in by a much wider cross-section of the population. The greater diversity of gaming platforms (such as smartphones and social networking sites) coupled with the greater social aspect of gaming has a psychological impact on users. This chapter will outline various definitions and types of games and describe key developments in the history of gaming. Following this, we will introduce the psychological theories and research that explore the motivations for and gratifications from playing video games, including the experience of presence and flow, and the use of "gamification". Finally, consideration will be given to problems associated with video gameplay such as intense forms of problematic use or "addiction" and the debate about the link between violent video games and aggressive behaviour.

Key Terms

Games that are played on a computer system and allow the player to interactively control graphics on some form of display may be termed **video games**. The individuals who interact with and control the actions within a video game are frequently referred to as **gamers**.

An Introduction to Video Gaming

Introduction

Video gaming has followed the exponential growth of computing, expanding from an activity initially engaged in by just a small number of the early computer hackers to one enjoyed by a diverse range of people from all ages and backgrounds. It is likely that you or someone close to you regularly play **video games**. This may involve spending hours at a time playing a massively

DOI: 10.4324/9781003092513-28

multiplayer online role-playing game (MMORPG) such as *World of Warcraft* on a custom gaming computer, spending a few spare minutes playing a casual game such as *Candy Crush* on a mobile device, or gameplay somewhere between these two ends of the gaming spectrum. Given the growth of gaming, diversification of player demographics, and increased social interaction facilitated by increased Internet connectivity it is vital to consider the psychological impact of these games on the players. Before delving into these psychological aspects, it is important to understand the context. What characteristics define a video game? How did games evolve to the diverse array of modern games we see today? What types of games are there? Who plays these games? This section aims to answer these questions.

What Are Video Games?

Before attempting to define the characteristics of a "video game", the term itself must be considered. Several alternative terms are also used, such as "computer game", "digital game", and "electronic game". The meaning of each of these terms may vary depending on the context and they are not always synonymous. For example, the term "computer game" is sometimes used to refer to games played on personal computers while the term video game sometimes refers exclusively to games on consoles such as the Sony PlayStation or Microsoft Xbox (Tavinor, 2008). For clarity, this chapter will use the term video game to refer to games that are played on any computer system and allow the player to interactively control graphics on some form of display.

Defining the term video game is not as straightforward as one might first imagine due to the variety of games encompassed by the term and the rate at which games evolve. Some of the key characteristics that define "traditional games" include conflict, rules, player effort, and valued outcomes. Most video games embody these characteristics within software that provides an interface to control the gameplay. This interface is the point at which the computer and human meet and typically includes input elements (e.g., keyboard, mouse, gamepad) and output elements (e.g., speakers, screen, haptic feedback). More detailed discussions of what makes a video game have been provided by Wolf (2002), Tavinor (2008), Karhulahti (2015), and Arjoranta (2019).

The Evolution of Video Games

William Higinbotham's *Tennis for Two* game, written in 1958 for an analogue computer and oscilloscope, is widely recognised as the first video game. It allowed two players to bounce a ball over a net on the oscilloscope display. Another notable early game, *Spacewar!*, was developed just three years later in 1961 by MIT student Steve Russell on a PDP-1 computer. It took another decade for computer hardware costs to reduce to a point where video games were commercially feasible. In 1971 Nolan Bushnell released the first arcade video game, *Computer Space*, which was not a commercial success. However, Nolan persevered and in 1972 founded his own company, Atari, and produced a ping-pong simulation, with the help of engineer Al Alcorn, named *Pong* that became the world's first commercially successful arcade video game and launched the video game industry.

The video game industry has grown and evolved dramatically since these early days. Wardyga (2019) has written a comprehensive history of video games, but the changes can be summarised in a few key categories:

- **Hardware**: The exponential improvements in computer hardware have had a huge impact on video games. Increasing memory sizes, improvements in graphics technologies, faster processor speeds, and new storage media (e.g., CD-ROMs and DVDs) allowed games to move from 2D to realistic 3D graphics and become larger and more complex. Reductions in the physical size of hardware devices have also facilitated the growth of mobile gaming.
- **Interfaces**: Linked to the improvements in computer hardware, the manner in which players interact with games has also evolved. Input devices evolved from simple joysticks to mouse and keyboard to touchscreens to motion-based controllers such as Valve's Index Controllers. Similarly, output devices have developed from low-resolution monochrome displays to modern high-definition displays to virtual reality headsets like the PlayStation VR.
- **Players**: The demographics of **gamers** shifted from predominantly young males to a wider cross-section of the population.
- **Connectivity**: The growth of the Internet and increasing ubiquity of always-on high-speed Internet connectivity, both wired and wireless, have led to an explosion of online gaming, mobile gaming, and casual gaming, and fuelled the rise of location-based augmented-reality games like *Pokémon GO*. Meanwhile, subscription-based services such as Xbox's Game Pass have changed how gamers access games by providing instant online access to hundreds of titles.
- **Game design**: Given the increasing diversification of the demographics of game players and game designers, new forms of gameplay are emerging to appeal to these different demographics.

What Types of Games Are There?

As with other forms of entertainment such as film and music, video games can be categorised by genre, or in many cases assigned to multiple genres. As video gaming evolves the genres also change; thus, it is impossible to give a definitive list of game genres that will not become outdated. However, Table 20.1, adapted from Rabin (2011, pp. 35–40), describes some of the most significant genres.

TABLE 20.1 Video Game Genres

Genre	Description	Example
Action	Quick and accurate reactions are required to succeed.	*Pong*
Adventure	Players, typically taking the role of a single character, can explore and interact with other characters and the game world. Gameplay focuses on puzzle-solving and problem-solving rather than action/combat.	*Zork*
Action-adventure	A combination of the two genres above.	*The Legend of Zelda*
Platformer	Run and jump from platform to platform to reach required goals.	*Super Mario Bros*
Fighting	Engage in combat, typically hand-to-hand, with other players or the computer.	*Street Fighter*
First-person shooter	The player's view of the world is from the perspective of the character they are playing.	*Call of Duty*
Strategy	Focus on planning, strategic thinking, and decision-making. The player is typically given a top-down view of the game world. May be either real-time or turn-based.	*Command and Conquer*
Role-playing game (RPG)	Gameplay is based on traditional tabletop role-playing games.	*Dungeons & Dragons*
Massively multiplayer online role-playing game	RPGs in which thousands of players simultaneously play in the same persistent virtual world in real-time.	*World of Warcraft*
Simulation	Designed to simulate a real or imaginary reality.	*Microsoft Flight Simulator*
Rhythm	Require the player to match their actions to the musical beat, typically focusing on players playing simulated musical instruments or dancing.	*Guitar Hero*
Casual	Targeted at casual gamers, i.e., players who do not wish to commit large amounts of time and effort to playing games.	*Angry Birds*
Social	Involve an element of social interaction with other human players.	*FarmVille*
Sandbox	Give players lots of freedom over how to play and what to do in game. Usually involve open-world environments that players are free to roam, and gameplay systems that allow for considerable player creativity.	*Grand Theft Auto V*

FEATURE BOX: WHO PLAYS GAMES?

The classic stereotype of a gamer is that of a reclusive, adolescent male. However, the statistics show that this is a grossly inaccurate picture of the modern game-playing audience. Reports by industry bodies reveal that in the US and Europe the average gamer is around 31 years old, while 45–47% of gamers identify as female (Entertainment Software Association (ESA), 2021; Interactive Software Federation of Europe-European Games Developer Federation, 2021). In 2021, an estimated 3 billion people played video games and spent $175.8 billion on this pastime (Newzoo, 2021), further emphasising that video games are far from a niche activity. Perceptions of gaming as anti-social are also misguided, with US gamers spending an average of 7.5 hours playing with others online and 4.5 hours playing with others in-person each week (ESA, 2021). Together, these statistics demonstrate that gaming is a highly popular and social activity, enjoyed by a large and diverse audience. Thus, it is crucial to consider the psychological impacts of gaming. But also, it is crucial to do so in a way that is inclusive and representative of the wide variety of gamers.

The Psychology of Video Gaming

Why Do People Play Video Games?

Psychological Gratifications

Since the rise in video games, media psychologists have tried to explain why people engage in such game-playing activities. Much of this work has focused on predicting the enjoyment that gamers experience, yet scholars have increasingly recognised the importance of game *appreciation* for understanding the appeal of video games (Oliver et al., 2016). Whereas enjoyment relates to hedonic (pleasure-focused) needs, appreciation is characterised by meaning-making, insight, and feeling moved (Oliver & Bartsch, 2010). In general, research exploring the motivations for playing video games has referred to several common benefits or "gratifications" that may contribute to a gamer's enjoyment and/or appreciation of a game. Recently, Scharkow et al. (2015) proposed a model of gaming gratifications comprising individual, social, and content gratifications. Here, individual gratifications relate to a desire to explore the game world (exploration), to experience things that are not possible in the real world and take on different roles (fantasy), and to develop one's gaming skills (competence). Social gratifications involve wanting to compete (competition) or cooperate (teamplay) with others and a desire to meet people (social capital). Finally, content gratifications relate to the importance of the game's graphics/mechanics (mechanics) and topic/story (narration) for the player. Using this model, Possler et al. (2020) found that narration, mechanics, fantasy, and competence were associated with both enjoyment and appreciation, while exploration was only associated with enjoyment and social capital and teamplay only influenced appreciation. Yet the authors note that this last finding may have been driven by the game used, as significant links between game enjoyment and social gratifications have been demonstrated elsewhere (cf. Rogers, 2017).

The benefits (and appeal) of video games are also encapsulated within the self-determination theory (SDT) model of video game engagement (Przybylski et al., 2010). This model proposes that the popularity of a game is based upon its ability to satisfy basic psychological needs. According to SDT, people want to feel various degrees of competence (a sense of ability), autonomy (freedom and individuality), and relatedness (social connection). More recently, Oliver et al. (2016) proposed a complementary need for *insight* and found that autonomy and competence were associated with game enjoyment, while relatedness and insight predicted game appreciation.

Altered States of Consciousness

Psychologists have also theorised about the benefits of video gameplay in terms of the altered states of consciousness it might produce. Playing video games commonly (and necessarily) alters a player's state of consciousness. When playing video games, players often lose awareness of their (real) surroundings and become engulfed in the world of the game. They may not notice the time go by or events that are taking place in the same room. However, even during particularly intense video game experiences, players will often retain some awareness (on some level) of their surroundings and the context in which they are engaging in the activity (Banos et al., 2004; Singer & Witmer, 1999). This is necessary for their popularity, as an extreme dissociation from reality or hallucinogenic effect of video gameplay would be unusual and unsettling, if not traumatic.

The altered state of consciousness is an integral part of the way in which video games work and has been explored in various fields of study, including psychology, game studies, philosophy, computer science, and user experience (UX). This broad interest in the area has generated the use of different terms for the changes in consciousness when playing. This can make studying the area tricky sometimes because these terms can be overlapping and yet have a slightly different focus.

One of the most common terms associated with the experience of video gameplay is "**presence**". The term was first introduced as "telepresence" by Minsky (1980) and in film studies has been referred to as the diegetic effect (Burch, 1979). Presence is a player's *subjective* sensation of "being in" the game (Michailidis et al., 2018). Lombard and Ditton (1997) define it as "a perceptual illusion of non-mediation", that is, the extent to which a player is unaware that they are playing a game. Researchers exploring presence have distinguished between the contributing aspects of the medium (the video game or interface) on one hand and the psychological processes of the player on the other. These researchers have used a related but different term, **immersion**, to define the characteristics of the technology. Immersive technologies are those that offer a higher quality or quantity of sensory information to the user (Slater, 1999). Thus, the modern gaming experience is becoming increasingly immersive. So, it would make sense if modern gamers are feeling more presence when they play; that there would be a relationship between the immersiveness of the game and the amount of presence that the player feels. Several empirical studies have demonstrated that feelings of presence tend to increase as the level of immersion increases (Pallavicini et al., 2019; Seibert & Shafer, 2018). However, Wirth et al. (2007) argue that we cannot assume such a relationship is simple and one-way. They point out that there are other factors that affect feelings of presence such as the characteristics of the game (e.g., novelty or genre) and the individual gamer's preferences.

The state of "**flow**" is another common and overlapping psychological construct from the literature and while the term flow is not solely reserved for video gameplay, it has become a useful construct for exploring the way in which gamers can engage with the activity. The term was coined by the Hungarian psychologist Mihaly Csikszentmihalyi (pronounced *CHEEK-sent-me-hi-ee*) and can be seen as a related concept to the idea of presence. To be in a state of flow is to be focused and engaged in gameplay (or another activity) and includes a feeling of enjoyment, being one with the game, and a distorted perception of time. It occurs in a moment when the player achieves a balance between the skill or effort required and the difficulty or challenge faced (Csikszentmihalyi & Csikszentmihalyi, 1988).

Despite the prevalence of enjoyable flow, playing a video game is not always a positive experience; games can cause us to feel a range of negative emotions such as anger, anxiety, fear, and frustration (Porter & Goolkasian, 2019). Indeed, games that arouse negative emotions such as the game series *Call of Duty*, *Resident Evil*, and *Assassins' Creed* are among the most popular games currently available (NPD, 2021). How can we explain the appeal of games that make us feel negative emotions? Emotions like fear and anxiety can be experienced as highly enjoyable as a result of excitation transfer – where the high levels of arousal associated with these emotions are interpreted in a positive light when the threat is removed (e.g., the gamer escapes a monster in a horror game) or if there is a positive ending (Bartsch, 2017). Separately, strong emotions, both positive and negative, may stimulate self-reflection (Bopp et al., 2016) and the process of meaning-making (Bartsch, 2017). Thus, it is proposed that experiencing all emotions (whether positive or negative) is enjoyable and beneficial.

Learning and Honing Adaptive Skills

This idea is also in line with researchers such as Steen and Owens (2001) and Tan (2008), who have explored the evolutionary function of engaging with entertainment such as video games. They argue that playing video games is an "adaptive activity". In other words, humans are motivated to play video games, because they, in some way contribute to human prosperity. According to Tan (2008), such activity allows us to learn and practice skills that are helpful for everyday life, in a way that is safe and enjoyable. What sort of skills? You would be forgiven for thinking that the average person would never need the skills of dragon-slaying or zombie-killing in their day-to-day lives. Of course! But embedded in these activities are opportunities to develop a range of other skills that are useful, such as problem-solving, planning, social skills, and emotion regulation (e.g., keeping calm in a stressful situation). Psychologists have argued that playing games might be beneficial because they allow us to hone skills in a way that is perhaps more enjoyable than, say, formally learning social skills from a textbook.

The idea that games make learning fun offers a possible explanation as to why people might engage in video gameplay. Furthermore, this idea offers an opportunity to capitalise on the popularity of gaming to increase engagement towards all sorts of activities. Nick Pelling (2011) referred to this activity by coining the phrase "**gamification**" in 2002. This is where an existing challenge or activity is re-designed with gaming principles or mechanics to make the task into an enjoyable game. For example, *Recyclebank* is an application that has gamified various tasks such as recycling, conserving water, or online learning about sustainable living. Players earn points for these activities that can be redeemed for rewards like discounts on various products or services. More recently, some enterprising psychologists and other researchers have also begun to use gamification to bring about health and education benefits within entertaining video games. For example, Coyle et al. (2017) designed a video game called *Pesky gNATs* that supports the delivery of a cognitive behaviour therapy intervention for children experiencing anxiety or depression (see Chapter 12 for further information on *Pesky gNATs*).

The Negative Aspects of Computer Gaming

As gaming in its various forms has become ubiquitous, the "downsides", or negative aspects, of gaming have been discussed heavily in the general media and scientific literature alike. The conversation ranges from anecdotes about people losing out on sleep after becoming immersed in a game, to stories of genuine addictive behaviours, and even to games being considered significant factors in acts of violence such as mass shootings in schools in the United States. A topic that reaches such a large cross-section of society, with such serious implications and emotions attached to it, has led to heated debate among psychologists. However, the field remains divided on key questions.

The Debate

In essence, the debate surrounding video game playing behaviour boils down to two questions:

1. Does playing for excessive lengths of time classify as an addiction or is it over-enthusiastic behaviour, i.e. is the behaviour pathological or problematic?
2. Does playing (violent) video games have a genuine and lasting effect on (aggressive) behaviour in real life?

Theories of How Games Affect People

Theoretical attempts to explain how gaming impacts players are largely the same as those that have been suggested for viewing violent or aggressive media. The foundational model is social learning theory (Bandura & Walters, 1977), which posits that behaviour can be learned by modelling the observed actions of others, even without partaking in the behaviour itself. This theory has been applied to gaming where there is ample opportunity to learn from the behaviour of non-player characters (NPCs) and other players online. Building on this, social cognitive theory (Bandura & National Institute of Mental Health, 1986) suggests that exposure to violent or aggressive media leads to the priming of aggressive "scripts", or pre-programmed ways of behaving. These theories also incorporate desensitisation, where a player becomes accustomed to violent stimulus, something that has been related to in-game violent behaviours that are common in many video games. Competing theories include the catalyst model (Ferguson et al., 2008), which regards violent media as much less important than early social experiences, and moral panic theory (Cohen, 1973), which would argue that the general fear of a new medium, though highly influential, is cyclical and will be replaced by fear of the next new medium.

Pathological or Problematic Behaviour?

In the publication of the ICD-11 (World Health Organization, 2019), "gaming disorder" was included as a diagnosable addiction. To be diagnosed, an individual must display impaired control over their online/offline gaming, prioritise gaming over other interests and activities, and continue/escalate their gaming activities despite the negative consequences this entails, where these include marked distress or significant impairment of functioning. Though the decision to recognise pathological gaming as a formal disorder was welcomed by many, others argue that it is premature (van Rooij et al., 2018). Specifically, scholars point to the poor quality of the evidence basis, the risk of inappropriate diagnoses and accompanying pathologising of normal gaming activities, a lack of practical utility of the disorder, and a lack of a strong rationale for focusing on gaming over other behaviours. Furthermore, in a recent survey of video game scholars, Ferguson and Colwell (2020) reported that while the majority believe that pathological gaming could be a formal disorder, only 56.5% agreed that the ICD-11 criteria were valid.

Given these issues, it may be more appropriate to consider the negative consequences associated with gaming in terms of *problematic* rather than *pathological* behaviour. In this context, research has increasingly focused on maladaptive coping strategies as a key driver of problematic gaming (Melodia et al., 2020). In other words, problematic gaming is prompted by an individual's use of video games to escape or avoid their real-world problems. Di Blasi et al. (2019) further suggest that those with an inability to control/regulate their emotions (emotional dysregulation) are more likely to use games as a coping mechanism and, thus, to engage in problematic gaming. Chapter 12 considers additional aspects of pathological gaming.

Gaming and Violence

The other key flashpoint around which researchers frequently clash is whether playing violent video games (VVGs) creates genuine violent trends in players, and therefore whether they should be considered a risk factor for committing acts of violence in the real world. Over the past three decades, researchers have produced a considerable body of work on the topic, including several meta-analytic reviews that pool the results of individual studies. However, the authors of these reviews typically fall into one of two camps based on their views of VVGs, with each side directing scathing (sometimes personal) attacks against the other. Consequently, whenever a meta-analysis reports significant (or no) links between VVGs and aggressive behaviour, aggressive cognition, aggressive affect, and/or decreased empathy and pro-social behaviour (cf. American Psychological Association, 2015), it is invariably followed up by a paper which provides extensive criticism of that review's methodology and findings, and occasionally includes a re-examination of the data (cf. Ferguson et al., 2020). Both camps also point to broader issues in the literature, with those advocating null or trivial effects of VVGs highlighting the issue of publication bias favouring significant findings and several methodological issues such as the use of inappropriate controls and unstandardised measures (Ferguson et al., 2020). Meanwhile, those who propose significant links between VVGs and violence/aggression have raised concerns over small sample sizes, inappropriate measures, and a lack of appropriate controls, among a host of other issues (Bushman & Anderson, 2021).

Given all of the above and despite decades of empirical research, we still do not have a definitive answer as to whether VVGs have genuine and lasting effects on violent and aggressive behaviour. To make meaningful progress, Ferguson (2020) points to the need for preregistered studies, standardised measures, matched violent/non-violent games (in terms of story, difficulty, competitiveness, etc.), multivariate controls (e.g., gender, trait aggressiveness), and the use of standardised regression coefficients in meta-analyses.

Negative Gaming Behaviour

Aside from the above questions, which dominate the field and the media coverage, there are other negative aspects to gaming that run under the radar of large research projects. These negatives are behaviours like in-game cyber-bullying, **trolling,** and griefing. Such behaviours can be considered to arise due to the anonymity created by the technological medium. This phenomenon is not a new discovery and has been noted in technologies such as CB radios in the 1970s, where communication without identifiable features or profiles allows people to communicate without repercussions. Chapter 5 considers negative online behaviours in more detail.

Conclusion

The video game medium is one that is constantly evolving in tandem with technological advances and cultural shifts. The popularity of this medium is also increasing and finding new audiences beyond those that were typical in the past. Going forward it will be increasingly important to study the psychological impact of gameplay on this diverse and growing population of gamers. Such studies should provide an insight into the psychological effects of gameplay and thus allow players to avoid the negative aspects of gaming and prioritise the potential positive elements. Similarly, game designers should be cognizant of the psychological factors at play when creating games.

Activity

If someone experiences "flow" while playing a video game their perception of time can be distorted (Nakamura & Csikszentmihalyi, 2009). To explore this yourself, ask someone to play a video game that they like (this is important if they are to experience flow) for a specific period of time and then stop them after a certain amount of time and ask them to estimate how long they've been playing. Make sure they don't know that you're going to ask them to estimate their playing time because knowing this might disrupt their ability to experience flow. You will also need to make sure that there is no time display feature as part of the game.

Did they experience flow? Was their estimate of elapsed time accurate? If not, was it longer or shorter than the correct amount? In other words, did time fly while they were having fun?

Discussion Questions

1. Video games are good for society. Do you agree with this statement? Discuss the reasons why/why not.

2. Can you think of any reasons for playing video games that did not feature within the presented theories?
3. How much do you think the principles of gamification could be applied in formal education? Could everything in school be taught through a game?
4. Media reports on violent events in society, particularly those involving young males, often draw a link between video game violence and real-life violence. Discuss the evidence for and against this link.

Recommended Reading List

This book covers a host of different topics relating to the psychology of video games, including the use of games for learning and behavioural change, video game addiction and violence, and discrimination and inequality in gaming, among others.

> Kowert, R., & Quandt, T. (Eds.). (2021). *The video game debate 2: Revisiting the physical, social, and psychological effects of video games*. Routledge.

This book provides a review of the psychology of video game motivation and engagement, addressing both the positive and negative aspects of gameplay. It is based on years of research with thousands of gamers.

> Rigby, S., & Ryan, R. (2011). *Glued to games how video games draw us in and hold us spellbound*. Praeger.

This article reviews the theoretical arguments that explore why people engage with entertainment (including video games) and then proposes a theoretical model to explain how and why people feel strong emotions towards entertainment that they know is fabricated and fictional.

> Tan, E. S. H. (2008). Entertainment is emotion: The functional architecture of the entertainment experience. *Media Psychology, 11*(1), 28–51. https://doi.org/10.1080/15213260701853161

Game researcher Nick Yee has used player surveys, psychological experiments, and in-game data to study online fantasy gameplay.

> Yee, N. (2014). *The proteus paradox: How online games and virtual worlds change us- and how they don't*. Yale University Press.

Glossary

Flow: Similar to presence, flow refers to a heightened state of engagement with a video game activity (or other activity) that is characterised by feelings of presence, energised focus, and enjoyment; being at one with the game. Flow typically involves distortions of time perception.

Gamer: A video game player.

Gamification: The application of game principles or mechanisms to a task or problem to encourage increased engagement with the activity.

Immersion: An objective characteristic of the medium that describes the quality or quantity of sensory information provided to a person from a video game (or other audio-visual technology).

Presence: The subjective feeling of being in a video game (or other virtual environment); an illusion that renders the viewer unaware of the medium (the screen, the interface)

Trolling: The negative behaviours engaged in by some gamers to bother other gamers, which can include deliberate annoyance or disruption, sexism, racism, and faking.

Video game: Games that are played on any computer system and allow the player to interactively control graphics on some form of display.

References

American Psychological Association. (2015). *Technical report on the review of the violent video game literature.* https://www.apa.org/pi/families/review-video-games.pdf

Arjoranta, J. (2019). How to define games and why we need to. *The Computer Games Journal, 8*(3–4), 109–120. https://doi.org/10.1007/s40869-019-00080-6

Bandura, A., & National Institute of Mental Health. (1986). *Social foundations of thought and action: A social cognitive theory.* Prentice-Hall, Inc.

Bandura, A., & Walters, R. H. (1977). *Social learning theory* (Vol. 1). Prentice Hall.

Banos, R. M., Botella, C., Alcaniz, M., Liano, V., Guerrero, B., & Rey, B. (2004). Immersion and emotion: Their impact of sense of presence. *Cyberpsychology and Behavior, 7*(6), 734–741. http://doi.org/10.1089/cpb.2004.7.734

Bartsch, A. (2017). Content effects: Entertainment. In P. Rössler (Ed.), *International encyclopedia of media effects* (pp. 1–15). Wiley. https://doi.org/10.1002/9781118783764.wbieme0128

Blasi, M. D., Giardina, A., Giordano, C., Coco, G. L., Tosto, C., Billieux, J., & Schimmenti, A. (2019). Problematic video game use as an emotional coping strategy: Evidence from a sample of MMORPG gamers. *Journal of Behavioral Addictions, 8*(1), 25–34. https://doi.org/10.1556/2006.8.2019.02

Bopp, J. A., Mekler, E. D., & Opwis, K. (2016, May 7). *Negative emotion, positive experience? Emotionally moving moments in digital games* [Paper presentation]. 2016 CHI Conference on Human Factors in Computing Systems. https://doi.org/10.1145/2858036.2858227

Burch, N. (1979). *To the distant observer.* University of California Press.

Bushman, B. J., & Anderson, C. A. (2021). Solving the puzzle of null violent media effects. *Psychology of Popular Media.* Advance online publication. https://doi.org/10.1037/ppm0000361

Cohen, S. (1973). *Folk devils and moral panics.* Paladin.

Coyle, D., O'Reilly, G., van der Meulen, H., Tunney, C., Cooney, P., & Jackman, C. (2017, October). Pesky gNATs: Using games to support mental health interventions for adolescents [Paper presentation]. ACM SIGCHI Annual Symposium on Computer-Human Interaction in Play (CHI Play 2017), Amsterdam, The Netherlands. http://hdl.handle.net/10197/9310

Csikszentmihalyi, M., & Csikszentmihalyi, I. (1988). *Optimal experience: Psychological studies of flow in consciousness.* Cambridge University Press.

Entertainment Software Association. (2021). *2021 essential facts about the computer and video game industry.* The Entertainment Software Association. https://www.theesa.com/wp-content/uploads/2021/08/2021-Essential-Facts -About-the-Video-Game-Industry-1.pdf

Ferguson, C. J. (2020). Aggressive video games research emerges from its replication crisis (sort of). *Current Opinion in Psychology, 36,* 1–6. https://doi .org/10.1016/j.copsyc.2020.01.002

Ferguson, C. J., & Colwell, J. (2020). Lack of consensus among scholars on the issue of video game "addiction". *Psychology of Popular Media, 9*(3), 359–366. https://doi.org/10.1037/ppm0000243

Ferguson, C. J., Copenhaver, A., & Markey, P. (2020). Reexamining the findings of the American Psychological Association's 2015 task force on violent media: A meta-analysis. *Perspectives on Psychological Science, 15*(6), 1423–1443. https://doi.org/10.1177/1745691620927666

Ferguson, C. J., Rueda, S., Cruz, A., Ferguson, D., Fritz, S., & Smith, S. (2008). Violent video games and aggression: Causal relationship or byproduct of family violence and intrinsic violence motivation? *Criminal Justice and Behavior, 35*(3), 311–332. https://doi.org/10.1177/0093854807311719

Interactive Software Federation of Europe-European Games Developer Federation. (2021). *2021 key facts.* Interactive Software Federation of Europe. https://www.isfe.eu/wp-content/uploads/2021/08/2021-ISFE-EGDF-Key -Facts-European-video-games-sector-FINAL.pdf

Karhulahti, V.-M. (2015). Defining the videogame. *Game Studies, 15*(2). http:// gamestudies.org/1502/articles/karhulahti

Lombard, M., & Ditton, T. (1997). At the heart of it all: The concept of presence. *Journal of Computer-Mediated Communication, 3*(2), Article JCMC321. https:// doi.org/10.1111/j.1083-6101.1997.tb00072.x

Melodia, F., Canale, N., & Griffiths, M. D. (2020). The role of avoidance coping and escape motives in problematic online gaming: A systematic literature review. *International Journal of Mental Health and Addiction.* Advance online publication. https://doi.org/10.1007/s11469-020-00422-w

Michailidis, L., Balaguer-Ballester, E., & He, X. (2018). Flow and immersion in video games: The aftermath of a conceptual challenge. *Frontiers in Psychology, 9,* Article 1682. https://doi.org/10.3389/fpsyg.2018.01682

Minsky, M. (1980, June). *Telepresence.* OMNI Magazine. https://web.media.mit .edu/~minsky/papers/Telepresence.html

Nakamura, J., & Csikszentmihalyi, M. (2009). Flow theory and research. In C. R. Snyder & S. Lopez (Eds.), *The Oxford handbook of positive Psychology* (pp. 195–206). Oxford University Press.

Newzoo. (2021). *Global games market report 2021 free version.* Newzoo. https:// newzoo.com/insights/trend-reports/newzoo-global-games-market-report -2021-free-version/

NPD. (2021, August 13). Top 10 video games. NPD. https://www.npd.com/news /entertainment-top-10/2021/top-10-video-games/

Oliver, M. B., & Bartsch, A. (2010). Appreciation as audience response: Exploring entertainment gratifications beyond hedonism. *Human Communication Research, 36*(1), 53–81. https://doi.org/10.1111/j.1468-2958.2009.01368.x

Oliver, M. B., Bowman, N. D., Woolley, J. K., Rogers, R., Sherrick, B. I., & Chung, M.-Y. (2016). Video games as meaningful entertainment experiences. *Psychology of Popular Media Culture, 5*(4), 390–405. https://doi.org/10.1037/ ppm0000066

Pallavicini, F., Pepe, A., & Minissi, M. E. (2019). Gaming in virtual reality: What changes in terms of usability, emotional response and sense of presence compared to non-immersive video games? *Simulation and Gaming, 50*(2), 136–159. https://doi.org/10.1177/1046878119831420

Pelling, N. (2011, August 9). The (short) prehistory of gamification… . *Funding Startups (& Other Impossibilities).* http://nanodome.wordpress.com/2011/08 /09/the-short-prehistory-of-gamification/

Porter, A. M., & Goolkasian, P. (2019). Video games and stress: How stress appraisals and game content affect cardiovascular and emotion outcomes. *Frontiers in Psychology, 10*, Article 967. https://doi.org/10.3389/fpsyg.2019 .00967

Possler, D., Kümpel, A. S., & Unkel, J. (2020). Entertainment motivations and gaming-specific gratifications as antecedents of digital game enjoyment and appreciation. *Psychology of Popular Media, 9*(4), 541–552. https://doi.org/10 .1037/ppm0000248

Przybylski, A. K., Rigby, C. S., & Ryan, R. M. (2010). A motivational model of video game engagement. *Review of General Psychology, 14*(2), 154–166. https:// doi.org/10.1037/a0019440

Rabin, S. (2011). *Introduction to game development* (2nd ed.). Cengage Learning.

Rogers, R. (2017). The motivational pull of video game feedback, rules, and social interaction: Another self-determination theory approach. *Computers in Human Behavior, 73*, 446–450. https://doi.org/10.1016/j.chb.2017.03.048

Scharkow, M., Festl, R., Vogelgesang, J., & Quandt, T. (2015). Beyond the "core-gamer": Genre preferences and gratifications in computer games. *Computers in Human Behavior, 44*, 293–298. https://doi.org/10.1016/j.chb.2014.11.020

Seibert, J., & Shafer, D. M. (2018). Control mapping in virtual reality: Effects on spatial presence and controller naturalness. *Virtual Reality, 22*(1), 79–88. https://doi.org/10.1007/s10055-017-0316-1

Singer, M. J., & Witmer, B. G. (1999). On selecting the right yardstick. *Presence, 8*(5), 566–573. https://doi.org/10.1162/105474699566486

Slater, M. (1999). Measuring presence: A response to the Witmer and Singer questionnaire. *Presence, 8*(5), 560–565. https://doi.org/10.1162 /105474699566477

Steen, F. F., & Owens, S. A. (2001). Evolution's silent pedagogy: An adaptationist model of pretense and entertainment. *Journal of Cognition and Culture, 1*(4), 289–321. https://doi.org/10.1163/156853701753678305

Tan, E. S. H. (2008). Entertainment is emotion: The functional architecture of the entertainment experience. *Media Psychology, 11*(1), 28–51. https://doi.org /10.1080/15213260701853161

Tavinor, G. (2008). Definition of videogames. *Contemporary Aesthetics, 6.* http:// hdl.handle.net/2027/spo.7523862.0006.016

van Rooij, A. J., Ferguson, C. J., Carras, M. C., Kardefelt-Winther, D., Shi, J., Aarseth, E., Bean, A. M., Bergmark, K. M., Brus, A., Coulson, M., Deleuze J., Dullur, P., Dunkels, E., Edman, J., Elson, M., Etchells, P. J., Fiskaali, A., Granic, I., Jansz, J., … Przybylski, A. K. (2018). A weak scientific basis for gaming disorder: Let us err on the side of caution. *Journal of Behavioral Addictions, 7*(1), 1–9. https://doi.org/10.1556/2006.7.2018.19

Wardyga, B. J. (2019). *The video games textbook.* CRC Press.

Wirth, W., Hartmann, T., Böcking, S., Vorderer, P., Klimmt, C., Schramm, H., Saari, T., Laarni, J., Ravaja, N., Gouveia, F. R., Biocca, F., Sacau, A., Jäncke, L., Baumgartner, T., & Jäncke, P. (2007). A process model of the formation of spatial presence experiences. *Media Psychology, 9*(3), 493–525. https://doi.org /10.1080/15213260701283079

Wolf, M. (2002). *The medium of the video game*. University of Texas Press.

World Health Organization. (2019). *International classification of diseases* (11th rev.). https://icd.who.int/

Psychological Applications of Virtual and Augmented/ Mixed Reality

Gráinne Kirwan

Chapter Overview

Virtual environments (VEs) are a prominent aspect of cyberpsychology, both in relation to desktop software (such as immersive games) and dedicated three-dimensional (3D) viewing technologies, such as head mounted displays (HMDs). After a brief description of some of the equipment used in augmented reality (AR) and virtual reality (VR), this chapter will describe the phenomenon of **presence**, a sense of immersion in the virtual environment that is essential for many of the research, therapeutic, diagnostic, and educational applications which are then described.

Key Terms

Virtual reality (VR) refers to highly immersive worlds, where users are unaware of their actual physical environment, while **augmented reality (AR)** or **mixed reality (MR)** usually involves the placement of digital objects or holograms into real physical environments. Users sometimes inhabit virtual bodies, known as **avatars** within VR worlds, and they can interact with other individuals or **agents** (characters controlled by the computer). Because of the 3D nature of these worlds they are often more immersive than VEs which are depicted via traditional, two-dimensional monitors. Consequentially, users may experience an increase in **presence** – a sensation of being immersed in a virtual world. Recent years have seen the development of relatively cheap HMDs targeted at a consumer audience, and this has resulted in the technology receiving increased attention from both the media and the general public, despite a lull in general interest since the term was initially popularised decades ago.

DOI: 10.4324/9781003092513-29

Virtual Reality Equipment

The most commonly used type of VR equipment are HMDs, but there is a variety of other display and interaction technologies which can also be utilised. Some of these will be briefly described in this section.

Head Mounted Displays

HMDs are relatively lightweight headsets, often incorporating headphones for sound (an example of one is shown in Figure 21.1). Many HMDs require a computer, games console, or smartphone to run the virtual environment, the visual portrayal of which is then presented in the headset. However some HMDs are standalone devices, requiring no additional equipment.

HMDs induce a sensation of three-dimensional viewing by presenting slightly different images to each of the user's eyes. This mimics vision in the real world, where each eye sees a slightly different view because of the small distance between the eyes. In this way the HMD fools the brain into thinking that the two-dimensional image being portrayed actually depicts "normal" three-dimensional space. The HMD also includes devices which detect the position and orientation of the user's head, and adjusts the image that is seen accordingly. This means that if a user decides to look over their shoulder, or down to

Figure 21.1
Virtual reality head mounted display (courtesy of Dr Brendan Rooney and the Media and Entertainment Psychology Lab, University College Dublin).

the floor, the technology will detect this, and ensure that the image portrayed reflects this changed visual orientation.

For many of the psychological applications described later in this chapter, it is helpful if the researcher or therapist is able to determine exactly what the user is looking at throughout their experience. For this reason, they may sometimes use a supplemental traditional monitor to show this. For certain purposes, such as the treatment of anxiety disorders, it is also helpful for the therapist to be able to examine if the stimuli in the virtual world elicited a physiological reaction and so physiological monitoring devices are sometimes attached to the user.

Other Virtual Reality Equipment

While HMDs are one of the most common types of VR devices, they are far from the only technology used. Other VR display systems include projection-based systems, or systems similar to those used within cinemas to show 3D films. Such devices usually require the user to wear special sets of glasses which, combined with the display, allow different images to be portrayed to both eyes in a similar manner to that described above for HMDs. Such projection systems allow the user to still view aspects of the real world (such as their own body) while experiencing the virtual world. However, projection-based systems are expensive and difficult to transport, and this type of VR may feel less immersive to some users.

It should be noted that whichever device is used, it is important that the technology is also capable of replicating sound in three dimensions. If this is not achieved, the user will consciously or unconsciously realise that there is a mismatch between the auditory and visual stimuli, which may reduce their sensation of presence. Other senses, such as touch, smell, and taste, have received less attention from researchers in VR. Datagloves and other haptic devices provide one possible method of allowing touch sensations to be transmitted to the user, but the added complexity in the virtual world that this requires, along with the additional costs of the equipment, mean that these are rarely utilised. Indeed, it may be possible for researchers and therapists to add tactile cues without the technological requirements of haptic devices – as early as 1997, Carlin, Hoffman, and Weghorst used a furry toy spider in addition to a VR environment to treat a woman with a spider phobia (arachnophobia), a technique known as **tactile augmentation**. Such a technique can greatly reduce the costs and technological requirements of adding the extra tactile sensations. Some centres specialising in the treatment of aviation phobias will also ask clients to sit in actual airplane seats in order to enhance the sense of realism.

The user of a virtual world can interact with it in many ways. These can include remote controls (sometimes called "wands") and other devices such as keyboards, control panels, and even a normal computer mouse. Technologies are also available which can recognise gestures and hand position without additional devices, allowing for a more intuitive control of the virtual world (see Figure 21.2). Depending on the system, the user might also be able to explore the virtual world by physically walking around real space and having their movements tracked – such a system allows an enhanced sense of realism and freedom to explore the virtual world, although care must be taken to ensure that the user does not walk into a wall or trip over an obstacle as their visual perception of the real world is blocked by the VR headset.

When using VR, users should always be conscious of a phenomenon known as **cybersickness**. This is a form of motion sickness caused by discrepancies between visual and proprioceptive cues, and is very similar to carsickness or seasickness. Symptoms include nausea, vomiting, postural instability, and disorientation, but often the earlier stages of cybersickness can be identified by carefully observing the user for other symptoms, such as pallor or even yawning. Cybersickness can occur in any user, and in any virtual world, but it can be more common in virtual worlds which do not respond sufficiently quickly to user movement (lag) or those with misaligned optical components or slow frame refresh rates. In the vast majority of cases, simply turning off the VR or removing the person from the simulation will resolve any cybersickness within moments. However, care should also be taken with any potential VR users who have certain medical conditions, such as epilepsy, vestibular problems, or some heart conditions. It is advisable that such individuals seek advice from a medical professional before being exposed to any VR environment.

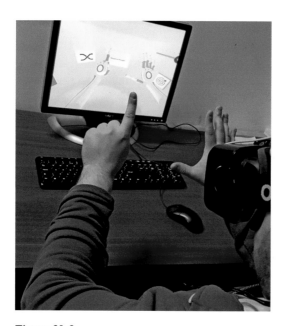

Figure 21.2
Gesture recognition in virtual reality (courtesy of Dr Brendan Rooney and the Media and Entertainment Psychology Lab, University College Dublin).

Mixed Reality and Augmented Reality

While not specifically VR, the related concepts of **MR** and **AR** are also worth describing here. These technologies are very similar to each other, and involve virtual objects being used to supplement a real scene using technologies such as headsets, holograms, cameras, and screens. While there is some disagreement as to the exact usage of these terms, usually MR refers to situations where there is some interaction between the virtual and physical object, while AR suggests a simpler overlay of the virtual object on a physical scene – although this is not universally agreed, and some sources do not distinguish between the two. There are several smartphone applications which allow users to experience AR/MR, and these have been particularly popular for tourism, where the user can view information about buildings, monuments, and other tourist attractions by pointing their phone at the landmark. It has also been used for some museum exhibits – at a dinosaur exhibition at the Museum of New Zealand Te Papa Tongarewa in Wellington, visitors could interact with an AR dinosaur which would pace around the person (although the dinosaur was only visible on a giant monitor nearby and not in the real space surrounding the visitor).

While AR and MR will not be examined in detail in this chapter, it is worth noting that there are many practical psychological uses for the technology. For example, it has been used as a method of inducing the mirror box illusion for individuals experiencing phantom limb pain (see, for example, Lendaro et al., 2020). It is also possible that AR could be used as an alternative to VR for many of the purposes outlined below – early research by Botella et al. (2010) examined the potential of AR in the treatment of cockroach phobias, and more recently, Zimmer et al. (2021) examined the use of a smartphone-based AR application to reduce fear of spiders.

Presence

It is interesting to attend cinemas full of individuals watching horror movies, if only to see the audience physically jump or crouch down in their seats as the tension builds. Sometimes their reaction is more subtle, such as holding their breath or an increase in heart rate, sometimes more obvious, such as hiding behind their popcorn or a cushion. Rationally, they know that what is happening on screen is not real, and that the villain, monster, or other malevolent creature cannot actually harm them. But the film has drawn them in, causing them to feel fear, which has observable effects on their behaviour and physiology. The individual is experiencing a sense of immersion in the film, a phenomenon more commonly identified in VR literature as **presence** (see also Chapter 20). In short, presence is the extent to which the person allows themselves to be convinced that they are somewhere other than their actual physical location. Riva et al. (2014, p. 10) suggest that the sensation of presence requires three components:

1 That the multimodal input from the virtual world is combined so as to be experienced as a reality.
2 That the integration occurs from an egocentric perspective – specifically that the user feels that they are within the environment, rather than observing it from an external vantage point.
3 That the virtual experience is recognised as having meaning and relevance.

Consider again the fear that emerged from watching the film in the cinema – to experience such terror the viewer needs to set aside the knowledge that the events portrayed are not actually occurring at that moment, in that location. They need to ignore the fact that they are in a cinema, with other people, watching the events occur on the screen. In essence, in order to experience presence, the viewer needs to enter the world of the film and to have "an illusion that [the] mediated experience is not mediated" (Lombard & Ditton, 1997, paragraph 1). Various occurrences can break that illusion – for example, a phone might ring during the film, or some other patrons may start talking – and part of the annoyance that occurs in the viewer as a result of these experiences is likely due to the disruption of the sensation of presence. Other factors that can disrupt presence include the cybersickness or lag problems mentioned above.

Presence is necessary for many of the psychological applications of VR to be effective – the user needs to feel immersed in the environment portrayed. The remainder of this chapter will briefly describe some of the psychological applications of VR, particularly those related to treatment, diagnosis, pain management, and psychological research.

Virtual Reality as a Treatment Tool

Virtual reality has opened up new possibilities in the treatment of several conditions. Most notably these include anxiety disorders and addictions, although researchers and therapists have also identified other conditions which might be effectively treated with VR. While this chapter will focus on psychological conditions, VR training has also been used to help individuals with a variety of physical conditions (see, for example, Sevcenko & Lindgren, 2022). There are many potential benefits available through the use of VR in such settings, but there are also a variety of ethical and legal considerations which must be remembered, such as information overload, depersonalisation, and specific concerns relating to vulnerable populations (Parsons, 2021), and so care must be taken when using VR for these purposes.

Anxiety Disorders

When VR technologies were still very new, many therapists identified them as potential aids in the treatment of various psychological conditions. This was particularly true for anxiety disorders such as phobias and post-traumatic stress disorder (PTSD), where VEs could be used to elicit anxiety responses in clients undergoing therapy. Such responses can also be elicited using other techniques, such as in-vivo exposure (where the client confronts the feared situation or object in real life) and imaginal exposure (where the client visualises the feared situation or object). However, both of these techniques have limitations which in-virtuo (VR) exposure can help to overcome (Wiederhold & Wiederhold, 2014). Many clients are too afraid to face their fear during in-vivo treatments, or may never seek such treatment due to the anxiety that they know it will bring. Clients may also have problems visualising the feared object or situation in sufficient detail for imaginal exposure to be effective. However, potential clients are more open to facing their fears in virtual worlds and do not have to visualise the stimulus themselves.

It is important to note that the virtual world is not an alternative to traditional therapy, but rather should be seen as an adjunct to it. The presence of the therapist remains as important as it is for other forms of treatment, as they provide guidance to clients on how to manage their responses and overcome their phobias as they explore the virtual world. While in the virtual world, the therapist helps the client to extinguish their initial response to the feared object or situation by repeatedly exposing them to cues related to their fear, preventing them from avoiding the feared situation, and providing them with techniques which help them to face the situation when it occurs. As these techniques are learned, and the urge to flee is extinguished, the client learns to manage and overcome their fears.

In virtual worlds the environment can be adapted to best treat the client. For a person with a fear of spiders, early stages of the therapy might involve a single virtual spider at the far end of a virtual room, or one enclosed within a glass box. As the client masters their fear, then the number of virtual spiders can be increased, and their proximity to the client in the virtual world can be adapted.

In addition to phobias, VR therapy has also been successfully utilised in the treatment of other anxiety disorders, including PTSD, generalised anxiety disorder, panic disorder, and obsessive-compulsive disorder. A systematic review by Freitas et al. (2021) noted that **virtual reality exposure therapy (VRET)** tends to have a positive effect, but that for some specific phobias, it is not as effective as in-vivo treatments.

Addictions and Eating Disorders

The treatment of addictions and some eating disorders using VR follows a similar basic premise to that of anxiety disorders. The client is exposed to cues in the virtual world (objects or situations) which would normally elicit a reaction in the real world. For example, an individual with problematic drinking behaviours might associate specific environments, such as hotels, bars, and restaurants, with consuming alcoholic beverages. They may also find their cravings increase as they are exposed to certain cues, such as advertisements or items on display at supermarkets or other public places. In a similar way to the treatment of phobias and other anxiety disorders, VRET can be used to reduce the client's responses to these cues by displaying them in a carefully controlled virtual environment and providing the client with techniques for managing, resisting, and reducing their cravings.

Many studies have examined first the potential for virtual reality cues to induce cravings in individuals (cue-reactivity), and then the use of VR as a method of reducing those cravings. These papers have considered the potential of VR in the treatment of smoking addictions (see, for example, the systematic review by Keijsers et al., 2021), problem drinking (see, for example, the systematic review by Ghiţă & Gutiérrez-Maldonado, 2018), illegal drugs (see, for example, Skeva et al., 2021), and even pathological gambling (see, for example, Mazza et al., 2021). Similar methodologies can be employed in the treatment of eating disorders (see, for example, Riva et al., 2021).

Virtual Reality as a Diagnostic Tool: Paranoia and Attention Deficit Hyperactivity Disorder

While VR has been demonstrated to be an effective treatment tool for many conditions, there are some psychological conditions for which it can also be used as a diagnostic tool. These include paranoia and attention deficit hyperactivity disorder (ADHD), although it should be noted that VR can also be used in the assessment of a wide range of conditions, including neurological assessments (Parsons et al., 2022).

When assessing a client who may have unusually high levels of paranoia, it is sometimes difficult to be certain if their actions and reactions are actually warranted. For example, a person complains that others are especially impolite towards them, or take advantage of them, and this may be a delusion or an accurate observation. Questionnaires and even some clinical interviews may have problems in differentiating between these circumstances. It is helpful if we can observe the client's reactions to other individuals, but it is difficult to sufficiently control such circumstances so that the other individuals maintain a standardised response to the client. Researchers such as Daniel Freeman have used VR simulations of a library and an underground train to assess the cognitions of individuals regarding the computer-controlled agents within those worlds (see, for example, Fornells-Ambrojo et al., 2015; Freeman et al., 2010). While many users see the agents in these worlds as benevolent or neutral, some users demonstrated paranoid appraisals of the agents, despite seeing them react in exactly the same way. When users show such paranoid appraisals, it may be an indication of an underlying condition. Neutral environments such as these can then also be used as part of a treatment and assessment protocol (see, for example, Brown et al., 2020).

In a similar way, Albert "Skip" Rizzo and his colleagues developed an immersive VR classroom which is designed to assess symptoms of ADHD in children (see, for example, Bioulac et al., 2012; Parsons et al., 2007; Stokes et al., 2022). The virtual classroom has been developed and updated through several iterations, and it resembles a traditional classroom, including a teacher and a board/screen, and the child is required to perform a task related to the content on the board/screen. Occasional distractions are introduced into the environment (such as a paper airplane, passing vehicles, or a phone on a classmate's desk) and the child's reactions to these distractions are noted, as well as their effects on the child's scores on the task.

VR can also be used as a therapeutic tool for paranoia and ADHD, and the interested reader can review the work of Freeman, Rizzo, and others to see the developments in these areas. The technology also has therapeutic value in realms other than psychological disorders, and its use as a distractor for pain is considered in the following section.

Virtual Reality as Pain Management

Have you ever noticed a bump, cut, or bruise on your body that you have no memory of receiving? The probability is that at the time that you received that injury, you were either asleep, or you were distracted. For some people, the knowledge that they are about to experience pain (for example, while receiving a vaccination) can lead to a heightened state of anxiety, which might result in an intensification of the pain experience.

Such phenomena were noticed by early researchers of pain and integrated into a model known as the gate control theory of pain, which was developed by Melzack and Wall (1965). This theory suggests that the perception of pain is complex, and the severity of the pain experienced can vary depending on factors such as the extent of the injury, the emotional status of the person, and the extent to which the person is distracted. The use of VR in pain management depends on this last factor, providing sufficient distraction to the user so that their experience of pain is reduced. This distraction might be used in addition to, or as an alternative to, pharmacological analgesics.

The use of VR in the diagnosis and treatment of psychological conditions as outlined in the previous sections relies on the virtual world recreating an environment containing specific cues which will elicit precise reactions from the user – such as the fear in anxiety disorders or the craving in substance abuse. In contrast, the use of VR in the management of pain often does not require cues specific to the condition, but rather the distraction from the non-virtual world instead, so while the content of the world might be tailored to the user's condition, it does not have to be, and research has even examined the use of commercially available VR systems in the use of pain management (Boylan et al., 2018).

An example of a virtual world which has been specifically designed for the type of pain that the user is suffering from is "SnowWorld", which was developed by Hunter Hoffman and his colleagues for the distraction of burn pain (see, for example, Hoffman et al., 2011, 2020). SnowWorld and other virtual worlds for pain distraction have demonstrated potential in reducing the subjective discomfort of individuals undergoing painful procedures, and have even been identified to work alongside other pain reduction methods, such as hypnosis (Patterson et al., 2021). In a similar way, VR has also been demonstrated to affect the perception of the passage of time in patients undergoing intravenous chemotherapy (Schneider et al., 2011), with patients tending to underestimate the duration of the treatment when experiencing VR. However other research has indicated that people undergoing chemotherapy do not necessarily experience time distortion when using VR (Janssen et al., 2022).

Virtual Reality in Psychological Research

A final application of VR for psychology is the potential for the use of virtual worlds in psychological research. In perception research an experimenter can fully immerse a participant within a virtual world, where there are no other visual or auditory distractions. If the experimenter decides that they do want to see how the participant's scores change when subjected to distraction, they can add very specific additional stimuli into the visual field, and these stimuli will appear in exactly the same place at exactly the same time for each participant.

VR has long been identified as a useful tool for social psychological research, allowing for high levels of experimental control over relatively realistic environments (see, for example, Blascovich et al., 2002; Pan & Hamilton, 2018). For example, research by Rooney et al. (2017) used a virtual simulation "Coffee without Words" to see how users interact with a virtual agent who displays varying degrees of eye-contact, while all other variables are kept constant. However this simulation also allows for the impact of environment to be investigated, where all variables are kept constant except for the setting (see Figure 21.3). This high degree of control over the environment and behaviour of the interacting partner is not possible in non-VR social psychology research. Indeed VR-based methodologies have numerous benefits for social psychological research, and a wider review of studies in this field is outlined by Yaremych and Persky (2019).

While VR can be used to examine traditional topics in social psychology, the nature of the virtual environment can also allow new phenomena to be uncovered. For example, Yee and Bailenson (2007) noted that participants' behaviour "conforms to their digital self-representation independent of how others perceive them" (p. 271), with individuals who were assigned taller or

Figure 21.3
Virtual cafe scenario with a variety of settings (courtesy of Dr Brendan Rooney and
the Media and Entertainment Psychology Lab, University College Dublin).

more attractive avatars proceeding to act more confidently and intimately
respectively. Yee and Bailenson termed this the **Proteus effect**, and it has
been identified across a variety of behaviours (see the meta-analysis by Ratan
et al., 2020). As this effect has been demonstrated to last for some time after
immersion in a virtual world, these findings are of immense importance in the
potential of VR to alter human behaviours.

VR as a research tool has expanded in recent years, and its merits have now
been noted in other areas such as health psychology (Martingano & Persky,
2021) and psycholinguistics (Peeters, 2019). Vasser and Aru (2020) provide a set
of guidelines on the use of immersive VR in psychological research, considering factors such as reliability and validity, which are useful for those considering using VR as a research tool.

FEATURE BOX: USING VIRTUAL REALITY TO REDUCE PREJUDICE

The Proteus effect has been examined in a wide range of contexts, perhaps most interestingly when it has been employed to reduce prejudice against certain groups. For example,
Peck et al. (2013) used VR embodiments of various ethnic backgrounds and discovered that
in some circumstances it reduced implicit racial bias. Similarly, Kotani et al. (2022) noted that
empathy towards elderly people can be increased by using elderly avatars to elicit a Proteus
effect. It is possible that the Proteus effect may therefore be a powerful tool in reducing prejudice and bias across a range of factors.

Conclusion

As is evident from the research presented in this chapter, psychology has long appreciated the potential for VR in research, assessment, and therapy. As the technologies become more affordable and mainstream, it is possible that these developments will increase in number and potential. It should also be noted that VR has a wide variety of uses that are not described here, including engineering, architecture, entertainment, data visualisation, training, and education. However, up to now, VR therapy has generally been used as an additional tool in conjunction with a human therapist, and it will be interesting to see if artificial intelligence technologies might in the future be incorporated into VR devices in order to allow the client to progress independently of the therapist. The psychological applications of artificial intelligence will be considered in the next chapter.

Activity

Consider when you have felt the most presence in a film, book, or video game. What was your subjective experience of that immersion? What elements of the media enhanced that sense of immersion?

Discussion Questions

1 What other psychological applications might virtual reality have?
2 Considering the Proteus effect identified by Yee and Bailenson, what are the ethical and practical implications of research in this field?
3 VR is becoming more mainstream, and the concept of a "metaverse", which has historically been limited to fiction, will potentially be widely available in the near future. How might the psychological applications discussed here change or evolve if VR becomes a technology which people use every day?
4 What other psychological conditions might virtual reality be useful in the diagnosis and/or treatment of?

Recommended Reading List

Ratan et al. (2020) provide a meta-analysis of the Proteus effect, outlining the support which has been demonstrated for this phenomenon in the empirical literature.

Ratan, R., Beyea, D., Li, B. J., & Graciano, L. (2020). Avatar characteristics induce users' behavioral conformity with small-to-medium effect sizes:

A meta-analysis of the proteus effect. *Media Psychology, 23*(5), 651–675. https://doi.org/10.1080/15213269.2019.1623698

Two papers by Vasser and Aru (2020) and Pan and Hamilton (2018) provide very useful guidelines and caveats concerning the use of VR for psychological research.

Vasser, M., & Aru, J. (2020). Guidelines for immersive virtual reality in psychological research. *Current Opinion in Psychology, 36*, 71–76. https://doi.org/10.1016/j.copsyc.2020.04.010

Pan, X., & Hamilton, A. F. D. C. (2018). Why and how to use virtual reality to study human social interaction: The challenges of exploring a new research landscape. *British Journal of Psychology, 109*(3), 395–417. https://doi.org/10.1111/bjop.12290

Thomas Parsons provides clear guidance and caveats in the use of VR for the assessment and treatment of a variety of psychological conditions in this paper relating to the ethical challenges involved.

Parsons, T. D. (2021). Ethical challenges of using virtual environments in the assessment and treatment of psychopathological disorders. *Journal of Clinical Medicine, 10*(3), 378. https://doi.org/10.3390/jcm10030378

Jeremy Bailenson's book *Experience on Demand* provides an excellent overview of the potential of virtual reality in a variety of psychological settings, outlining the potential benefits and dangers in the technology.

Bailenson, J. N. (2018). *Experience on demand: What virtual reality is, how it works, and what it can do.* W.W. Norton.

Glossary

Agent: Virtual world characters controlled by the computer.

Augmented reality (AR): The visual portrayal of virtual objects over real world settings using technologies such as headsets, cameras, screens, and holograms.

Avatar: An online representation of a user, especially in three-dimensional virtual worlds.

Cybersickness: A form of motion sickness caused by discrepancies between visual and proprioceptive cues.

Head mounted displays (HMDs): Virtual reality technology where the environment is presented to the user via screens in a headset.

Mixed reality (MR): Technology which is similar to augmented reality as it uses a combination of real and virtual objects

Presence: The subjective feeling of being in a virtual environment (such as a video game or virtual reality): an illusion that renders the viewer unaware of the technological medium through which the environment is presented.

Proteus effect: Proposed by Yee and Bailenson (2007), this refers to a change in online and offline self-perception based on the features or behaviours of a user's avatar.

Tactile augmentation: Using a real item to induce a sensation of touch when a user is in a virtual world.

Virtual reality (VR): The use of computer technologies to create three-dimensional virtual worlds or objects which users can interact with.

Virtual reality exposure therapy (VRET): The use of VR to present cues or stimuli to a user to treat a psychological condition such as an anxiety disorder or addiction.

References

Bioulac, S., Lallemand, S., Rizzo, A., Philip, P., Fabrigoule, C., & Bouvard, M. P. (2012). Impact of time and task on ADHD patients' performances in a virtual classroom. *European Journal of Paediatric Neurology, 16*(5), 514–521. https://doi .org/10.1016/j.ejpn.2012.01.006

Blascovich, J., Loomis, J., Beall, A. C., Swinth, K. R., Hoyt, C. L., & Bailenson, J. N. (2002). Immersive virtual environment technology as a methodological tool for social psychology. *Psychological Inquiry: An International Journal for the Advancement of Psychological Theory, 13*(2), 103–124. https://doi.org/10 .1207/S15327965PLI1302_01

Botella, C., Bretón-López, J., Quero, S., Baños, R., & García-Palacios, A. (2010). Treating cockroach phobia with augmented reality. *Behaviour Therapy, 41*(3), 401–413. https://doi.org/10.1016/j.beth.2009.07.002

Boylan, P., Kirwan, G. H., & Rooney, B. (2018). Self-reported discomfort when using commercially targeted virtual reality equipment in discomfort distraction. *Virtual Reality, 22*(4), 309–314. https://doi.org/10.1007/s10055 -017-0329-9

Brown, P., Waite, F., Rovira, A., Nickless, A., & Freeman, D. (2020). Virtual reality clinical-experimental tests of compassion treatment techniques to reduce paranoia. *Scientific Reports, 10*(1), 1–9. https://doi.org/10.1038/s41598 -020-64957-7

Carlin, A. S., Hoffman, H. G., & Weghorst, S. (1997). Virtual reality and tactile augmentation in the treatment of spider phobia: A case report. *Behaviour Research and Therapy, 35*(2), 153–158. https://doi.org/10.1016/S0005 -7967(96)00085-X

Fornells-Ambrojo, M., Freeman, D., Slater, M., Swapp, D., Antley, A., & Barker, C. (2015). How do people with persecutory delusions evaluate threat in a controlled social environment? A qualitative study using virtual reality. *Behavioural and Cognitive Psychotherapy, 43*(1), 89–107. https://doi.org/10.1017 /S1352465813000830

Freeman, D., Pugh, K., Vorontsova, N., Antley, A., & Slater, M. (2010). Testing the continuum of delusional beliefs: An experimental study using virtual reality. *Journal of Abnormal Psychology, 119*(1), 83–92. https://doi.org/10.1037 /a0017514

Freitas, J. R. S., Velosa, V. H. S., Abreu, L. T. N., Jardim, R. L., Santos, J. A. V., Peres, B., & Campos, P. F. (2021). Virtual reality exposure treatment in phobias: A systematic review. *Psychiatry Quarterly, 92*(4), 1685–1710. https://doi.org/10 .1007/s11126-021-09935-6

Ghiţă, A., & Gutiérrez-Maldonado, J. (2018). Applications of virtual reality in individuals with alcohol misuse: A systematic review. *Addictive Behaviors*, *81*, 1–11. https://doi.org/10.1016/j.addbeh.2018.01.036

Hoffman, H. G., Chambers, G. T., Meyer III, W. J., Arceneaux, L. L., Russell, W. J., Seibel, E. J., Richards, T. L., Sharar, S. R., & Patterson, D. R. (2011). Virtual Reality as an adjunctive non-pharmacological analgesic for acute burn pain during medical conditions. *Annals of Behavioural Medicine*, *41*(2), 183–191. https://doi.org/10.1007/s12160-010-9248-7

Hoffman, H. G., Patterson, D. R., Rodriguez, R. A., Peña, R., Beck, W., & Meyer, W. J. (2020). Virtual reality analgesia for children with large severe burn wounds during burn wound debridement. *Frontiers in Virtual Reality*, *1*, 32. https://doi.org/10.3389/frvir.2020.602299

Janssen, A., Fletcher, J., Keep, M., Ahmadpour, N., Rouf, A., Marthick, M., & Booth, R. (2022). Experiences of patients undergoing chemotherapy with virtual reality: Mixed methods feasibility study. *JMIR Serious Games*, *10*(1), e29579. https://doi.org/10.2196/29579

Keijsers, M., Vega-Corredor, M. C., Tomintz, M., & Hoermann, S. (2021). Virtual reality technology use in cigarette craving and smoking interventions (I "virtually" quit): Systematic review. *Journal of Medical Internet Research*, e24307. https://doi.org/10.2196/24307

Kotani, K., Yamazaki, H., Sakata, Y., Asao, T., & Suzuki, S. (2022). Does the proteus effect with elderly simulation kit improve empathy enhancement to the elderly? In V. G. Duffy, Q. Gao, J. Zhou, M. Antona, C. Stephanidis (Eds.), *HCI international 2022 – Late breaking papers: HCI for health, well-being, universal access and healthy aging*. HCII 2022. Lecture Notes in Computer Science, Vol. 13521. Springer. https://doi.org/10.1007/978-3-031-17902-0_32

Lendaro, E., Middleton, A., Brown, S., & Ortiz-Catalan, M. (2020). Out of the clinic, into the home: The in-home use of phantom motor execution aided by machine learning and augmented reality for the treatment of phantom limb pain. *Journal of Pain Research*, *13*, 195–209. https://doi.org/10.2147/JPR.S220160

Lombard, M., & Ditton, T. (1997). At the heart of it all: The concept of presence. *Journal of Computer-Mediated Communication*, *3*(2). https://doi.org/10.1111/j.1083–6101.1997.tb00072.x.

Martingano, A. J., & Persky, S. (2021). Virtual reality expands the toolkit for conducting health psychology research. *Social and Personality Psychology Compass*, *15*(7), e12606. https://doi.org/10.1111/spc3.12606

Mazza, M., Kammler-Sücker, K., Leménager, T., Kiefer, F., & Lenz, B. (2021). Virtual reality: A powerful technology to provide novel insight into treatment mechanisms of addiction. *Translational Psychiatry*, *11*(1), 1–11. https://doi.org/10.1038/s41398-021-01739-3

Melzack, R., & Wall, P. D. (1965). Pain mechanisms: A new theory: A gate control system modulates sensory input from the skin before it evokes pain perception and response. *Science*, *150*(3699), 971–979. https://doi.org/10.1126/science.150.3699.971

Pan, X., & Hamilton, A. F. D. C. (2018). Why and how to use virtual reality to study human social interaction: The challenges of exploring a new research landscape. *British Journal of Psychology*, *109*(3), 395–417. https://doi.org/10.1111/bjop.12290

Parsons, T. D. (2021). Ethical challenges of using virtual environments in the assessment and treatment of psychopathological disorders. *Journal of Clinical Medicine*, *10*(3), 378. https://doi.org/10.3390/jcm10030378

Parsons, T. D., Bowerly, T., Buckwalter, J. G., & Rizzo, A. A. (2007). A controlled clinical comparison of attention performance in children with ADHD in a Virtual Reality classroom compared to standard neuropsychological methods. *Child Neuropsychology: A Journal on Normal and Abnormal Development in Childhood and Adolescence, 13*(4), 363–381. https://doi.org/10 .1080/13825580600943473

Parsons, T. D., Kane, R., & Duffield, T. C. (2022). Virtual-reality-based neuropsychological assessments of everyday functioning. In T. D. Marcotte et al. (Eds.), *Neuropsychology of everyday functioning* (2nd ed.) (pp. 336–371). Guildford Publications.

Patterson, D. R., Hoffman, H. G., Chambers, G., Bennetts, D., Hunner, H. H., Wiechman, S. A., Garcia-Palacios, A., & Jensen, M. P. (2021). Hypnotic enhancement of virtual reality distraction analgesia during thermal pain: A randomized trial. *International Journal of Clinical and Experimental Hypnosis, 69*(2), 225–245. https://doi.org/10.1080/00207144.2021.1882259

Peck, T. C., Seinfeld, S., Aglioti, S. M., & Slater, M. (2013). Putting yourself in the skin of a black avatar reduces implicit bias. *Consciousness and Cognition, 22*(3), 779–787. https://doi.org/10.1016/j.concog.2013.04.016

Peeters, D. (2019). Virtual reality: A game-changing method for the language sciences. *Psychonomic Bulletin and Review, 26*(3), 894–900. https://doi.org/10 .3758/s13423-019-01571-3

Ratan, R., Beyea, D., Li, B. J., & Graciano, L. (2020). Avatar characteristics induce users' behavioral conformity with small-to-medium effect sizes: A meta-analysis of the proteus effect. *Media Psychology, 23*(5), 651–675. https:// doi.org/10.1080/15213269.2019.1623698

Riva, G., Malighetti, C., & Serino, S. (2021). Virtual reality in the treatment of eating disorders. *Clinical Psychology and Psychotherapy, 28*(3), 477–488. https://doi.org/10.1002/cpp.2622

Riva, G., Mantovani, F., & Bouchard, S. (2014). Presence. In B. K. Wiederhold & S. Bouchard (Eds.), *Advances in virtual reality and anxiety disorders* (pp. 9–34). Springer.

Rooney, B., Burke, C., Bálint, K., O'leary, T., Parsons, T., Lee, C. T., & Mantei, C. (2017). Virtual reality, presence and social cognition: The effect of eye-gaze and narrativity on character engagement. In *23rd international conference on virtual system & multimedia (VSMM)* (pp. 1–6). IEEE.

Schneider, S. M., Kisby, C. K., & Flint, E. P. (2011). Effect of virtual reality on time perception in patients receiving chemotherapy. *Supportive Care in Cancer, 19*(4), 555–564. https://doi.org/10.1007/s00520-010-0852-7

Sevcenko, K., & Lindgren, I. (2022). The effects of virtual reality training in stroke and Parkinson's disease rehabilitation: A systematic review and a perspective on usability. *European Review of Aging and Physical Activity, 19*(1), 4. https://doi.org/10.1186/s11556-022-00283-3

Skeva, R., Gregg, L., Jay, C., & Pettifer, S. (2021). Views of practitioners and researchers on the use of virtual reality in treatments for substance use disorders. *Frontiers in Psychology, 12*, 1852. https://doi.org/10.3389/fpsyg .2021.606761

Stokes, J. D., Rizzo, A., Geng, J. J., & Schweitzer, J. B. (2022). Measuring attentional distraction in children with ADHD using virtual reality technology with eye-tracking. *Frontiers in Virtual Reality, 3*, 855895. https://doi.org/10.3389/ frvir

Vasser, M., & Aru, J. (2020). Guidelines for immersive virtual reality in psychological research. *Current Opinion in Psychology, 36*, 71–76. https://doi .org/10.1016/j.copsyc.2020.04.010

Wiederhold, B. K., & Wiederhold, M. D. (2014). Introduction. In B. K. Wiederhold & S. Bouchard (Eds.), *Advances in virtual reality and anxiety disorders* (pp. 3–8). Springer.

Yaremych, H. E., & Persky, S. (2019). Tracing physical behavior in virtual reality: A narrative review of applications to social psychology. *Journal of Experimental Social Psychology, 85*, 103845. https://doi.org/10.1016/j.jesp.2019.103845

Yee, N., & Bailenson, J. (2007). The Proteus Effect: The effect of transformed self-representation on behaviour. *Human Communication Research, 33*(3), 271–290. https://doi.org/10.1111/j.1468-2958.2007.00299.x

Zimmer, A., Wang, N., Ibach, M. K., Fehlmann, B., Schictanz, N. S., Bentz, D., Michael, T., Papassotiropoulos, A., & de Quiervain, D. J. F. (2021). Effectiveness of a smartphone-based, augmented reality exposure app to reduce fear of spiders in real-life: A randomized controlled trial. *Journal of Anxiety Disorders, 82*, 102442. https://doi.org/10.1016/j.janxdis.2021.102442

22 The Psychology of Artificial Intelligence

Gráinne Kirwan

Chapter Overview

Artificial intelligence (AI) plays an important, yet often invisible, role in our online lives. Interactions such as searches, online recommendations, and gaming are often based on AI. The role of Non-Player Characters (NPCs) in gaming is a clear example – the realism of these characters and their responses to player actions can have a significant impact on the perceived quality of a game. The rise in the quality of "chatbots" (interactive communicative agents), and their use in customer/user interfaces on websites is an interesting development, as is the inclusion of such chatbots as interaction devices on smartphones and mobile devices. The potential use of artificially intelligent robots as companion devices is explored, and the observed effects on specific populations are examined. The potential future role of artificial intelligence in human life is considered.

Key Terms

Several definitions of **artificial intelligence** (AI) have been proposed, including "the science and engineering of making intelligent machines, especially intelligent computer systems" (McCarthy, 2007, p. 2) and "the field that studies the synthesis and analysis of computational agents that act intelligently" (Poole & Mackworth, 2010, p. 3). Often AI is associated with **robotics**, the creation of programmed machines which may or may not have some degree of autonomy, although many AIs do not have robotic forms. Some researchers are particularly interested in robots that can interact socially with other robots or humans with some degree of adherence to social and/or cultural norms, a field known as **social robotics**.

Despite the prevalence of features of AI in modern society, there are many problems in defining an agreed standard of AI. Also, individuals may demonstrate the **AI effect**, where they refute the existence of intelligence in some technologies that actually demonstrate one or more elements of AI.

357

DOI: 10.4324/9781003092513-30

Defining and Testing Artificial Intelligence

One of the main problems in defining AI comes from the definition of "intelligence" itself. Even within humans, there are many types of intelligence. For example, maybe you have a friend who is extremely good at languages and who can help you when you need to proofread or translate a document. But it might be a different friend who is the most helpful if you need to build a wall, or set up a new laptop. Gardner (1983) suggests that there are multiple intelligences that people can have, including linguistic, musical, logical–mathematical, spatial, bodily–kinaesthetic, and personal intelligences. While some individuals may have high levels of many of these intelligence types, sometimes people differ widely on their levels, being exceptionally good at some, while being quite poor in other areas.

Often when we see artificially intelligent beings portrayed in science fiction, they demonstrate high intelligence across many of the types that Gardner suggests (although almost always their "personal" intelligences are relatively low). Because of this, it is somewhat unsurprising that most people fall victim to the AI effect with regard to current technologies. It is extremely difficult to build a physically agile robot that is also capable of creativity, learning, natural language processing, planning, perception, decision making, problem-solving, and holding vast quantities of knowledge. Nevertheless, it is worth considering how far AI has come in a relatively short period of time. In 1967, AI researcher Marvin Minsky said "within a generation … the problem of creating 'artificial intelligence' will substantially be solved" (Minsky, 1967, as cited in Crevier, 1993, p. 109). With the benefit of hindsight, it is easy to think that Minsky was overly optimistic, yet the advances that have been made in this field should not be underestimated. While we may not yet have the types of AI displayed in science fiction movies, we do now have self-driving cars, autonomous robots, chatbots with natural language processing, and AI agents on our smartphones and tablets which can interpret our requests and complete a wide variety of tasks.

Probably the most famous test to determine if we have actually achieved artificial intelligence is known as the **Turing test** (although when originally conceived by Turing in 1950, he proposed it as the "Imitation Game"). This test determines that, if a computer can have a conversation with a human without the human being aware that they are talking to a machine, then the AI is deemed to have passed the test. There have been many attempts to create machines with this goal in mind, and competitions are held annually to assess entries.

There are arguments against the validity of the Turing test as a measure of artificial intelligence, the most famous being the "Chinese room argument" developed by John Searle in 1980. It offers the example of a person inside a room who does not speak Chinese, but who does have a library of "if …, then …" rules which indicate which character strings are the appropriate response

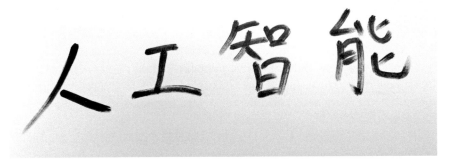

Figure 22.1
Searle's "Chinese room argument" is a critique of the validity of the Turing test as a measure of artificial intelligence. (The characters in this image are those for "artificial intelligence" and were prepared by Ng Yin Lu.)

to other written strings of characters (similar to those in Figure 22.1). These inputs can be submitted to the room by people outside. If the person in the room follows the "if ..., then ..." rules, they can respond in such a way that it appears that they understand the conversation, even though they have no idea what they are communicating about. In short, Searle argues that a computer could pass the Turing test while only having **weak AI** (i.e. only a simulation of intelligence) rather than **strong AI** (where the computer actually possesses the intelligence that it appears to have).

There are, of course, further counterarguments against Searle's position. For example, we accept that many of the people that we meet on a daily basis have true intelligence based only on the responses that they give during conversations. We make judgements about people based only on what we can see, and the Turing test suggests a similar goal for machine intelligence. This is a topic of much philosophical argument within the field, and further elaboration can be found in texts such as Epstein et al. (2008).

Some of the most recent developments in AI involve the use of machine learning – where the technology imitates the way that we learn through the use of various types of data and algorithms. This learning can take many forms, such as learning the rules and strategies for playing a computer game, the best way for a car to drive itself, how to communicate with humans, and even how to cure medical conditions.

Social Robotics

While the philosophy of AI is a very interesting topic, psychologists are frequently more interested in how humans interact with the AI, particularly when the AI is embedded in a robot. **Social robotics** examines how humans interact socially with robots, and even how robots interact with each other. A prominent example of a research group in this area is the Massachusetts Institute of Technology Personal Robots Group, which develops social robots and assesses how users interact with them and what their potential applications might be.

However, social robotics can also consider many of the higher-end commercially available toys that simulate pets and contain a certain degree of AI (for example, they may learn behaviours, or adopt certain personalities depending on how they are treated by their owners). Heerink et al. (2012) examined how children experienced and interacted with a robot dinosaur, noting that their interactions with it were prevalently social, rarely treating the robot as an object. Similarly, Díaz et al. (2011) noted that when children interacted with different types of robots, the robots' appearance and performance altered the interactions that children engaged in with them, including affecting attachment. More recently, Pelikan et al. (2020) also analysed how users interacted with a toy that simulated various emotions.

Our interactions with robots are usually dependent on our interpretations of the robot's actions and intentions. Correct interpretations are not always easy to achieve, at least immediately (Erden & Tapus, 2010). Errors in human–robot interactions (HRI) can cause multiple problems, including "social errors" which affect the "user's perception of a robot's socio-affective competence" (Tian & Oviatt, 2021, p. 1). However, it is possible that our interpretations of the robot's actions can affect how we feel about interacting with the robot. For example, Park et al. (2012) found that, when interacting with robots that were programmed to demonstrate facial expressions associated with either introverted

Figure 22.2
Young children frequently give their toys personalities and ascribe human-like characteristics to them. (Photograph by Glen Lockhart).

or extroverted personalities, users tended to be most comfortable around robots with similar personalities to themselves.

Social robotics is a very important topic when psychologists consider the role of AI in human interactions, and we will return to consider some aspects of this in more detail when discussing the potential for companion robots below. However, it should be remembered that in cutting-edge research it is sometimes better for investigators to know how a human would engage with a robot before they start to program the AI itself (hence they know how to design the robot better, or what features to focus on, or they can test features that are not yet technically possible). To allow this, some research is conducted as a "**Wizard of Oz**" study, where the robot or agent is not actually autonomous but is instead controlled by the researchers so that it acts in a way that the agent actually would if it was developed. There are several ethical implications with studies of this type – if the participant knows that they are really engaging with a human being they may behave differently than if they think that they are interacting with a robot. However, they may also make personal disclosures to an entity that they think is artificial which they would not to a human researcher, or they may believe themselves to be alone and engage in behaviours that they would not do if another person (rather than just a robot) was present.

Applications of Artificial Intelligence

There are many applications of AI. Sometimes we are conscious that we are interacting with an AI agent (for example, if we are interacting with a smart assistant device, such as those developed by Google, Amazon, Apple, and others), while sometimes the application that we are using utilises a basic level of AI without our realising it. Here we will consider various reasons why psychologists have an interest in artificial intelligence. These include gaming, customer service/user interfaces, psychotherapy, and companionship. However, we will start with a brief explanation of how AI can aid psychologists to develop a greater understanding of cognitive psychology.

Cognitive Psychology

Cognitive psychologists try to understand how human cognition works. They wish to determine why we make the decisions that we do, how we solve problems, how we perceive the world, and how we store and retrieve items in our memories. Unfortunately, the methods by which these processes occur can be quite difficult to accurately determine. We can observe a person encountering a situation where they have to make a choice, but even if we encourage them to talk out loud while they are making their decision, it is possible that we will miss steps in their cognitive processing (and indeed, by asking them to talk through their reasoning, we may alter the decision that they will make).

Early cognitive psychologists developed theories to help to understand what happened while people underwent cognitive processes, but these could be vague and quite difficult to test. They then began to develop flowcharts – diagrams describing a process in terms of questions, responses, and outcomes, which included more detail on the stages involved. The accuracy of these flowcharts could be tested by coding them into computers using AI languages. The researchers could then provide the computer with the same input that they gave human participants. If the computer model came up with the same response that humans made, then it was likely that the model predicted by the flowchart was correct. Of course, for this to be true, the computer program needed to make the same types of errors that the human participants did. The researchers were not looking to create a computer that would always provide the "correct" answer – instead, they attempted to create a computer that provided the same output that a human did when given the same set of data. If this occurred, then the flowchart was likely an accurate depiction of how humans thought, perceived, and reasoned as well.

Gaming

While we don't often think about artificial intelligence while gaming, it contributes significantly to the feeling of realism that we experience. This is particularly so for NPCs – characters within the game that the gamer does not control. These might be the opponents in a sports game or the villains in an adventure or shooter game. They may also be "helper" characters who form a team that you are leading, or who are designed to provide advice or help at various stages of a game. If designed well, they can enhance the game significantly, but if the NPC behaves in certain ways, it may break the player's sense of immersion (Johansson et al., 2014).

There is some evidence that individuals can form attachments to such NPCs, depending on their personalities and motivations, as well as the behaviours and physical attractiveness of the NPC (Coulson et al., 2012). To achieve a higher quality of interaction and increase social relations, it is necessary for the designers of the NPC to consider many psychological factors. Chowanda et al. (2014) describe how rules can be generated that guide the actions of NPCs, and that these actions could be dependent on aspects such as "observed social and emotional signals, the agent's personality, and the social relation between agent and player" (p. 134).

In some ways, we can consider the AI behind NPCs in gaming as a type of Turing test. The character needs to be able to respond in ways that convince us of their identity – as a helper, as an opponent, or as any other type of character. If the NPC behaves in ways that are incongruent with that identity or converses in ways which a real-life person in the same circumstances would not, then it will have an effect on how we perceive the game and our relationship with the character.

Customer Services and User Interfaces

As chatbots grow closer to passing the Turing test, various potential commercial applications have been explored. Probably the most widely used of these are customer service chatbots and user interfaces on smartphones which utilise natural language processing to interpret user requests. These chatbots help users to find out information and carry out tasks in as natural a way as possible – as if they were asking a friend, colleague, or human customer service agent to help them to achieve a goal. In some cases, it is even helpful to analyse similar human conversations in order to determine the best way to create and program the chatbot (Jenkins et al., 2007). However, there is little research evaluating the benefits of chatbots in customer service roles, and what does exist does not always show that such interaction agents are preferred to standard web-based interfaces (see, for example, May & Kirwan, 2014). More recent research indicates that chatbots may not meet customer expectations, but that some design features, such as anthropomorphic design, may affect user interactions (Adam et al., 2021).

However, one way in which artificially intelligent user interfaces could surpass traditional ones is their ability to react and adjust to the user. For example, Saadatian et al. (2014) suggest the use of probabilistic mood estimation (PME) to determine the user's mood through information such as location, physical activity, and so on. This could then be used to alter the behaviour of an AI virtual companion on a smartphone (which could feasibly include the user interface AI) so that it behaves in a manner that complements the user at that time (e.g. happy, relaxed, or sleepy). Similar research by Adam and Lorini (2014) suggests that an agent which can interpret user emotion could be used to suggest coping strategies (such as positive reinterpretation of events) to help the person to improve their well-being.

Psychotherapy

With enhanced conversational abilities, other opportunities arise for chatbots beyond customer service and user interfaces. There are various aspects of psychotherapy that AI could be utilised in, such as clinical training, psychological assessment, clinical decision making, and treatment (Luxton, 2014). As early as 1988, Binik et al. considered the potential for AI in therapeutic practice for clients with sexual dysfunction.

While never intended to actually conduct any psychotherapy itself, one of the first chatbots was created as a parody of a Rogerian psychotherapist. Her name was Eliza, and she was created by Joseph Weizenbaum (1966) to study natural language processing between humans and computers. Weizenbaum chose this persona for his chatbot because of the nature of conversation between a therapist and client. For example, a therapist might turn the last statement made by the client into a question, while adding little detail (e.g. a client might say "I feel sad", while Eliza might respond "why do you feel sad?"). Adopting such an identity for his chatbot allowed Weizenbaum to avoid providing the program with vast quantities of general knowledge.

While quite basic by today's standards, Weizenbaum's chatbot still had an interesting effect on users. He later noted that his secretary held conversations with the chatbot, preferring to have these in private. This, along with similar observations, led to the development of the term the "**Eliza effect**" – defined by Hofstadter (2008) as "the susceptibility of people to read far more understanding than is warranted into strings of symbols – especially words – strung together by computers" (p. 157).

Since Eliza, there have been several other examples of chatbots imitating psychotherapists, although often these have been designed to help in the training of psychotherapists rather than being intended to provide therapy themselves. For example, Gutiérrez-Maldonado et al. (2008) created a three-dimensional environment where trainee psychotherapists can interact with a group of AI clients. The trainee therapists are required to make a diagnosis based on the actions and statements of the virtual clients.

More recent reviews, such as that by Luxton (2014), highlight the advancements in AI for clinical psychological practice, while noting that there are some problems that clinicians need to be aware of. Certainly, AI programs would have some advantages over human psychotherapists – for example, they would be immune to countertransference, and would have a memory for details that most human psychotherapists could only dream of. Nevertheless, they would also have failings – they may not be able to pick up on nuance or subtlety, and their inability to empathise may cause problems during therapeutic interventions (research by Liu and Shyam Sundar in 2018 indicates that sympathy and empathy from chatbots are preferred over the "unemotional provision of advice", p. 625). Martinez-Martin and Kreitmair (2018) also note other potential disadvantages of using chatbots in this manner, including a lack of lines of accountability, a potential lack of ethical obligations, privacy concerns, and queries regarding what should be done if the individual is in extreme distress.

Companionship

One of the main applications of social robotics is companionship, with research often specifically focusing on the use of robots as companions for older adults and children. While many positive aspects have been identified, there are also many concerns regarding such use.

Some researchers have investigated the use of therapeutic robots in hospitals and elder-care settings. Such robots are often designed to have the same advantages as are found in animal therapy but without the risks of infection or injury which real animals bring. Some research has identified potential benefits (see, for example, Jøranson et al., 2016; Shibata & Wada, 2008), but there are indications that many elderly users might reject the robot, feeling it might be suitable for others who are more dependent or lonely than themselves (Neven, 2010). Still others admit the benefits of such robots but indicate that the ethical concerns of their use, especially with patients with dementia, need to be carefully considered (Calo et al., 2011). Similar robots have also been demonstrated to reduce stress and increase positive mood in children and students (Aminuddin & Sharkey, 2017; Crossman et al., 2018).

It should be noted that the AI companion does not need to have a robotic form, and many "virtual" pets are presented within games or smartphone apps. It should be remembered that whether or not the AI is housed in a robot form can impact on how users interact with it. Segura et al. (2012) noted that participants preferred a robotic companion to a virtual agent presented on a normal screen when completing secretarial tasks, finding it to have greater social presence and to be less annoying. Similarly, Syrdal et al. (2013) noted that sharing physical space in real-time might be important for companionship.

The use of AI as companions may also pose problems. For example, Borenstein and Pearson (2013) discuss child–robot interaction (CRI), arguing that while a robotic companion for children might have many benefits, there are ethical issues that may impact on the healthy emotional development of the child. It has already been evidenced that children can attribute emotions and human-like rights to robots (see, for example, Beran et al., 2011; Kahn et al., 2012). The ethical difficulties are not limited to the reactions of children. Wilks et al. (2015) describe the development of CALONIS, a companion for a veteran with damage to the brain resulting in memory problems. In a Wizard of Oz type study, they found that the robot enhanced communication with the patient, but that ethical issues arose regarding the relationship between the companion and the patient, and the dissemination of the patient's communications to their caregiver.

Scheutz (2012) queries whether humans might become emotionally dependent on social robots, particularly as a result of the "unidirectional emotional bonds" that could occur, where humans have feelings regarding the robots, while the robots do not have any emotions at all. Similarly, Sharkey and Sharkey (2012) discuss several ethical concerns regarding the use of robotic care for the elderly, including loss of privacy, deception, loss of control, and a potential reduction in human contact. However, they do note that robots could improve the lives of the elderly and reduce dependence, provided that they were implemented carefully. Borenstein and Pearson (2010) also consider robots as caregivers but emphasise that they may not be flexible enough to predict what a patient might do and that they would fail to offer emotional support, while the use of the technology might also lead to erosion of the relationships between human caregivers and the patients.

FEATURE BOX: CRITICAL THINKING – SOCIAL ROBOTICS ACROSS THE LIFESPAN

While a lot of the research regarding chatbots, NPCs, and other AIs focuses on adult interactions with the technology, social robotics research has had a strong focus on examining interactions between robots and either elderly people or children. This focus on specific age groups has been noted by various commentators in the field, and is something which is worth critical evaluation. Young children frequently give their toys personalities and ascribe human-like characteristics to them, and so it could be argued that any research involving interactions between this age group and social robots needs to take this pre-existing tendency into account before drawing conclusions. Similarly, any research which focuses on interactions between social robots and individuals with dementia should also carefully consider the characteristics of this group. It seems likely that considerably more research needs to focus on individuals who do not fall into these categories in order to achieve a wider perspective on human interactions with social robots.

Artificial Intelligence in the Future

Many of the sections above have considered the short-term developments that we can likely expect in psychological applications of AI, but newer developments such as machine learning have broadened the possibilities of what may happen in the future. Many philosophers, authors, and researchers also consider the longer-term possibilities, such as what will happen when AI reaches and surpasses human intelligence (e.g., Bostrom, 2014; Kurzweil, 2005; Tegmark, 2017). For some, it is a moment to be feared, while others are hopeful that at such a time it will be possible for humans to attain immortality by being able to upload themselves into a machine. Researchers in AI refer to a time in the future known as the **singularity,** although sometimes with different definitions. Some authors take it to be the point in time when the advances in AI become uncontrollable; some take it to be the time when AI surpasses human intelligence in every way and becomes a **superintelligence.** Predictions for what will happen after the singularity are hypothetical, although it has often been noted that humanity will need to be prepared for such an event and that care needs to be taken in the development of AI to ensure that a positive outcome is reached.

Conclusion

This chapter has considered the relationship between psychology and AI. In particular, it has examined how AI is defined, and the applications of AI with psychological relevance – especially gaming, user interfaces, customer service agents, psychotherapy, companionship, and the greater understanding of cognitive science. While there are notable benefits to AI in all of these areas, it is clear that a greater understanding of how humans interact and behave around AI will be extremely useful as the technology develops.

Activity

Find two or three chatbots online and have a conversation with each (you can find them easily by using the word "chatbot" in a search engine). Try to include Eliza among them, as well as one or two newer chatbots. What are the techniques used by each chatbot? Does it have a personality? What does it do when faced with a question or statement that it does not have an appropriate answer for? Does the more recent chatbot feel qualitatively different to Eliza, or are they broadly similar?

Discussion Questions

1. Is the Turing test an accurate measure of AI?
2. What role might companion robots have to play for older adults and children in the future? Will they have a similar role to play for younger adults?
3. AI is playing a more significant role in customer service and user interfaces. What features might make them more liked or accepted by users?
4. Should AI be used in place of human psychotherapists?

Recommended Reading List

Alan Turing's 1950 paper proposing the "Imitation Game" (later known as the "Turing test") is accessible, even to those without a technical or strongly mathematical background.

> Turing, A. M. (1950). Computing machinery and intelligence. *Mind*, *49*(236), 433–460. https://doi.org/10.1093/mind/LIX.236.433

While now a little dated, Jay Friedenberg's textbook remains fascinating as it has a particular focus on how AI can help us to understand cognitive science and examines what an artificial person would need to be able to do.

> Friedenberg, J. (2008). *Artificial psychology: The quest for what it means to be human*. Psychology Press.

Max Tegmark's *Life 3.0* is an interesting introduction to artificial intelligence as a field, with particular focus on the development of AI in the future.

> Tegmark, M. (2017). *Life 3.0: Being human in the age of artificial intelligence*. Knopf Publishing Group.

David Duffy's humorous, touching, and thought-provoking book explores what can happen when a group of researchers attempt to recreate the conversational style of a human in an android. It is an easy read, yet encourages us to consider what the future may hold.

> Duffy, D. (2012). *Losing the Head of Philip K. Dick: A Bizarre but True Tale of Androids, Kill Switches and Left Luggage*. Oneworld Publications.

Glossary

AI effect: A phenomenon where users discount technologies that include some degree of AI as not really being intelligent.

Artificial intelligence (AI): The creation of intelligent machines and computer systems.

Chatbots: Artificial agents that can hold conversations with a user.

Eliza effect: A phenomenon where people read understanding into computer-generated actions and communications.

Non-player characters (NPCs): Characters in games that are controlled by the computer rather than the gamer.

Robotics: The creation of programmed machines which may or may not have autonomy.

Singularity: A future time where advances in AI become uncontrollable or where AI becomes a superintelligence.

Social robotics: Research examining how robots interact socially with other robots or humans.

Strong AI: A computer that actually possesses the intelligence that it appears to have.

Superintelligence: A level of intelligence reached by an AI where it surpasses human intelligence in every way.

Turing test: A standard of AI proposed by Alan Turing, where the computer is deemed to have passed if a human conversing with it cannot tell that it is not human.

Weak AI: A simulation of intelligence, where no real intelligence exists.

Wizard of Oz study: A research methodology common in AI where it appears that a robot or computer is behaving intelligently, but instead it is being controlled by a human.

References

Adam, C., & Lorini, E. (2014). A BDI emotional reasoning engine for an artificial companion. In J. M. Corchado, J. Bajo, J. Kozlak, P. Pawlewski, J. M. Molina, B. Gaudou, V. Julian, R. Unland, F. Lopes, K. Hallenborg & P. G. Teodoro (Eds.), *Highlights of practical applications of heterogeneous multi-agent systems: The PAAMS collection* (pp. 66–78). Springer International Publishing. https://doi.org/10.1007/978-3-319-07767-3_7

Adam, M., Wessel, M., & Benlian, A. (2021). AI-based chatbots in customer service and their effects on user compliance. *Electronic Markets*, *31*(2), 427–445. https://doi.org/10.1007/s12525-020-00414-7

Aminuddin, R., & Sharkey, A. (2017, September). A Paro robot reduces the stressful effects of environmental noise. In *Proceedings of the European conference on cognitive ergonomics 2017* (pp. 63–64). http://doi.org/10.1145/3121283.3121420

Beran, T. N., Ramirez-Serrano, A., Kuzyk, R., Fior, M., & Nugent, S. (2011). Understanding how children understand robots: Perceived animism in child-robot interaction. *International Journal of Human-Computer Studies*, *69*(7–8), 539–550. https://doi.org/10.1016/j.ijhcs.2011.04.003

Binik, Y. M., Servan-Schreiber, D., Freiwald, S., & Hall, K. S. (1988). Intelligent computer-based assessment and psychotherapy: An expert system for sexual dysfunction. *Journal of Nervous and Mental Disease*, *176*(7), 387–400. https://doi.org/10.1097/00005053-198807000-00001

Borenstein, J., & Pearson, Y. (2010). Robot caregivers: Harbingers of expanded freedom for all? *Ethics and Information Technology*, *12*(3), 277–288. https://doi.org/10.1007/s10676-010-9236-4

Borenstein, J., & Pearson, Y. (2013). Companion robots and the emotional development of children. *Law, Innovation and Technology*, *5*(2), 172–189. https://doi.org/10.5235/17579961.5.2.172

Bostrom, N. (2014). *Superintelligence: Paths, dangers, strategies*. Oxford University Press.

Calo, C. J., Hunt-Bull, N., Lewis, L., & Metzler, T. (2011, August). Ethical implications of using the Paro robot. In *2011 AAAI Workshop (WS-2011–2012)*.

Chowanda, A., Blanchfield, P., Flintham, M., & Valstar, M. (2014, January). ERiSA: Building emotionally realistic social game-agents companions. In T. Bickmore, S. Marsella & C. Sidner (Eds.) *Intelligent virtual agents* (pp. 134–143). Springer International Publishing.

Coulson, M., Barnett, J., Ferguson, C. J., & Gould, R. L. (2012). Real feelings for virtual people: Emotional attachments and interpersonal attraction in video games. *Psychology of Popular Media Culture*, *1*(3), 176–184. https://doi.org/10.1037/a0028192

Crevier, D. (1993). *AI: The tumultuous search for artificial intelligence*. Basic Books.

Crossman, M. K., Kazdin, A. E., & Kitt, E. R. (2018). The influence of a socially assistive robot on mood, anxiety, and arousal in children. *Professional Psychology: Research and Practice*, *49*(1), 48–56. https://doi.org/10.1037/pro0000177

Díaz, M., Nuno, N., Saez-Pons, J., Pardo, D. E., & Angulo, C. (2011, March). Building up child-robot relationship for therapeutic purposes: From initial attraction towards long-term social engagement. In *Automatic face & gesture recognition and workshops 2011 IEEE*. https://doi.org/10.1109/FG.2011.5771375

Epstein, R., Roberts, G., & Beber, G. (Eds.) (2008). *Parsing the turing test: Philosophical and methodological issues in the quest for the thinking computer*. Springer.

Erden, M. S., & Tapus, A. (2010, June). *Postural expressions of emotions in a humanoid robot for assistive applications*. Robotics Science and Systems-RSS Workshop on Learning for Human–Robot Interaction Modeling. Zaragoza, Spain.

Gardner, H. (1983). *Frames of mind: The theory of multiple intelligences*. Basic Books.

Gutiérrez-Maldonado, J., Alsina, I., Ferrer, M., & Aguilar, A. (2008, June). *Virtual reality and artificial intelligence to train abilities of diagnosis in psychology and psychiatry.* Paper presented at the World Conference on Educational Multimedia, Hypermedia and Telecommunications, Chesapeake, VA.

Heerink, M., Diaz, M., Albo-Canals, J., Angulo, C., Barco, A., Casacuberta, J., & Garriga, C. (2012, September). *A field study with primary school children on perception of social presence and interactive behaviour with a pet robot.* Paper presented at RO-MAN 2012 IEEE, Paris, France. https://doi.org/10.1109/ROMAN.2012.6343887.

Hofstadter, D. R. (2008). *Fluid concepts and creative analogies: Computer models of the fundamental mechanisms of thought.* Basic books.

Jenkins, M. C., Churchill, R., Cox, S., & Smith, D. (2007). Analysis of user interaction with service oriented chatbot systems. In J. A. Jacko (Ed.), *Human–computer interaction: HCI intelligent multimodal interaction environments* (pp. 76–83). Springer.

Johansson, M., Strååt, B., Warpefelt, H., & Verhagen, H. (2014). Analyzing the social dynamics of non-player characters. In S. A. Meijer & R. Smeds (Eds.), *Frontiers in gaming simulation* (pp. 173–187). Springer International Publishing.

Jøranson, N., Pedersen, I., Rokstad, A. M. M., & Ihlebaek, C. (2016). Change in quality of life in older people with dementia participating in Paro-activity: A cluster-randomized controlled trial. *Journal of Advanced Nursing, 72*(12), 3020–3033. https://doi.org/10.1111/jan.13076

Kahn, P. H. Jr., Kanda, T., Ishiguro, H., Freier, N. G., Severson, R. L., Gill, B. T., Ruckert, J. H. & Shen, S. (2012). 'Robovie, you'll have to go into the closet now': Children's social and moral relationships with a humanoid robot. *Developmental Psychology, 48*(2), 303–314. https://doi.org/10.1037/a0027033

Kurzweil, R. (2005). *The singularity is near: When humans transcend biology.* Penguin.

Liu, B., & Sundar, S. S. (2018). Should machines express sympathy and empathy? Experiments with a health advice chatbot. *Cyberpsychology, Behavior, and Social Networking, 21*(10), 625–636. https://doi.org/10.1089/cyber.2018.0110

Luxton, D. D. (2014). Artificial intelligence in psychological practice: Current and future applications and implications. *Professional Psychology: Research and Practice, 45*(5), 332–339. https://doi.org/10.1037/a0034559

Martinez-Martin, N., & Kreitmair, K. (2018). Ethical issues for direct-to-consumer digital psychotherapy apps: Addressing accountability, data protection, and consent. *JMIR Mental Health, 5*(2), e32. https://doi.org/10.2196/mental.9423

May, P., & Kirwan, G. (2014). Virtual Assistants: Trust and adoption in telecommunication customer support. In A. Power & G. Kirwan (Eds.), *Cyberpsychology and new media: A thematic reader* (pp. 75–90). Psychology Press.

McCarthy, J. (2007). What is artificial intelligence? http://jmc.stanford.edu/articles/whatisai/whatisai.pdf.

Neven, L. (2010). 'But obviously not for me': Robots, laboratories and the defiant identity of elder test users. *Sociology of Health and Illness, 32*(2), 335–347. https://doi.org/10.1111/j.1467-9566.2009.01218.x

Park, E., Jin, D., & del Pobil, A. P. (2012). The law of attraction in human–robot Interaction. *International Journal of Advanced Robotic Systems, 9*(35). https://doi.org/10.5772/50228.

Pelikan, H. R., Broth, M., & Keevallik, L. (2020, March). "Are you sad, Cozmo?" How humans make sense of a home robot's emotion displays. In *Proceedings of the 2020 ACM/IEEE international conference on human-robot interaction* (pp. 461–470). https://doi.org/10.1145/3319502.3374814

Poole, D. L., & Mackworth, A. K. (2010). *Artificial intelligence: Foundations of computational agents*. Cambridge University Press.

Saadatian, E., Salafi, T., Samani, H., De Lim, Y., & Nakatsu, R. (2014). Artificial Intelligence Model of a smartphone-based virtual companion. In Y. Pisan, N. M. Sgouros, & T. Marsh (Eds.), *Entertainment computing–ICEC 2014* (pp. 173–178). Springer.

Scheutz, M. (2012). The inherent dangers of unidirectional emotional bonds between humans and social robots. In P. Lin, K. Abney, & G. A. Bekey (Eds.), *Robot ethics: The ethical and social implications of robotics* (pp. 205–221). MIT Press.

Searle, J. R. (1980). Minds, brains, and programs. *Behavioral and Brain Sciences*, *3*(3), 417–457. https://doi.org/10.1017/S0140525X00005756

Segura, E. M., Kriegel, M., Aylett, R., Deshmukh, A., & Cramer, H. (2012, January). How do you like me in this: User embodiment preferences for companion agents. In Y. Nakano, M. Neff, A. Paiva, & M. Walker (Eds.), *Intelligent virtual agents* (pp. 112–125). Springer.

Sharkey, A., & Sharkey, N. (2012). Granny and the robots: Ethical issues in robot care for the elderly. *Ethics and Information Technology, 14*(1), 27–40. https://doi.org/10.1007/s10676-010-9234-6

Shibata, T., & Wada, K. (2008). Robot therapy at elder care institutions: Effects of long-term interaction with seal robots. In S. Helal, M. Mokhtari, & B. Abdulazarak (Eds.), *The engineering handbook of smart technology for aging, disability, and independence* (pp. 405–418). John Wiley & Sons. https://doi.org/10.1002/9780470379424.ch21

Syrdal, D. S., Dautenhahn, K., Koay, K. L., Walters, M. L., & Ho, W. C. (2013). Sharing spaces, sharing lives – The impact of robot mobility on user perception of a home companion robot. In G. Herrmann, M. J. Pearson, A. Lenz, P. Bremner, A. Spiers, & U. Leonards (Eds.), *Social robotics* (pp. 321–330). Springer International Publishing.

Tegmark, M. (2017). *Life 3.0: Being human in the age of artificial intelligence*. Knopf Publishing Group.

Tian, L., & Oviatt, S. (2021). A taxonomy of social errors in human-robot interaction. *ACM Transactions on Human-Robot Interaction (THRI), 10*(2), 1–32. https://doi.org/10.1145/3439720

Turing, A. M. (1950). Computing machinery and intelligence. *Mind, 49*(236), 433–460. https://doi.org/10.1093/mind/LIX.236.433

Weizenbaum, J. (1966). ELIZA – A computer program for the study of natural language communication between man and machine. *Communications of the ACM, 9*(1), 36–45. https://doi.org/10.1145/365153.365168

Wilks, Y., Jasiewicz, J. M., Catizone, R., Galescu, L., Martinez, K. M., & Rugs, D. (2015). CALONIS: An artificial companion within a smart home for the care of cognitively impaired patients. In C. Bodine, S. Helal, T. Gu, & M. Mokhtari (Eds.), *Smart homes and health telematics* (pp. 255–260). Springer International Publishing.

Glossary

Addiction: The state of being enslaved to a habit or practice or to something that is psychologically or physically habit-forming.

Advance fee fraud: A type of online fraud where a user is promised a significant financial reward should they meet what initially appear to be minor demands and fees.

ACM SIGCHI: Association for Computing Machinery's Special Interest Group on Computer–Human Interaction.

Agent: Virtual world characters controlled by the computer.

AI effect: A phenomenon where users discount technologies that include some degree of AI as not really being intelligent.

Anonymous: Your identity is hidden from others.

Anonymity: Nobody can identify you online.

Artificial intelligence: The creation of intelligent machines and computer systems.

Assessment: Any process by which learning is judged. It may lead to accreditation.

Asynchronous communication: Communications where it is expected that the users are not simultaneously communicating.

Attention: Directing the mind to any object of sense or thought.

Augmented reality (AR): The visual portrayal of virtual objects over real world displays using technologies such as cameras and screens. The visual portrayal of virtual objects over real world settings using technologies such as headsets, cameras, screens, and holograms.

Avatar: An online representation of a user, especially in three-dimensional virtual worlds.

Behavioural addictions: Involve a repeated compulsion to perform a particular behaviour.

Blended (hybrid) learning: Learning through a combination of classroom-based (face-to-face) learning and online learning.

Boundaryless mindset: The mindset of staff that are not restrained by traditional organisational boundaries. They may work collaboratively across teams and as part of multi-disciplinary teams.

Boundaryless organisations: Organisations where barriers between internal and external functions have been reduced. Organisational layers are reduced in the hope of achieving greater organisational efficiency and effectiveness.

Brand awareness: The ability to recognise and recall the brand from a relevant cue.

Bring your own devices (BYOD): Learners bring their own devices to the learning space.

Broadcasting: One-to-many with the primary flow outwards from the one.

Captology: The field of using computers as persuasive technologies.

CBT: Cognitive behavioural therapy: short-term psychotherapy developed by Aaron Beck and Albert Ellis.

cCBT: Computerised CBT.

CBT-(IA): Cognitive behavioural therapy – Internet addiction.

Chatbots: Artificial agents that can hold conversations with a user.

Communicating: Involves one-to-few with reciprocal exchanges.

Communication privacy management (CPM): A theory developed by Sandra Petronio (2002) describing how individuals view and share their private information.

Compliance: Public adherence to the requests of others.

Computer-mediated communication (CMC): Human communication that relies on the medium of computer technology for messaging.

Computer-supported co-operative work (CSCW): The use of computing technology to support work by groups.

Conceptual model: Developed early in the interface design process, the conceptual model incorporates high-level design decisions such as the overall structure of the interface and the basic interaction paradigm to be used.

Conditions of learning: The set of internal and external conditions that influence learning (Gagné et al., 1992).

Conformity: Change in our opinions, perceptions, attitudes, and behaviour that can be observed when we want others to believe that we agree with others around us.

Constant connectedness ("always on"): An intrinsic part of work practices today involving an expectation of being available 24 hours a day.

Consumer–brand relationship: What consumers think and feel about a brand and experience with a brand.

Contact hypothesis: Allport's idea of how to reduce bias by encouraging contact as equals between two individuals or groups.

Criminological psychology: A branch of psychology which deals mostly with understanding and reducing criminal behaviour.

Cues-filtered out: A description of CMC as a medium where there are limited non-verbal cues available (see also lean medium).

Customer segmentation: Dividing a customer base into groups of individuals who are similar in specific ways such as by demographics, lifestyle, and values, or by psychological factors such as personality and motivations.

Cyberbullying: Using technology to bully a person through hostile and/or threatening messages; various types of bullying that occur using technology.

Cybercrime: Any unlawful act which is conducted using computing technologies.

Cyberdeviant: A form of maladjusted Internet use at work that may be perpetuated by the lack of supervision in staff that works remotely.

Cyber obsessional pursuit (COP): Using technology-based stalking behaviours to harass someone or demand intimacy from them.

Cyberpsychology: "Is a scientific inter-disciplinary domain that focuses on the psychological phenomena which emerge as a result of the human interaction with digital technology, particularly the Internet" (British Psychological Society, n.d., Title section).

Cybersecurity: Cybersecurity is the process of protecting computer-based devices and systems from digital attacks from an unauthorised third party.

Cybersickness: A form of motion sickness caused by discrepancies between visual and proprioceptive cues.

Cyberslacking: Use of the Internet at work for personal reasons. Managers often fear that this can lead to loss of productivity and ultimately cost the organisation money.

Dark participation: A set of behaviours that can be considered as toxic, harmful, and anti-social in a digital gaming environment.

Deindividuation: The process by which you don't feel personally accountable for actions due to being part of a group.

Digital disruption: Alerts from devices signifying a new online message or email that disrupt the task at hand.

Digital inclusion: The process of creating equitable access to and of digital technologies with socially excluded groups.

Disinhibition: Behaving differently in the online world than in the real world.

Distance learning: Learning with teachers and learners in different physical spaces.

Distraction: Anything that prevents someone from concentrating on something else.

Door in the face technique (DITF): Two-step compliance technique where a large request is initially made, which is then followed by a second, more modest, request.

DSM-5-TR: The *Diagnostic and Statistical Manual of Mental Disorders, Fifth Edition Text Revision* (DSM-5-TR).

Educational technology: The technological artefacts and devices used in education, how the technologies are used in education and learning, and the context for their use (Selwyn, 2011).

eLearning: Learning with electronic technology.

Eliza effect: A phenomenon where people read understanding into computer-generated actions and communications.

eLoyalty: A favourable attitude towards an online business influencing the intention of the consumer to repurchase from a company and the likelihood of them recommending the brand to someone else.

Emojis: The use of symbols to indicate mood or to illustrate concepts in communication.

Emoticons: Variation of emojis, usually indicating facial expression.

Experiment: A research situation or activity that has been specifically designed and controlled so as to allow researchers to establish causal inference (i.e. the role of some condition or characteristic in causing some outcome).

Experiential learning: Learning through a cyclical process of doing, reflecting on action, identifying learning, and applying the new learning (Watkins et al., 2002).

Face-to-face learning (f2f): Teachers and learners are in the same physical space in classrooms, lecture theatres, labs, and studios.

Flaming: When personal insults are exchanged online.

Flipped classroom: Learners access concepts and ideas in their own time using video lectures and readings and the classroom (f2f or online) becomes a space for discussion and analysis enabling critical thinking and creativity.

Flow: Similar to presence, flow refers to a heightened state of engagement with a video game activity (or other activity) that is characterised by feelings of presence, energised focus, and enjoyment; being at one with the game. Flow typically involves distortions of time perception.

Fluidity: In CMC, refers to content that can be changed easily and frequently.

Focus groups: A variant of the interview method conducted with small groups of people, that allows for discussion to answer the interviewer's questions.

Foot in the door technique (FITD): Two-step compliance technique where a small request is first made, which is then followed up with a second, much larger, request.

Forensic psychology: "Is the application of psychology with people and organisations connected with the Court, Health or Justice systems" (British Psychological Society, n.d., "What Is Forensic Psychology?").

Formal learning: Learning takes place in formal settings such as schools and colleges or through courses. It often leads to accreditation.

Gamer: A video game player.

Gamification: The application of game principles or mechanisms to a task or problem to encourage increased engagement with the activity.

Gaming: The use of video games online or offline.

Gig economy:Workers work remotely on specific paid tasks through online labour platforms.

Graphical user interface (GUI): This is the layer between the human and the computer. The graphical user interface may consist of icons, buttons, text, windows, and other visual indicators.

Graphics (pictures): Static items such as illustrations, drawings, charts, maps, photographs, and dynamic items such as animation and video.

Group dynamics: The way individuals act in groups, the factors thought to influence group behaviour, and the processes thought to change group behaviour.

Group norms: The rules individuals are expected to obey as members of a particular group.

Group roles: The parts that individuals play within a group, or the positions they fill within a group. Such positions may be formal or informal.

Groupthink: "The tendency for cohesive groups to become so concerned about group consolidation that they fail to critically and realistically evaluate their decisions and antecedent assumptions" (Park, 1990, p. 229).

Halo effect: A cognitive bias that occurs when one element of the dating profile, usually the photograph, influences the observer's impressions of the profile as a whole.

Harm reduction therapy: Used to identify and treat any other issues, such as social isolation or depression, that could also be involved in the development of compulsive Internet use.

Head mounted displays (HMDs): Virtual reality technology where the environment is presented to the user via screens in a headset.

Heuristics: A set of guidelines or rules of thumb used to guide the design and/ or evaluation of an interface.

High-fidelity prototype: Similar in look and behaviour to the desired finished product. Typically computer-based, allowing the user to interact with the prototype using a mouse, touchscreen, etc.

Homophily: The tendency for people to like others similar to themselves.

Human–computer interaction: Refers to the field that studies the design and testing of interactive computer systems that exist at the point where humans and computers meet.

Hyperpersonal communication: A model by Walther (1996) describing how computer-mediated communication can lead to enhanced feelings of intimacy.

Identifiable: Your identity can be seen by others.

Identity: Recognition of one's potential and qualities as an individual, especially with social context.

Immersion: An objective characteristic of the medium that describes the quality or quantity of sensory information provided to a person from a video game (or other audio-visual technology).

Implicit association test (IAT): Allegedly measures attitudes that the person is unaware of or unwilling to admit to having.

Impression management: Selectively self-presenting or editing messages to reveal socially desirable attitudes and dimensions of the self.

Incels: Short for *involuntary celibates*. These are usually online groups of men who have been rejected by women or are unable to get a female romantic partner.

Informal learning: Learning takes place when someone decides to learn something from a book, a video, or another person generally from interest or need.

Instruction: All the events that affect learning.

Instructional design: "The systematic design of instruction to support learning" (Gagné et al., 1992).

Interaction design (IxD): A field similar to HCI, but wider in scope, incorporating any interactive experience.

Interface: The boundary between the human and the computer through which the two parties exchange information. Most commonly, this is represented on screen via a graphical user interface and the human provides commands by clicking or touching on screen interface elements such as icons or buttons.

Internet addiction disorder: A disorder associated with the overuse of the Internet.

Internet cookies: Data used by websites to record user activity.

Internet-enabled cybercrime: Crimes for which offline equivalents exist, but which Internet technologies enable or extend.

Internet gamers: Gamers who play online computer games.

Internet-specific cybercrime: Cybercrimes for which offline equivalents do not exist.

Interview (research): A method of data collection where questions are asked by the interviewer so as to collect information from the interviewee.

Knowing–doing gap: A situation where the user knows what the most secure behaviour is, but fails to behave in a way which promotes such security.

Lean medium: A description of CMC as a medium where limited non-verbal cues are available.

Learning: A change in behaviour.

Legal psychology: A branch of psychology which deals with the process of law.

Low-fidelity prototype: Often used early in the interaction design process, these prototypes are far from the finished product and may be developed using simple materials such as paper, offering no real user interaction.

Massive open online courses (MOOCs): These courses are available on the Internet and open to all who register at little or no charge and are often taken by large numbers of students.

Mastery of learning: "Achieved when learners are successful at learning tasks" (Gagné et al., 1992).

Media multitasking: Involves simultaneously engaging in more than one form of media or using alongside non-media activities.

Mental disorders: Cover a wide range of mental health issues. These include anxiety, stress, mood disorders, and addiction.

Mental health: Defined as a state of well-being in which every individual realises his or her potential, can cope with the normal stresses of life, can work productively and fruitfully, and can contribute to her or his community.

Mindfulness: Means paying attention in the present moment, on purpose and non-judgementally.

Mixed reality (MR): Technology which is similar to augmented reality as it uses a combination of real and virtual objects.

MMORPG: A massively multiplayer online role-playing game is an online game hosted on an online server where players play in a remote environment with each other.

Mobile computing: The use of smartphones, tablets, laptops, and other mobile devices as computers.

Multimedia: Any material that contains words and graphics.

Multimodality: The use of multiple modes of communication, such as text with video, images, or sound.

Multitasking: Involves doing more than one thing at once.

Negative automatic thoughts: Thoughts that are unhelpful and negative.

Next normal: Economic and social reality after COVID-19.

Nomophobia: The term refers to the fear of being out of mobile phone contact.

Non-player characters (NPCs): Characters in games that are controlled by the computer rather than the gamer.

Non-reactive data collection: When the researcher collects data using an unobtrusive observation method.

Observation (research): A non-experimental research method whereby the researcher observes behaviour.

Offender profiling: The creation of profiles of criminal suspects, sometimes by forensic psychologists.

Online counselling: The delivery of therapeutic interventions over the Internet.

Online dating: Searching for a romantic or sexual partner on the Internet, typically via a dedicated website.

Online disinhibition: Suler's (2004) theory that argues that social inhibitions that would normally would be present in face-to-face communication are loosened or removed when interacting online; a loosening or removal of social inhibitions when interacting online, that would normally be present in face-to-face communication.

Online games: A game played over a computer network.

Online gaming: Computer or console/video games that can be played over the Internet with other players.

Online learning: Use of communication networks for educational purposes mediated by the Web.

Online social capital: Resources accumulated through the relationships and interactions we have with people online.

Ostracism: When one is excluded or isolated from a group.

Paralanguage: Modifying meaning through the use of volume, intonation, or other adjustments; the visual appearance of written language, such as punctuation, spelling, grammar, and keyboard characters.

Peer pressure: Pressure to fit in with those we spend time with.

Persuasion: An attempt to bring about a change in attitude or behaviour.

Phishing: Emails which appear to be from a reputable source which are designed to elicit sensitive information from a user, leaving them vulnerable to identity theft.

PIU: Problematic Internet use.

Platform: The combination of hardware and software making up a computer system.

Prejudice: General term for any negative attitude towards a social group.

Presence: The subjective feeling of being in a video game (or other virtual environment); an illusion that renders the viewer unaware of the medium (the screen, the interface); the subjective feeling of being in a virtual environment (such as a video game or virtual reality); an illusion that renders the viewer unaware of the technological medium through which the environment is presented.

Primary research: When the researcher collects original data, specifically for their research project.

Privacy: The state or condition of not having personal information disclosed in public or semi-public settings.

Protection motivation theory: A theory proposed by Rogers (1975, 1983) which identified several factors which might trigger engagement in protective behaviours.

Proteus effect: Proposed by Yee and Bailenson (2007), this refers to a change in online and offline self-perception based on the features or behaviours of a user's avatar.

Prototype: A sample or model constructed to test an interface concept.

Psychopathology: The scientific study of mental disorders.

Questionnaire: A series of predefined questions or other statements distributed so as to collect information from respondents.

Research: The systematic process of collecting and analysing information in an effort to make a contribution to knowledge of a particular phenomenon.

Research population: The entire group of people (or animals or other things) with the characteristic(s) a researcher wishes to explore; the whole group of interest.

Research sample: A subset of the population, from which the researcher can collect data so as to make claims about the population.

Right to disconnect: Workers' right to disconnect from work tasks outside of working hours.

Robotics: The creation of programmed machines which may or may not have autonomy.

Secondary research: When the researcher collects, reviews, or synthesises existing research.

Self: A person's essential being that distinguishes them from others, especially considered as the object of introspection or reflexive action

Self-presentation: A strategic negotiation of how one presents one's self to audiences.

Sexual harassment online: An umbrella term for all forms of sexual harassment that can occur online. Can be considered as a form of gender-based violence.

Singularity: A future time where advances in AI become uncontrollable or where AI becomes a superintelligence.

Smileys: Variation of emoticons, usually indicating a smiling face.

Social identity theory: Theory by Tajfel and Turner (1979) which seeks to explain intergroup discrimination and how we form in-groups/out-groups.

Social influence: How we are affected by the real or imagined presence of others.

Social information processing theory (SIP): People encode and decode social information in the language they use in their text-based communications.

Social isolation: The lack of social contacts or having reduced social interactions with others which has a detrimental impact on the individual.

Social loafing: The reduction in effort exerted by some individuals when they perform as part of a group.

Social media: Websites, applications, and online social networks which individuals use to make contact with others and to communicate and share information online; websites and online social networks that individuals use to communicate and share information online.

Social networking: Using websites and applications to interact with other people, or to find people with similar interests to yours; the use of websites and other online technologies that enable individuals to communicate with each other and share information.

Social robotics: Research examining how robots interact socially with other robots or humans.

Strong AI: A computer that actually possesses the intelligence that it appears to have.

Superintelligence: A level of intelligence reached by an AI where it surpasses human intelligence in every way.

Synchronous communication: Communications where it is expected that users are simultaneously communicating, such as instant messaging.

Tactile augmentation: Using a real item to induce a sensation of touch when a user is in a virtual world.

Teaching: A key part of instruction; teachers (also called instructors) organise and plan the instruction for students and classes.

Techno-invasion: When technology invades our personal and family time.

Technology acceptance model (TAM): Designed to explain why people do or do not use technology in the context of the workplace; however, because online shoppers are also technology users, it has also been used to explain people's inclination to adopt technology in online shopping.

Technology-enhanced learning: The use of technology to support learning.

Telecommuters: Work independently from the "hub" and touch base only when necessary. They stay connected to the workplace by using a variety of digital technologies.

Text: Words printed on a screen or spoken.

Theory of reasoned action (TRA): The TRA examines people's intention to adopt certain behaviours, and that intention is determined by their attitude towards the behaviour and by subjective norms about the behaviour.

Trolling: Negative behaviours in online environments (such as social media and gaming) designed to provoke a reaction or sometimes cause harm; the negative behaviours engaged in by some gamers to bother other gamers, which can include deliberate annoyance or disruption, sexism, racism, and faking.

Turing test: A standard of AI proposed by Alan Turing, where the computer is deemed to have passed if a human conversing with it cannot tell that it is not human.

Twitter/X: A microblogging tool and online social network, where individuals post short messages (tweets) of up to 280 characters that their "followers" can read, favour, and retweet.

Uncertainty reduction: Strategies used at almost every stage in a relationship to reassure a person about aspects of their partner or relationship. Can include information seeking.

Usability: The extent to which users can achieve specified goals with effectiveness, efficiency, and satisfaction using a product.

User-centred design (UCD): A design philosophy that focuses on the needs, desires, and capabilities of the actual users of the product, rather than focusing on business goals, technologies, or other aspects.

User experience (UX): Involves a user's emotions and attitudes about interacting with a product.

User persona: A description of a hypothetical user with the same characteristics, motivations, and goals as the target user.

Video game: Games that are played on any computer system and allow the player to interactively control graphics on some form of display.

Virtual identity suicide: The removal of an online profile, sometimes to increase privacy.

Virtual environments (VE): A computer-generated 3D representation of a setting or situation.

Virtual learning environments (VLEs): Also called learning management systems (LMS) or course management systems (CMS) (Moore et al., 2011), these are web-based courses that support formal learning in schools and colleges.

Virtual organisation: Where members work for the same company but are geographically distant from each other and communicate by information technology.

Virtual reality: The use of computer technologies to create three-dimensional virtual worlds or objects which users can interact with; a realistic simulation of an environment, which has a 3D effect; a realistic simulation of an environment, including three-dimensional graphics, by a computer system using interactive software and hardware.

Virtual reality exposure therapy (VRET): The use of VR to present cues or stimuli to a user to treat a psychological condition such as an anxiety disorder or addiction.

Virtual teams: A virtual team is made up of a number of different people who work together collaboratively using web-based technologies. They may never meet in person.

Warranting principle: People are more likely to trust information online if it cannot be easily manipulated.

Weak AI: A simulation of intelligence, where no real intelligence exists.

Wearables: Electronic devices worn by a person (such as a watch/piece of clothing) that relay medical, biological, and exercise data to a database.

Web-enabled face-to-face learning: Learning in classrooms and at home with web resources and tools including VLEs.

Web facilitated: Where learning is supported by online course materials and activities.

Wikis: Collaborative websites.

Wizard of Oz study: A research methodology common in AI where it appears that a robot or computer is behaving intelligently, but instead it is being controlled by a human.

Working memory: The system for temporarily storing and managing the information required to carry out cognitive tasks such as learning and comprehension.

Word of mouth (WOM): Communication by a consumer to others actively influenced or encouraged by an organisation.

World Wide Web: An application of the Internet which allows the linking of documents online.

Zoom fatigue: A term used to encompass all video conferencing effects of exhaustion.

Index

Page numbers in **bold** indicate a table on the corresponding page